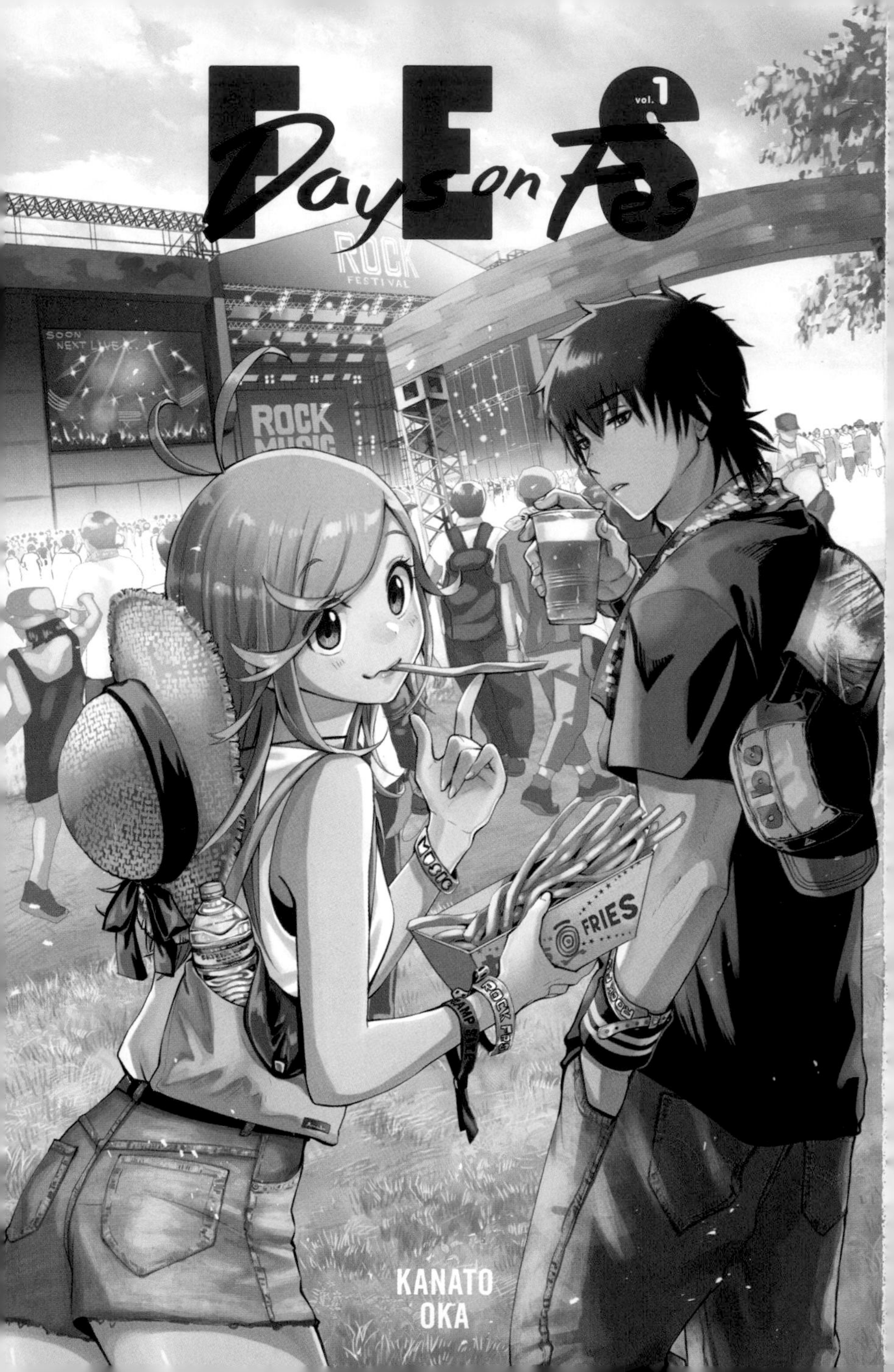
FES
vol. 1
Days on Fes
ROCK
FESTIVAL
SOON
NEXT LIVE...
ROCK
MUSIC
FRIES
KANATO
OKA

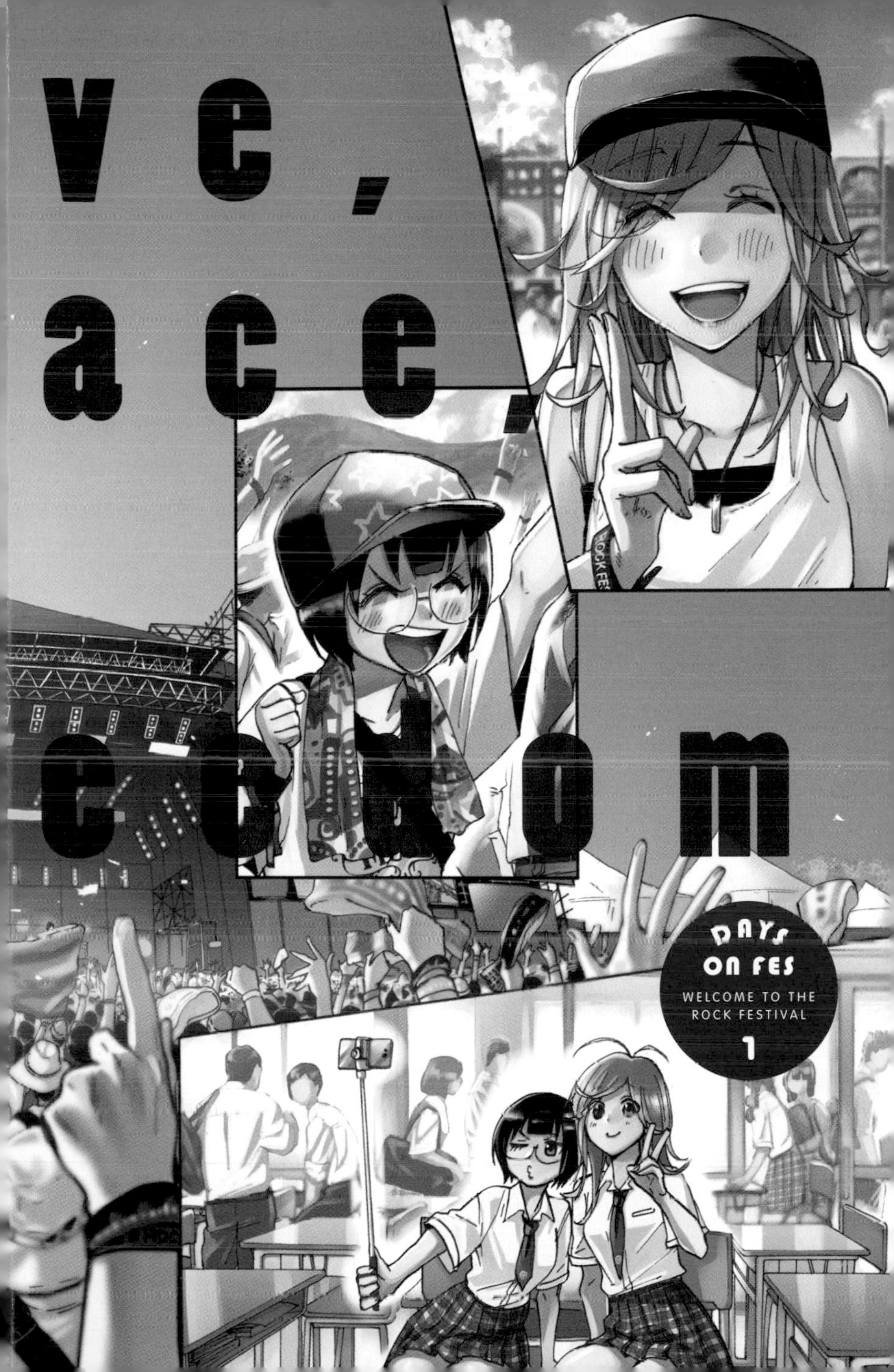
DAYS ON FES
WELCOME TO THE ROCK FESTIVAL
1

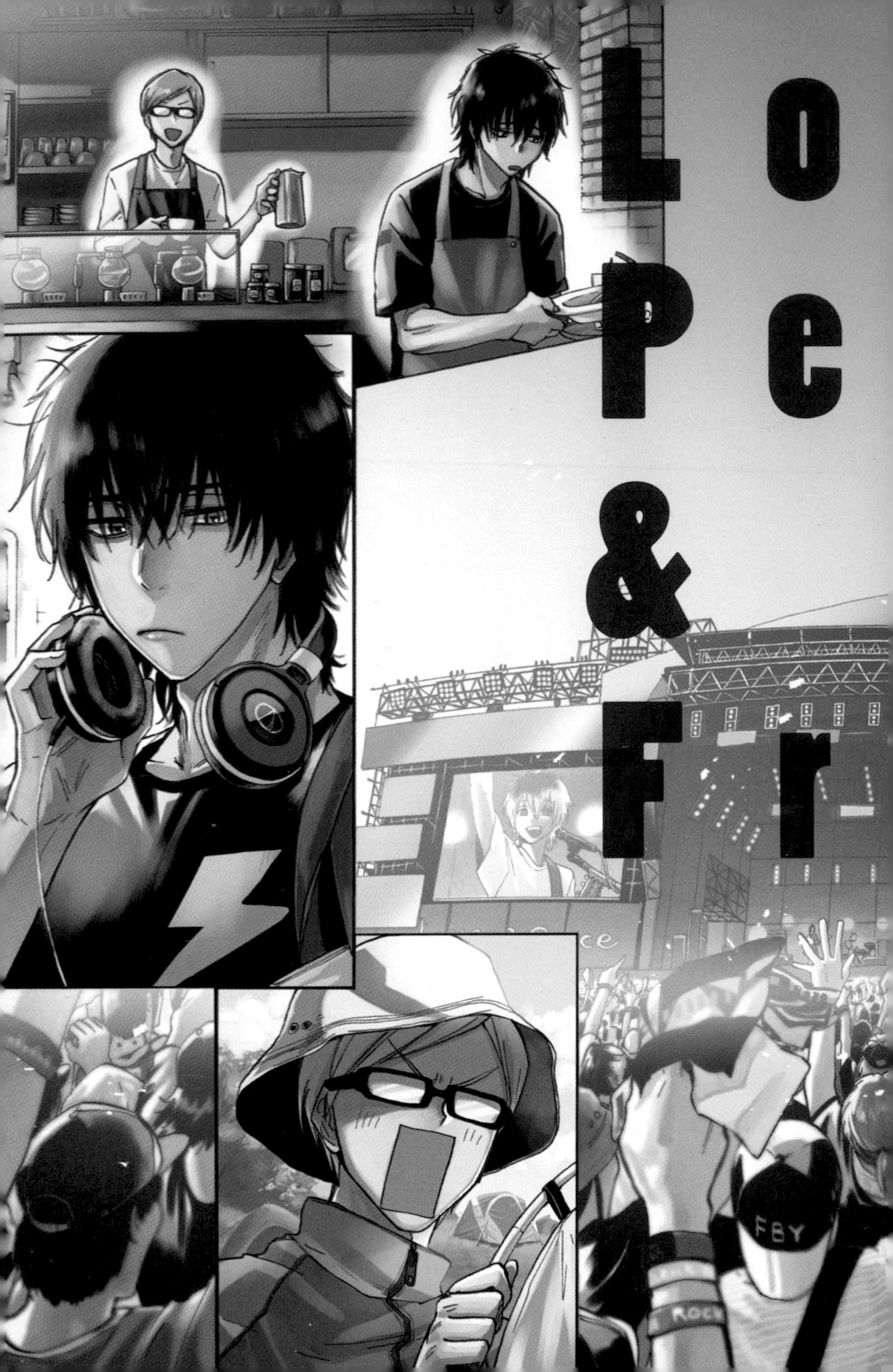
Lo
Pe
&
Fr
FBY
ROCK

contents

Days on Fes

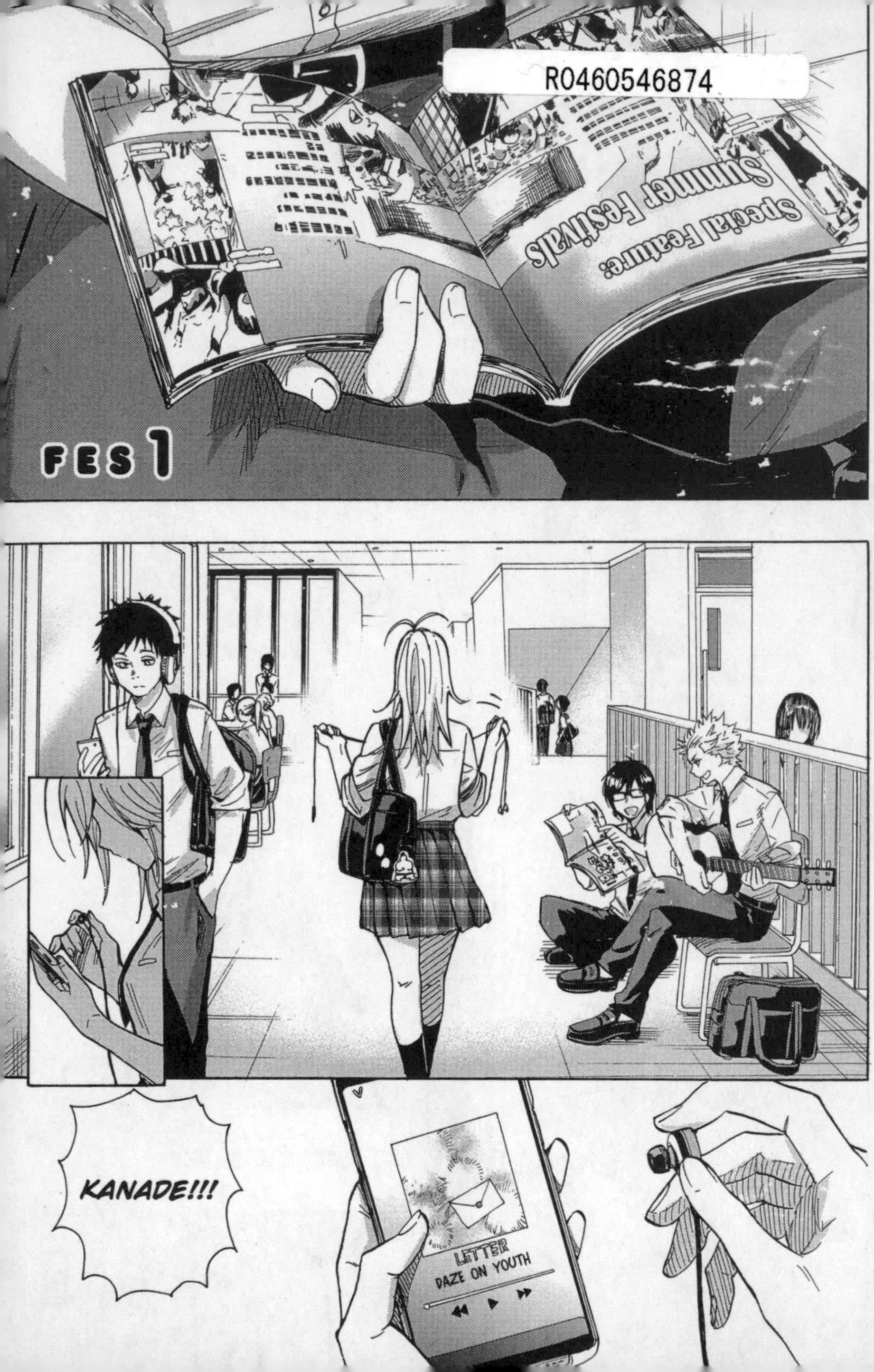
Special Feature:
Summer Festivals
FES 1
LETTER
DAZE ON YOUTH
KANADE!!!

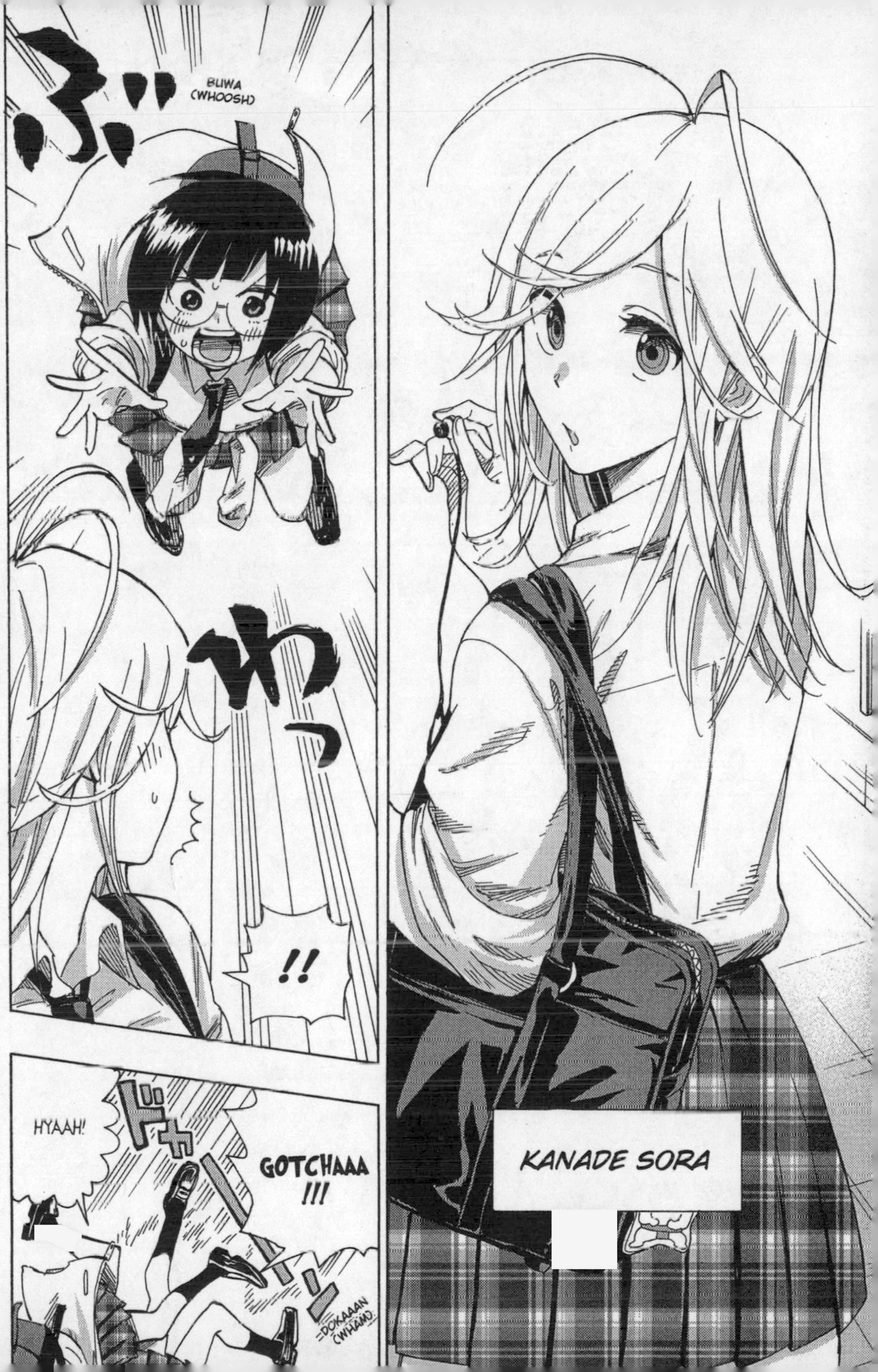
KANADE SORA
BUWA (WHOOSH)
わっ
!!
GOTCHAAA !!!
HYAAH!
DOKAAAN (WHAM)

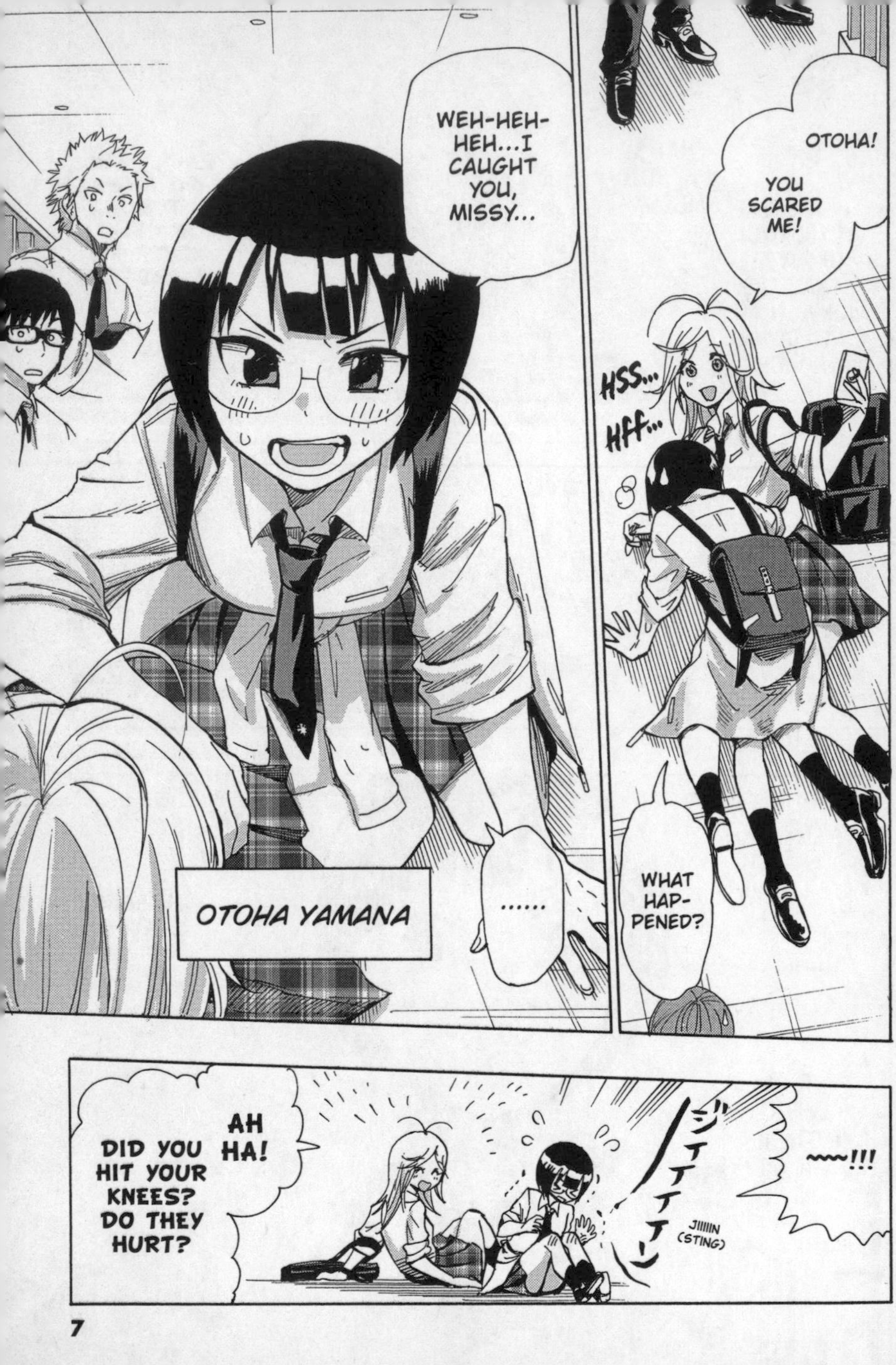
OTOHA!
YOU SCARED ME!
HSS...
HFF...
WHAT HAP-PENED?
WEH-HEH-HEH...I CAUGHT YOU, MISSY...
OTOHA YAMANA
......
~~~!!!
JIIIIIN (STING)
AH HA!
DID YOU HIT YOUR KNEES? DO THEY HURT?
~~~

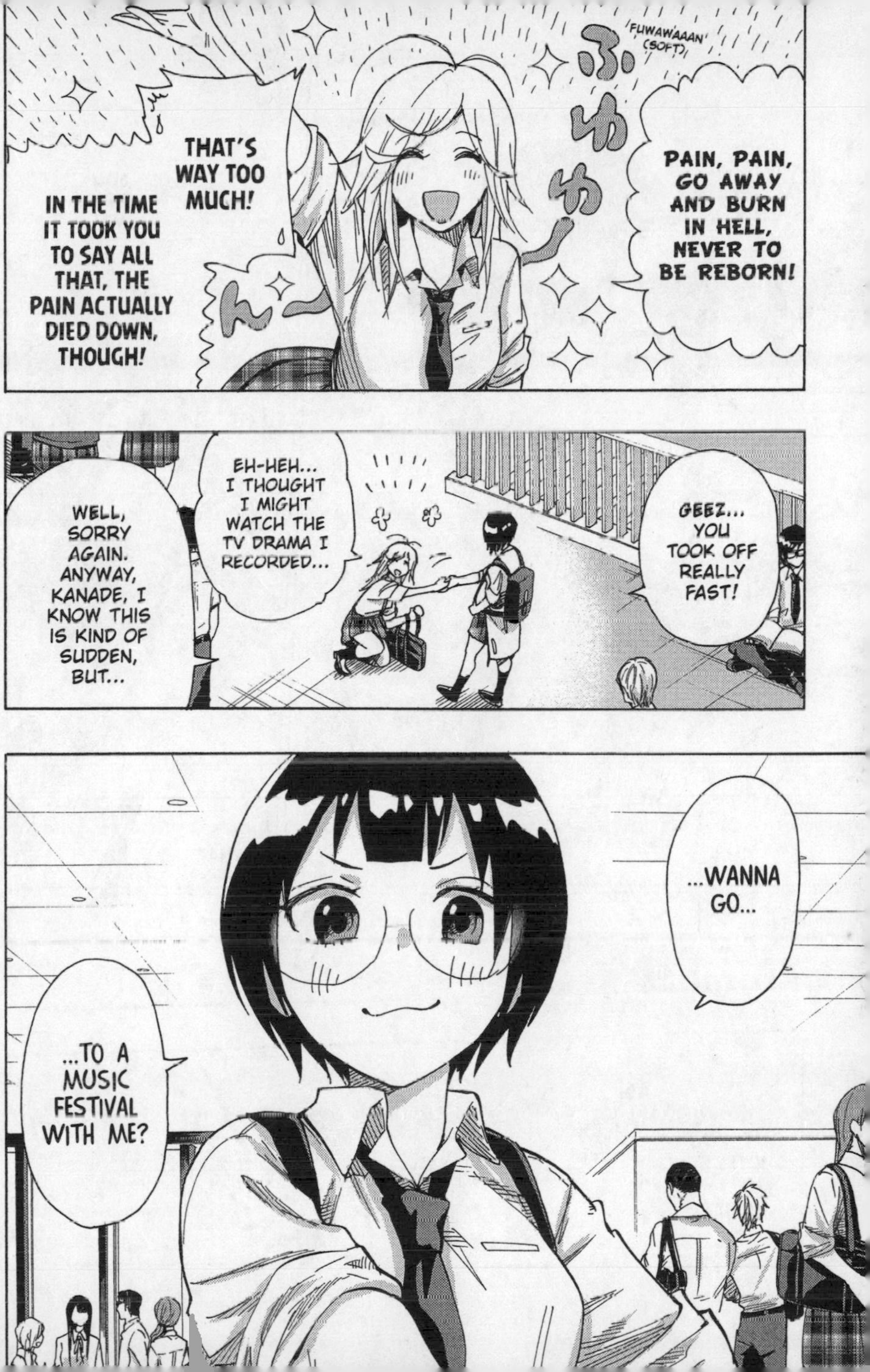
FUWAWAAAN (SOFT)
PAIN, PAIN, GO AWAY AND BURN IN HELL, NEVER TO BE REBORN!
THAT'S WAY TOO MUCH!
IN THE TIME IT TOOK YOU TO SAY ALL THAT, THE PAIN ACTUALLY DIED DOWN, THOUGH!
GEEZ... YOU TOOK OFF REALLY FAST!
EH-HEH... I THOUGHT I MIGHT WATCH THE TV DRAMA I RECORDED...
WELL, SORRY AGAIN. ANYWAY, KANADE, I KNOW THIS IS KIND OF SUDDEN, BUT...
...WANNA GO...
...TO A MUSIC FESTIVAL WITH ME?

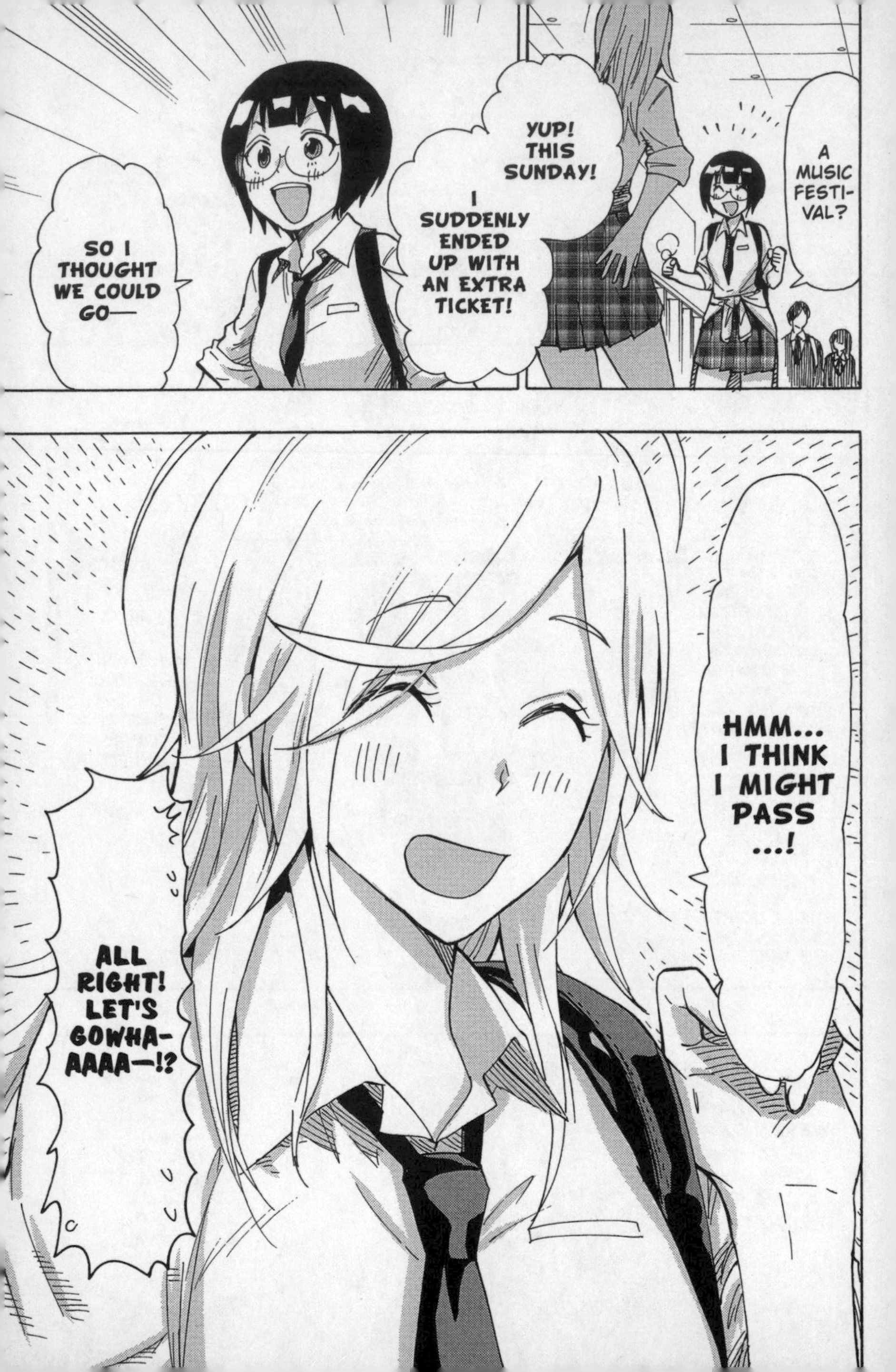
A MUSIC FESTI-VAL?
YUP! THIS SUNDAY!
I SUDDENLY ENDED UP WITH AN EXTRA TICKET!
SO I THOUGHT WE COULD GO—
HMM... I THINK I MIGHT PASS ...!
ALL RIGHT! LET'S GOWHA-AAAA—!?

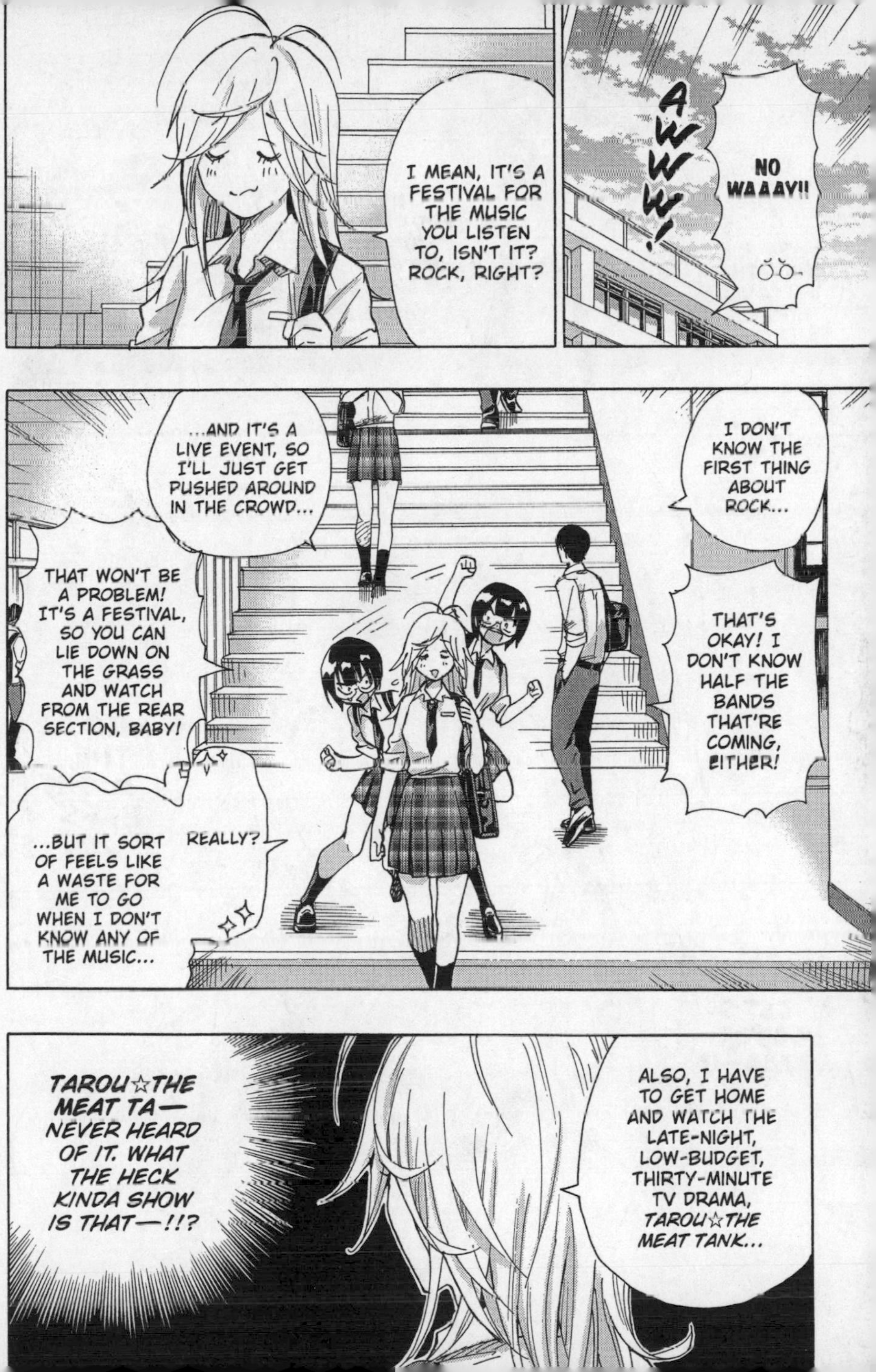
NO WAAAY!!
AWWWW!
I MEAN, IT'S A FESTIVAL FOR THE MUSIC YOU LISTEN TO, ISN'T IT? ROCK, RIGHT?
I DON'T KNOW THE FIRST THING ABOUT ROCK...
...AND IT'S A LIVE EVENT, SO I'LL JUST GET PUSHED AROUND IN THE CROWD...
THAT'S OKAY! I DON'T KNOW HALF THE BANDS THAT'RE COMING, EITHER!
THAT WON'T BE A PROBLEM! IT'S A FESTIVAL, SO YOU CAN LIE DOWN ON THE GRASS AND WATCH FROM THE REAR SECTION, BABY!
REALLY?
...BUT IT SORT OF FEELS LIKE A WASTE FOR ME TO GO WHEN I DON'T KNOW ANY OF THE MUSIC...
ALSO, I HAVE TO GET HOME AND WATCH THE LATE-NIGHT, LOW-BUDGET, THIRTY-MINUTE TV DRAMA, *TAROU☆THE MEAT TANK*...
TAROU☆THE MEAT TA— NEVER HEARD OF IT. WHAT THE HECK KINDA SHOW IS THAT—!!?

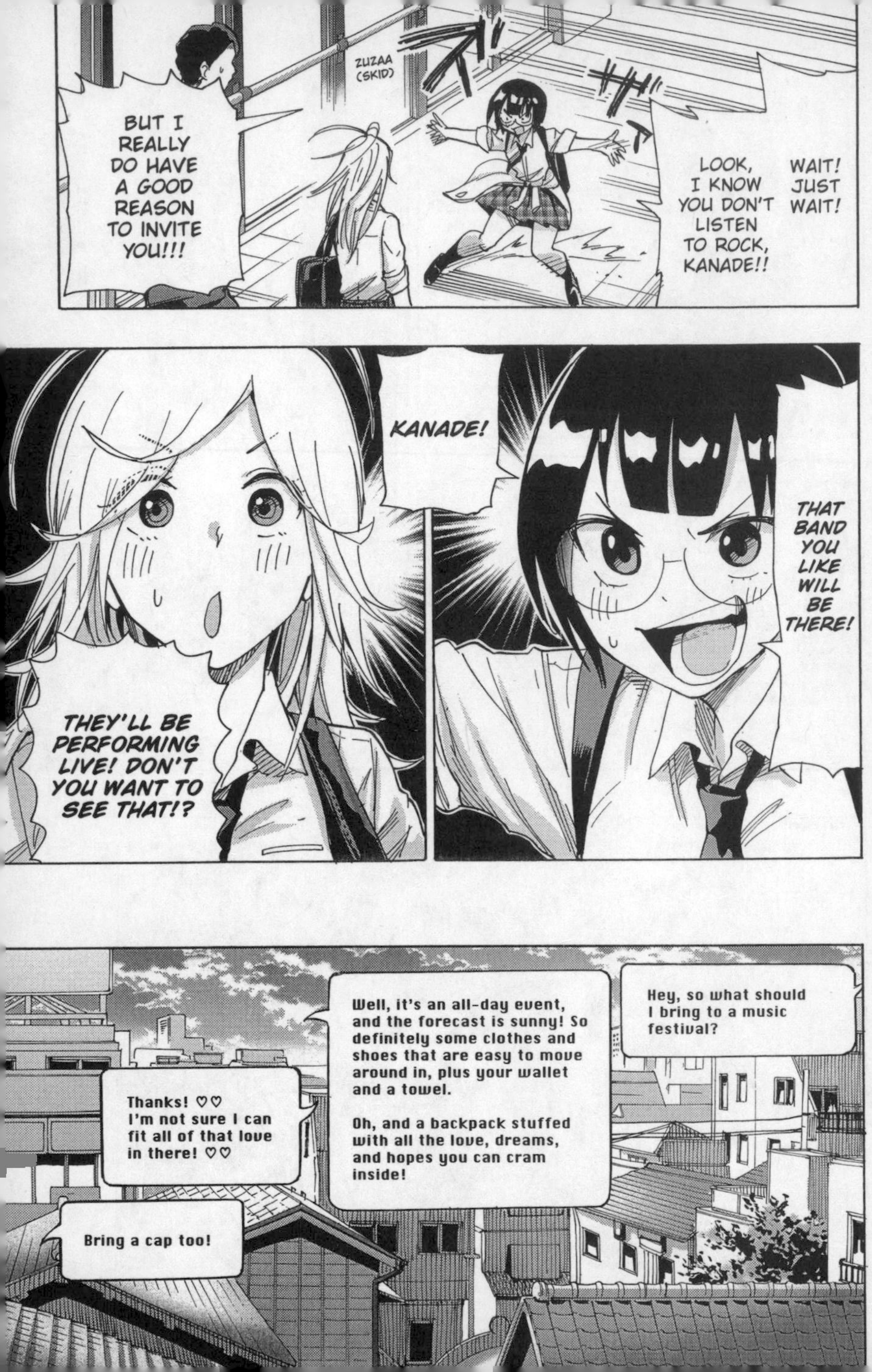
WAIT! JUST WAIT!
LOOK, I KNOW YOU DON'T LISTEN TO ROCK, KANADE!!
ZUZAA (SKID)
BUT I REALLY DO HAVE A GOOD REASON TO INVITE YOU!!!
KANADE!
THAT BAND YOU LIKE WILL BE THERE!
THEY'LL BE PERFORMING LIVE! DON'T YOU WANT TO SEE THAT!?
Hey, so what should I bring to a music festival?
Well, it's an all-day event, and the forecast is sunny! So definitely some clothes and shoes that are easy to move around in, plus your wallet and a towel.
Oh, and a backpack stuffed with all the love, dreams, and hopes you can cram inside!
Thanks! ♡♡ I'm not sure I can fit all of that love in there! ♡♡
Bring a cap too!

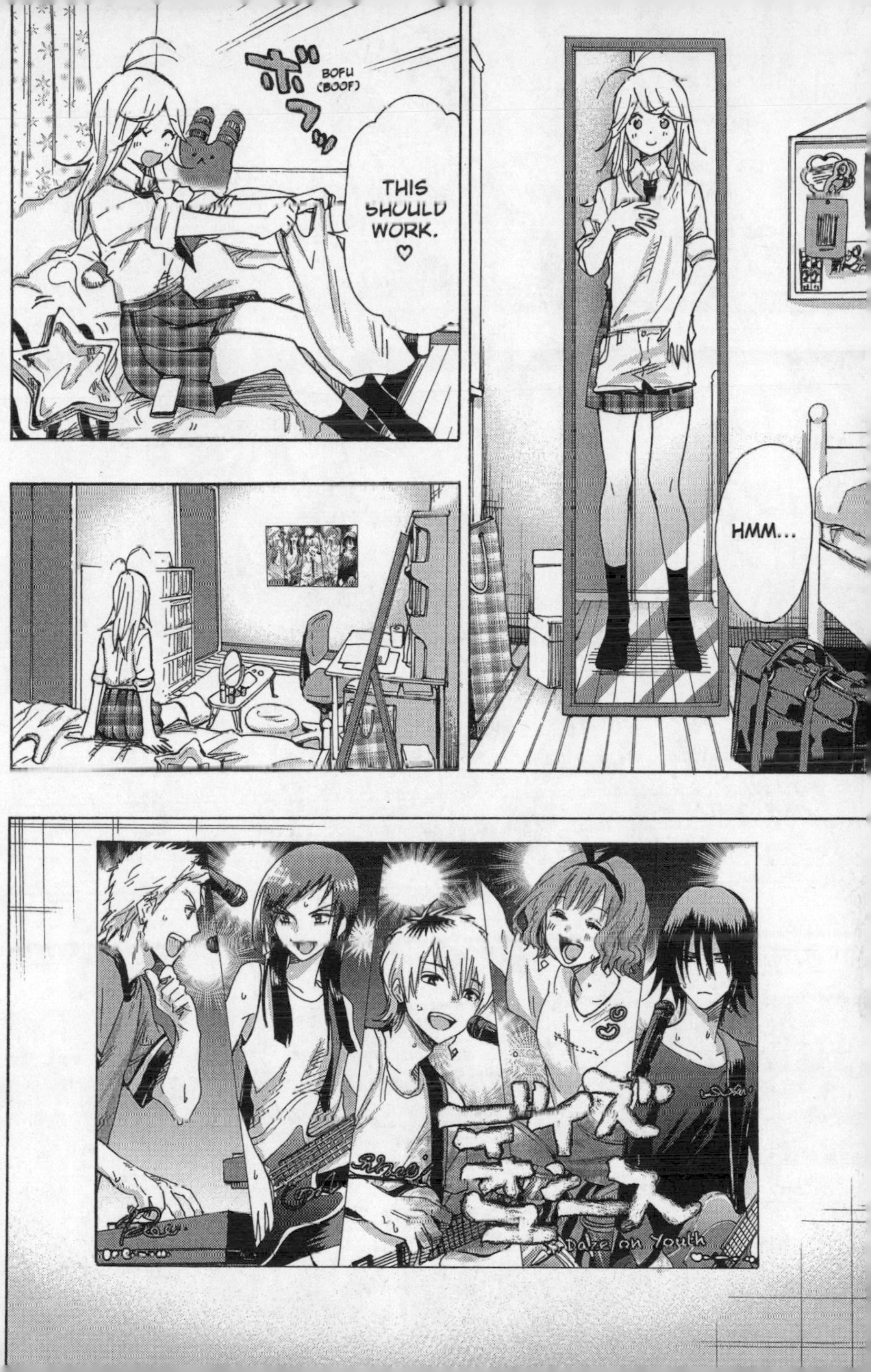
HMM...
BOFU (BOOF)
THIS SHOULD WORK. ♡
Daze on Youth

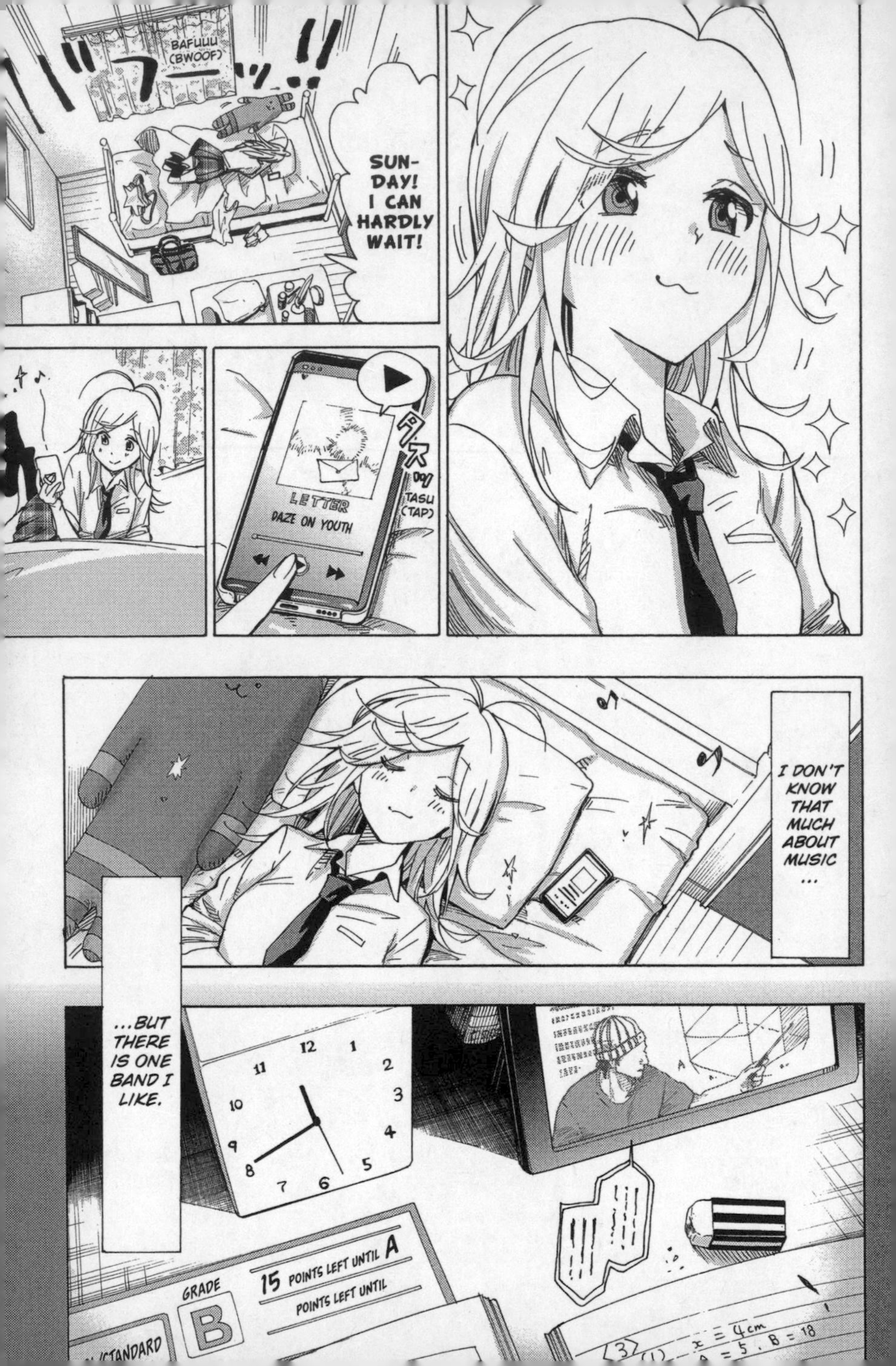
BAFUUU (BWOOF)
SUN-DAY! I CAN HARDLY WAIT!
TASU (TAP)
LETTER
DAZE ON YOUTH
I DON'T KNOW THAT MUCH ABOUT MUSIC...
...BUT THERE IS ONE BAND I LIKE.
15 POINTS LEFT UNTIL A
POINTS LEFT UNTIL
GRADE
B

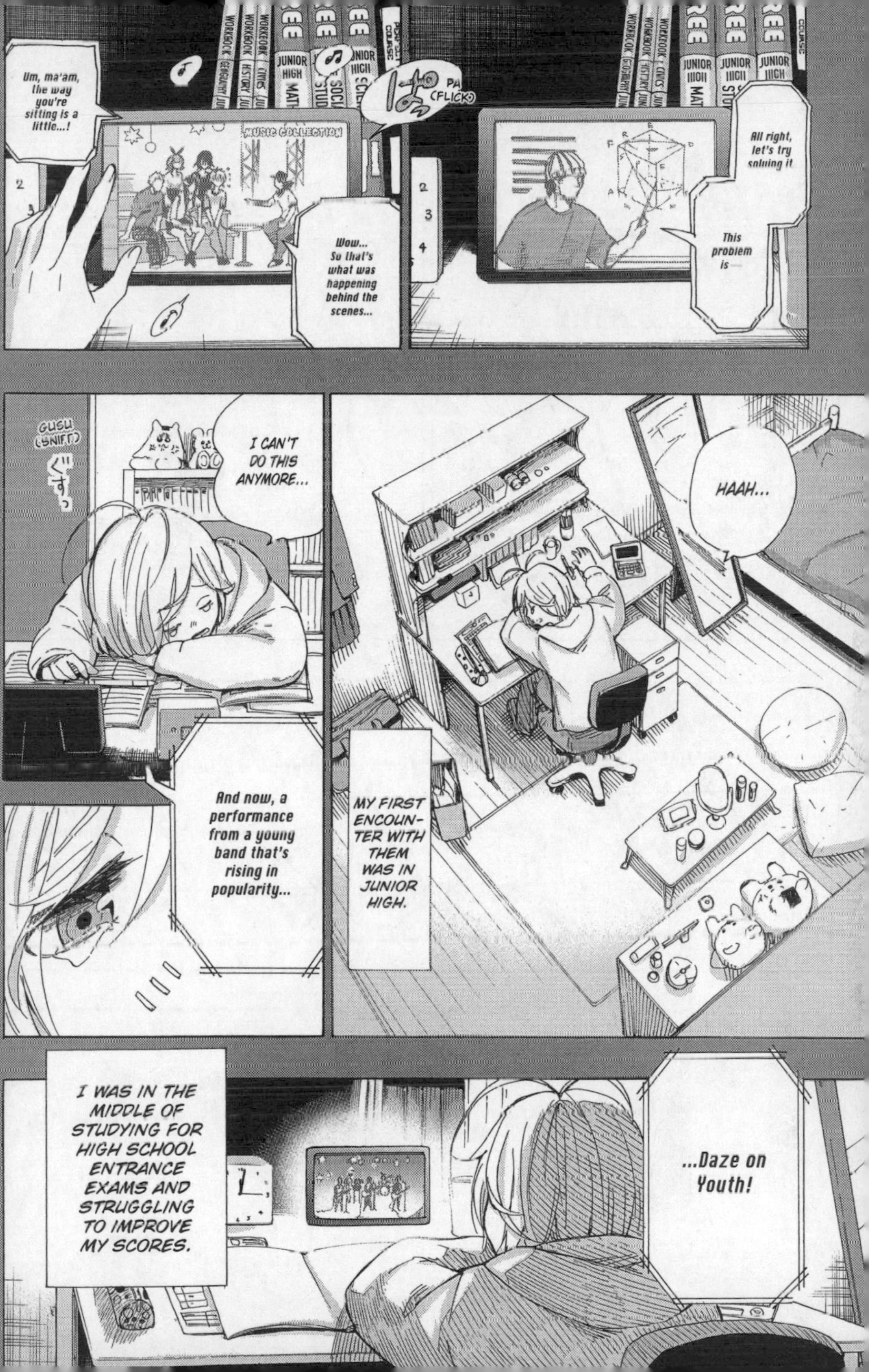
All right, let's try solving it
This problem is—
PA (FLICK)
Um, ma'am, the way you're sitting is a little...!
MUSIC COLLECTION
Wow... So that's what was happening behind the scenes...
HAAH...
MY FIRST ENCOUNTER WITH THEM WAS IN JUNIOR HIGH.
I CAN'T DO THIS ANYMORE...
GUSU (SNIFF)
ぐすっ
And now, a performance from a young band that's rising in popularity...
...Daze on Youth!
I WAS IN THE MIDDLE OF STUDYING FOR HIGH SCHOOL ENTRANCE EXAMS AND STRUGGLING TO IMPROVE MY SCORES.

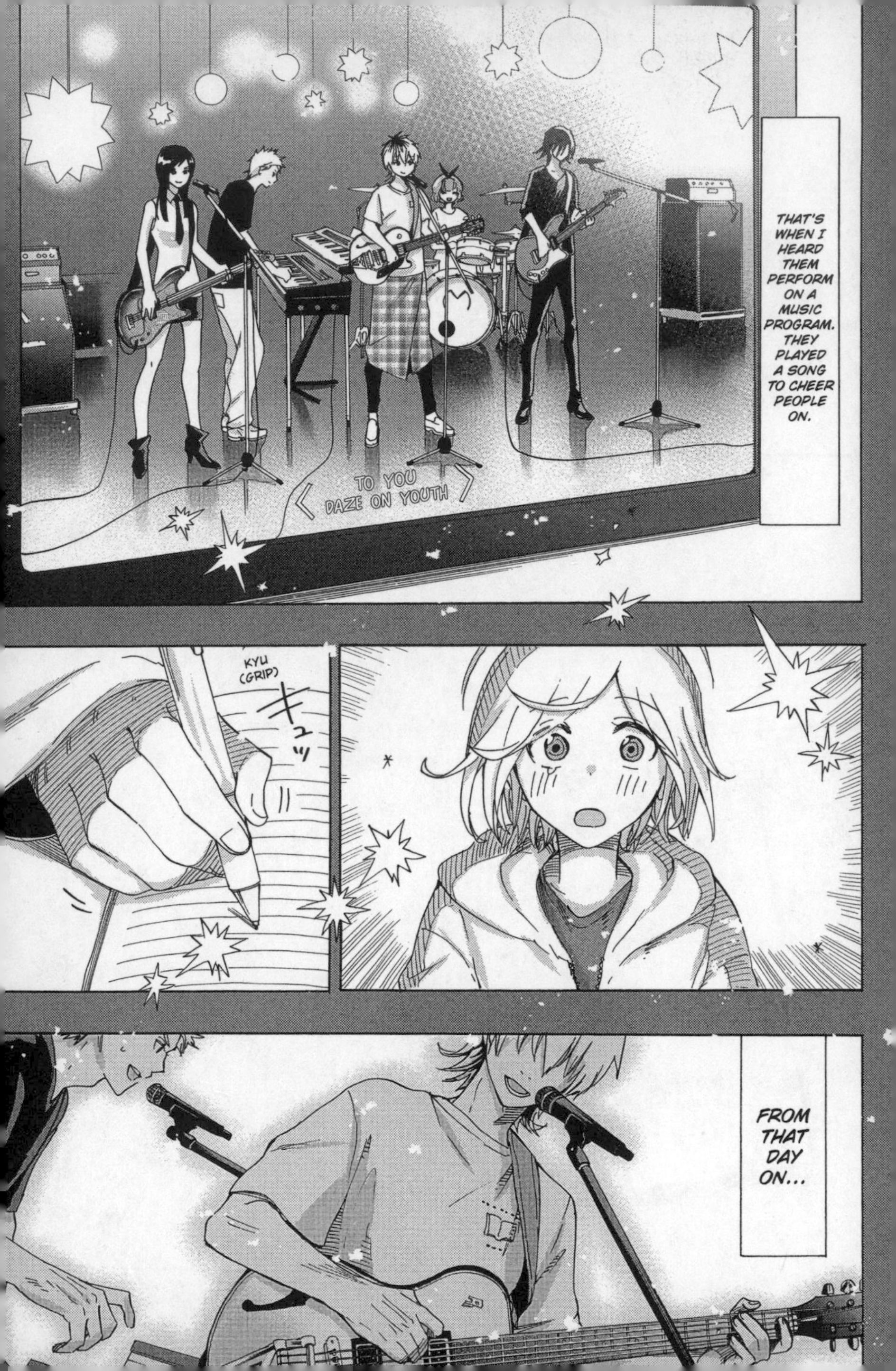
THAT'S WHEN I HEARD THEM PERFORM ON A MUSIC PROGRAM. THEY PLAYED A SONG TO CHEER PEOPLE ON.
〈TO YOU DAZE ON YOUTH〉
KYU (GRIP)
キュッ
FROM THAT DAY ON...

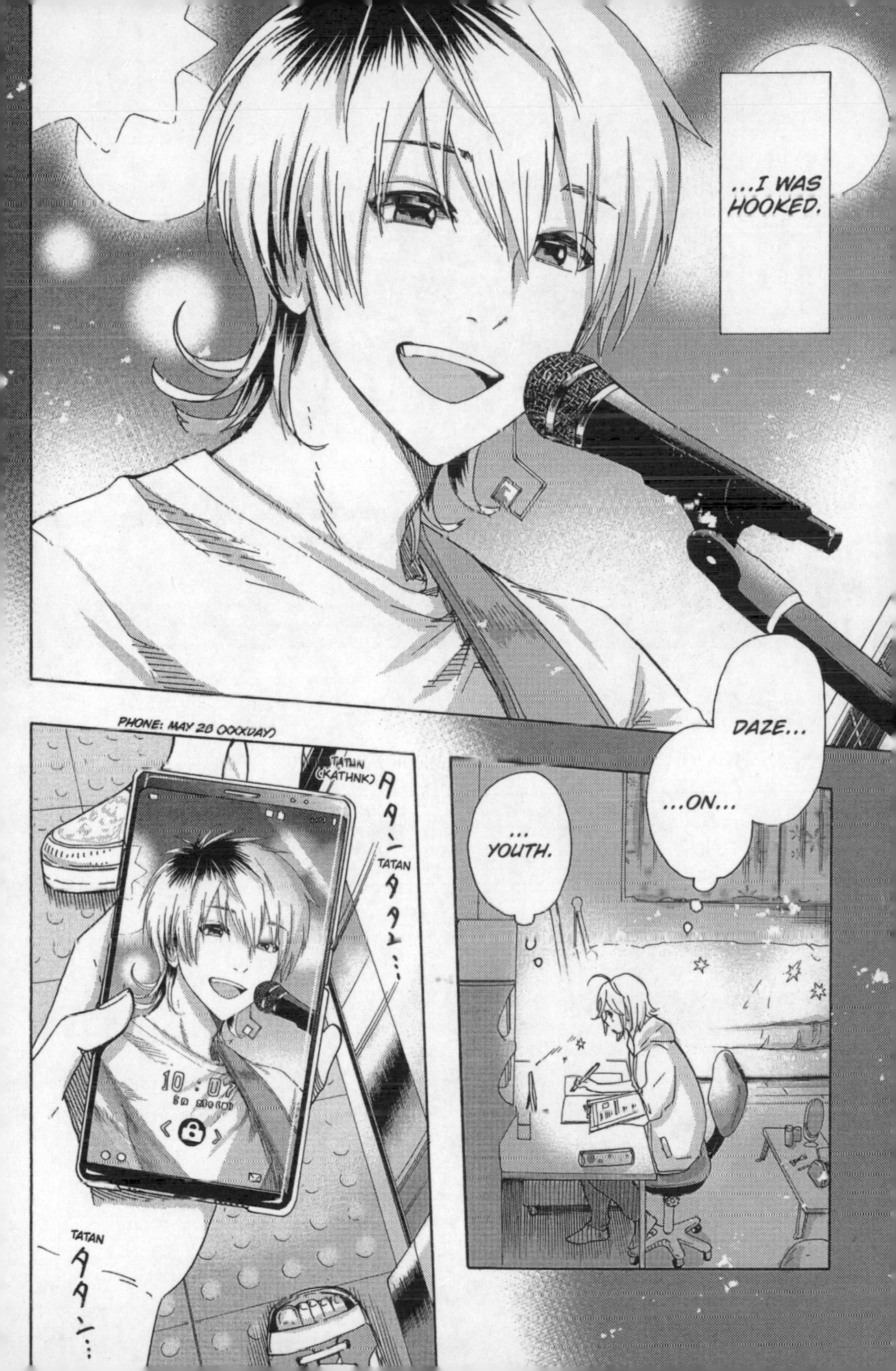
...I WAS HOOKED.
DAZE...
...ON...
...YOUTH.
PHONE: MAY 28 (XXXDAY)
TATUN (KATHNK)
TATAN
10:07
TATAN

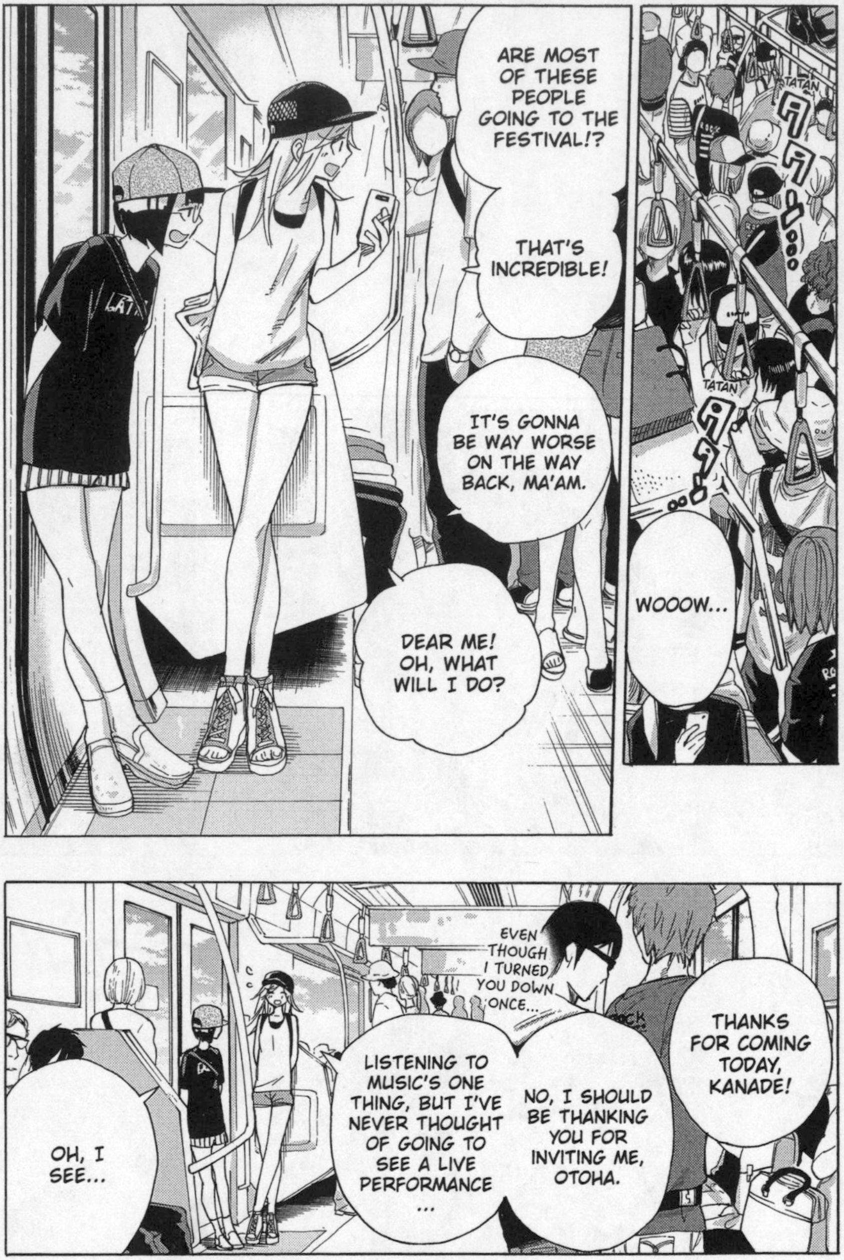
TATAN
TATAN
WOOOW...
ARE MOST OF THESE PEOPLE GOING TO THE FESTIVAL!?
THAT'S INCREDIBLE!
IT'S GONNA BE WAY WORSE ON THE WAY BACK, MA'AM.
DEAR ME! OH, WHAT WILL I DO?
THANKS FOR COMING TODAY, KANADE!
EVEN THOUGH I TURNED YOU DOWN ONCE...
NO, I SHOULD BE THANKING YOU FOR INVITING ME, OTOHA.
LISTENING TO MUSIC'S ONE THING, BUT I'VE NEVER THOUGHT OF GOING TO SEE A LIVE PERFORMANCE ...
OH, I SEE...

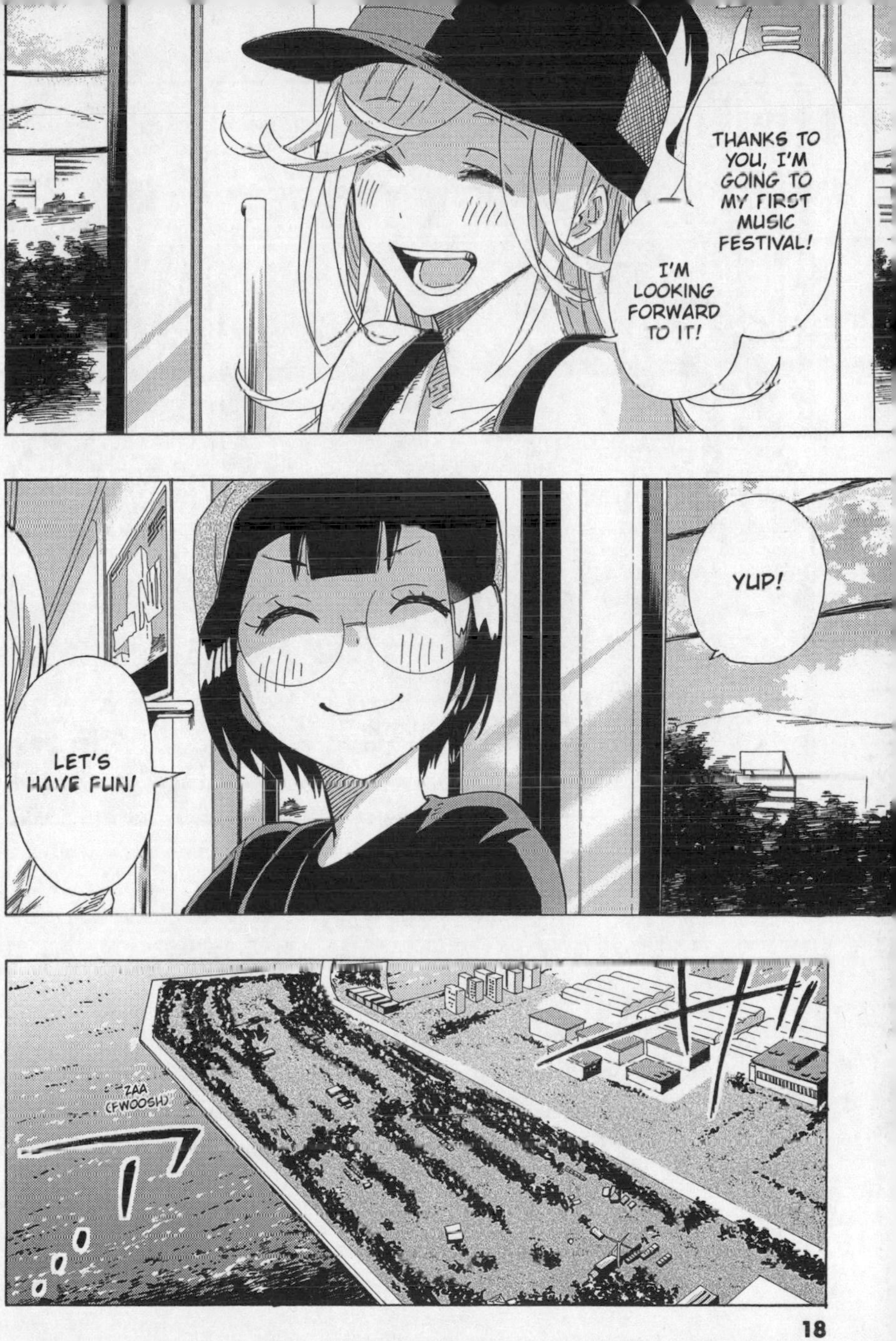
THANKS TO YOU, I'M GOING TO MY FIRST MUSIC FESTIVAL!
I'M LOOKING FORWARD TO IT!
YUP!
LET'S HAVE FUN!
ZAA (FWOOSH)

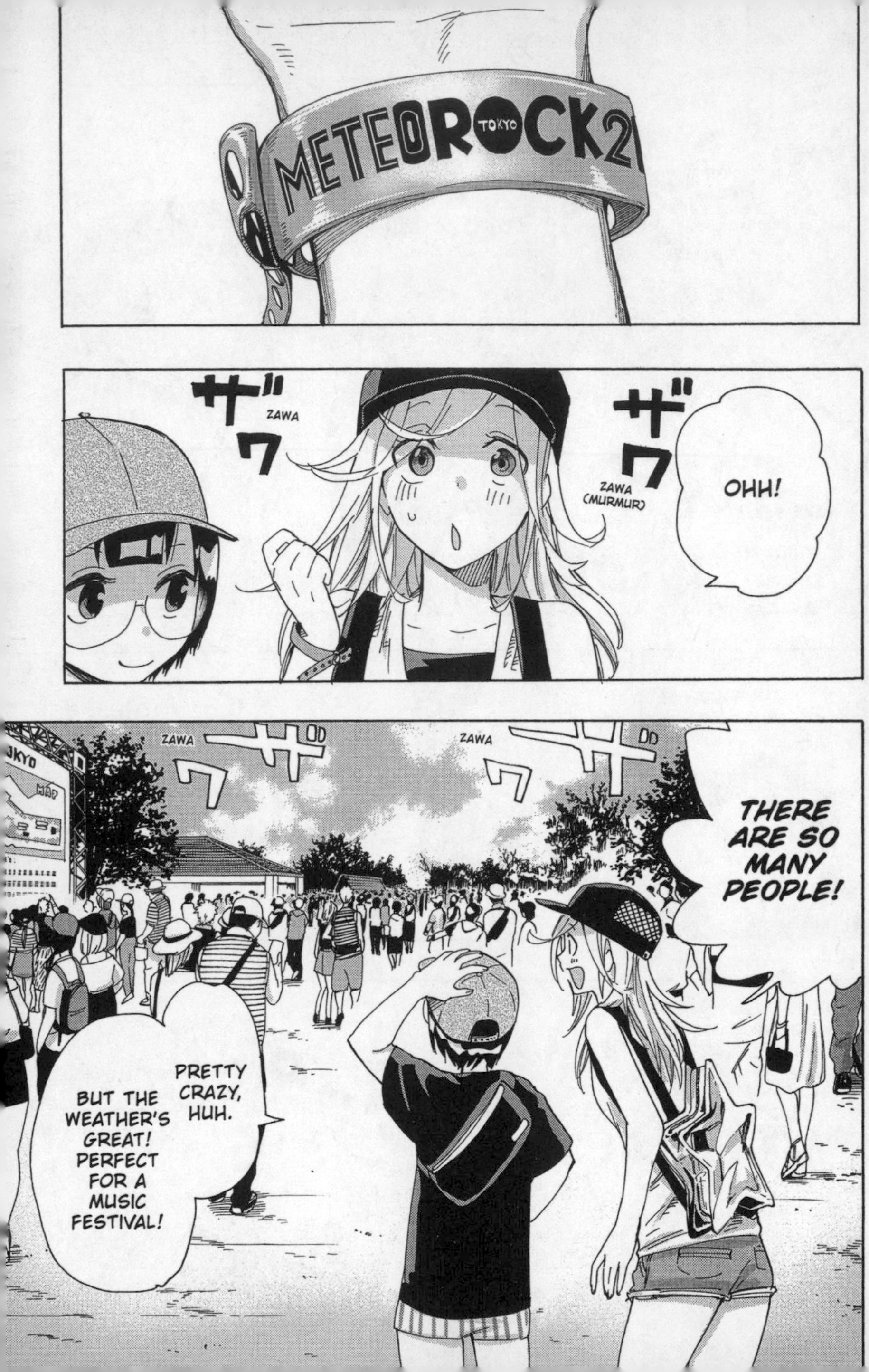

METEOROCK2
TOKYO
OHH!
ザワ
ZAWA (MURMUR)
ザワ
ZAWA
THERE ARE SO MANY PEOPLE!
ザワ
ZAWA
ザワ
ZAWA
PRETTY CRAZY, HUH.
BUT THE WEATHER'S GREAT! PERFECT FOR A MUSIC FESTIVAL!
MAP

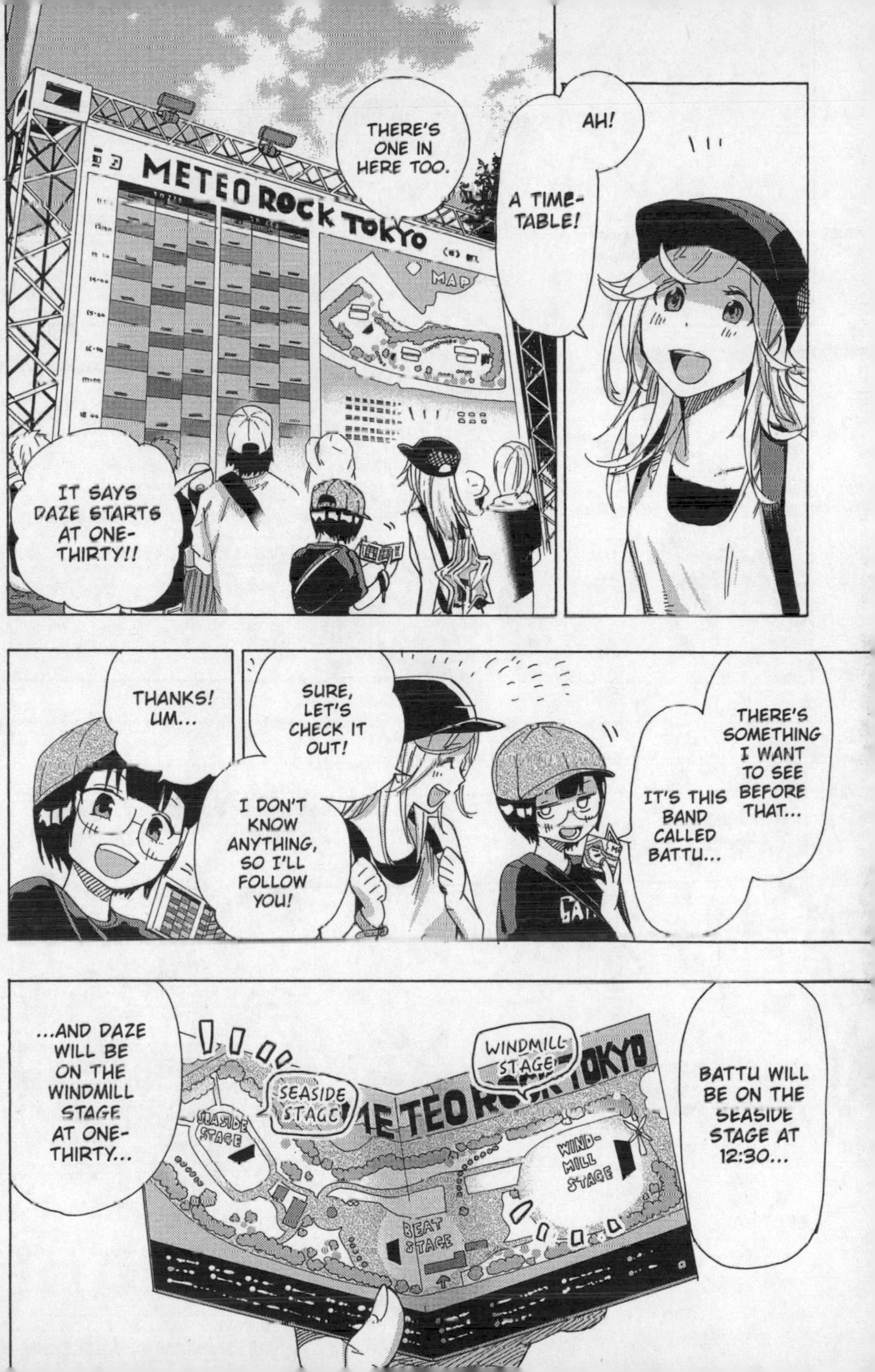
AH!
A TIME-TABLE!
THERE'S ONE IN HERE TOO.
METEO ROCK TOKYO
MAP
IT SAYS DAZE STARTS AT ONE-THIRTY!!
THERE'S SOMETHING I WANT TO SEE BEFORE THAT...
IT'S THIS BAND CALLED BATTU...
SURE, LET'S CHECK IT OUT!
I DON'T KNOW ANYTHING, SO I'LL FOLLOW YOU!
THANKS! UM...
BATTU WILL BE ON THE SEASIDE STAGE AT 12:30...
WINDMILL STAGE
SEASIDE STAGE
...AND DAZE WILL BE ON THE WINDMILL STAGE AT ONE-THIRTY...
SEASIDE STAGE
WIND-MILL STAGE
BEAT STAGE

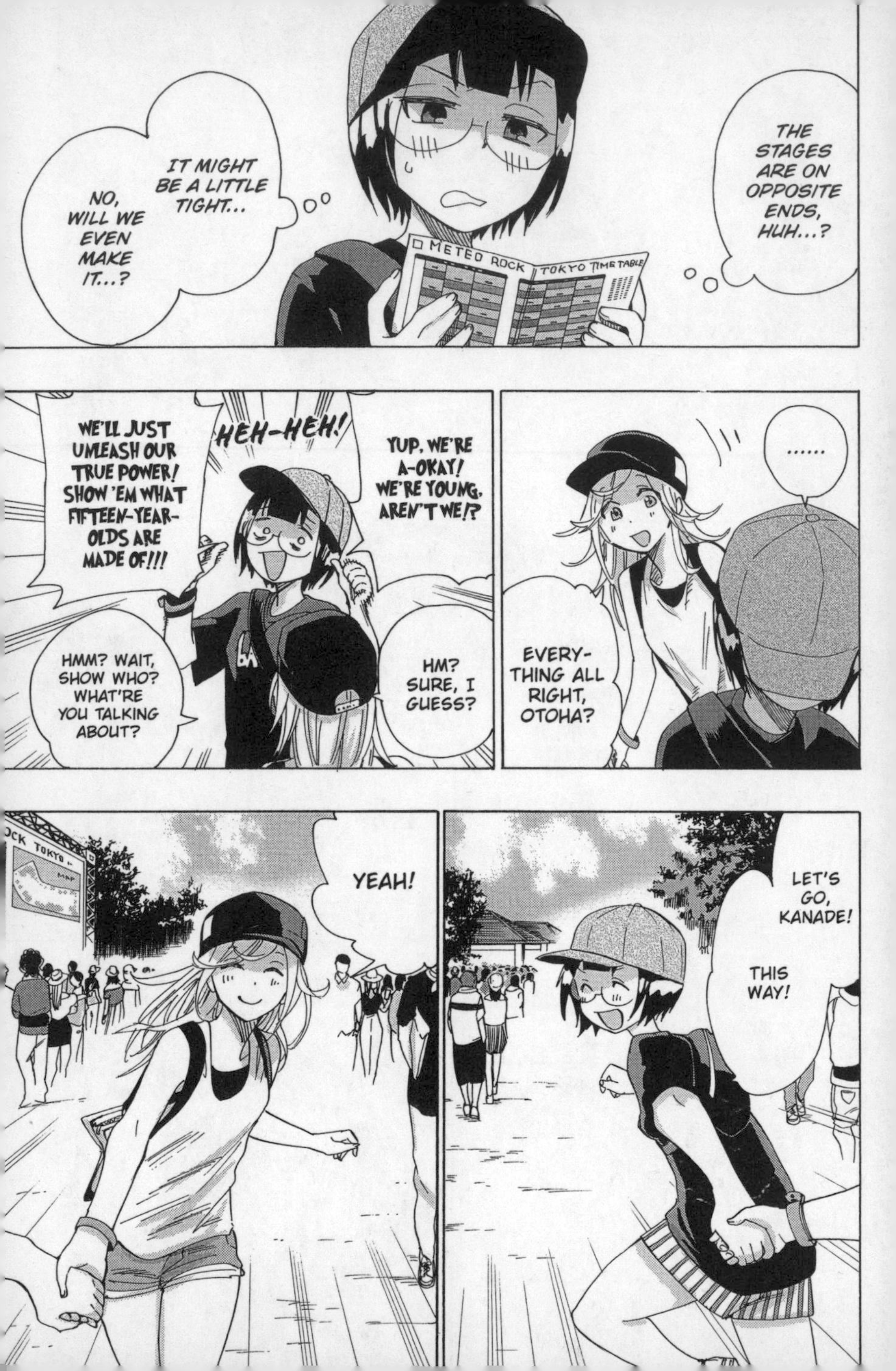
THE STAGES ARE ON OPPOSITE ENDS, HUH...?
METED ROCK TOKYO TIME TABLE
IT MIGHT BE A LITTLE TIGHT...
NO, WILL WE EVEN MAKE IT...?
......
EVERYTHING ALL RIGHT, OTOHA?
YUP, WE'RE A-OKAY! WE'RE YOUNG, AREN'T WE!?
HM? SURE, I GUESS?
HEH-HEH!
WE'LL JUST UNLEASH OUR TRUE POWER! SHOW 'EM WHAT FIFTEEN-YEAR-OLDS ARE MADE OF!!!
HMM? WAIT, SHOW WHO? WHAT'RE YOU TALKING ABOUT?
LET'S GO, KANADE!
THIS WAY!
YEAH!

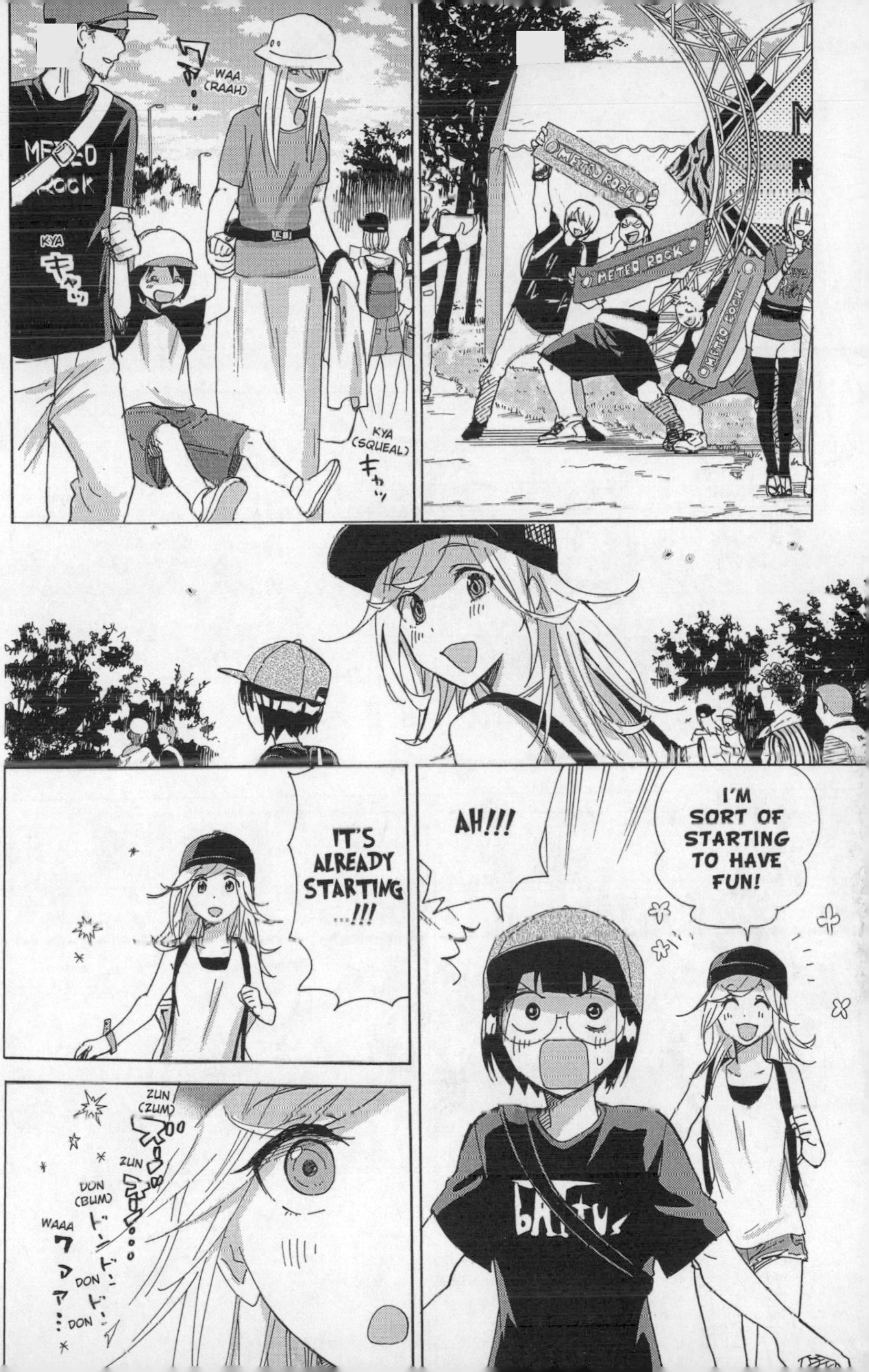
METEO ROCK
METEO ROCK
METEO ROCK
WAA (RAAH)
METEO ROCK
KYA
KYA (SQUEAL)
AH!!!
I'M SORT OF STARTING TO HAVE FUN!
IT'S ALREADY STARTING ...!!!
ZUN (ZUM)
ZUN
DON (BUM)
WAAA
DON
DON

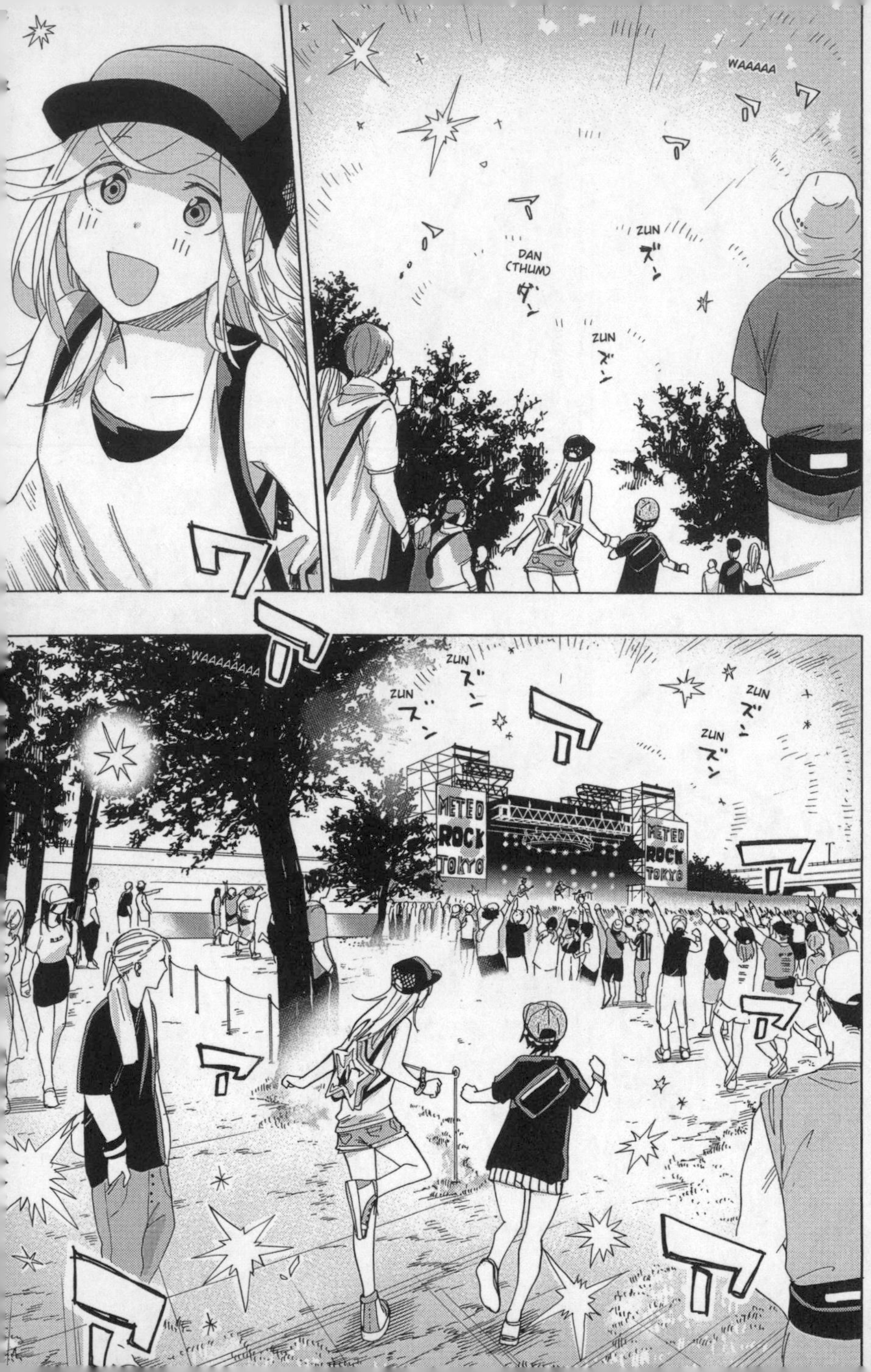

WAAAAA
アアアア
ZUN
ズン
DAN
(THUM)
ダン
ZUN
ズン
WAAAAAAAA
ZUN
ズン
ZUN
ズン
ZUN
ズン
ZUN
ズン
METEO ROCK TOKYO
METEO ROCK TOKYO

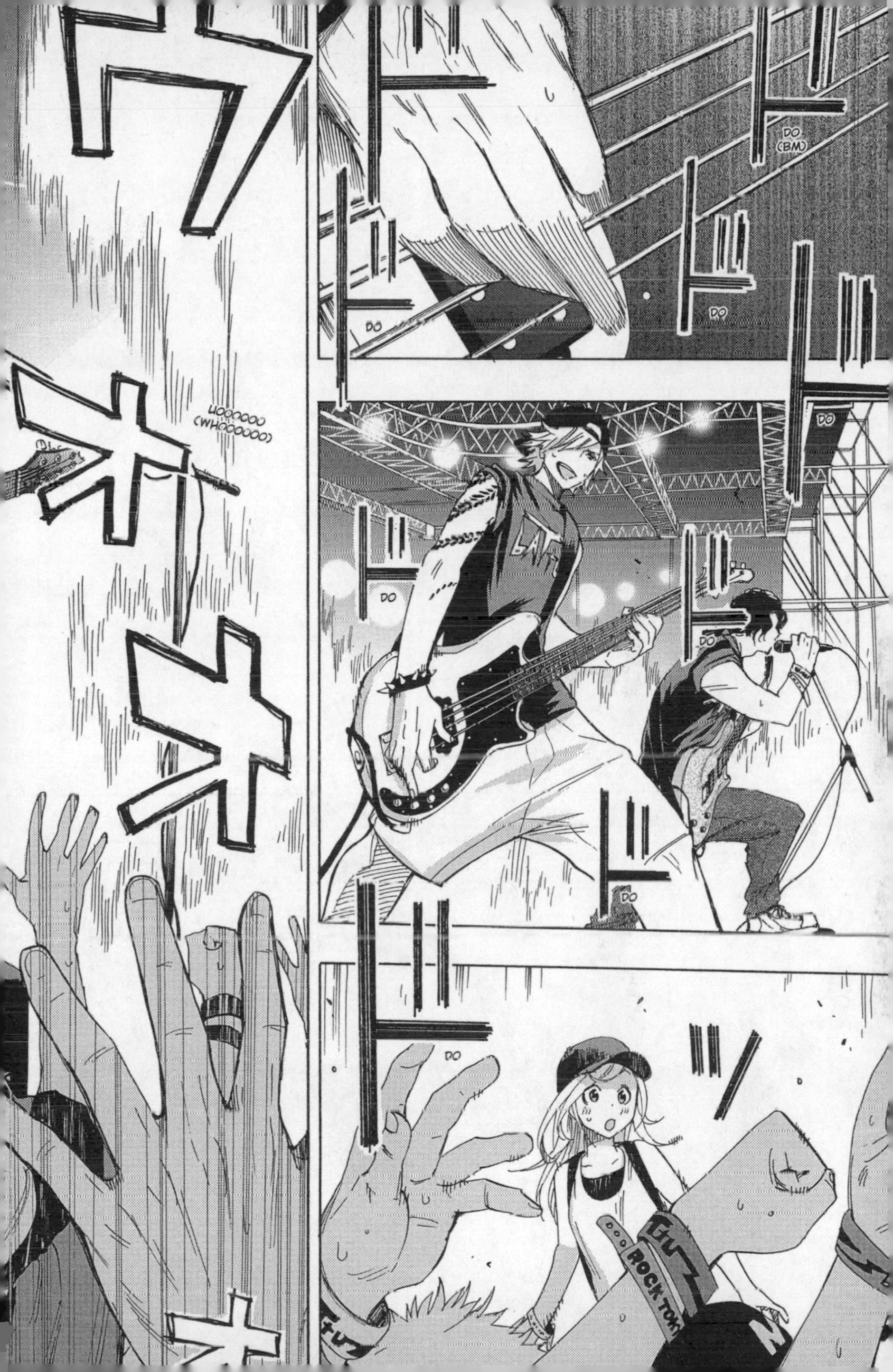
DO
(BM)
DO
DO
DO
DO
DO
DO
DO
ROCK
UOOOOOO
(WHOOOOOO)

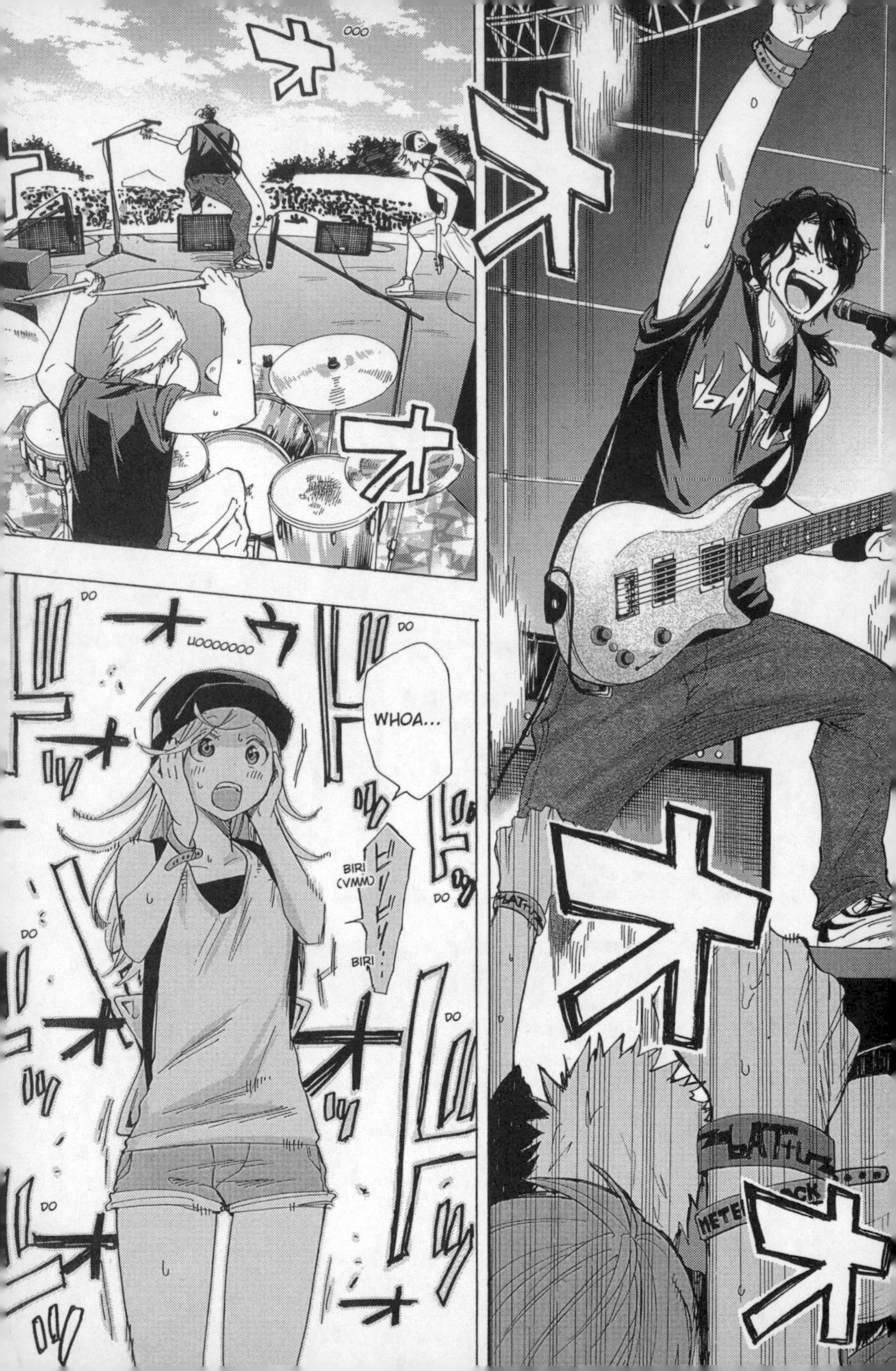

OOO
DO
UOOOOOOO
DO
WHOA...
BIRI
(VMM)
BIRI
DO
DO
DO
DO

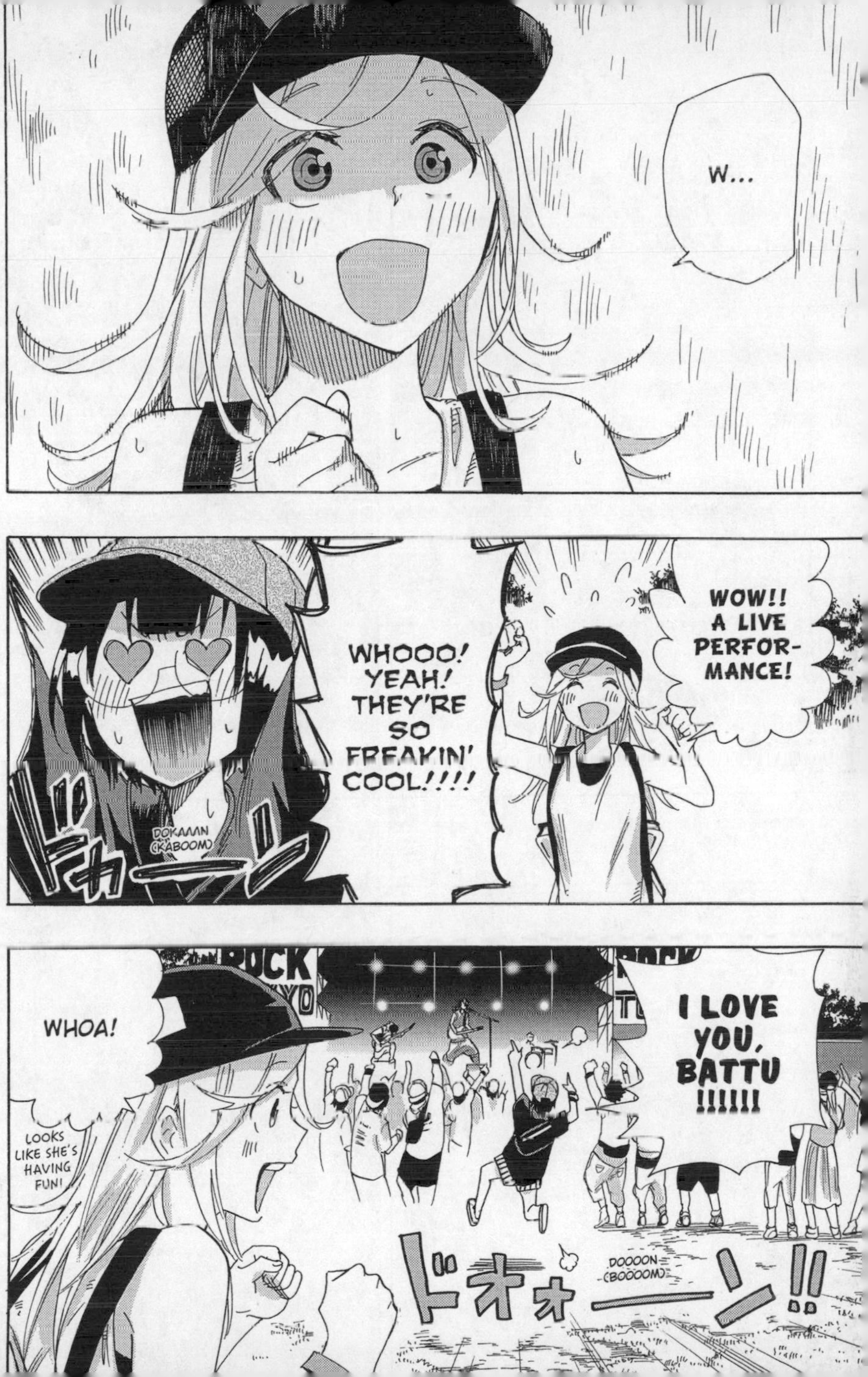
W...
WOW!! A LIVE PERFOR-MANCE!
WHOOOO! YEAH! THEY'RE SO FREAKIN' COOL!!!!
DOKAAAN (KABOOM)
I LOVE YOU, BATTU!!!!!!
ROCK
WHOA!
LOOKS LIKE SHE'S HAVING FUN!
DOOOON (BOOOOM)

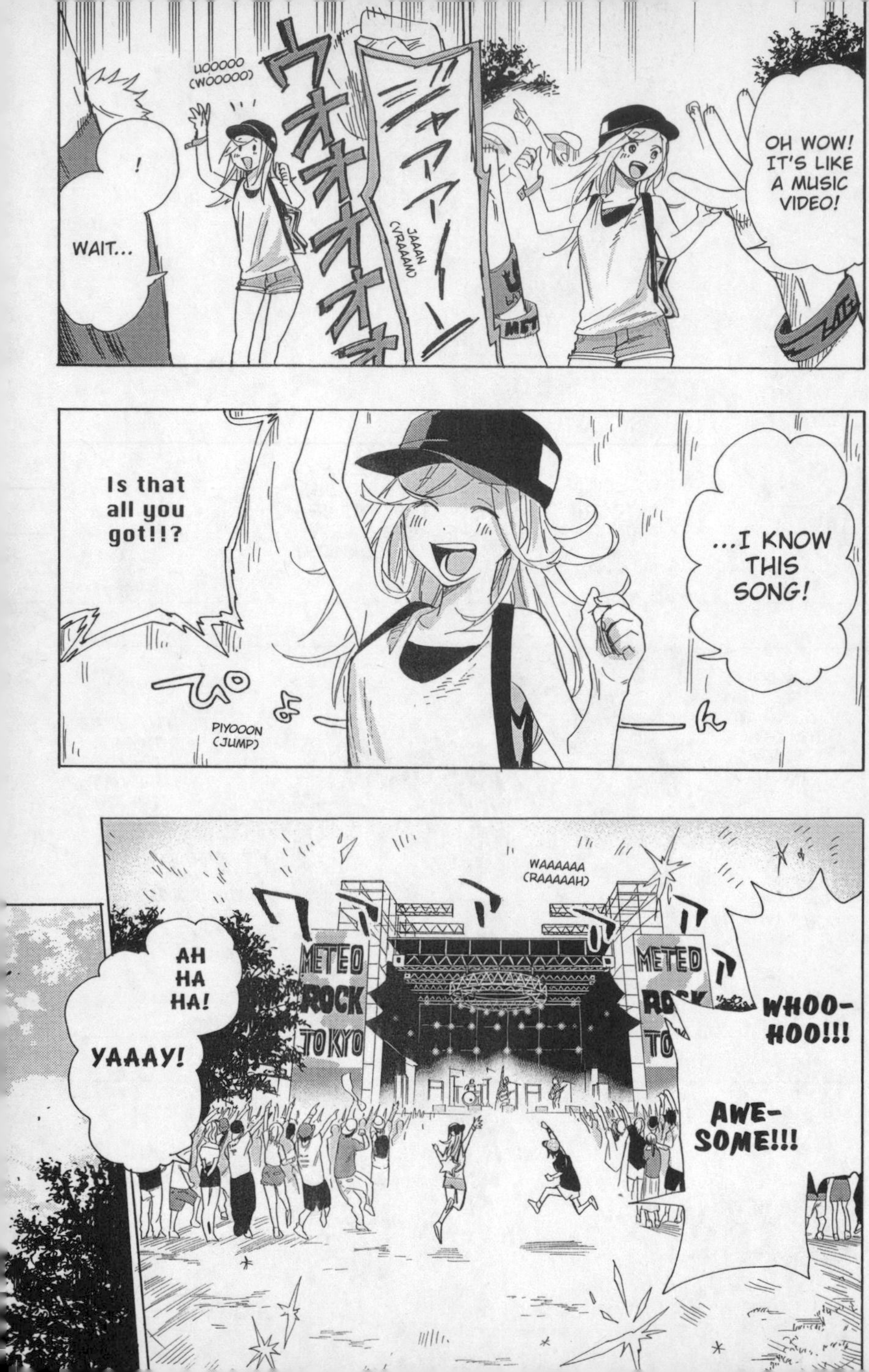
OH WOW! IT'S LIKE A MUSIC VIDEO!
ジャアアーン
JAAAN (VRAAAN)
ウオオオオ
UOOOOO (WOOOOO)
!
WAIT...
...I KNOW THIS SONG!
Is that all you got!!?
ぴょーーん
PIYOOON (JUMP)
WHOO-HOO!!!
AWE-SOME!!!
METEO ROCK TOKYO
WAAAAAA (RAAAAAH)
AH HA HA!
YAAAY!

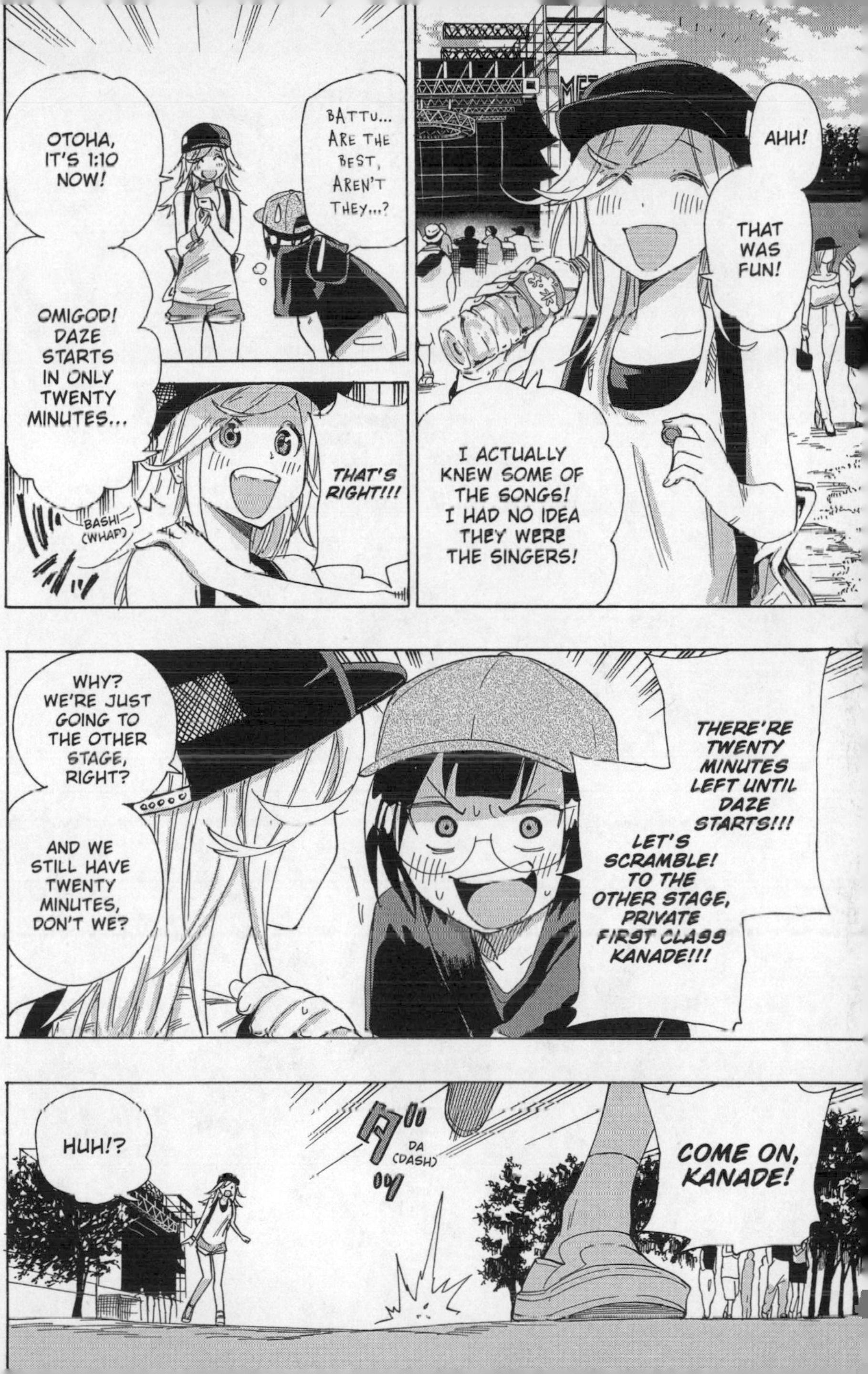
AHH!
THAT WAS FUN!
I ACTUALLY KNEW SOME OF THE SONGS! I HAD NO IDEA THEY WERE THE SINGERS!
BATTU... ARE THE BEST, AREN'T THEY...?
OTOHA, IT'S 1:10 NOW!
OMIGOD! DAZE STARTS IN ONLY TWENTY MINUTES...
THAT'S RIGHT!!!
BASHI (WHAP)
THERE'RE TWENTY MINUTES LEFT UNTIL DAZE STARTS!!!
LET'S SCRAMBLE! TO THE OTHER STAGE, PRIVATE FIRST CLASS KANADE!!!
WHY? WE'RE JUST GOING TO THE OTHER STAGE, RIGHT?
AND WE STILL HAVE TWENTY MINUTES, DON'T WE?
COME ON, KANADE!
DA (DASH)
HUH!?

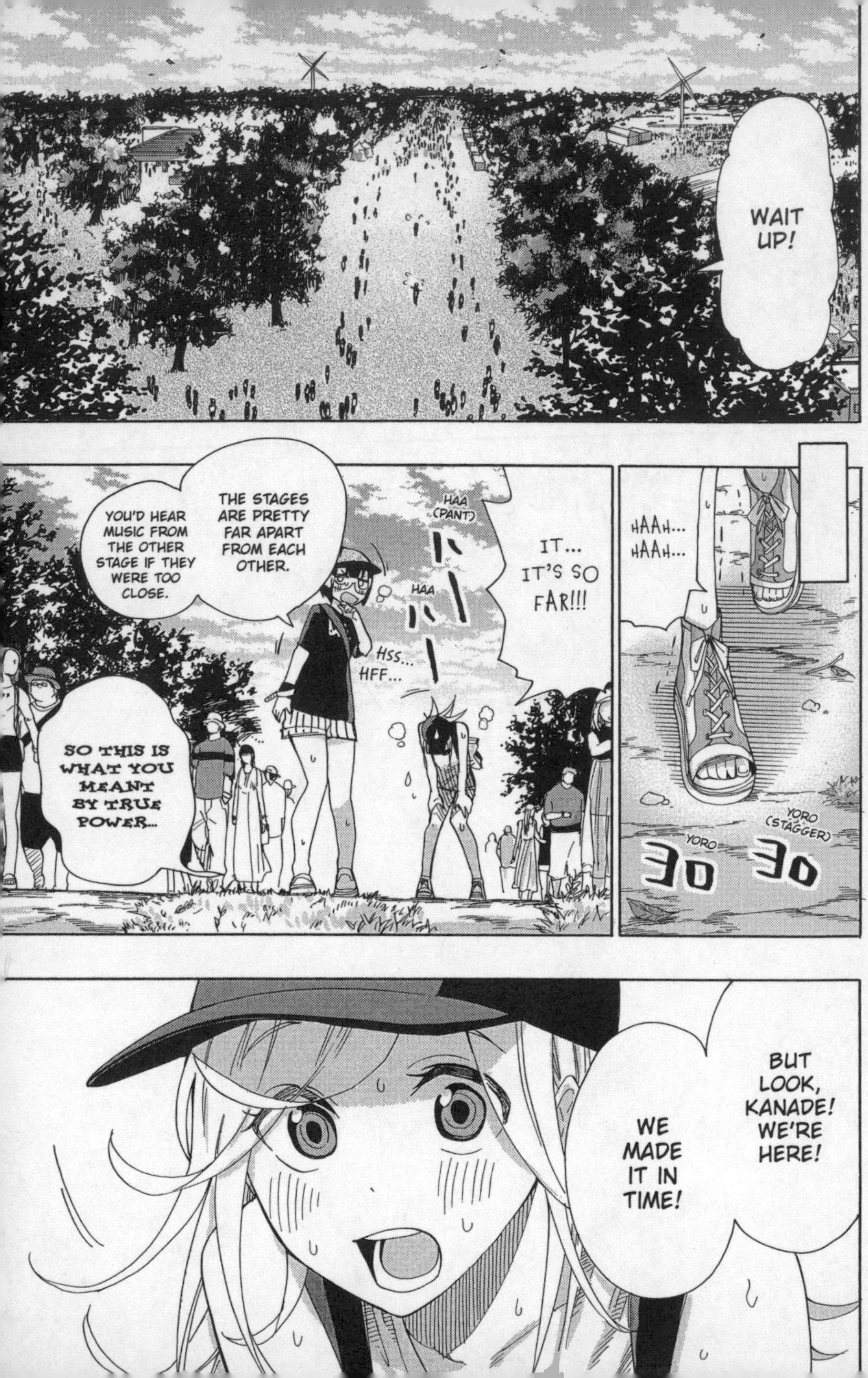
WAIT UP!
HAAH... HAAH...
YORO (STAGGER)
YORO
ヨロ ヨロ
IT... IT'S SO FAR!!!
HAA (PANT)
HAA
HSS... HFF...
THE STAGES ARE PRETTY FAR APART FROM EACH OTHER.
YOU'D HEAR MUSIC FROM THE OTHER STAGE IF THEY WERE TOO CLOSE.
SO THIS IS WHAT YOU MEANT BY TRUE POWER...
BUT LOOK, KANADE! WE'RE HERE!
WE MADE IT IN TIME!

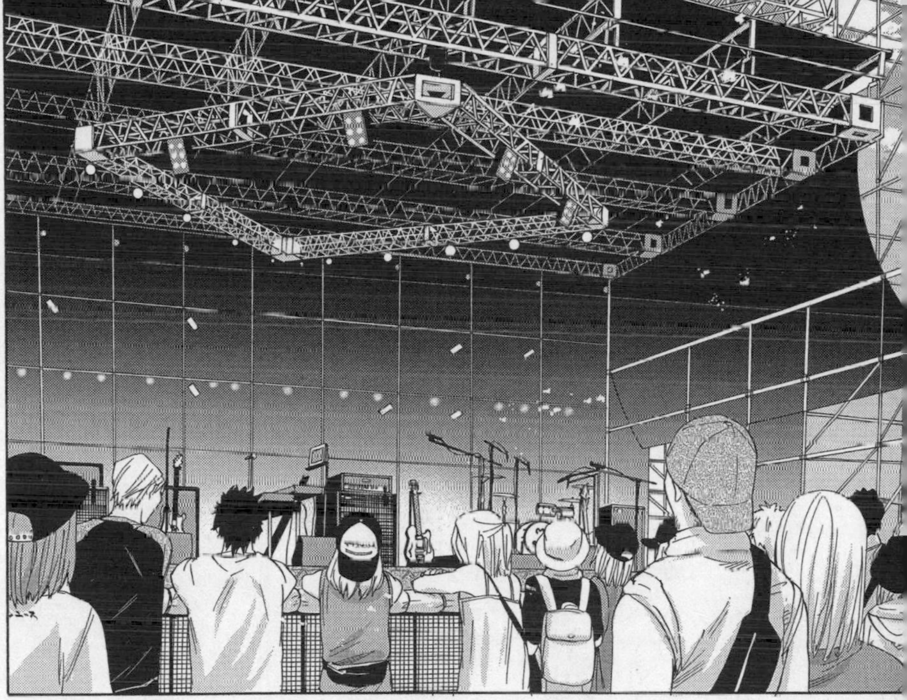
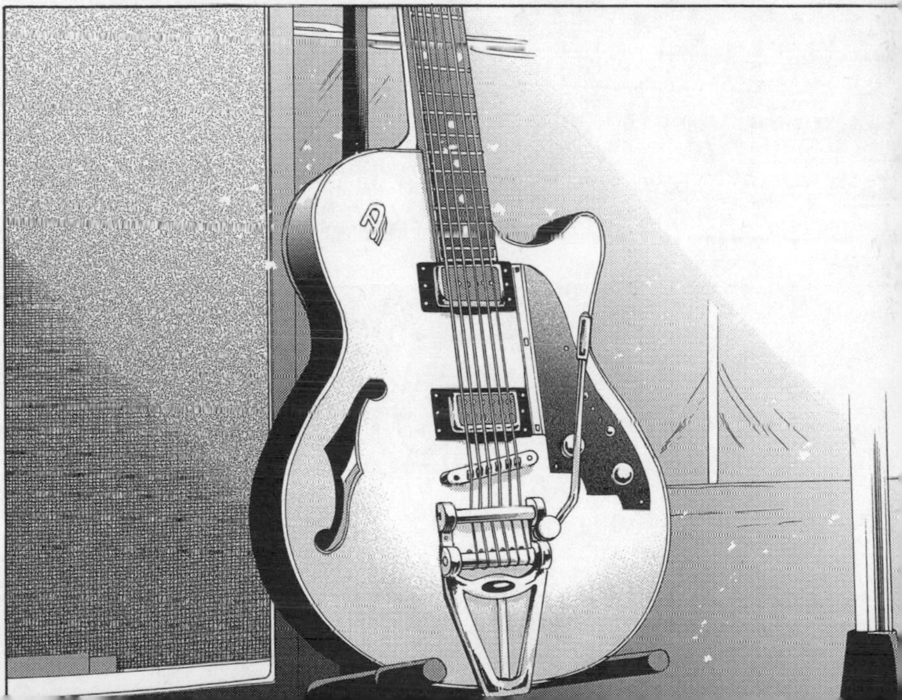

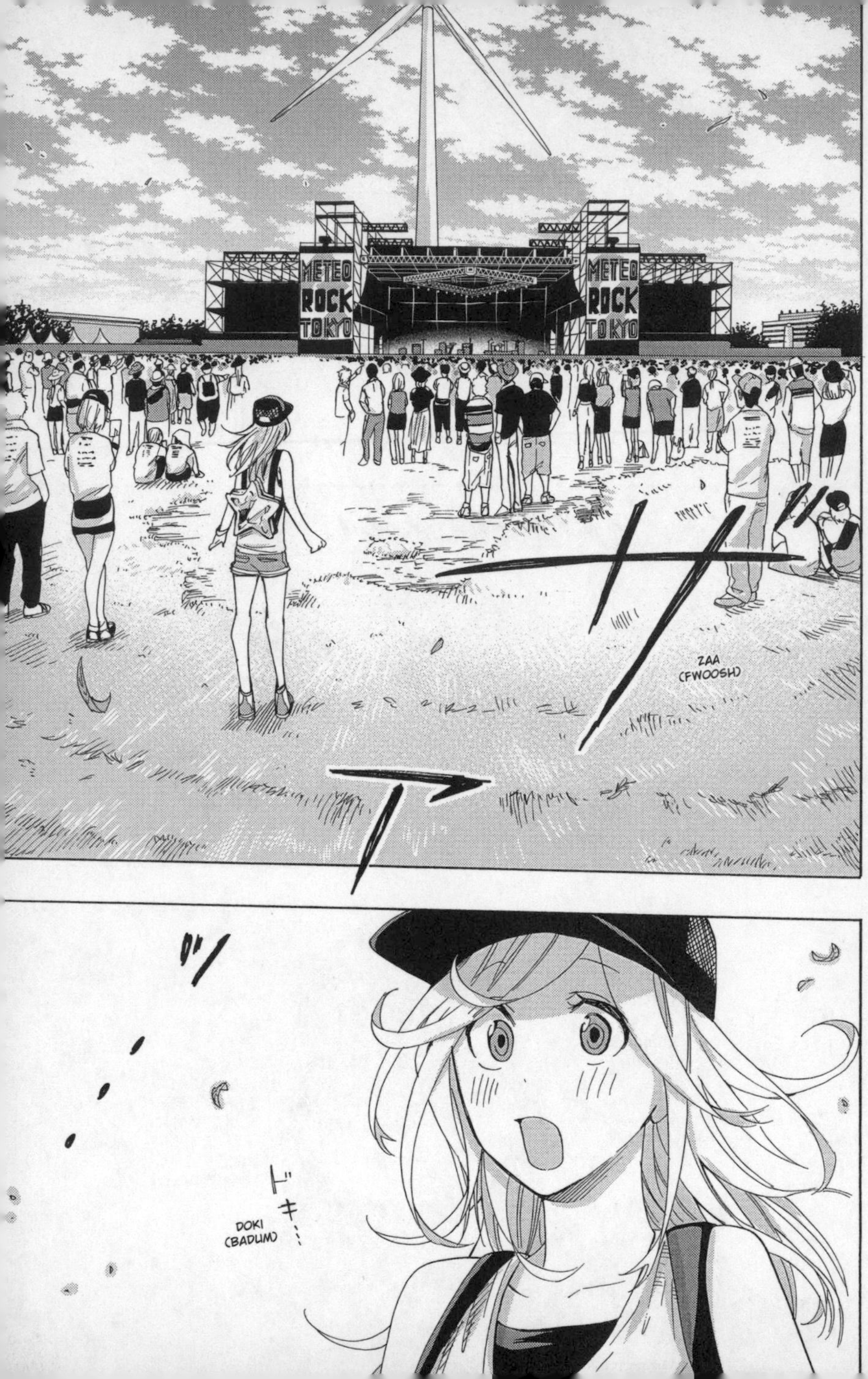

METEO ROCK TOKYO
METEO ROCK TOKYO
ZAA (FWOOSH)
ドキ…
DOKI (BADUM)

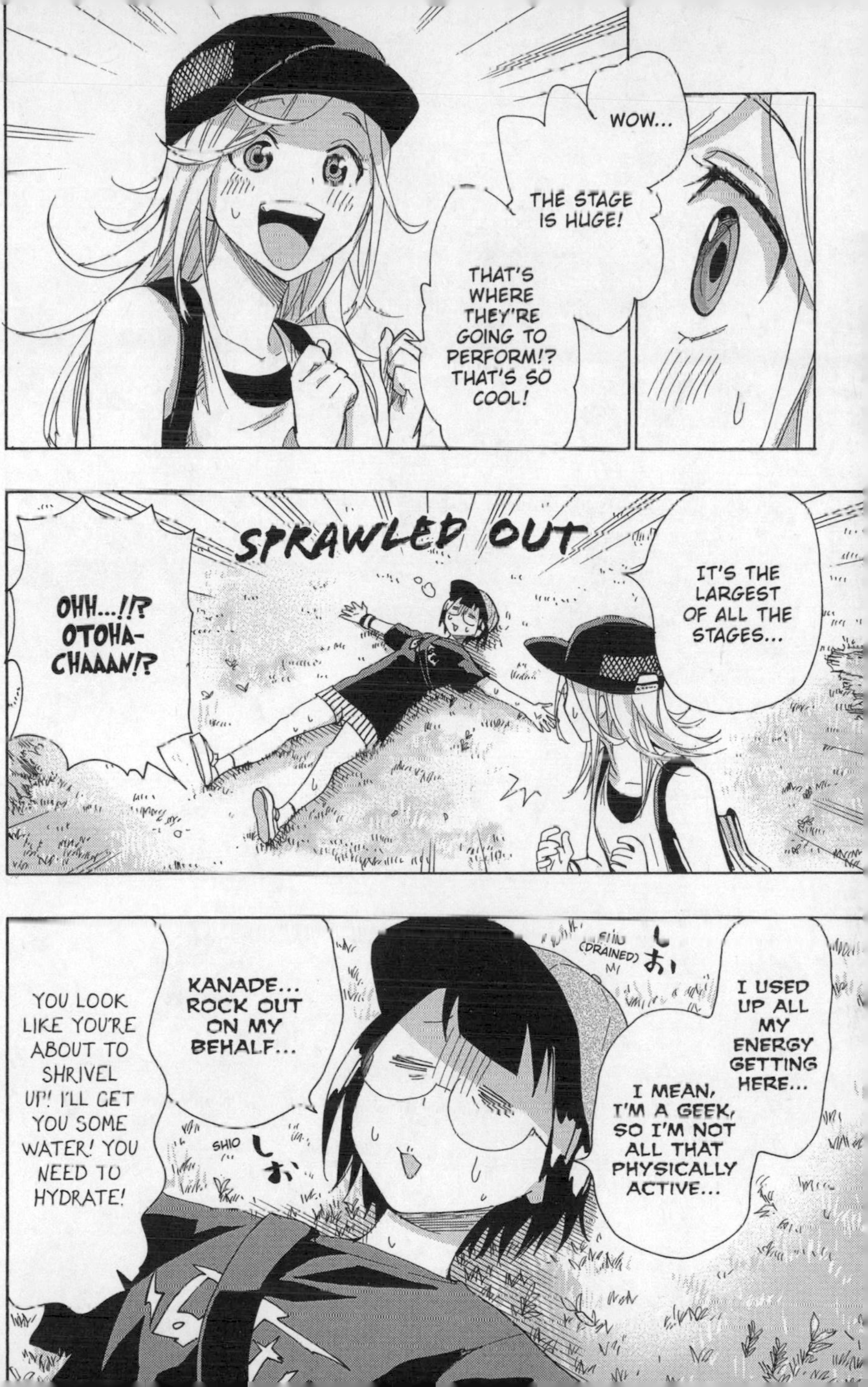
WOW...
THE STAGE IS HUGE!
THAT'S WHERE THEY'RE GOING TO PERFORM!? THAT'S SO COOL!
IT'S THE LARGEST OF ALL THE STAGES...
SPRAWLED OUT
OHH...!!? OTOHA-CHAAAN!?
I USED UP ALL MY ENERGY GETTING HERE...
I MEAN, I'M A GEEK, SO I'M NOT ALL THAT PHYSICALLY ACTIVE...
SHIO (DRAINED)
しお
KANADE... ROCK OUT ON MY BEHALF...
SHIO
しお
YOU LOOK LIKE YOU'RE ABOUT TO SHRIVEL UP! I'LL GET YOU SOME WATER! YOU NEED TO HYDRATE!

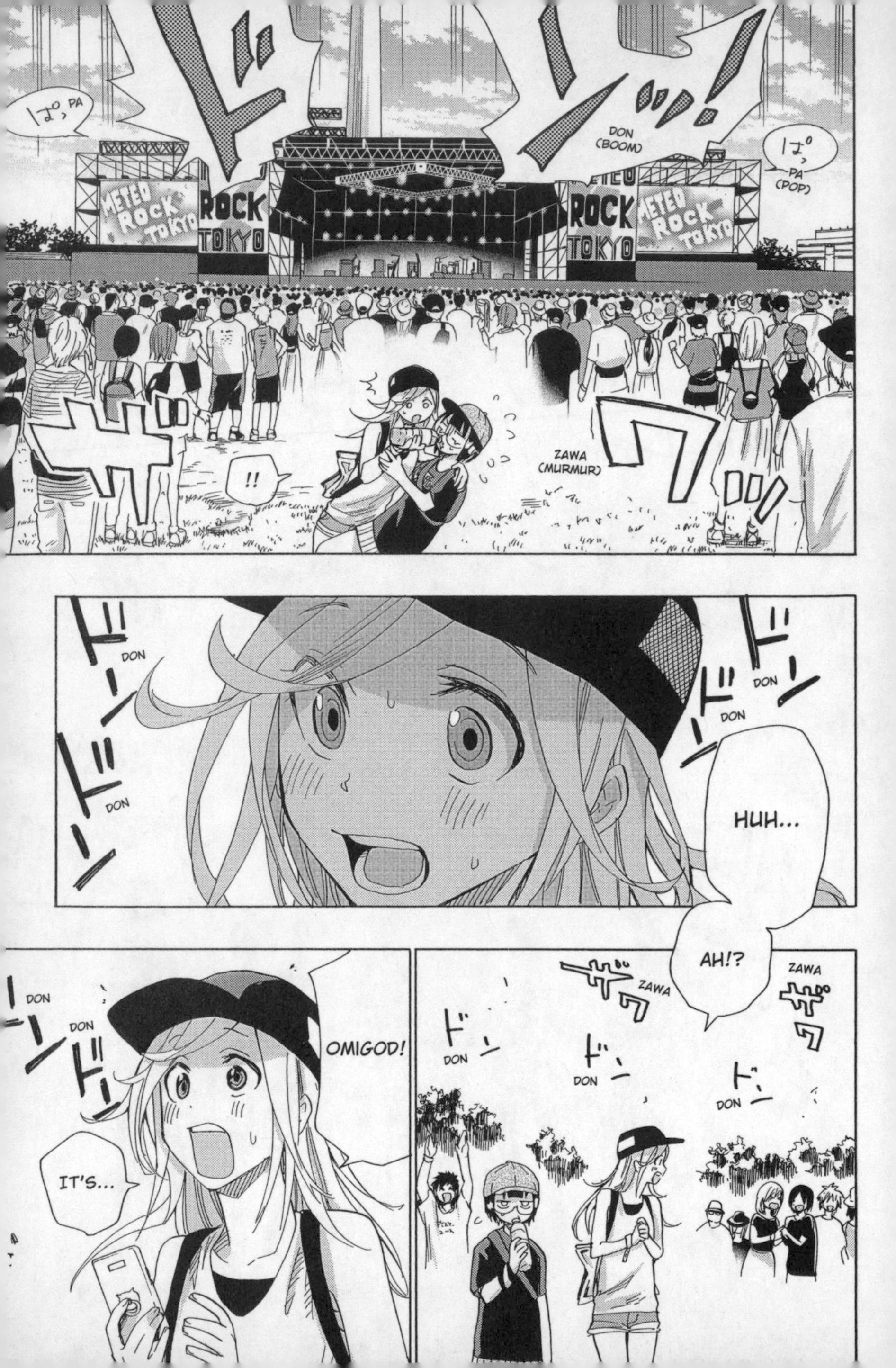
ぱっ
PA (POP)
DON (BOOM)
ぱっ PA
ZAWA (MURMUR)
!!
DON
DON
HUH...
DON
DON
ZAWA
AH!?
ZAWA
DON
DON
DON
OMIGOD!
DON
DON
IT'S...

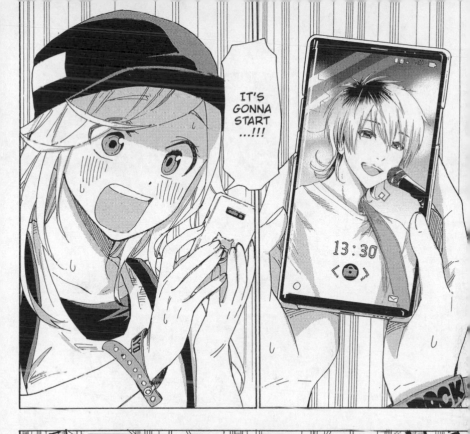

IT'S GONNA START ...!!!

13:30

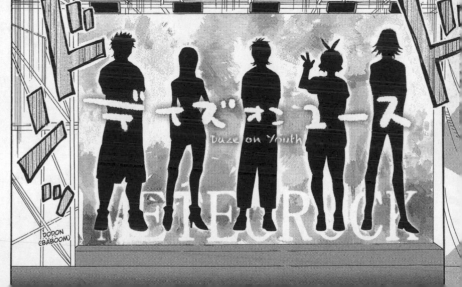

デイズオンユース
Daze on Youth

METEOROCK

DODON
CBABOOM

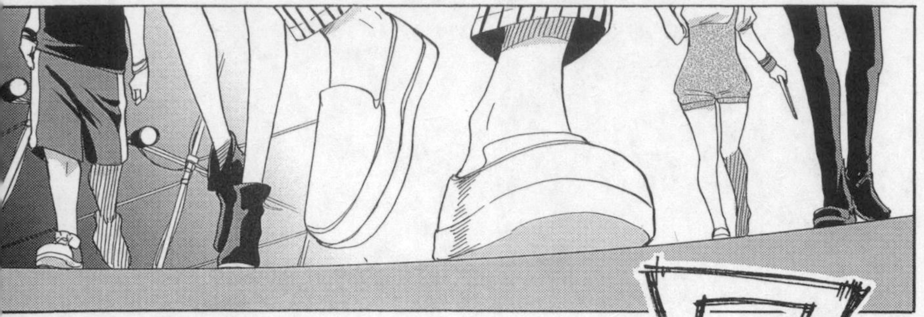
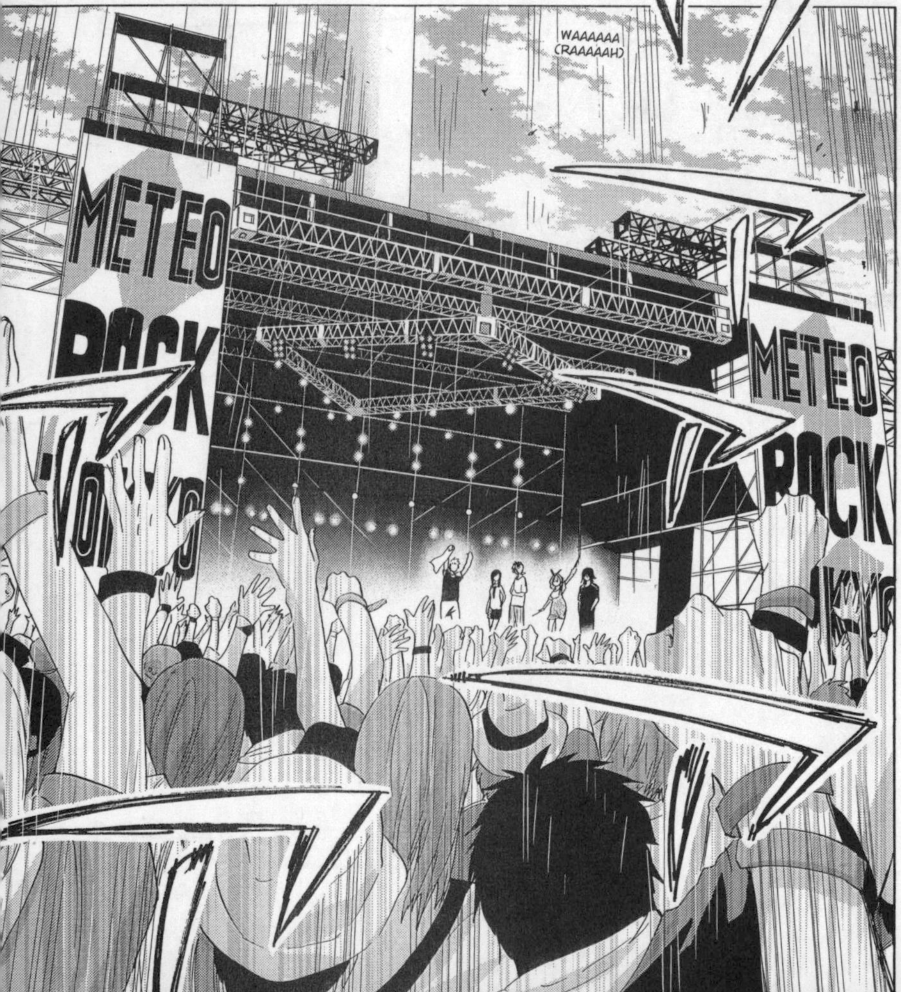
WAAAAAA
(RAAAAAH)

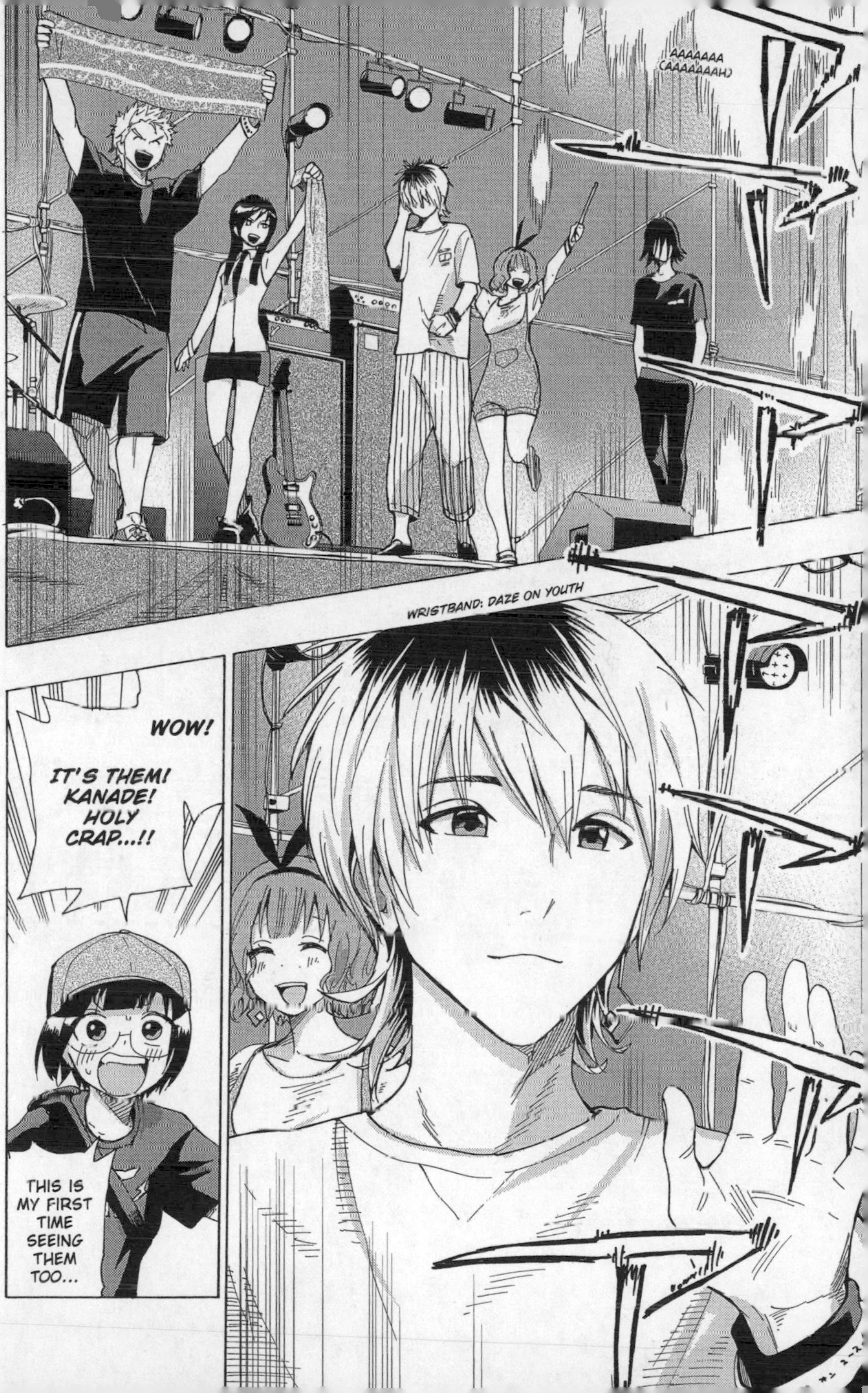
AAAAAAA (AAAAAAAH)
WRISTBAND: DAZE ON YOUTH
WOW!
IT'S THEM! KANADE! HOLY CRAP...!!
THIS IS MY FIRST TIME SEEING THEM TOO...

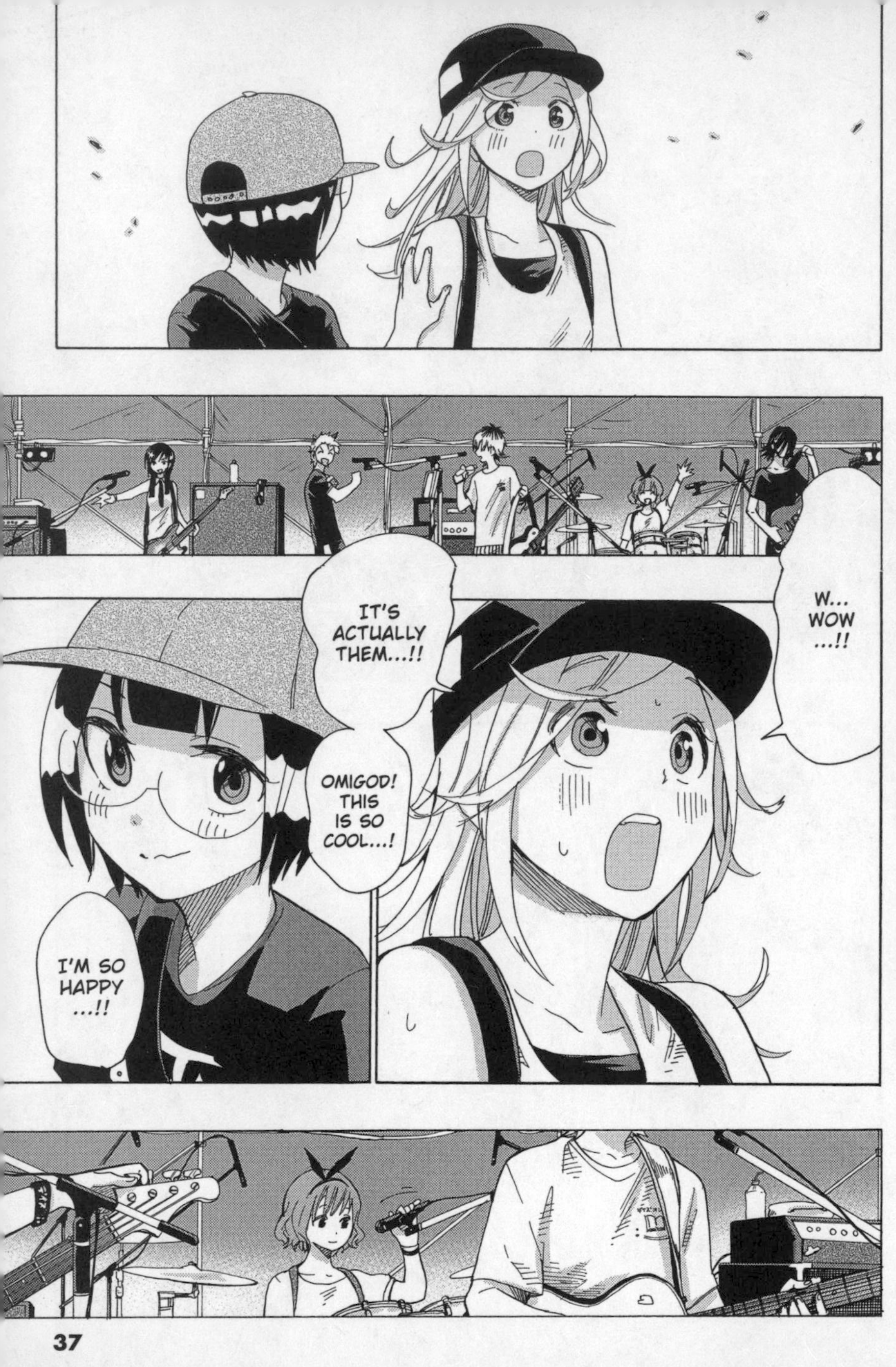
W... WOW ...!!
IT'S ACTUALLY THEM...!!
OMIGOD! THIS IS SO COOL...!
I'M SO HAPPY ...!!

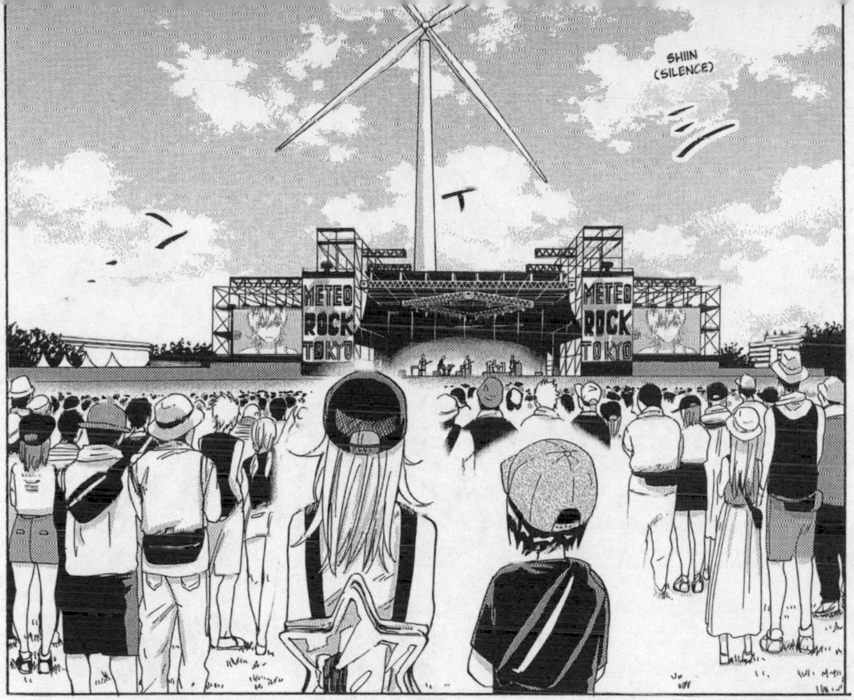
SHIIN
(SILENCE)
METEO ROCK TOKYO
METEO ROCK TOKYO

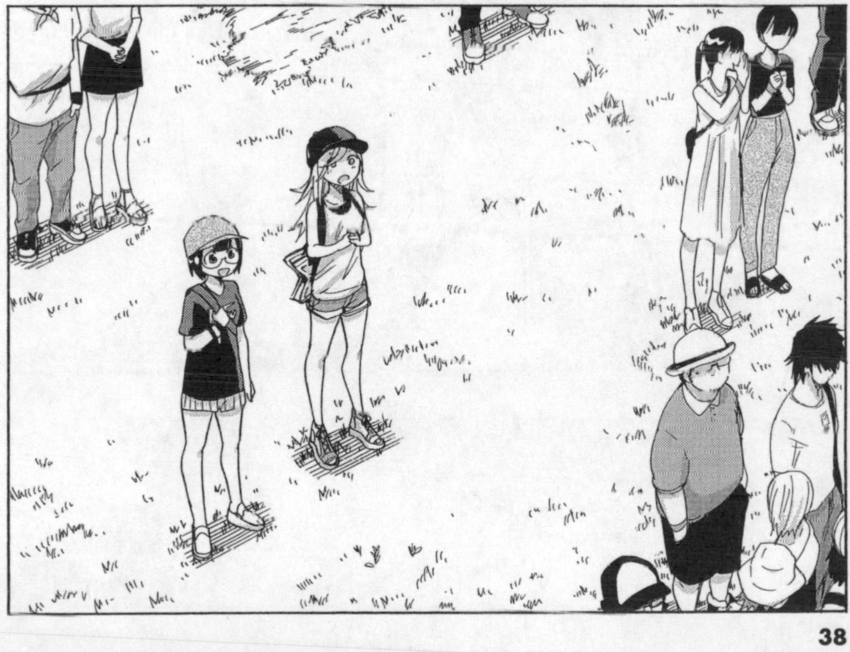

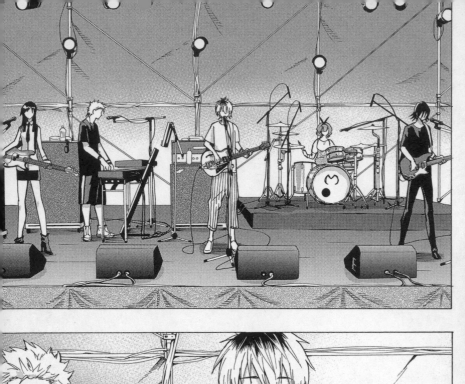

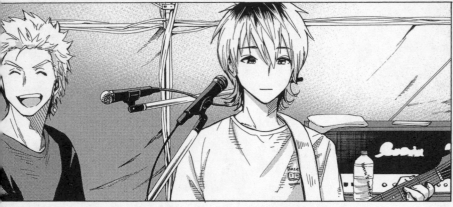

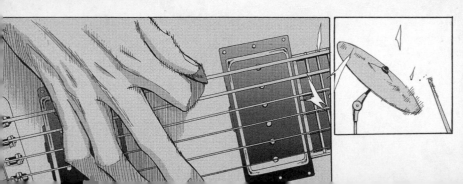

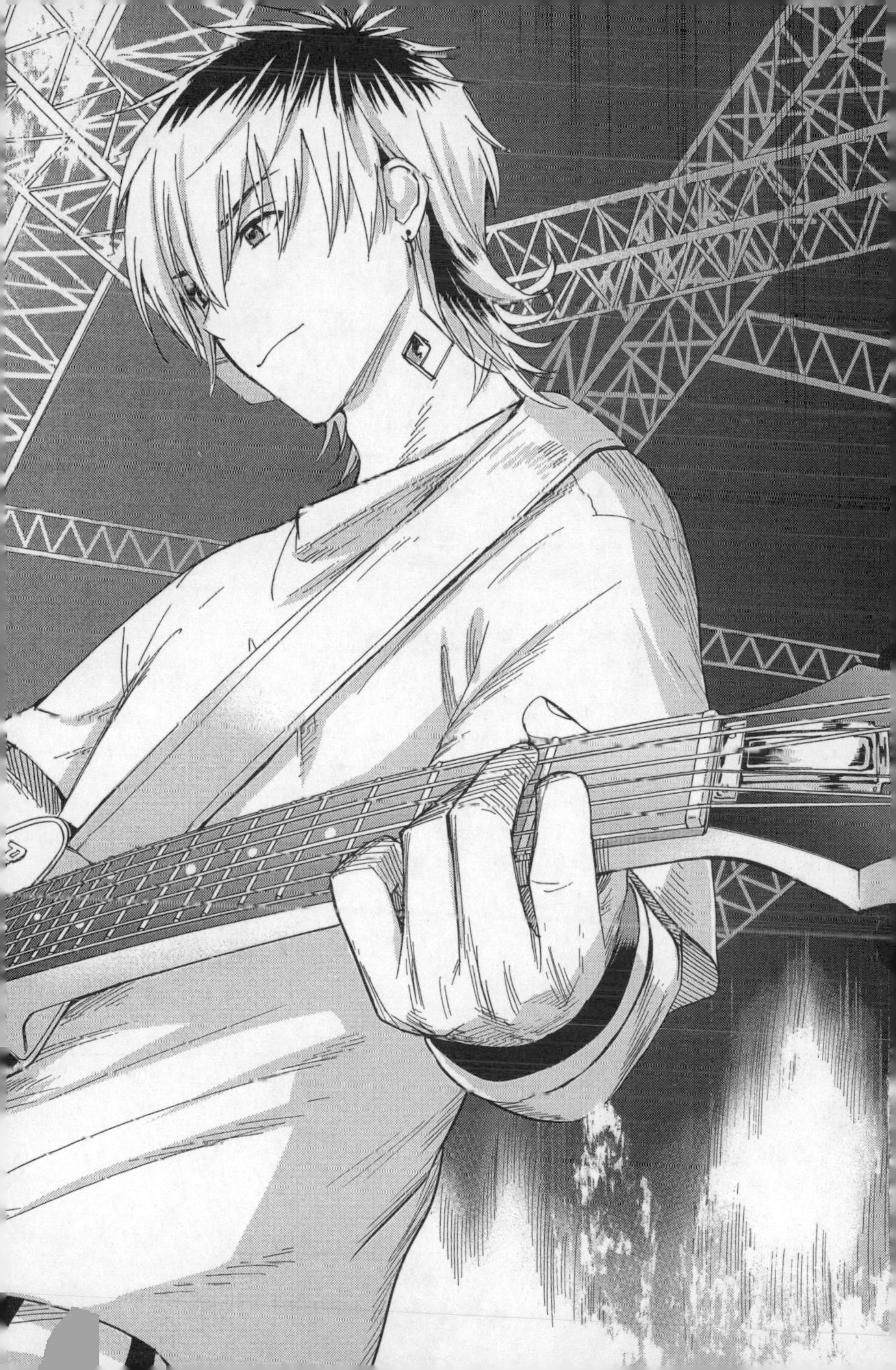

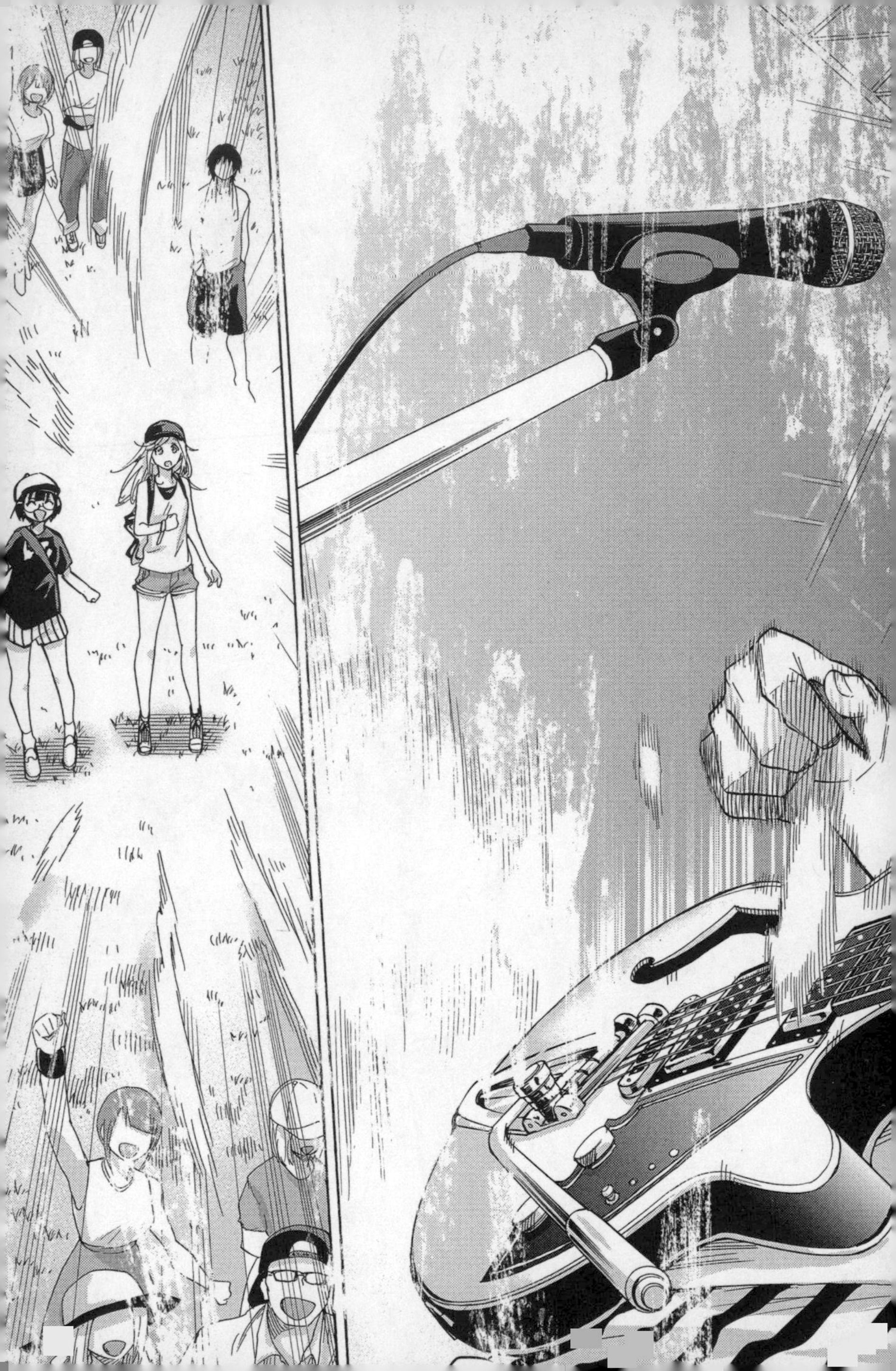

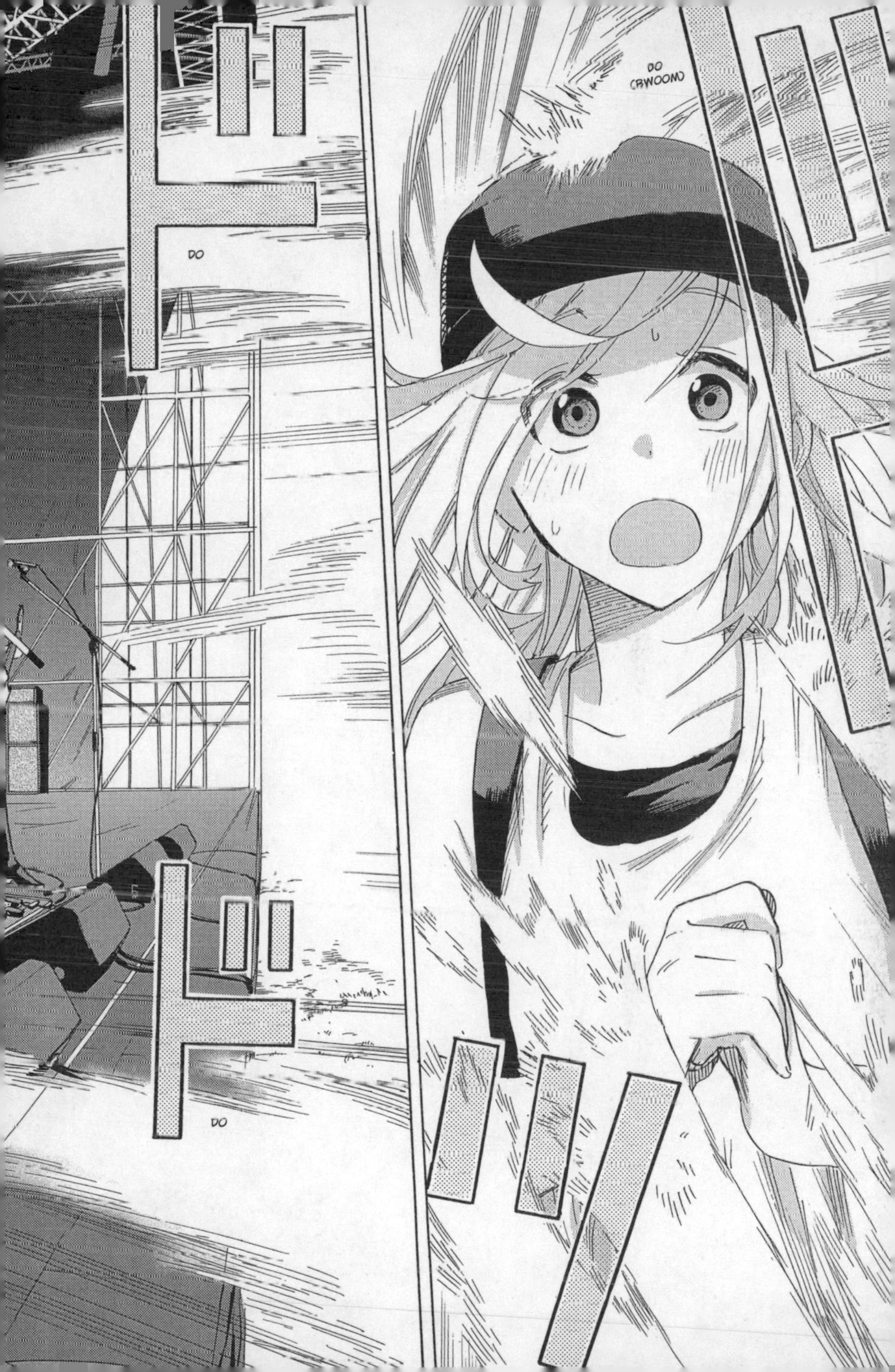
DO (BWOOM)
DO
DO

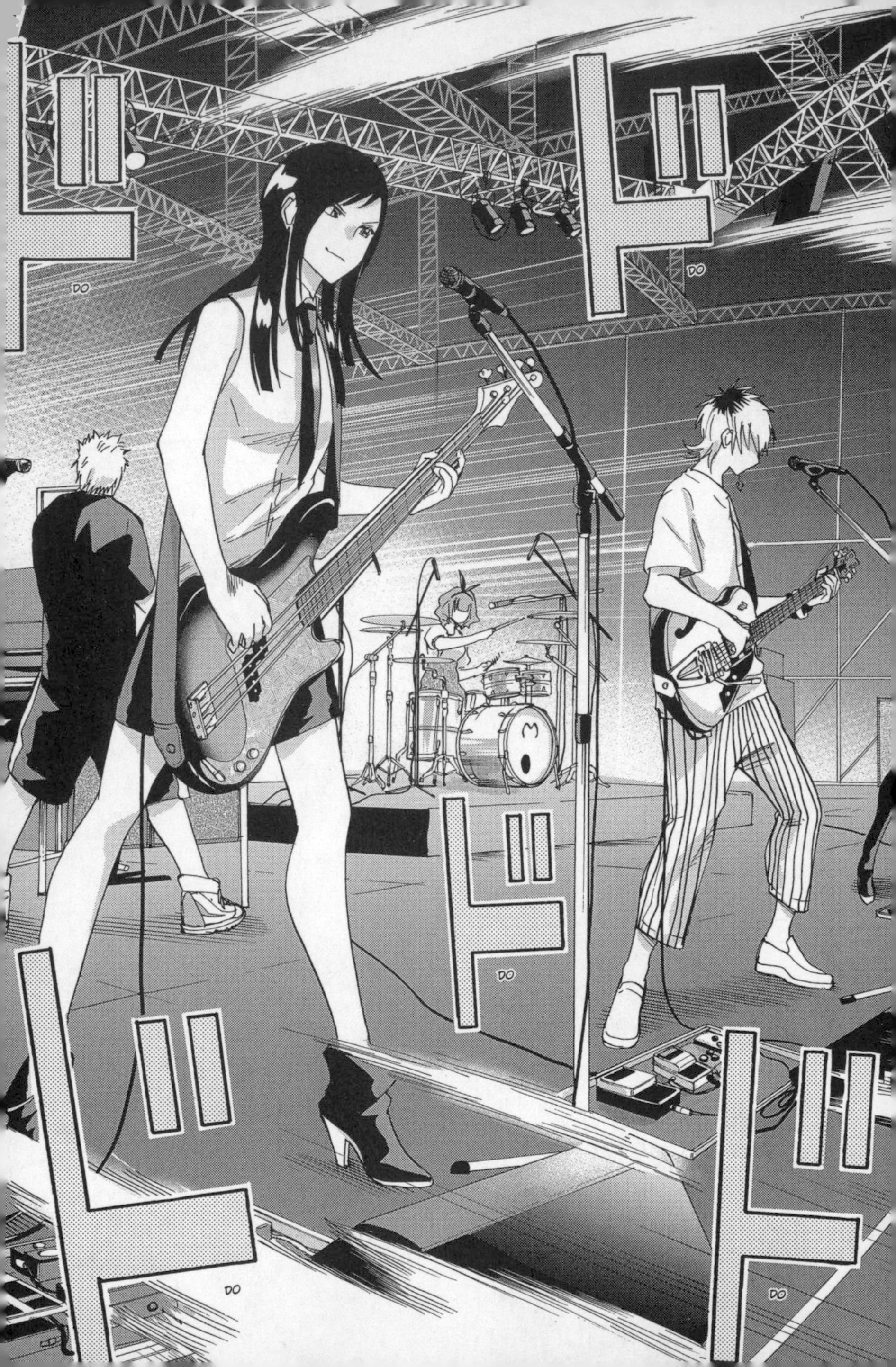

ド DO
ド DO
ド DO
ド DO
ド DO

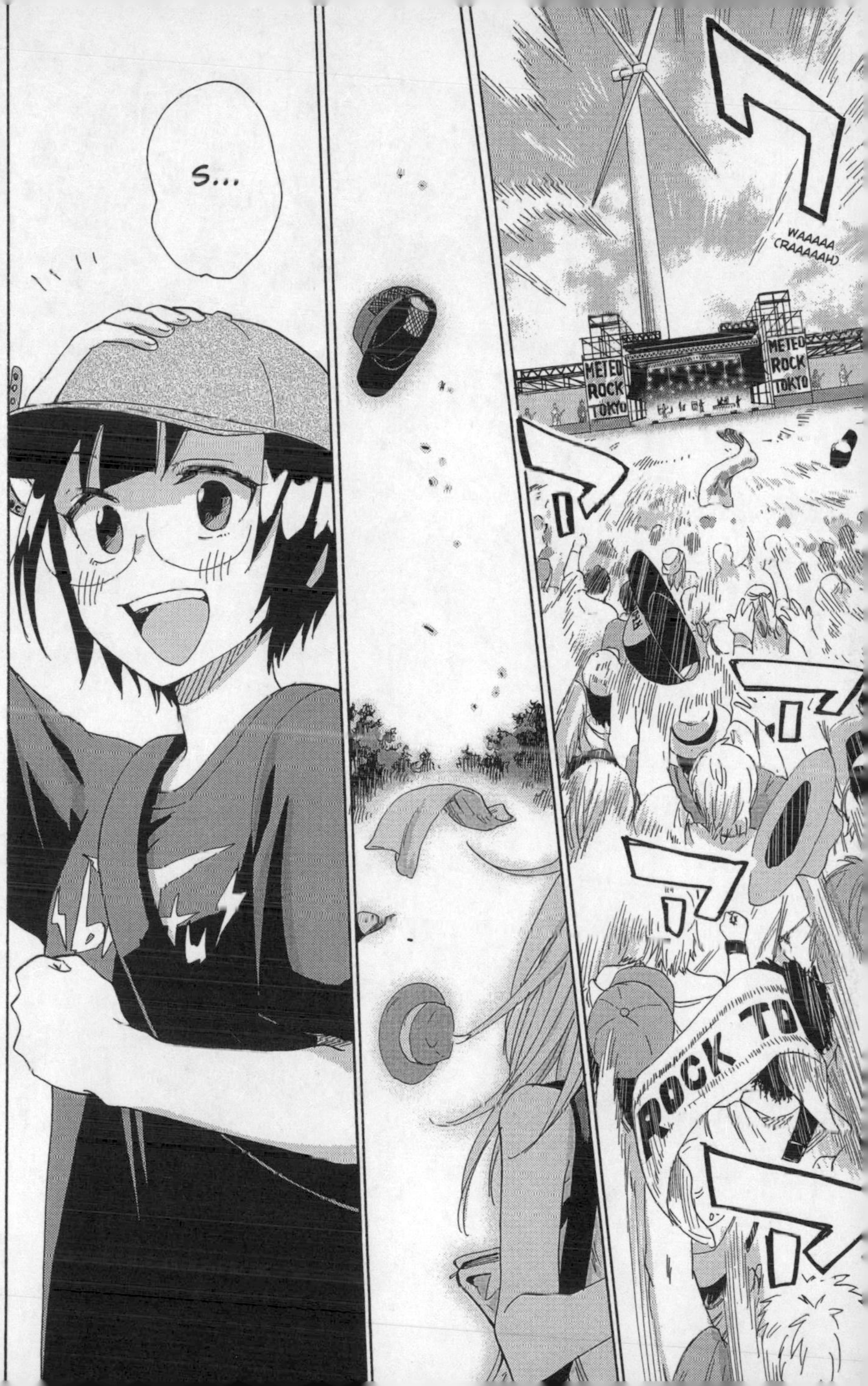
WAAAAA
(RAAAAAH)
METEO ROCK TOKYO
METEO ROCK TOKYO
ROCK TO
S...

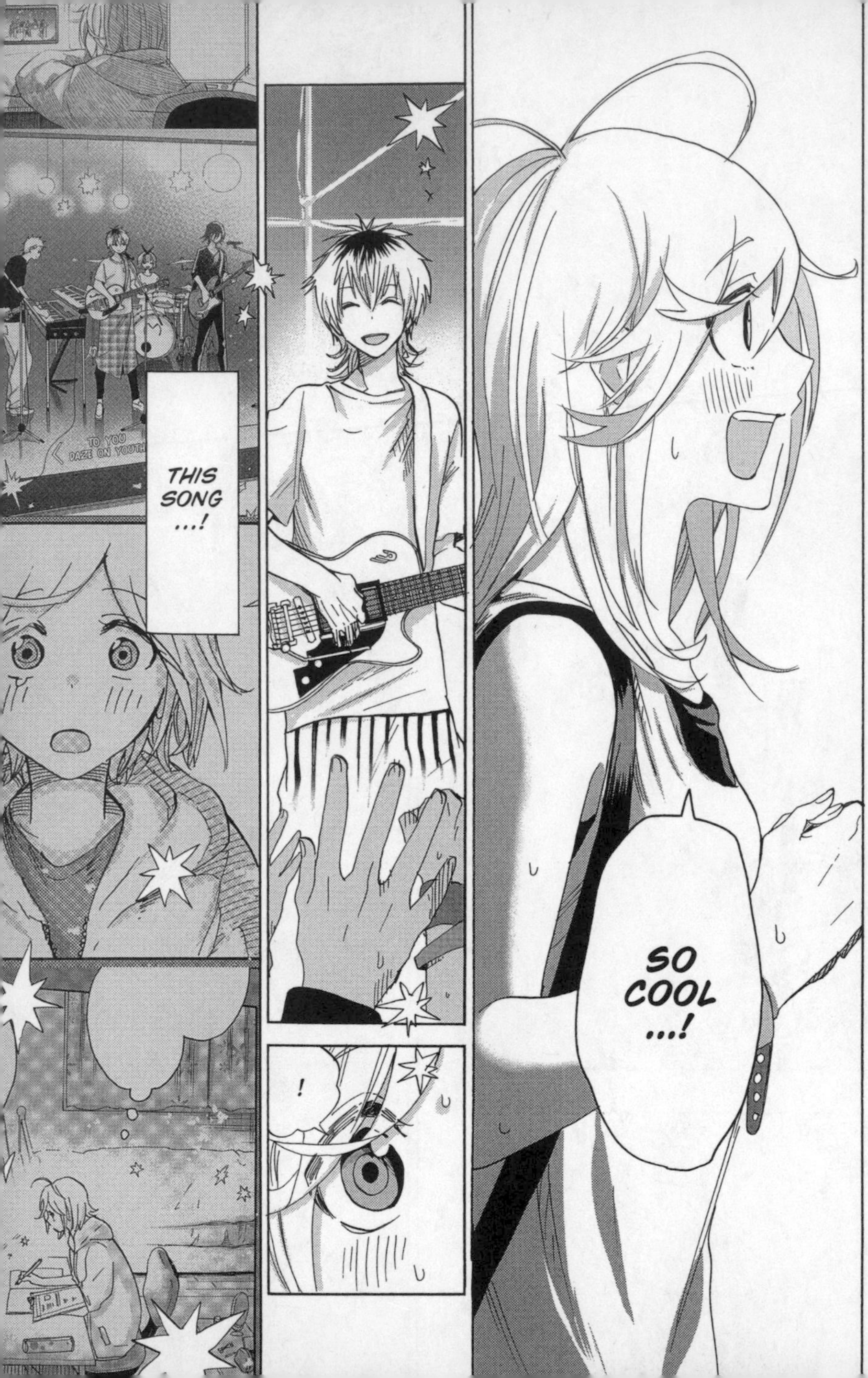
SO COOL ...!
!
TO YOU
DAZE ON YOUTH
THIS SONG ...!

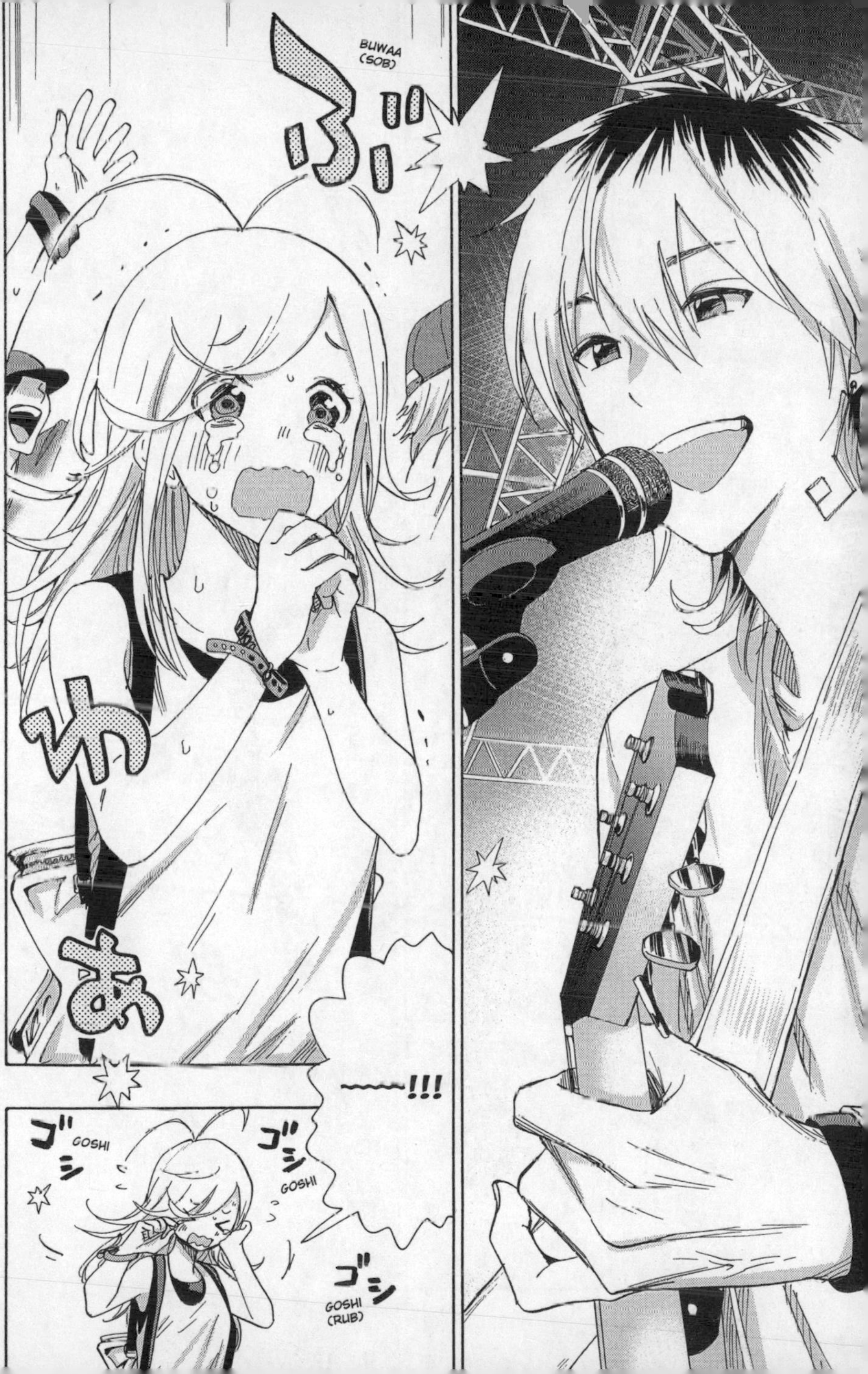

ぶ
BUWAA (SOB)
わあ
~~~!!!
ゴシ
GOSHI
ゴシ
GOSHI
ゴシ
GOSHI (RUB)
~~~

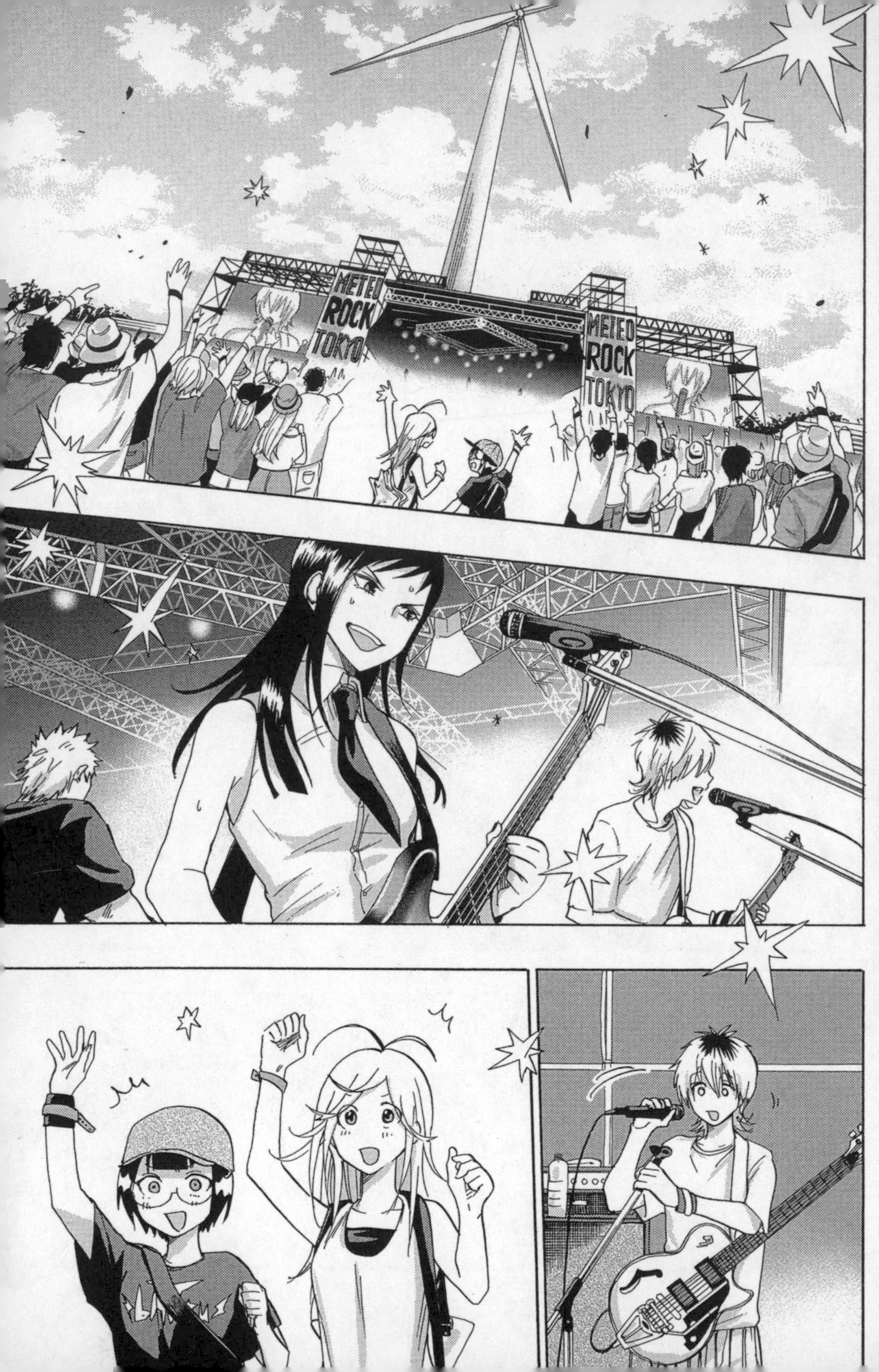
METEO ROCK TOKYO
METEO ROCK TOKYO

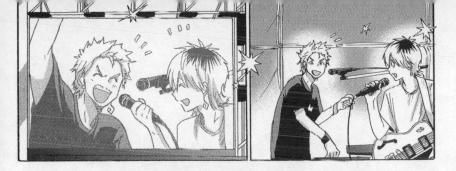

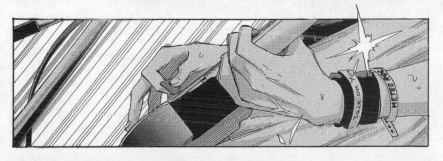

THEY'RE SO CUTE!!!

GYAAAN (SQUEE)

YAY! BEST-IES!!!

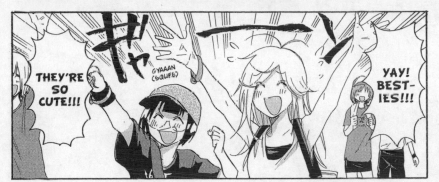

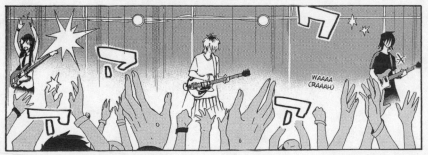

WAAAA (RAAAH)

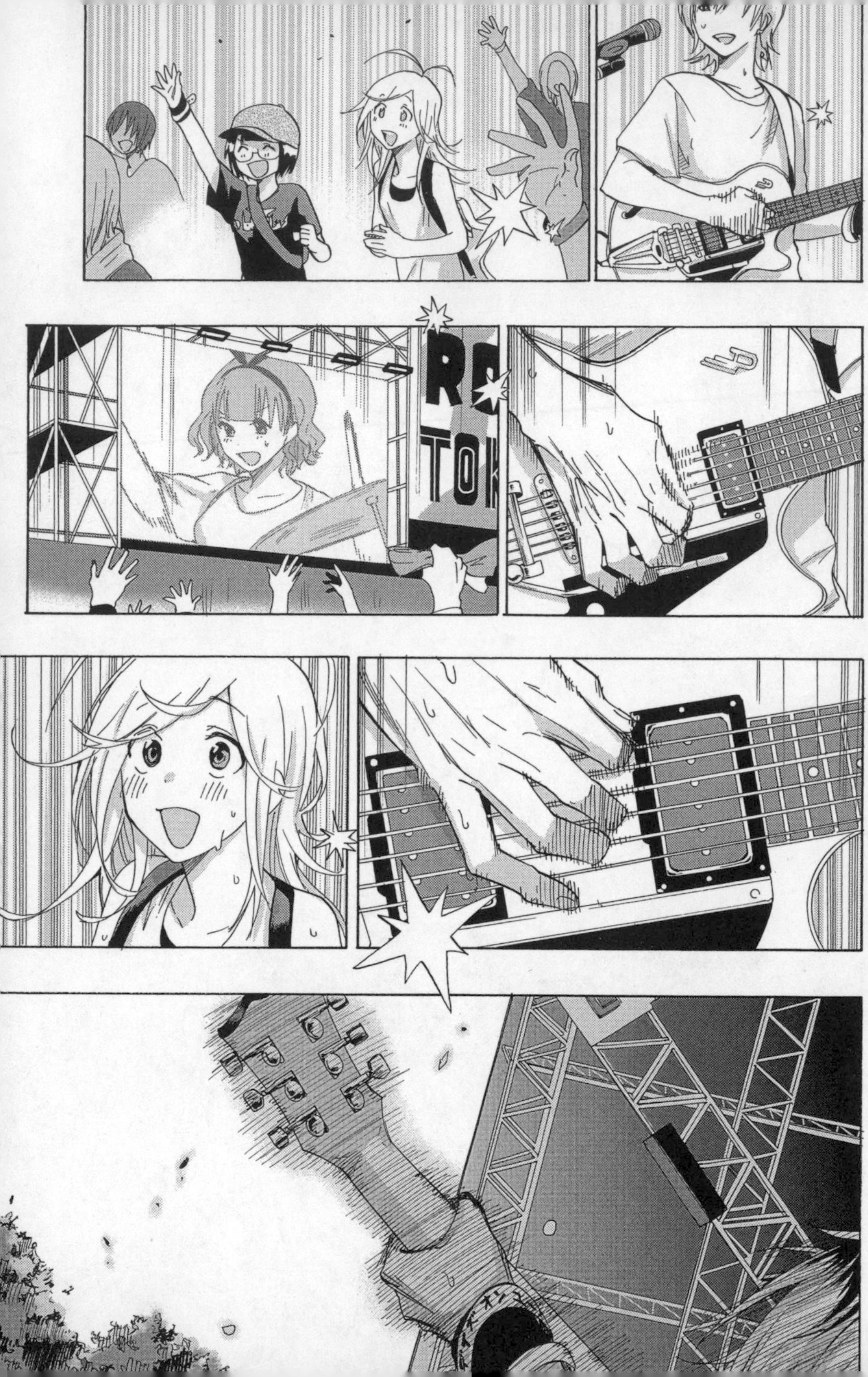

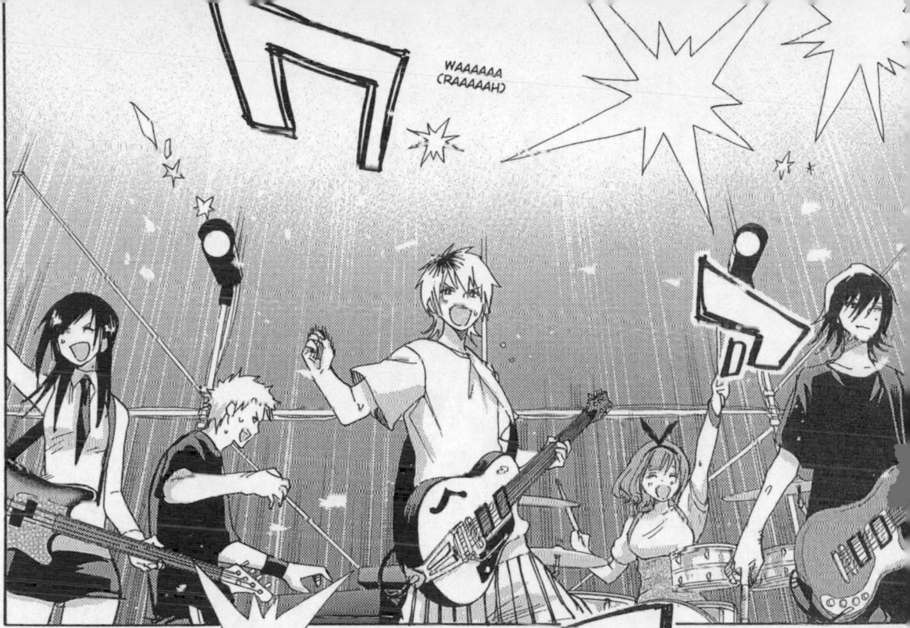
WAAAAAA
(RAAAAAH)
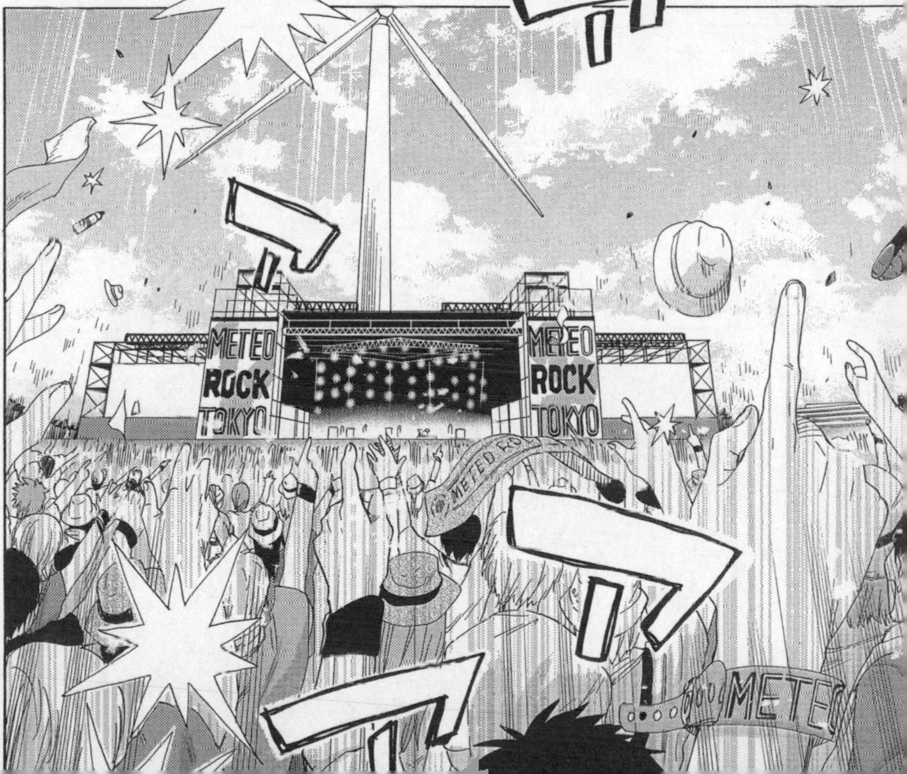
METEO
ROCK
TOKYO
METEO
ROCK
TOKYO
METEO

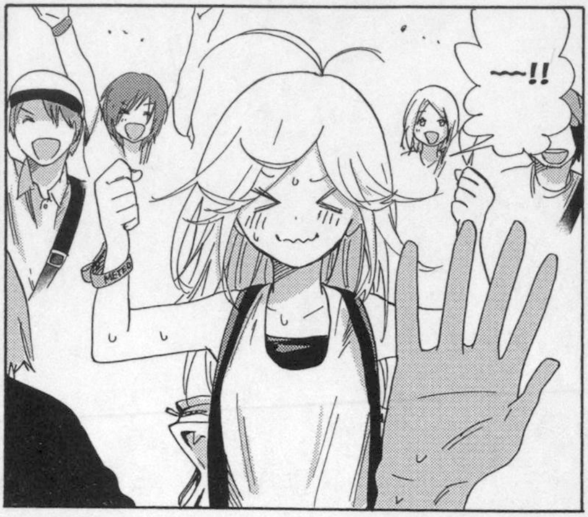
~~!!
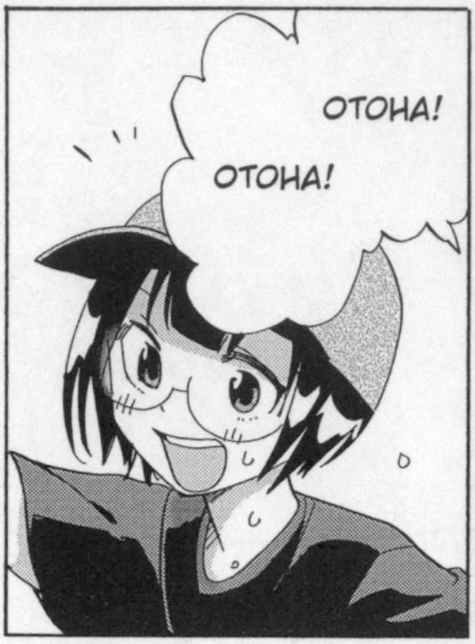
OTOHA!
OTOHA!
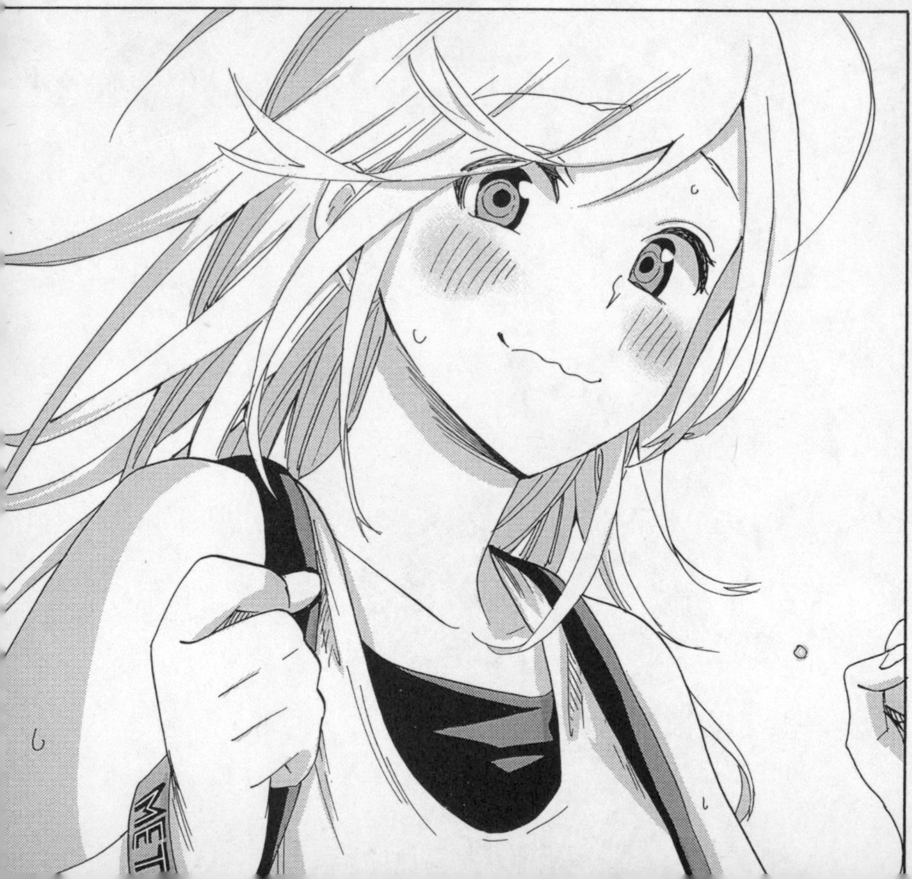

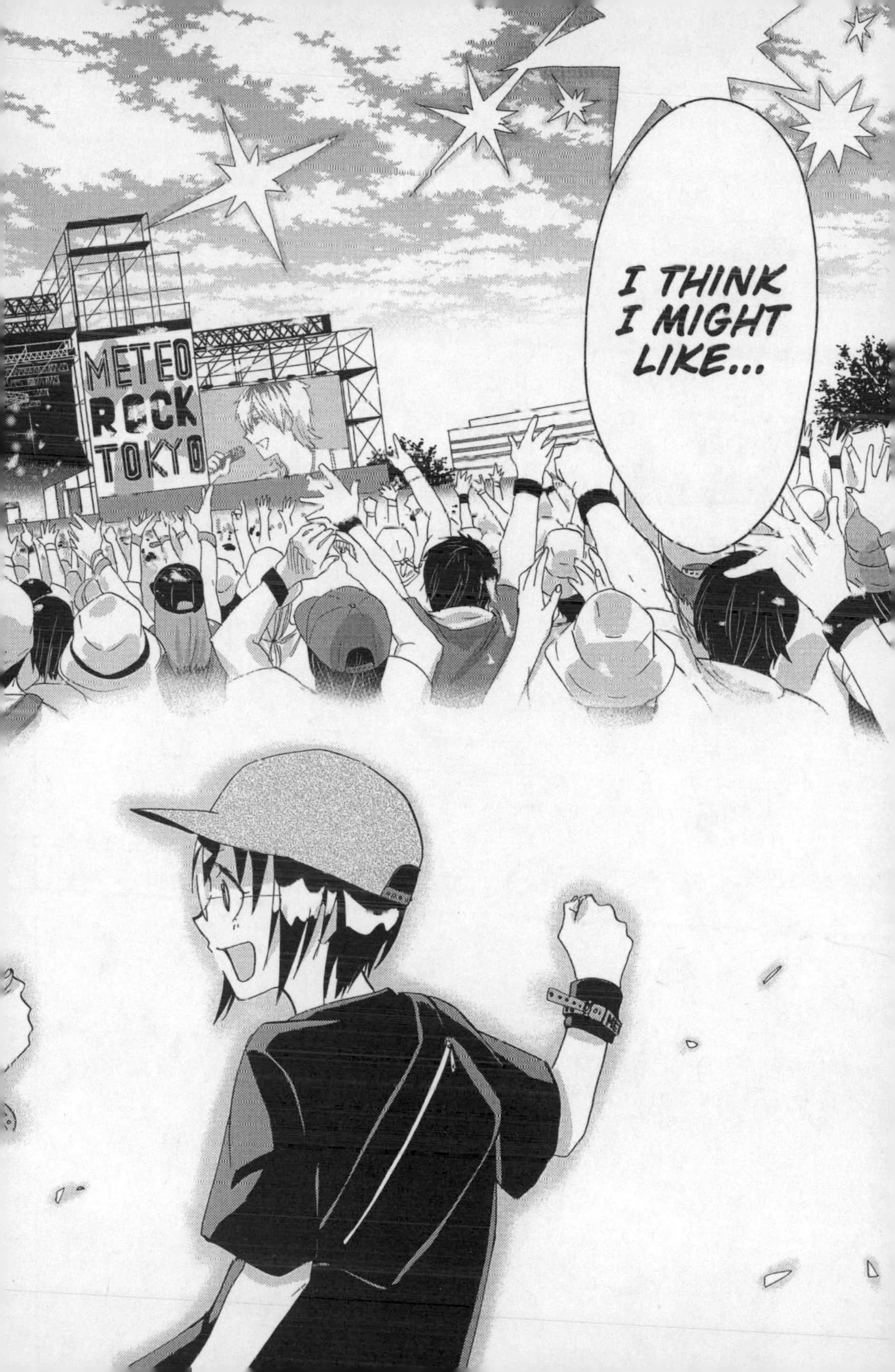
I THINK I MIGHT LIKE...
METEO ROCK TOKYO

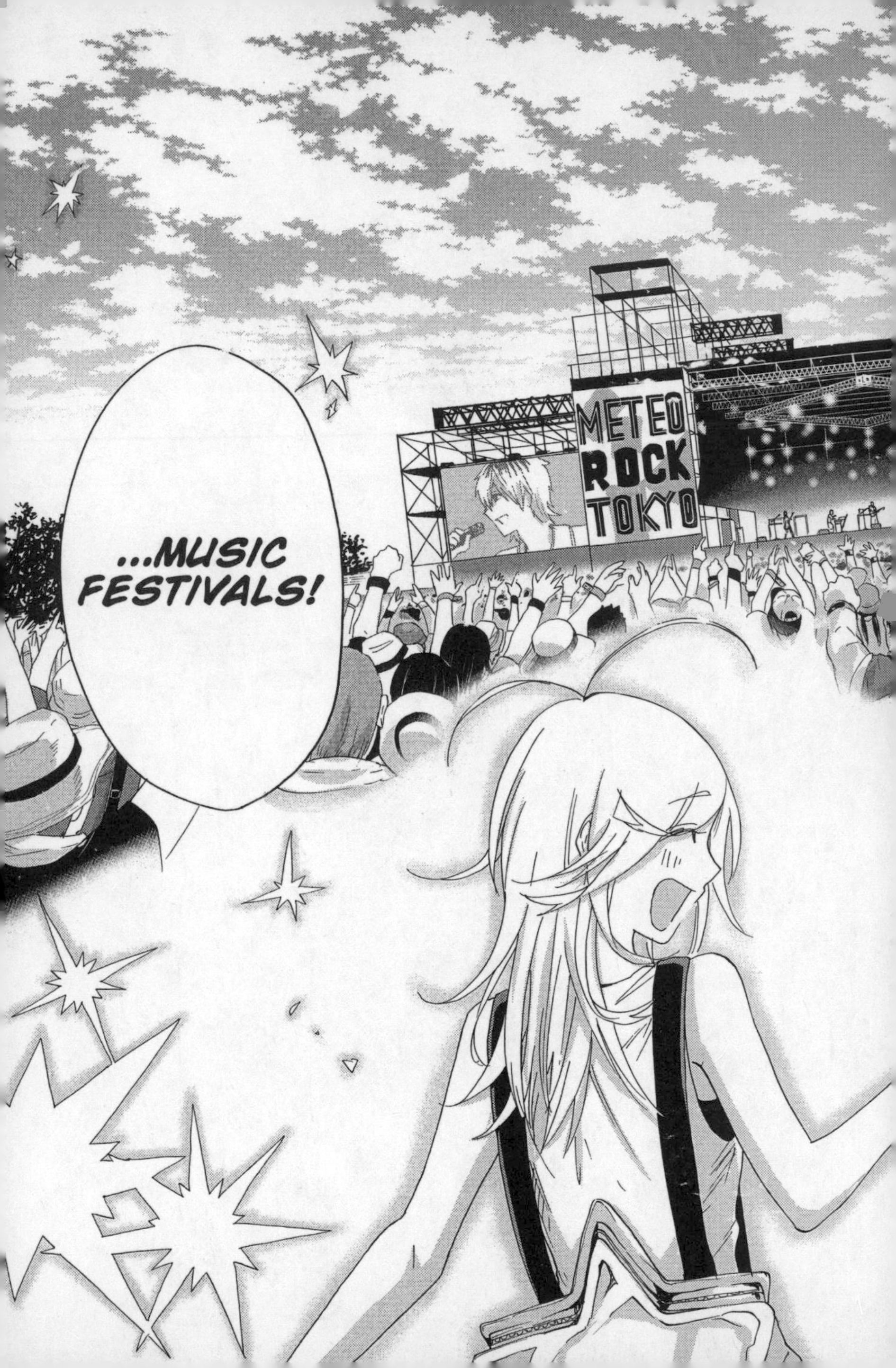
METEO ROCK TOKYO
...MUSIC FESTIVALS!

FES 1.5

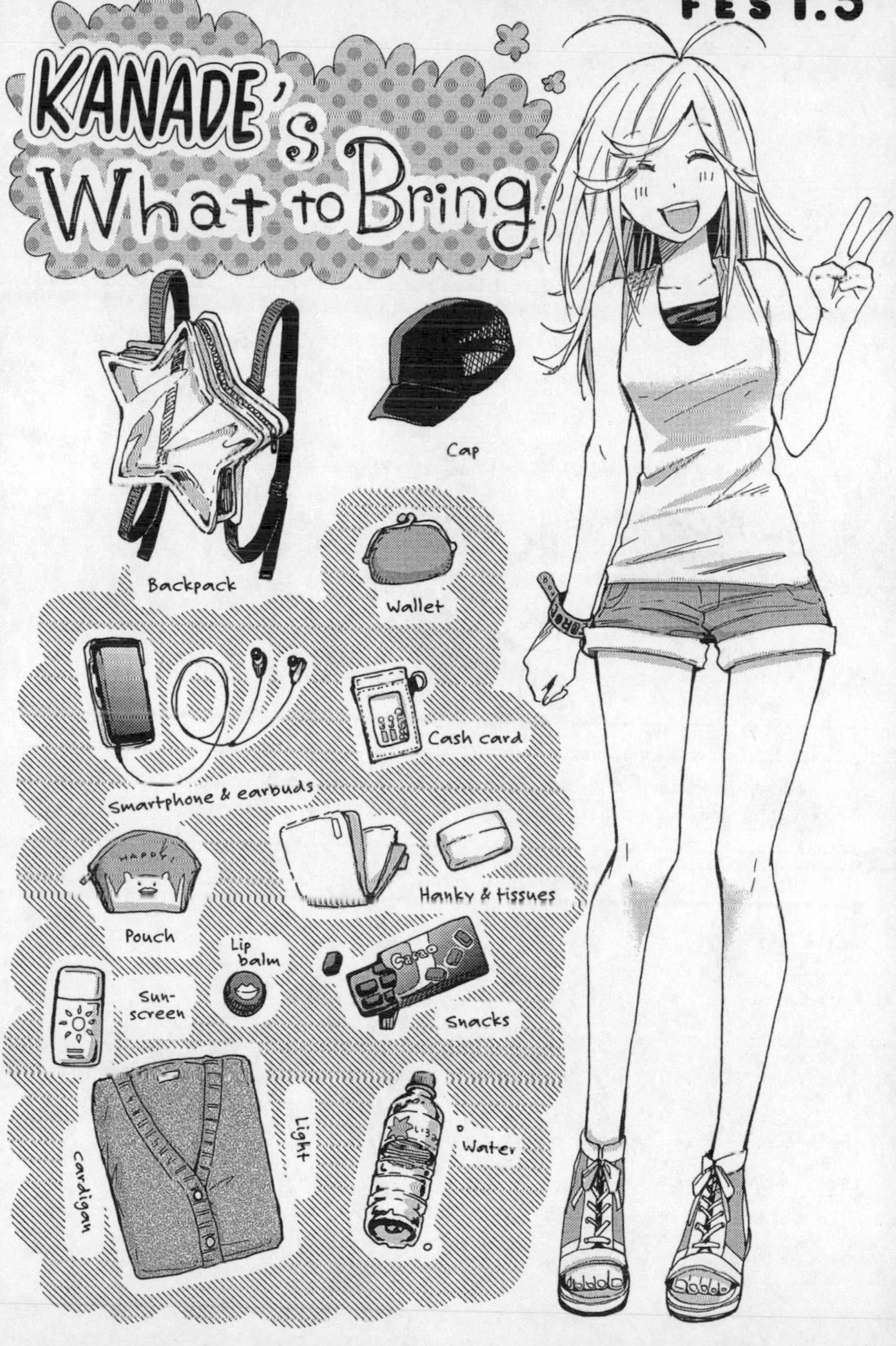
KANADE's What to Bring
Cap
Backpack
Wallet
Smartphone & earbuds
Cash card
HAPPY
Pouch
Hanky & tissues
Lip balm
Sun-screen
Cacao
Snacks
Light
Cardigan
Water

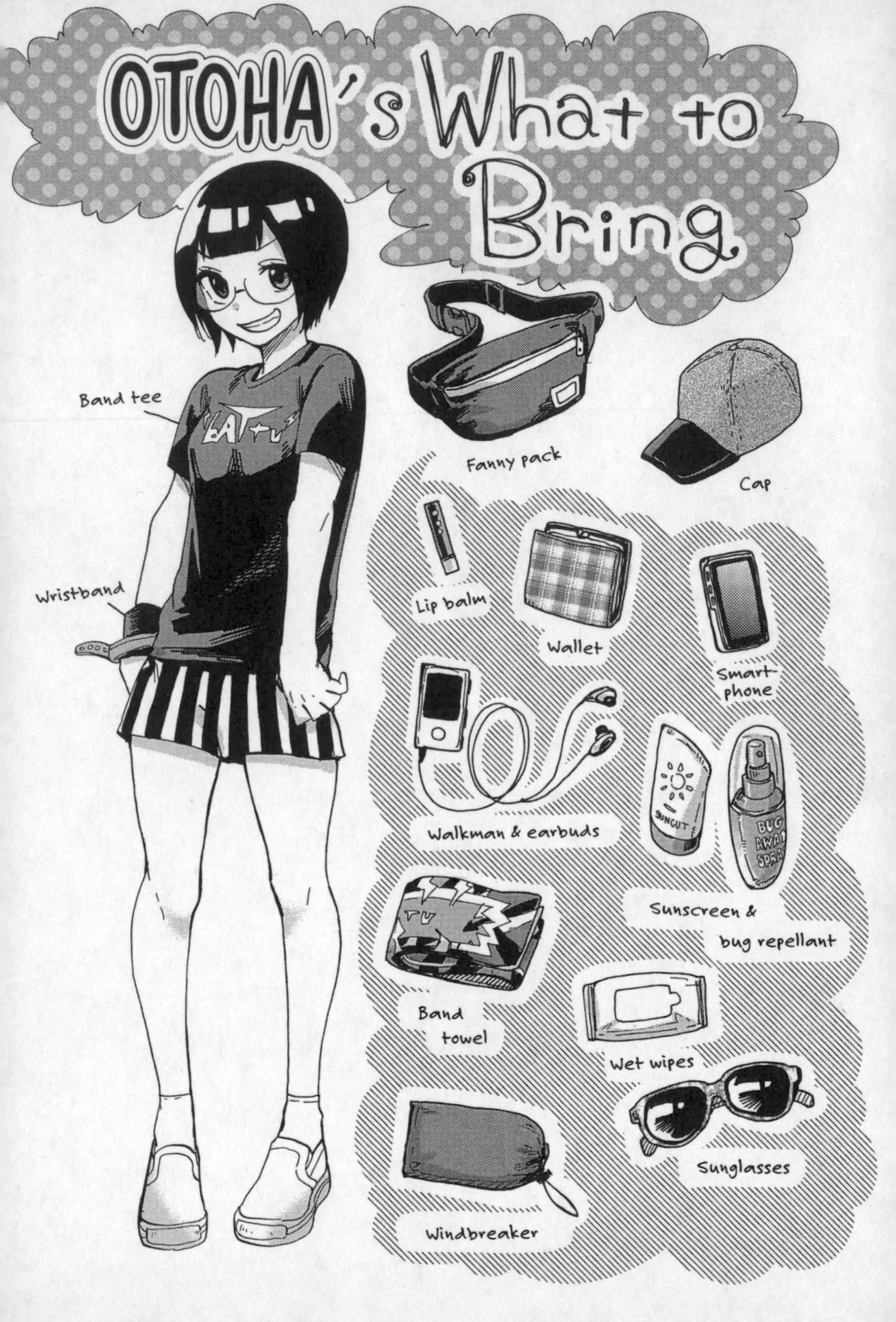
OTOHA's What to Bring
Band tee
Wristband
Fanny pack
Cap
Lip balm
Wallet
Smart-
phone
Walkman & earbuds
SUNCUT
BUG AWAY SPRAY
Sunscreen &
bug repellant
Band
towel
Wet wipes
Sunglasses
Windbreaker

Days on Fes

FES 2

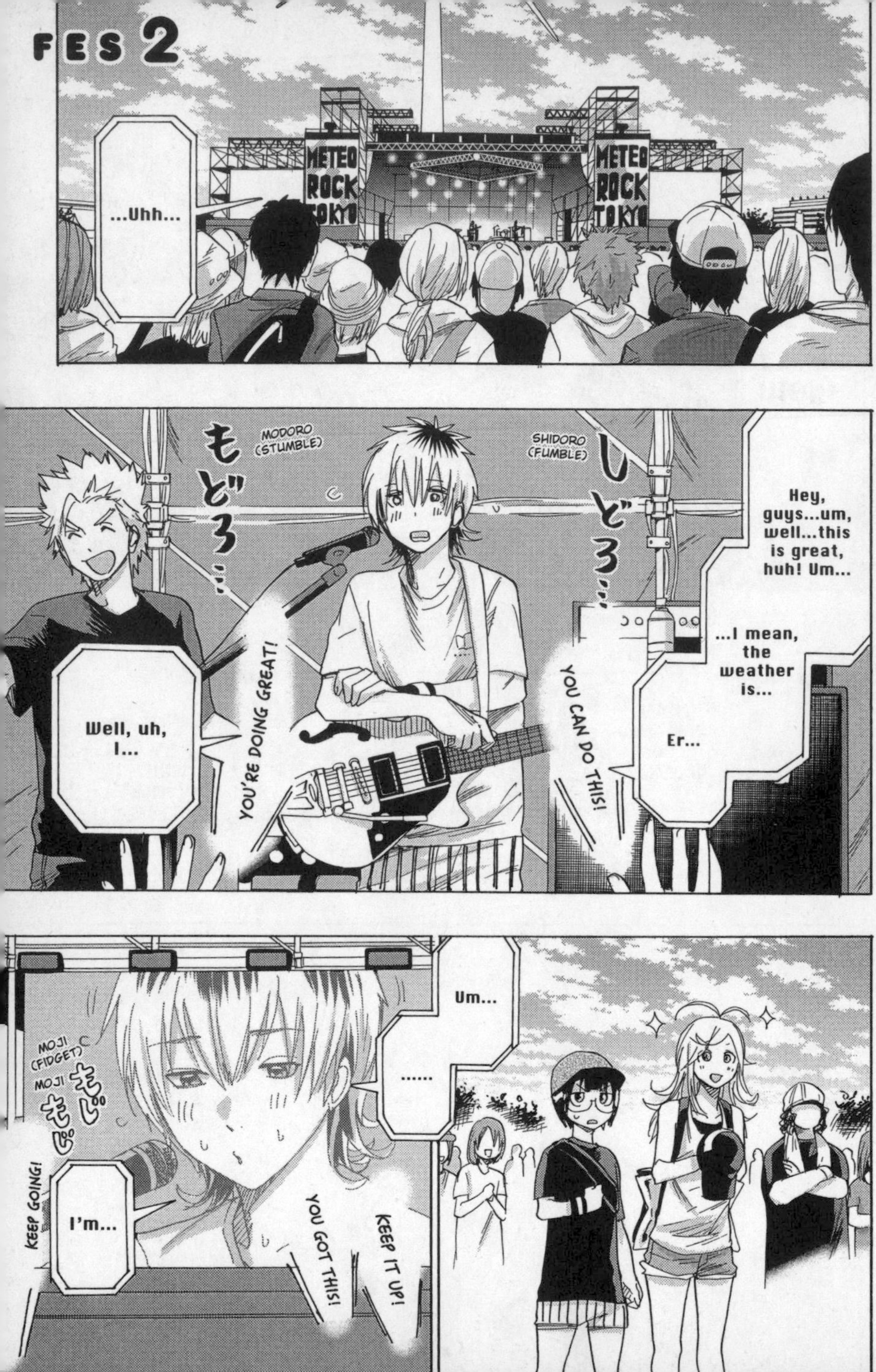
...Uhh...
METEO ROCK TOKYO
METEO ROCK TOKYO
Hey, guys...um, well...this is great, huh! Um...
...I mean, the weather is...
Er...
SHIDORO (FUMBLE) しどろ…
YOU CAN DO THIS!
YOU'RE DOING GREAT!
MODORO (STUMBLE) もどろ…
Well, uh, I...
Um...
......
KEEP IT UP!
YOU GOT THIS!
I'm...
MOJI (FIDGET) MOJI もじもじ
KEEP GOING!

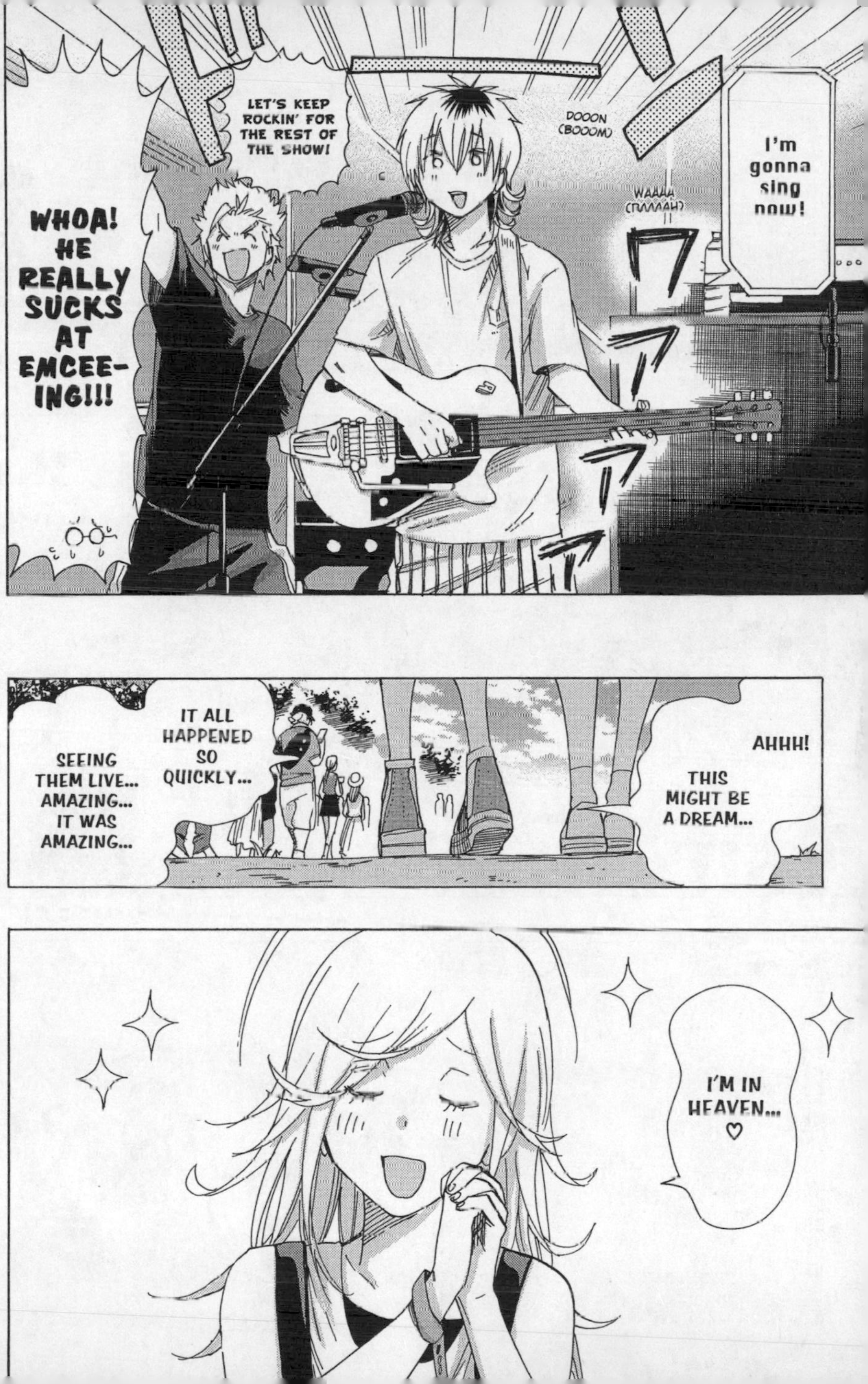
I'm gonna sing now!
DOOON (BOOOM)
WAAAA (RAAAAH)
LET'S KEEP ROCKIN' FOR THE REST OF THE SHOW!
WHOA! HE REALLY SUCKS AT EMCEE-ING!!!
AHHH!
THIS MIGHT BE A DREAM...
IT ALL HAPPENED SO QUICKLY...
SEEING THEM LIVE... AMAZING... IT WAS AMAZING...
I'M IN HEAVEN... ♡

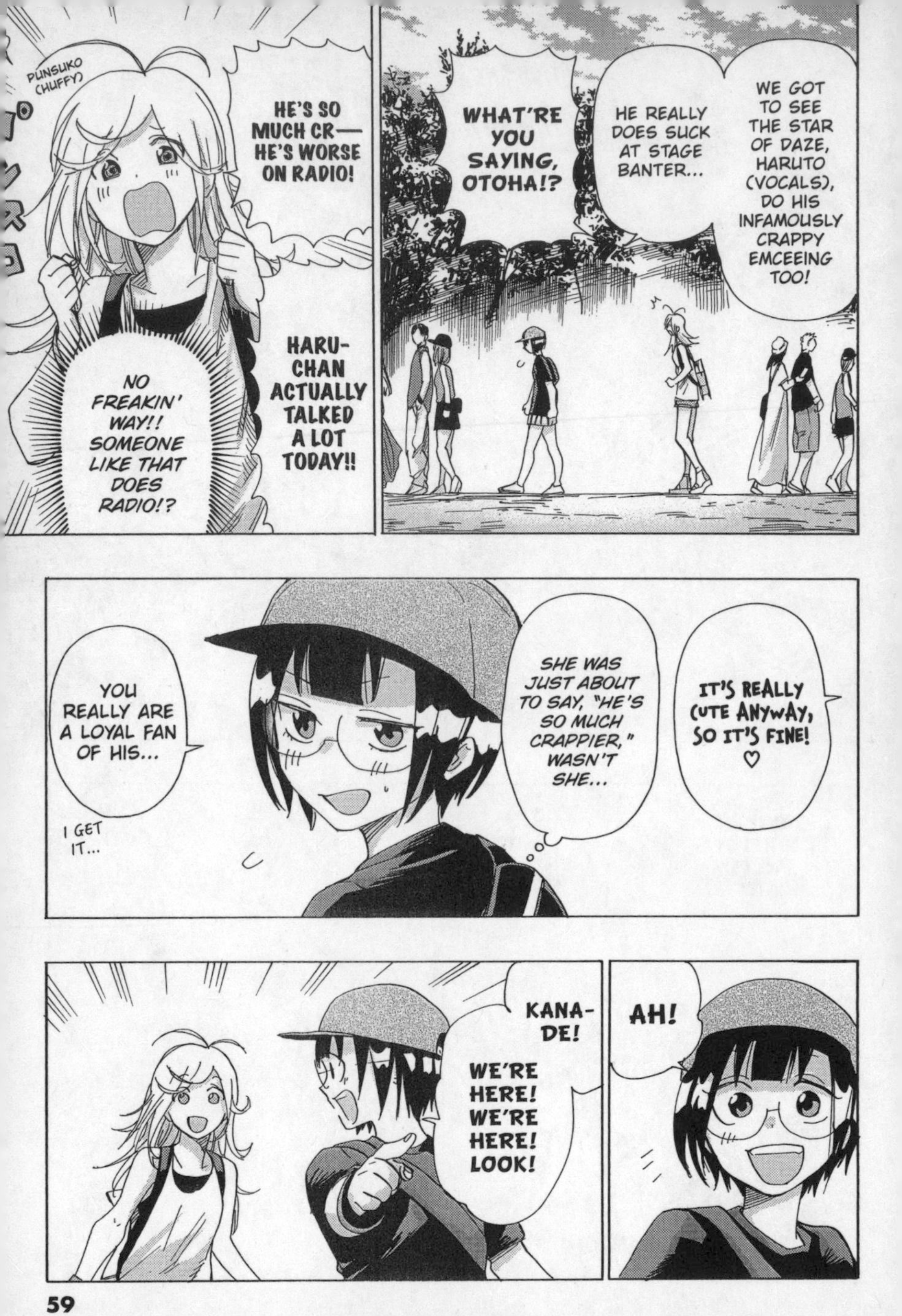
WE GOT TO SEE THE STAR OF DAZE, HARUTO (VOCALS), DO HIS INFAMOUSLY CRAPPY EMCEEING TOO!
HE REALLY DOES SUCK AT STAGE BANTER...
WHAT'RE YOU SAYING, OTOHA!?
HE'S SO MUCH CR— HE'S WORSE ON RADIO!
HARU-CHAN ACTUALLY TALKED A LOT TODAY!!
PUNSUKO (HUFFY)
NO FREAKIN' WAY!! SOMEONE LIKE THAT DOES RADIO!?
IT'S REALLY CUTE ANYWAY, SO IT'S FINE! ♡
SHE WAS JUST ABOUT TO SAY, "HE'S SO MUCH CRAPPIER," WASN'T SHE...
YOU REALLY ARE A LOYAL FAN OF HIS...
I GET IT...
AH!
KANA-DE!
WE'RE HERE! WE'RE HERE! LOOK!

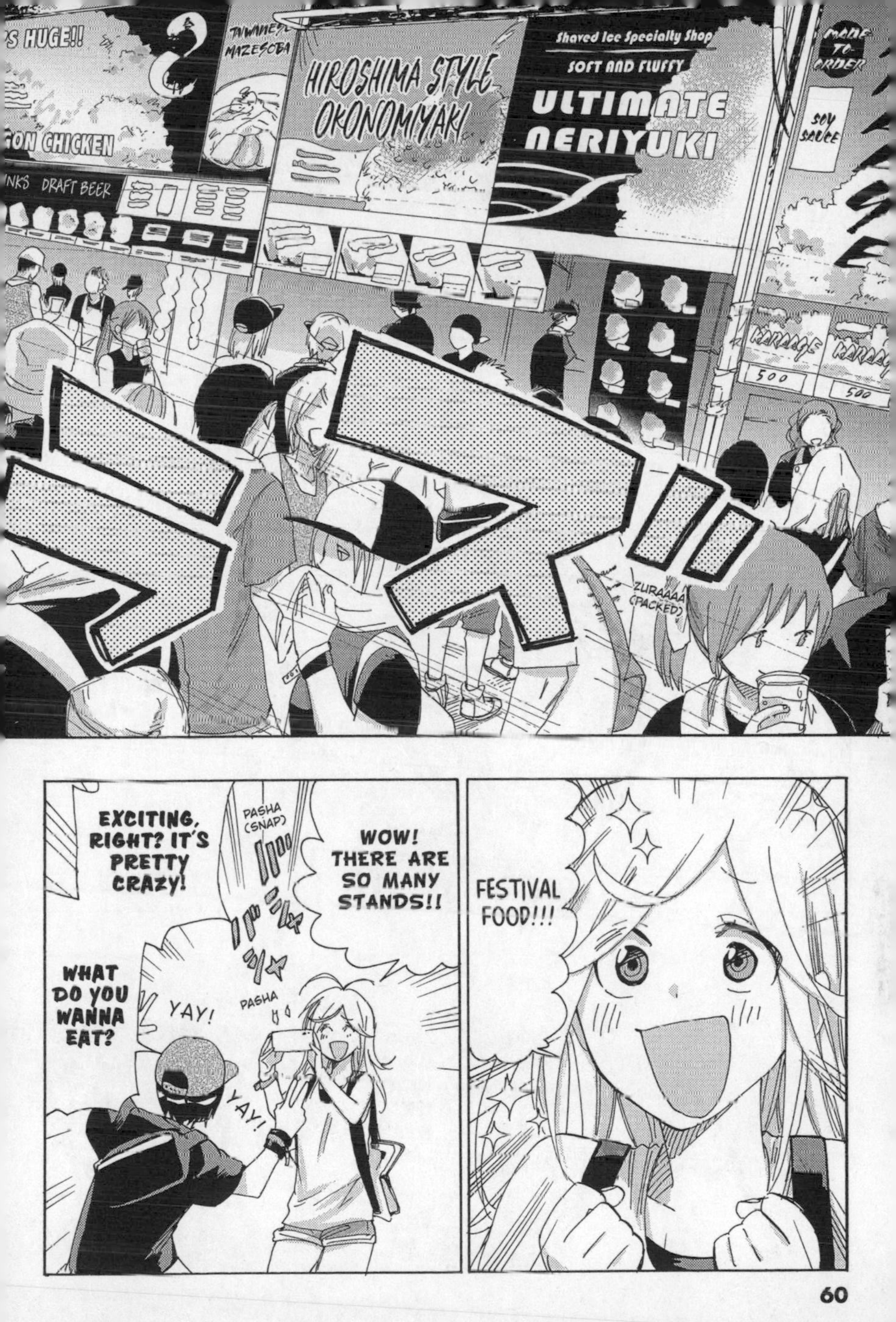
MADE-TO-ORDER
SOY SAUCE
Shaved Ice Specialty Shop
SOFT AND FLUFFY
ULTIMATE NERIYUKI
HIROSHIMA STYLE OKONOMIYAKI
TAIWANESE MAZESOBA
S HUGE!!
GON CHICKEN
NKS
DRAFT BEER
KARAAGE
500
KARAAGE
500
ZURAAAA (PACKED)
FESTIVAL FOOD!!!
WOW! THERE ARE SO MANY STANDS!!
PASHA (SNAP)
EXCITING, RIGHT? IT'S PRETTY CRAZY!
YAY!
WHAT DO YOU WANNA EAT?
PASHA
YAY!

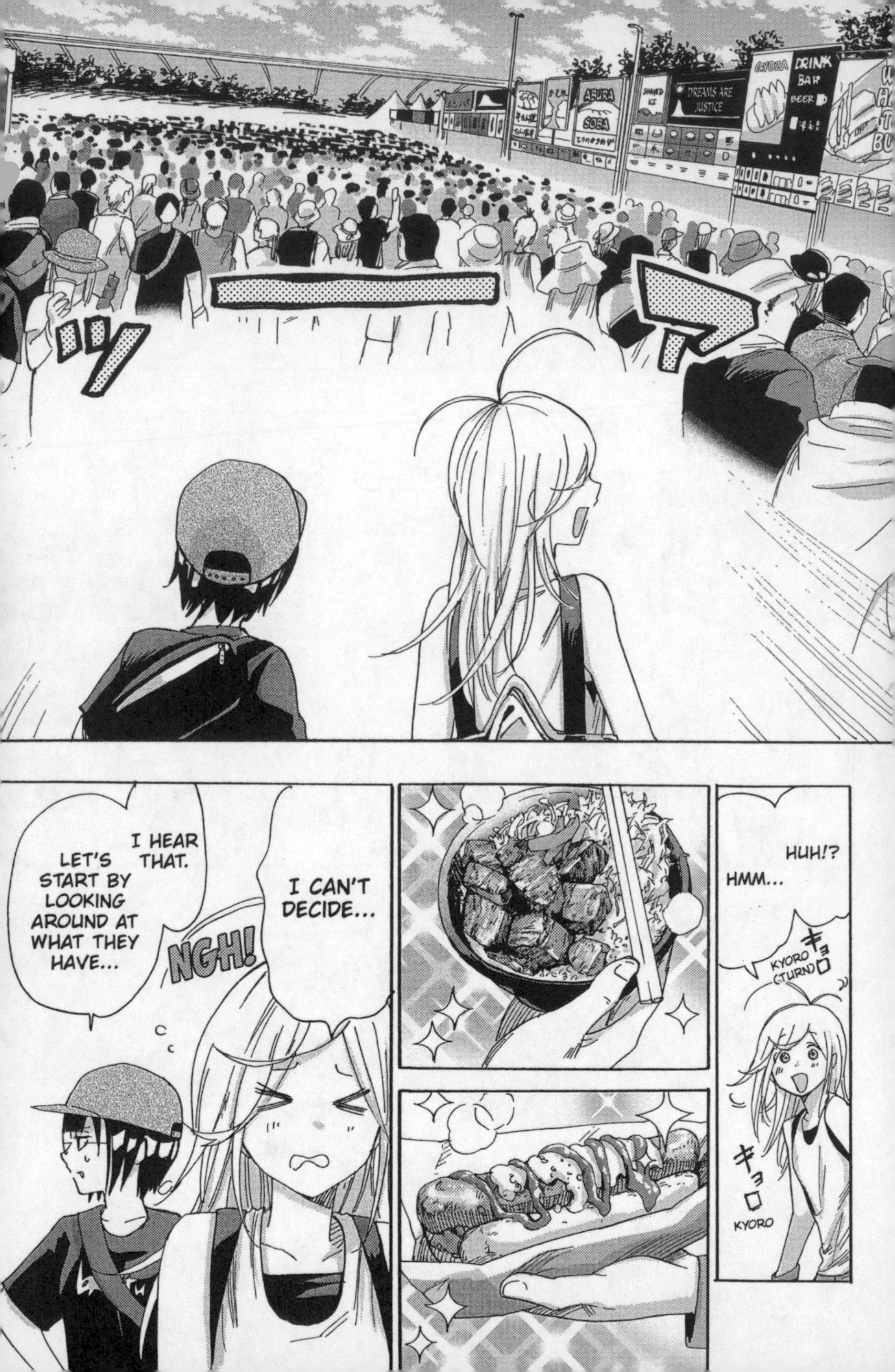

GYOZA
DRINK BAR BEER
DREAMS ARE JUSTICE
ABURA SOBA
HUH!?
HMM...
キョロ
KYORO (TURN)
キョロ
KYORO
I CAN'T DECIDE...
NGH!
I HEAR THAT.
LET'S START BY LOOKING AROUND AT WHAT THEY HAVE...

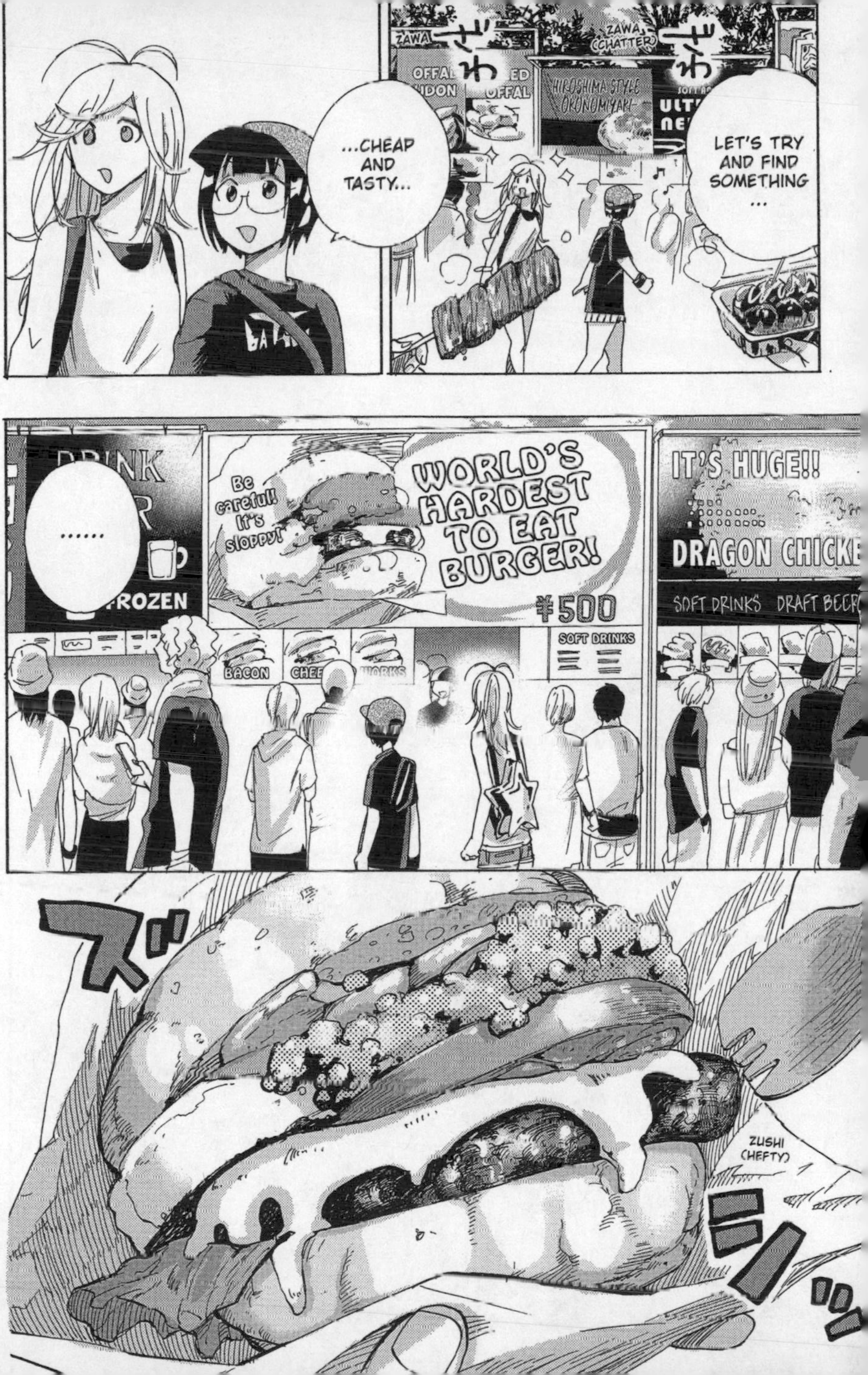
ZAWA
ZAWA (CHATTER)
OFFAL UDON
HIROSHIMA STYLE OKONOMIYAKI
LET'S TRY AND FIND SOMETHING ...
...CHEAP AND TASTY...
IT'S HUGE!!
DRAGON CHICKE
SOFT DRINKS
WORLD'S HARDEST TO EAT BURGER!
Be careful! It's sloppy!
¥500
SOFT DRINKS
BACON
WORKS
......
FROZEN
ZUSHI (HEFTY)

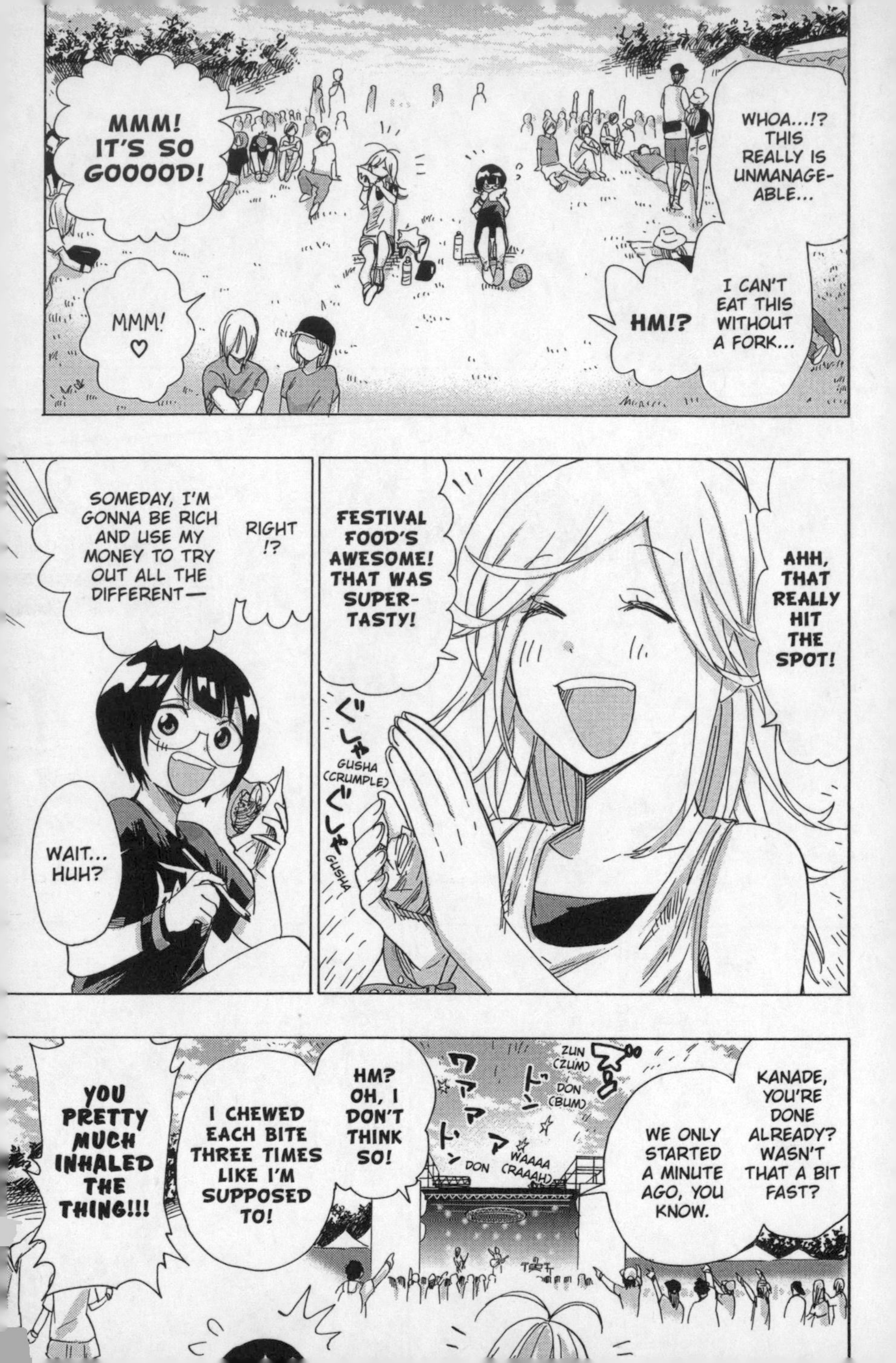

WHOA...!? THIS REALLY IS UNMANAGE-ABLE...
I CAN'T EAT THIS WITHOUT A FORK...
HM!?
MMM! IT'S SO GOOOOD!
MMM! ♡
AHH, THAT REALLY HIT THE SPOT!
FESTIVAL FOOD'S AWESOME! THAT WAS SUPER-TASTY!
ぐしゃ GUSHA (CRUMPLE)
ぐしゃ GUSHA
RIGHT!?
SOMEDAY, I'M GONNA BE RICH AND USE MY MONEY TO TRY OUT ALL THE DIFFERENT—
WAIT... HUH?
KANADE, YOU'RE DONE ALREADY? WASN'T THAT A BIT FAST?
WE ONLY STARTED A MINUTE AGO, YOU KNOW.
ズン ZUN (ZUM)
ドン DON (BUM)
ワァァ WAAAA (RAAAH)
ドン DON
HM? OH, I DON'T THINK SO!
I CHEWED EACH BITE THREE TIMES LIKE I'M SUPPOSED TO!
YOU PRETTY MUCH INHALED THE THING!!!

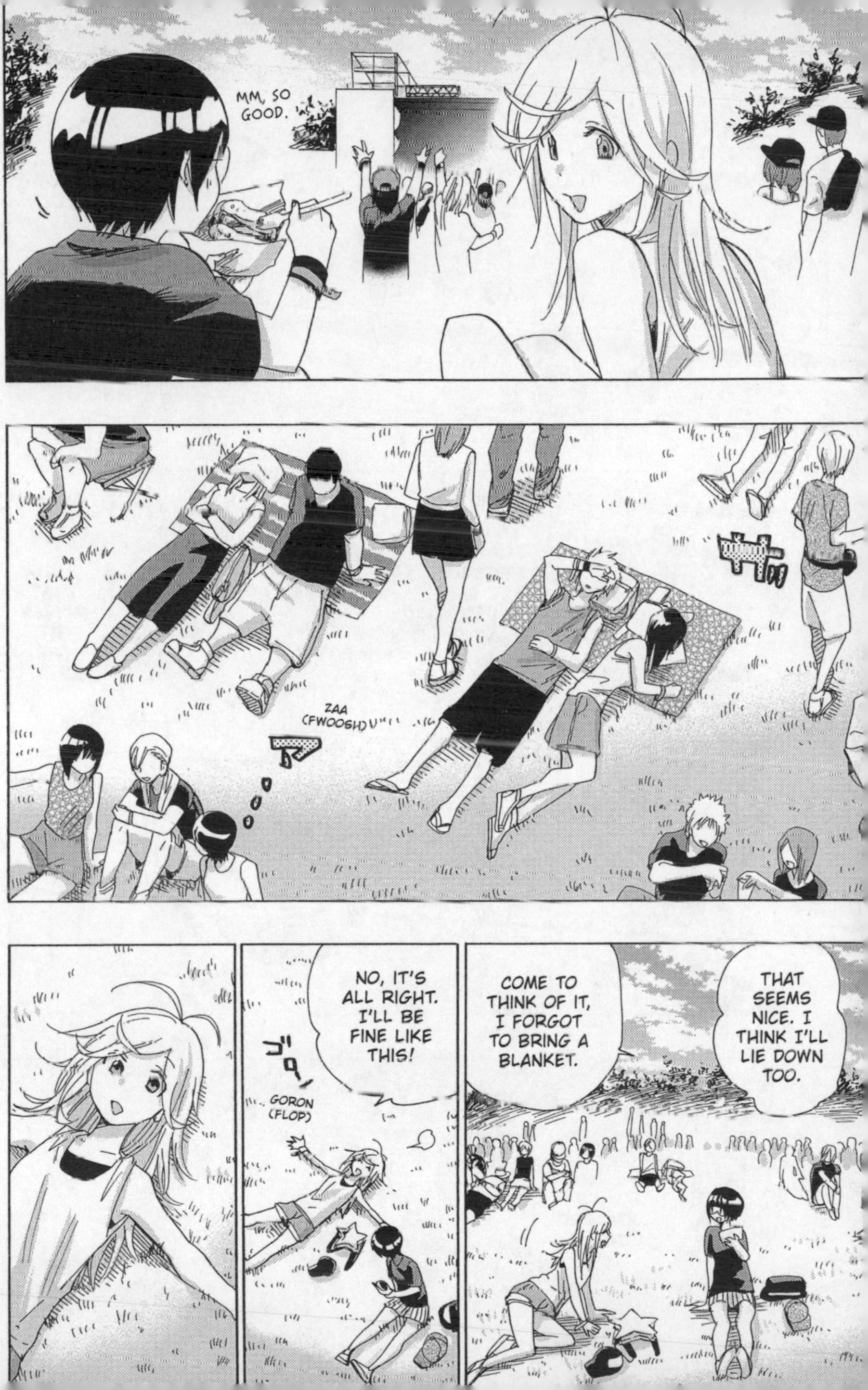
MM, SO GOOD.
ZAA (FWOOSH)
THAT SEEMS NICE. I THINK I'LL LIE DOWN TOO.
COME TO THINK OF IT, I FORGOT TO BRING A BLANKET.
NO, IT'S ALL RIGHT. I'LL BE FINE LIKE THIS!
GORON (FLOP)

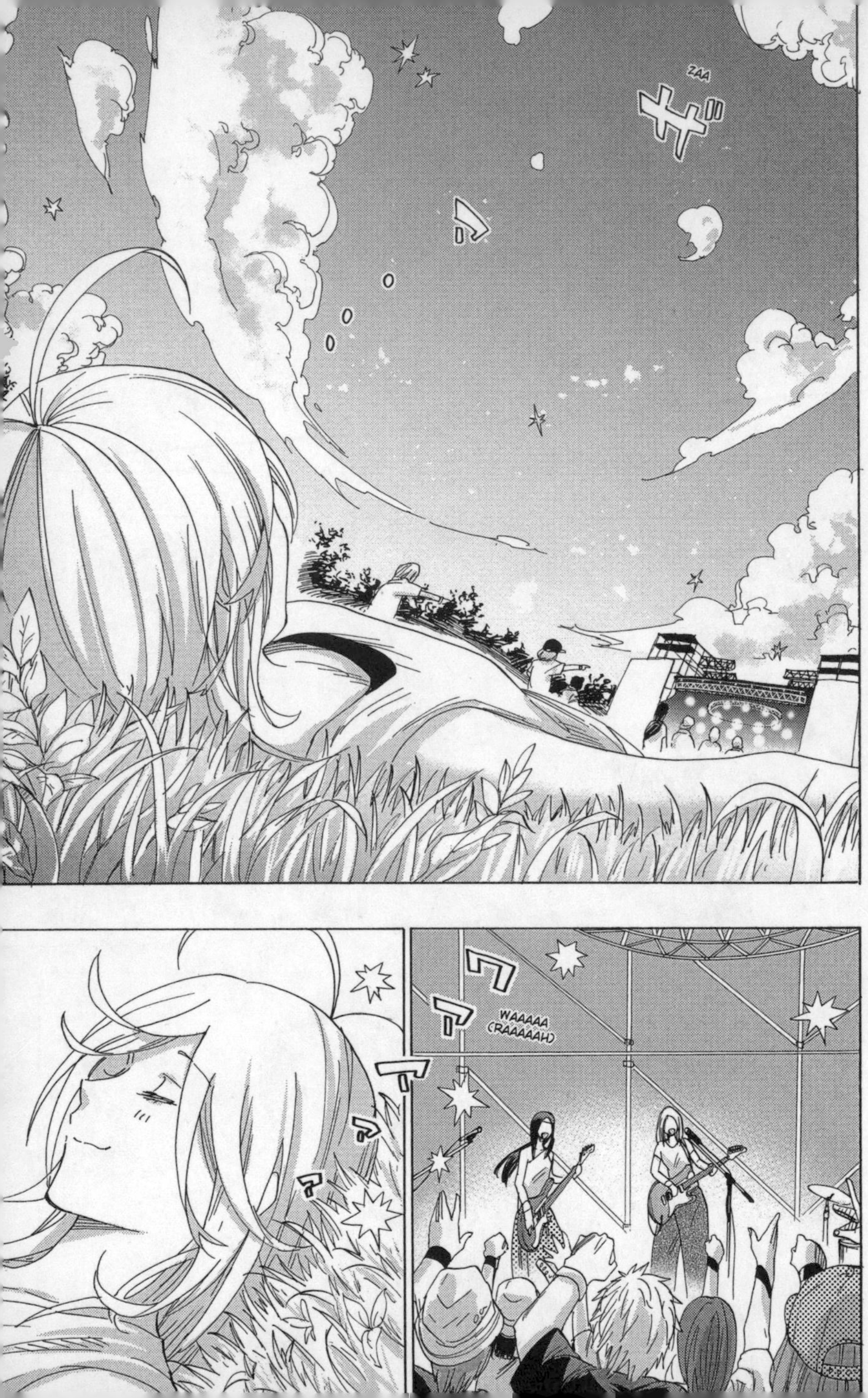
ZAA
WAAAAA
(RAAAAAH)

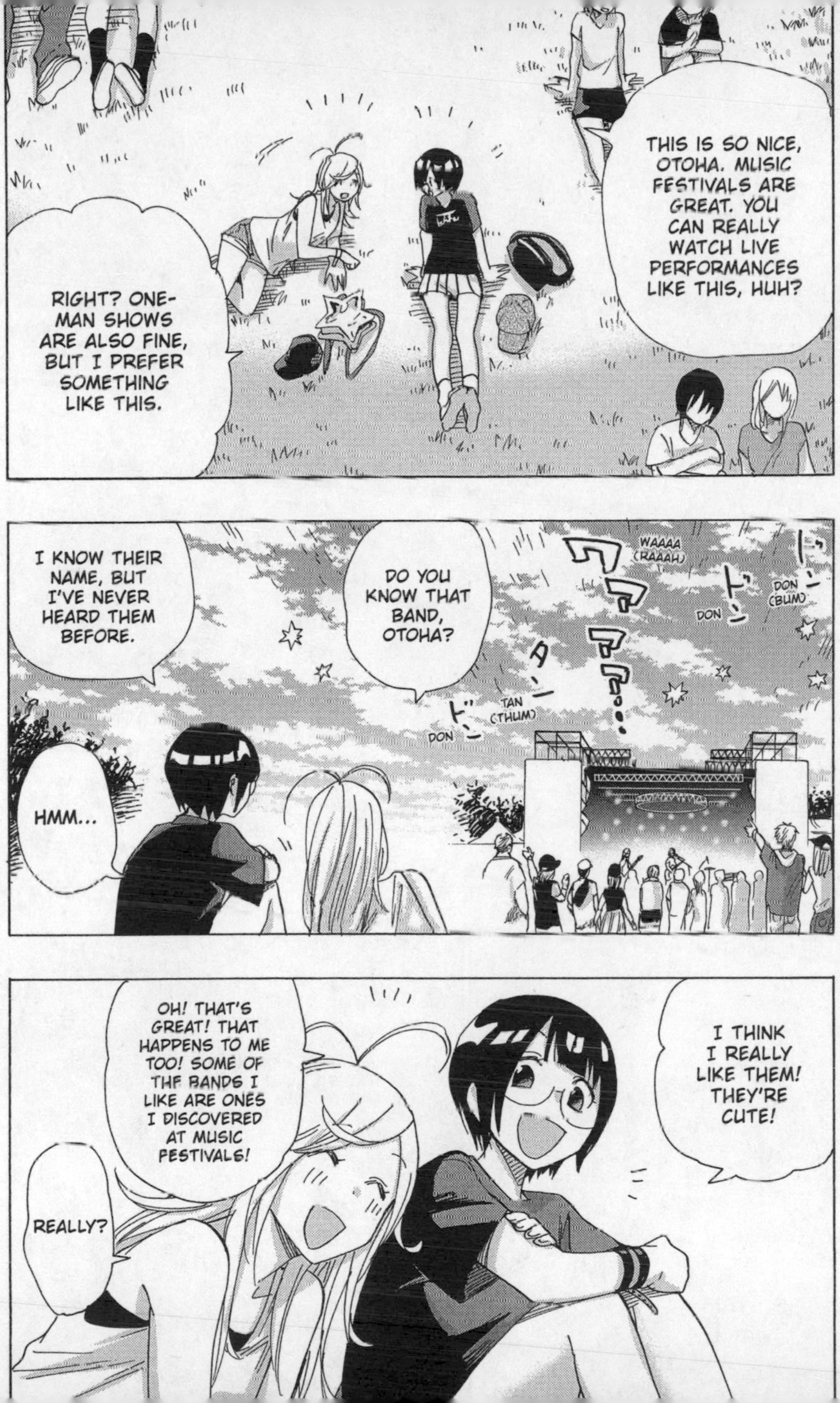
THIS IS SO NICE, OTOHA. MUSIC FESTIVALS ARE GREAT. YOU CAN REALLY WATCH LIVE PERFORMANCES LIKE THIS, HUH?
RIGHT? ONE-MAN SHOWS ARE ALSO FINE, BUT I PREFER SOMETHING LIKE THIS.
DON (BUM)
DON
WAAAA (RAAAH)
DO YOU KNOW THAT BAND, OTOHA?
TAN (THUM)
DON
I KNOW THEIR NAME, BUT I'VE NEVER HEARD THEM BEFORE.
HMM...
I THINK I REALLY LIKE THEM! THEY'RE CUTE!
OH! THAT'S GREAT! THAT HAPPENS TO ME TOO! SOME OF THE BANDS I LIKE ARE ONES I DISCOVERED AT MUSIC FESTIVALS!
REALLY?

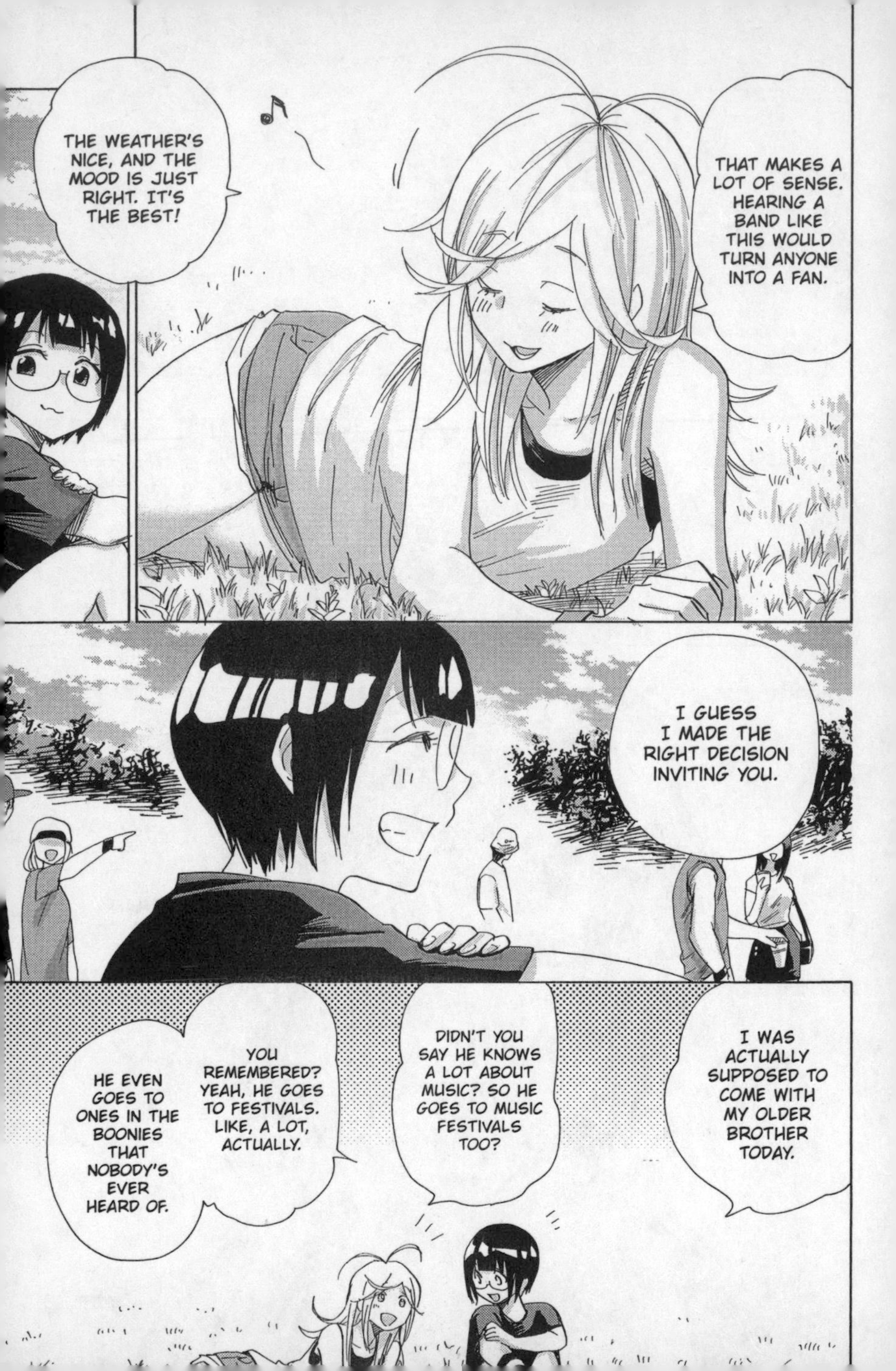
THAT MAKES A LOT OF SENSE. HEARING A BAND LIKE THIS WOULD TURN ANYONE INTO A FAN.
THE WEATHER'S NICE, AND THE MOOD IS JUST RIGHT. IT'S THE BEST!
I GUESS I MADE THE RIGHT DECISION INVITING YOU.
I WAS ACTUALLY SUPPOSED TO COME WITH MY OLDER BROTHER TODAY.
DIDN'T YOU SAY HE KNOWS A LOT ABOUT MUSIC? SO HE GOES TO MUSIC FESTIVALS TOO?
YOU REMEMBERED? YEAH, HE GOES TO FESTIVALS. LIKE, A LOT, ACTUALLY.
HE EVEN GOES TO ONES IN THE BOONIES THAT NOBODY'S EVER HEARD OF.

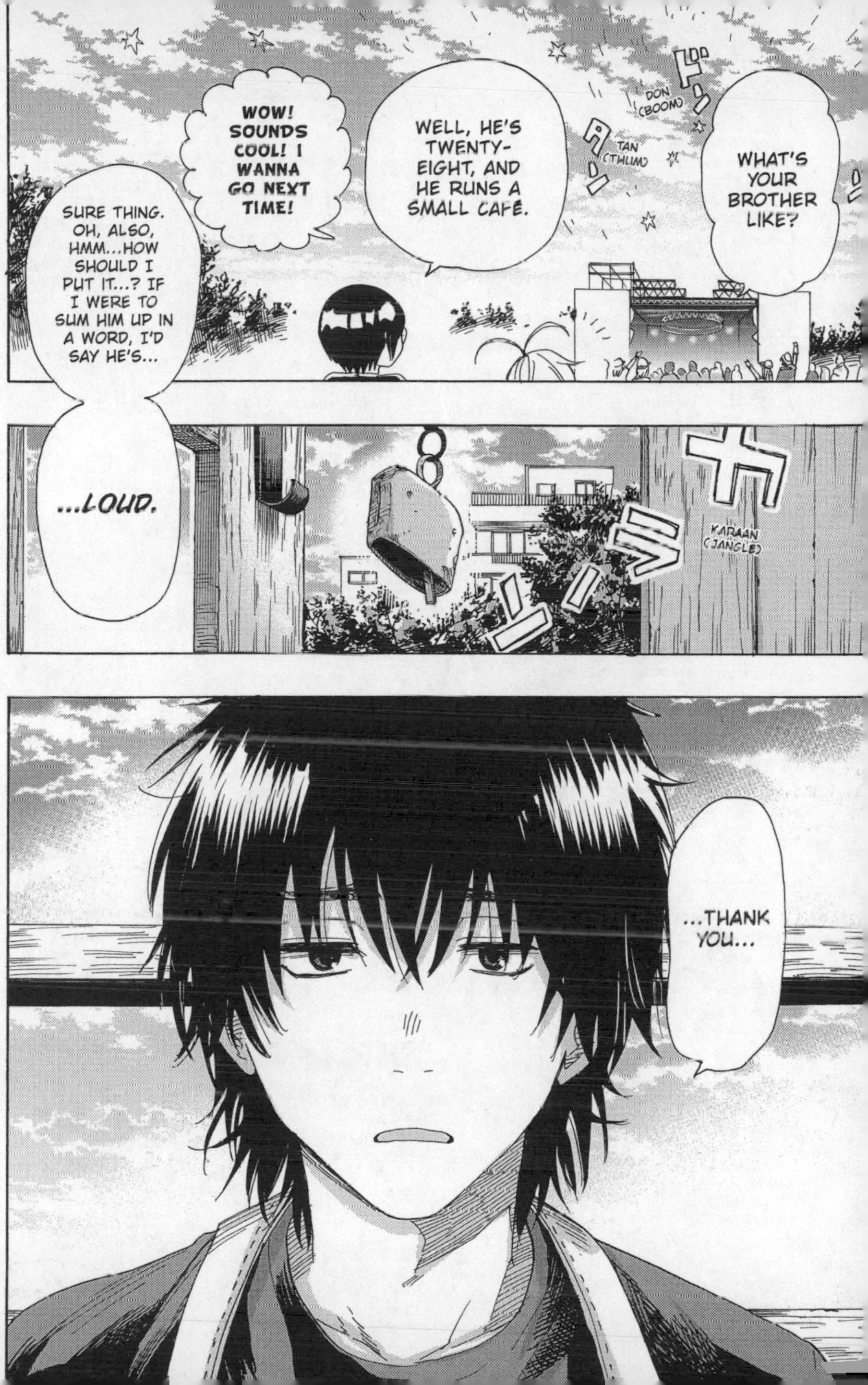
WHAT'S YOUR BROTHER LIKE?
DON (BOOM)
TAN (THUMP)
WELL, HE'S TWENTY-EIGHT, AND HE RUNS A SMALL CAFÉ.
WOW! SOUNDS COOL! I WANNA GO NEXT TIME!
SURE THING. OH, ALSO, HMM...HOW SHOULD I PUT IT...? IF I WERE TO SUM HIM UP IN A WORD, I'D SAY HE'S...
...LOUD.
KARAAN (JANGLE)
...THANK YOU...

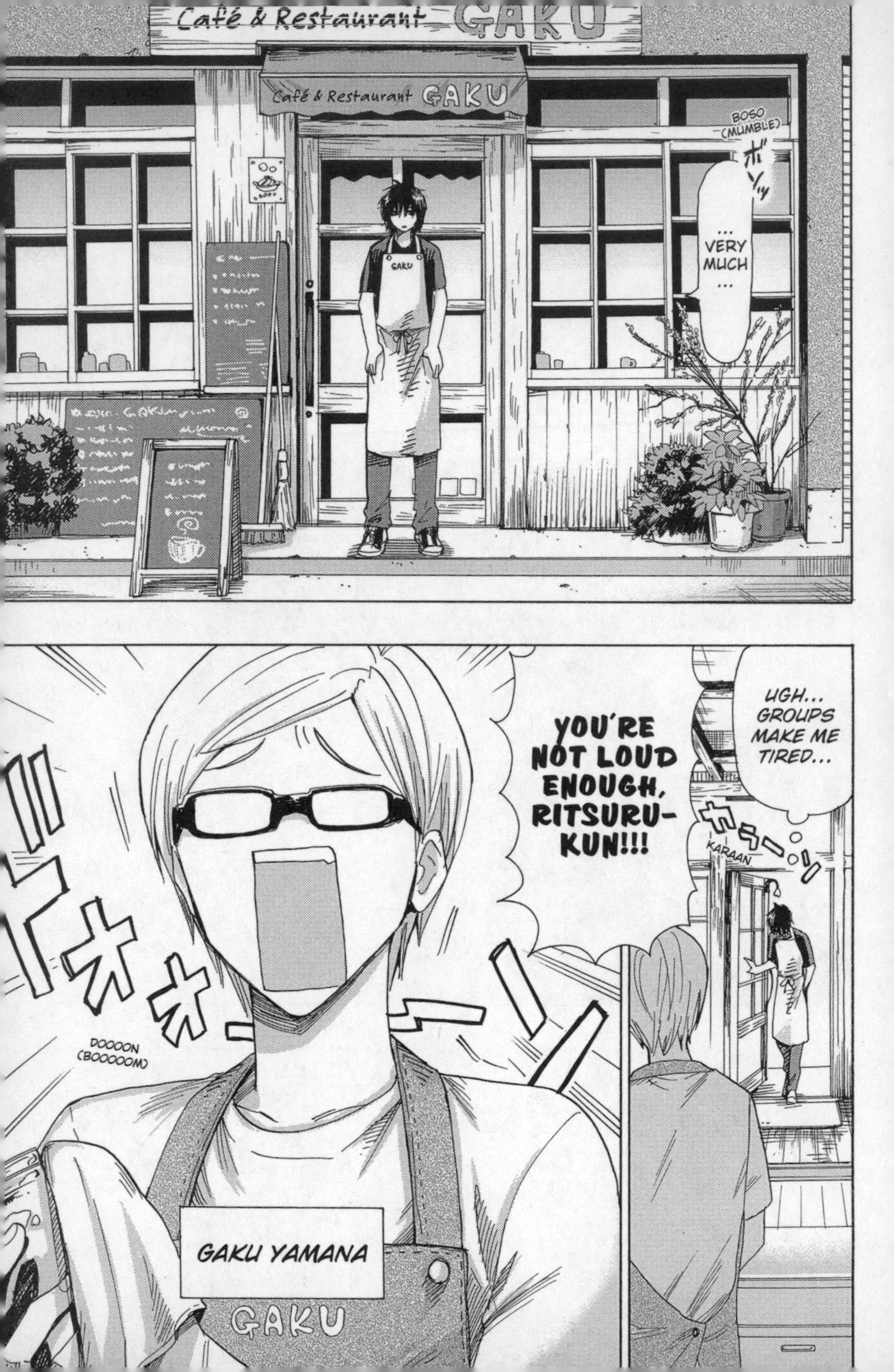
Café & Restaurant GAKU
Café & Restaurant GAKU
GAKU
BOSO (MUMBLE)
... VERY MUCH ...
UGH... GROUPS MAKE ME TIRED...
KARAAN
YOU'RE NOT LOUD ENOUGH, RITSURU-KUN!!!
DOOOON (BOOOOOM)
GAKU YAMANA
GAKU

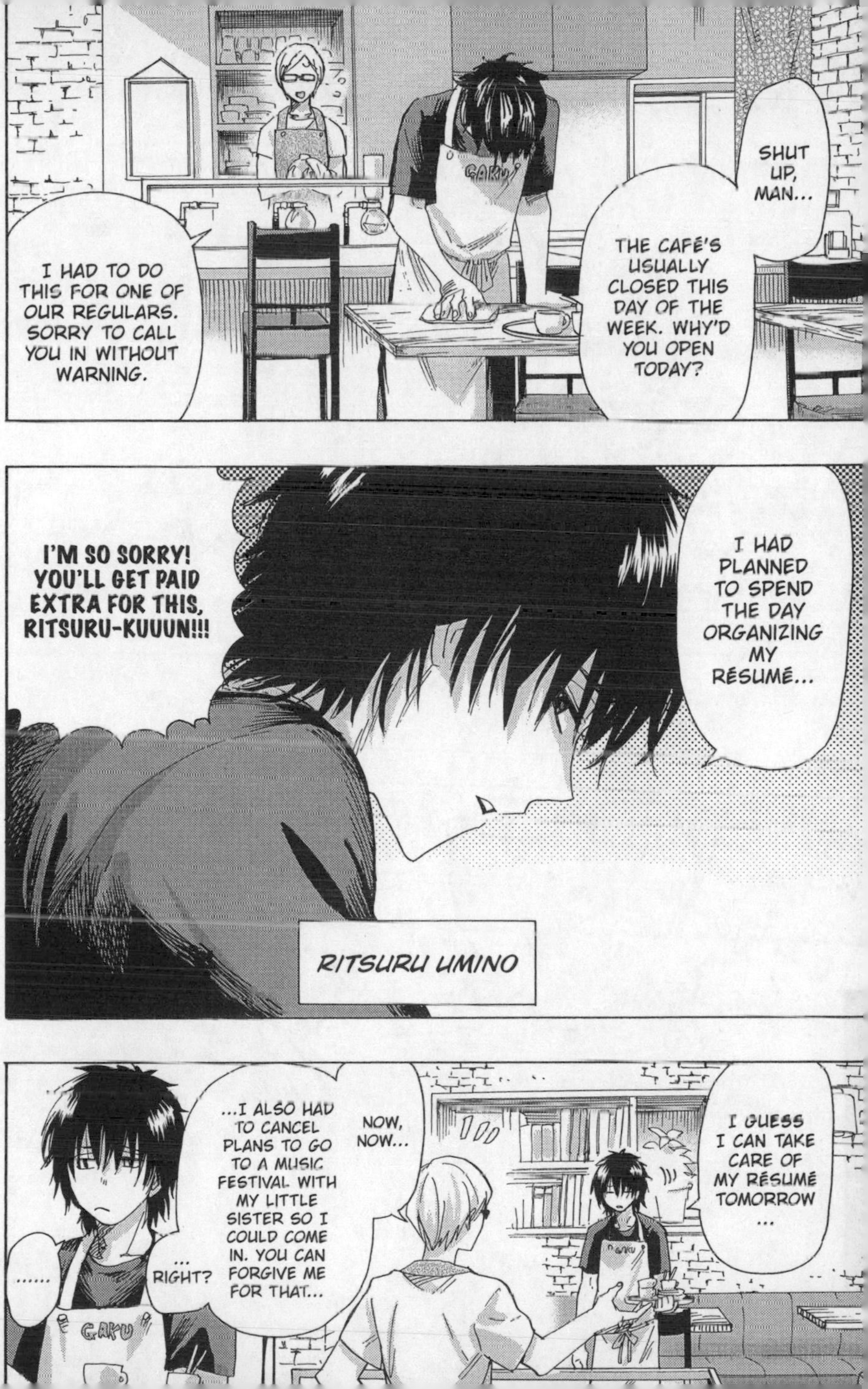
SHUT UP, MAN...
THE CAFÉ'S USUALLY CLOSED THIS DAY OF THE WEEK. WHY'D YOU OPEN TODAY?
I HAD TO DO THIS FOR ONE OF OUR REGULARS. SORRY TO CALL YOU IN WITHOUT WARNING.
I HAD PLANNED TO SPEND THE DAY ORGANIZING MY RÉSUMÉ...
I'M SO SORRY! YOU'LL GET PAID EXTRA FOR THIS, RITSURU-KUUUN!!!
RITSURU UMINO
I GUESS I CAN TAKE CARE OF MY RÉSUMÉ TOMORROW ...
NOW, NOW...
...I ALSO HAD TO CANCEL PLANS TO GO TO A MUSIC FESTIVAL WITH MY LITTLE SISTER SO I COULD COME IN. YOU CAN FORGIVE ME FOR THAT...
... RIGHT?
......

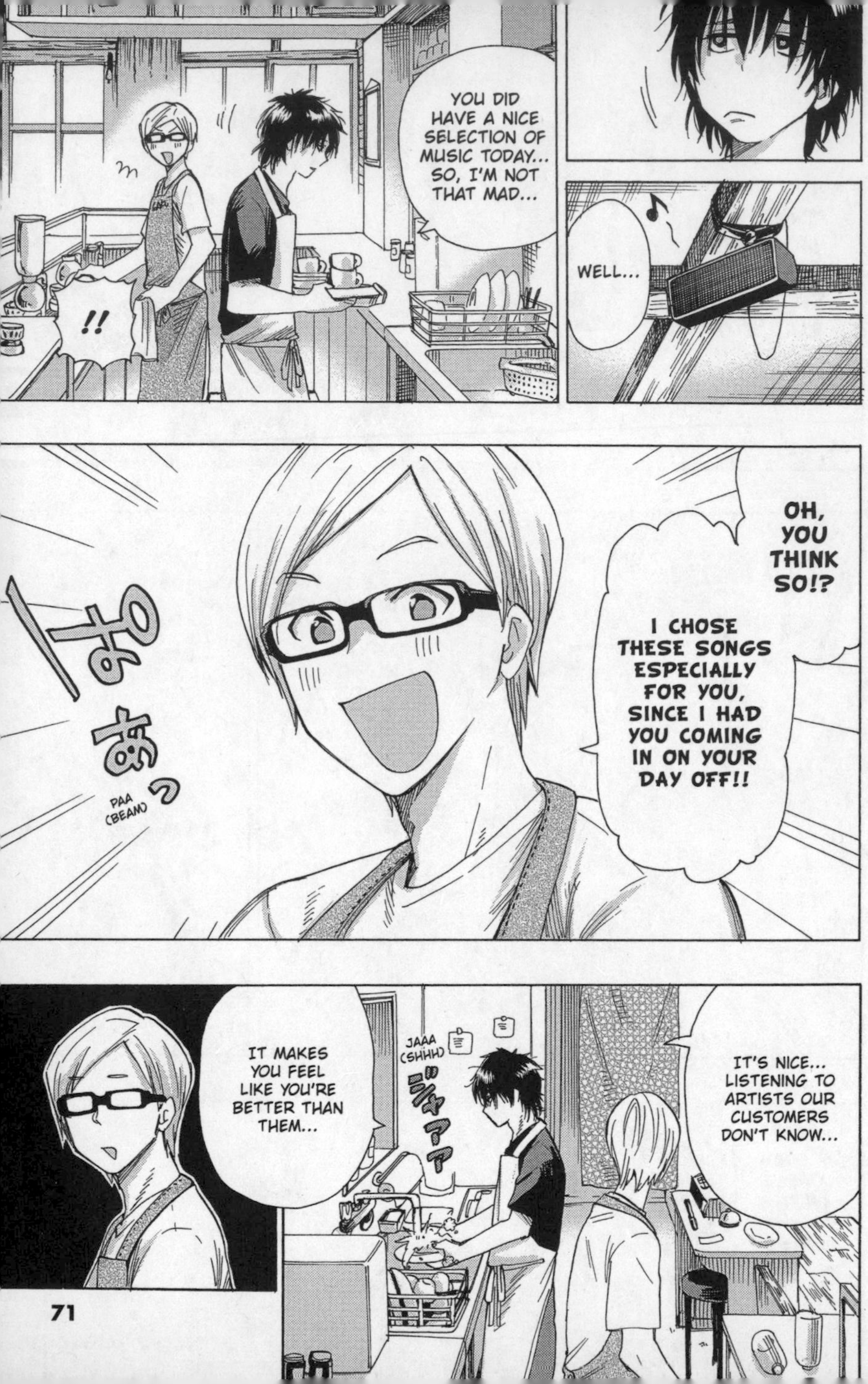
WELL...
YOU DID HAVE A NICE SELECTION OF MUSIC TODAY... SO, I'M NOT THAT MAD...
!!
OH, YOU THINK SO!?
I CHOSE THESE SONGS ESPECIALLY FOR YOU, SINCE I HAD YOU COMING IN ON YOUR DAY OFF!!
ぱぁっ
PAA (BEAM)
IT'S NICE... LISTENING TO ARTISTS OUR CUSTOMERS DON'T KNOW...
ジャアア
JAAA (SHHH)
IT MAKES YOU FEEL LIKE YOU'RE BETTER THAN THEM...

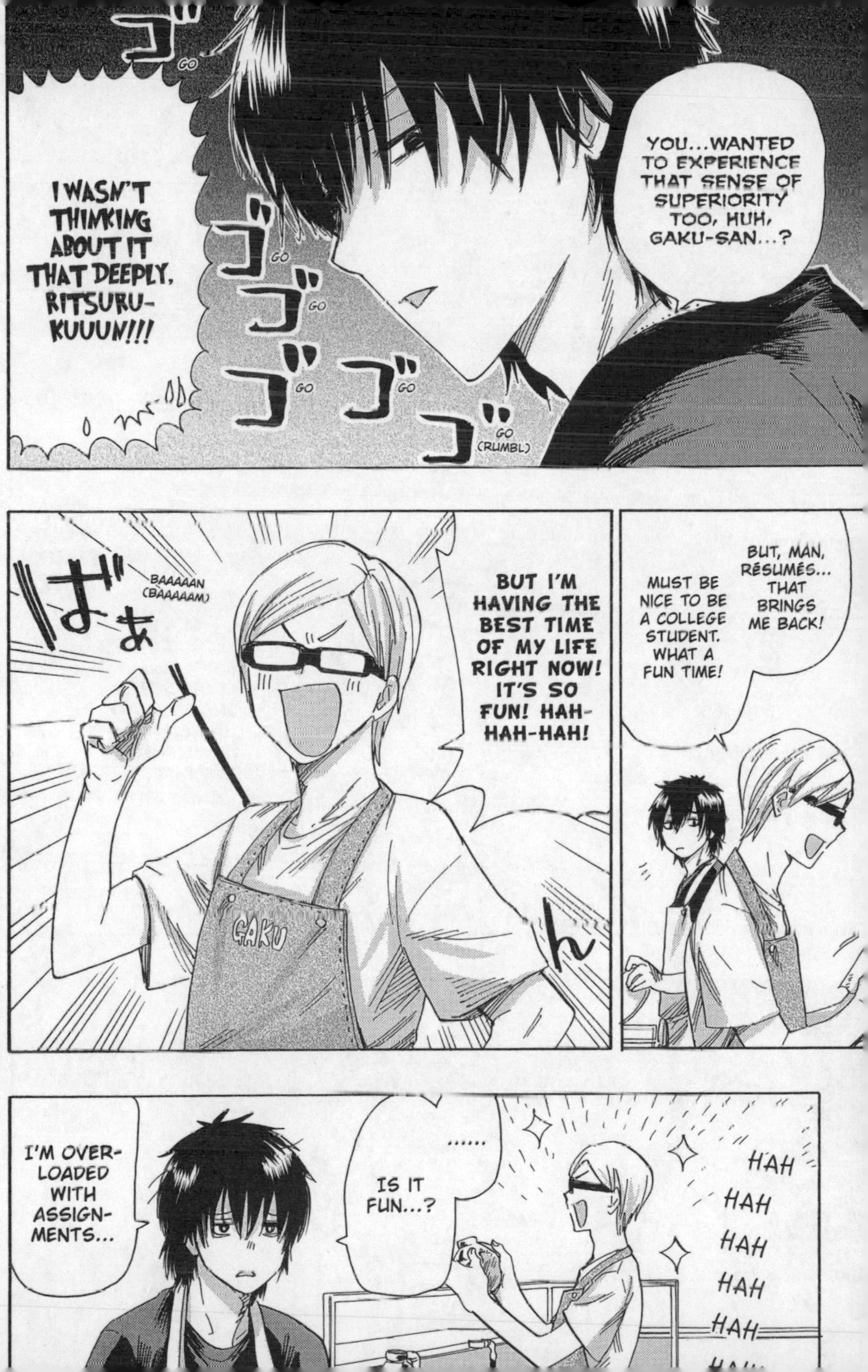
GO
YOU...WANTED TO EXPERIENCE THAT SENSE OF SUPERIORITY TOO, HUH, GAKU-SAN...?
GO GO GO GO GO
(RUMBL)
I WASN'T THINKING ABOUT IT THAT DEEPLY, RITSURU-KUUUN!!!
BUT, MAN, RÉSUMÉS... THAT BRINGS ME BACK!
MUST BE NICE TO BE A COLLEGE STUDENT. WHAT A FUN TIME!
BUT I'M HAVING THE BEST TIME OF MY LIFE RIGHT NOW! IT'S SO FUN! HAH-HAH-HAH!
GAKU
BAAAAAN (BAAAAAM)
HAH HAH HAH HAH HAH
......
IS IT FUN...?
I'M OVER-LOADED WITH ASSIGN-MENTS...

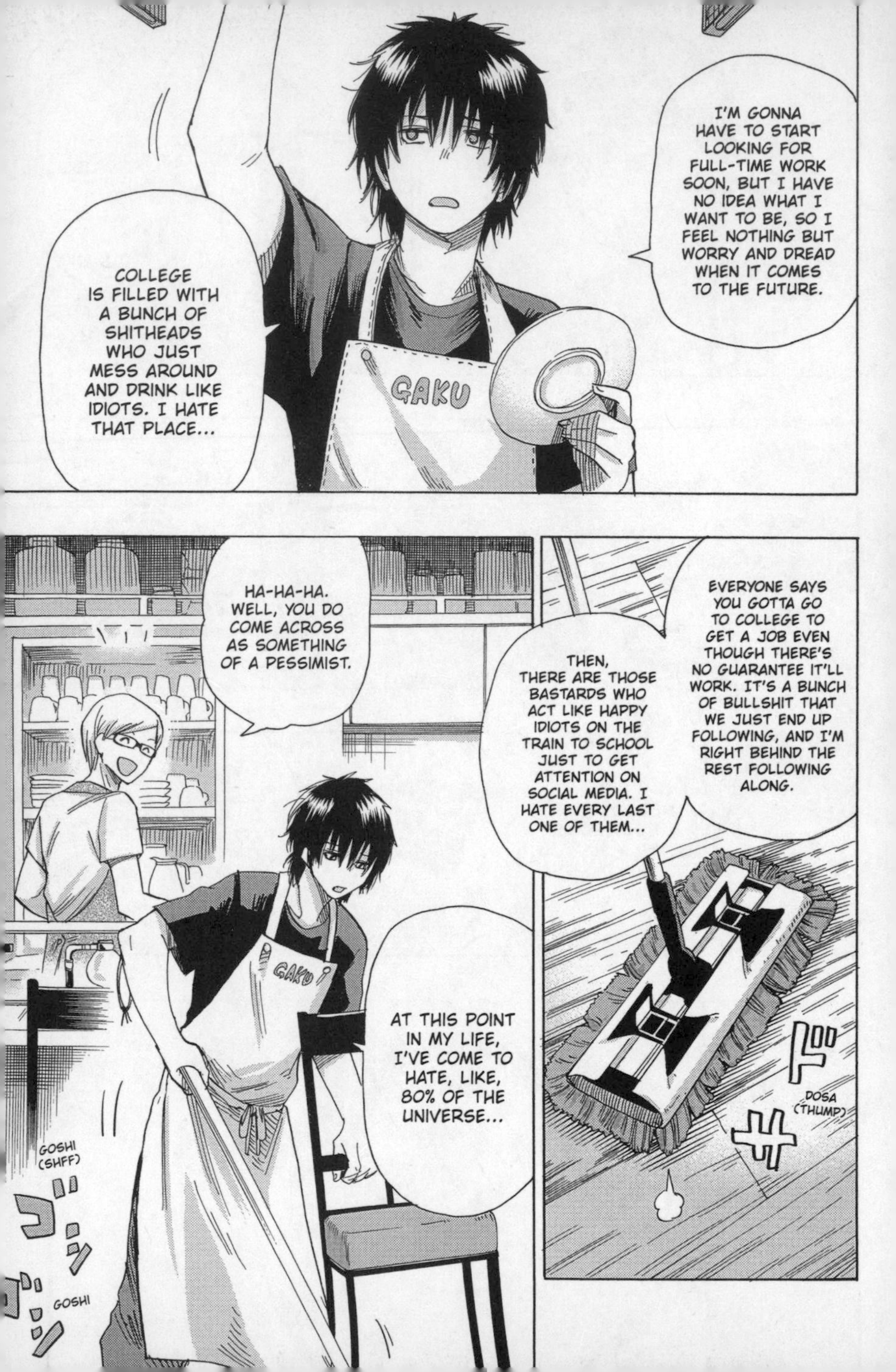
I'M GONNA HAVE TO START LOOKING FOR FULL-TIME WORK SOON, BUT I HAVE NO IDEA WHAT I WANT TO BE, SO I FEEL NOTHING BUT WORRY AND DREAD WHEN IT COMES TO THE FUTURE.
COLLEGE IS FILLED WITH A BUNCH OF SHITHEADS WHO JUST MESS AROUND AND DRINK LIKE IDIOTS. I HATE THAT PLACE...
GAKU
EVERYONE SAYS YOU GOTTA GO TO COLLEGE TO GET A JOB EVEN THOUGH THERE'S NO GUARANTEE IT'LL WORK. IT'S A BUNCH OF BULLSHIT THAT WE JUST END UP FOLLOWING, AND I'M RIGHT BEHIND THE REST FOLLOWING ALONG.
THEN, THERE ARE THOSE BASTARDS WHO ACT LIKE HAPPY IDIOTS ON THE TRAIN TO SCHOOL JUST TO GET ATTENTION ON SOCIAL MEDIA. I HATE EVERY LAST ONE OF THEM...
DOSA (THUMP)
HA-HA-HA. WELL, YOU DO COME ACROSS AS SOMETHING OF A PESSIMIST.
GAKU
AT THIS POINT IN MY LIFE, I'VE COME TO HATE, LIKE, 80% OF THE UNIVERSE...
GOSHI (SHFF)
GOSHI

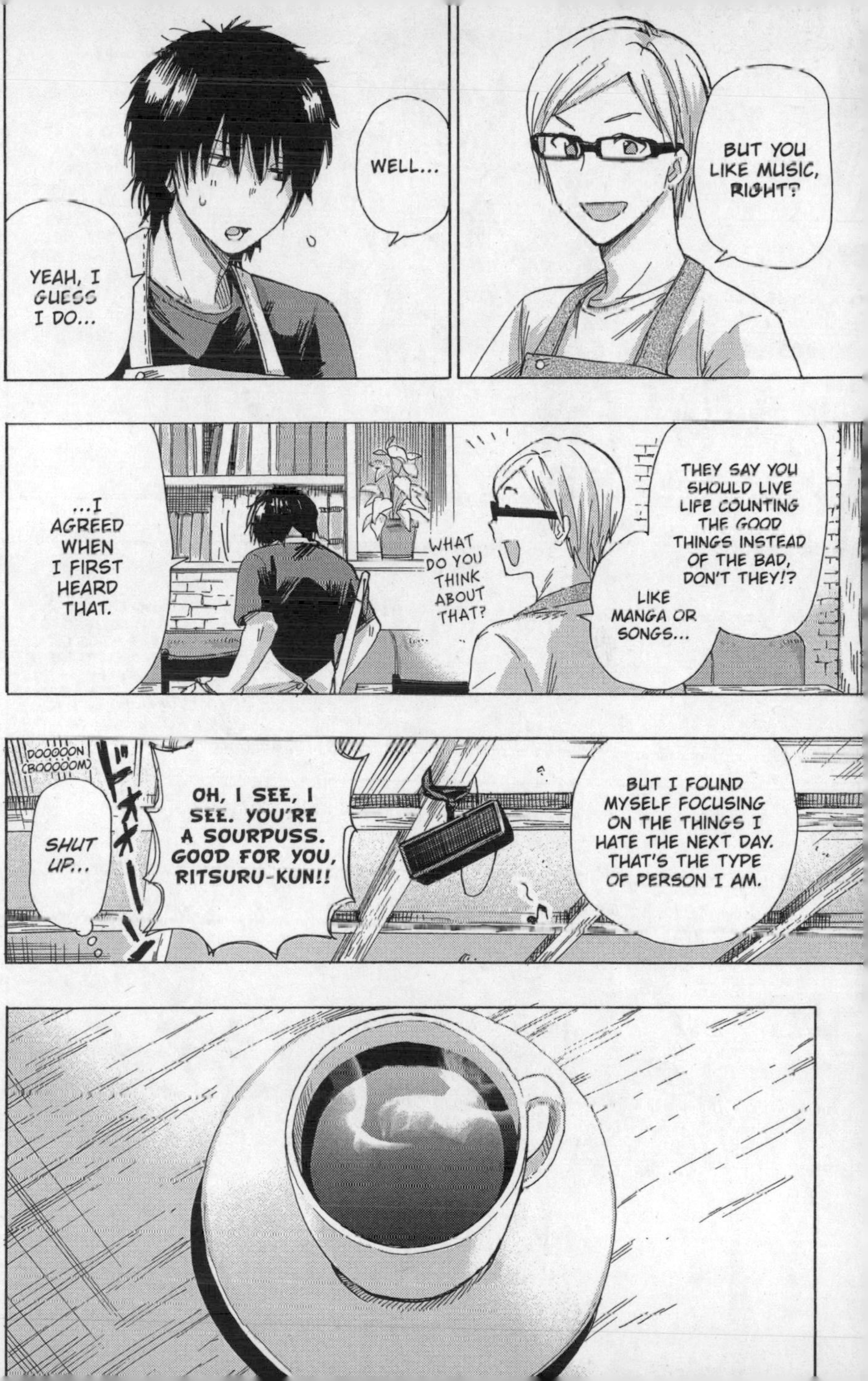
BUT YOU LIKE MUSIC, RIGHT?
WELL...
YEAH, I GUESS I DO...
THEY SAY YOU SHOULD LIVE LIFE COUNTING THE GOOD THINGS INSTEAD OF THE BAD, DON'T THEY!?
LIKE MANGA OR SONGS...
WHAT DO YOU THINK ABOUT THAT?
...I AGREED WHEN I FIRST HEARD THAT.
BUT I FOUND MYSELF FOCUSING ON THE THINGS I HATE THE NEXT DAY. THAT'S THE TYPE OF PERSON I AM.
OH, I SEE, I SEE. YOU'RE A SOURPUSS. GOOD FOR YOU, RITSURU-KUN!!
DOOOOON (BOOOOOM)
SHUT UP...

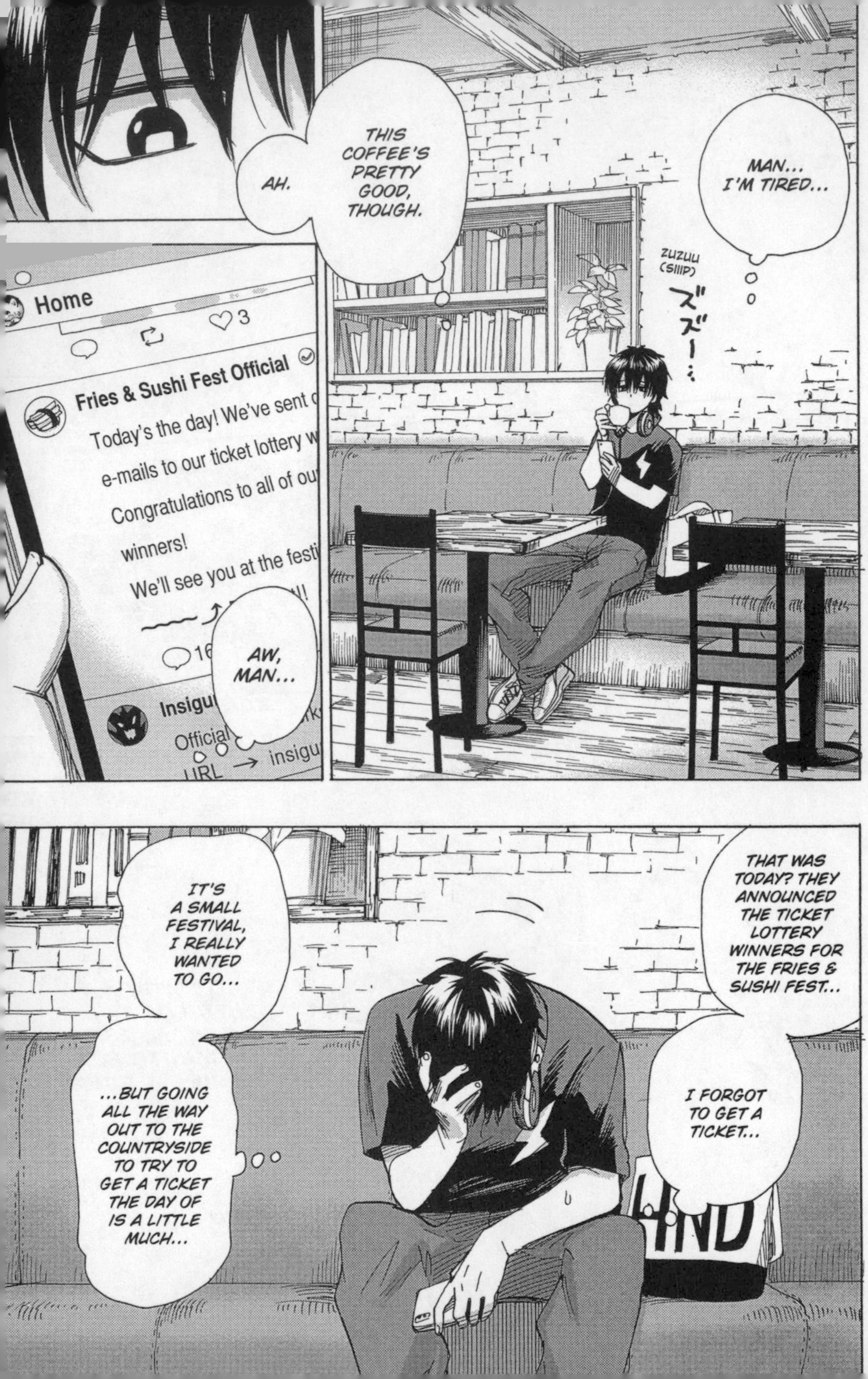

MAN... I'M TIRED...
ZUZUU (SIIIP)
ズズー…
AH.
THIS COFFEE'S PRETTY GOOD, THOUGH.
Home
3
Fries & Sushi Fest Official
Today's the day! We've sent
e-mails to our ticket lottery
Congratulations to all of
winners!
We'll see you at the
AW, MAN...
THAT WAS TODAY? THEY ANNOUNCED THE TICKET LOTTERY WINNERS FOR THE FRIES & SUSHI FEST...
I FORGOT TO GET A TICKET...
IT'S A SMALL FESTIVAL, I REALLY WANTED TO GO...
...BUT GOING ALL THE WAY OUT TO THE COUNTRYSIDE TO TRY TO GET A TICKET THE DAY OF IS A LITTLE MUCH...

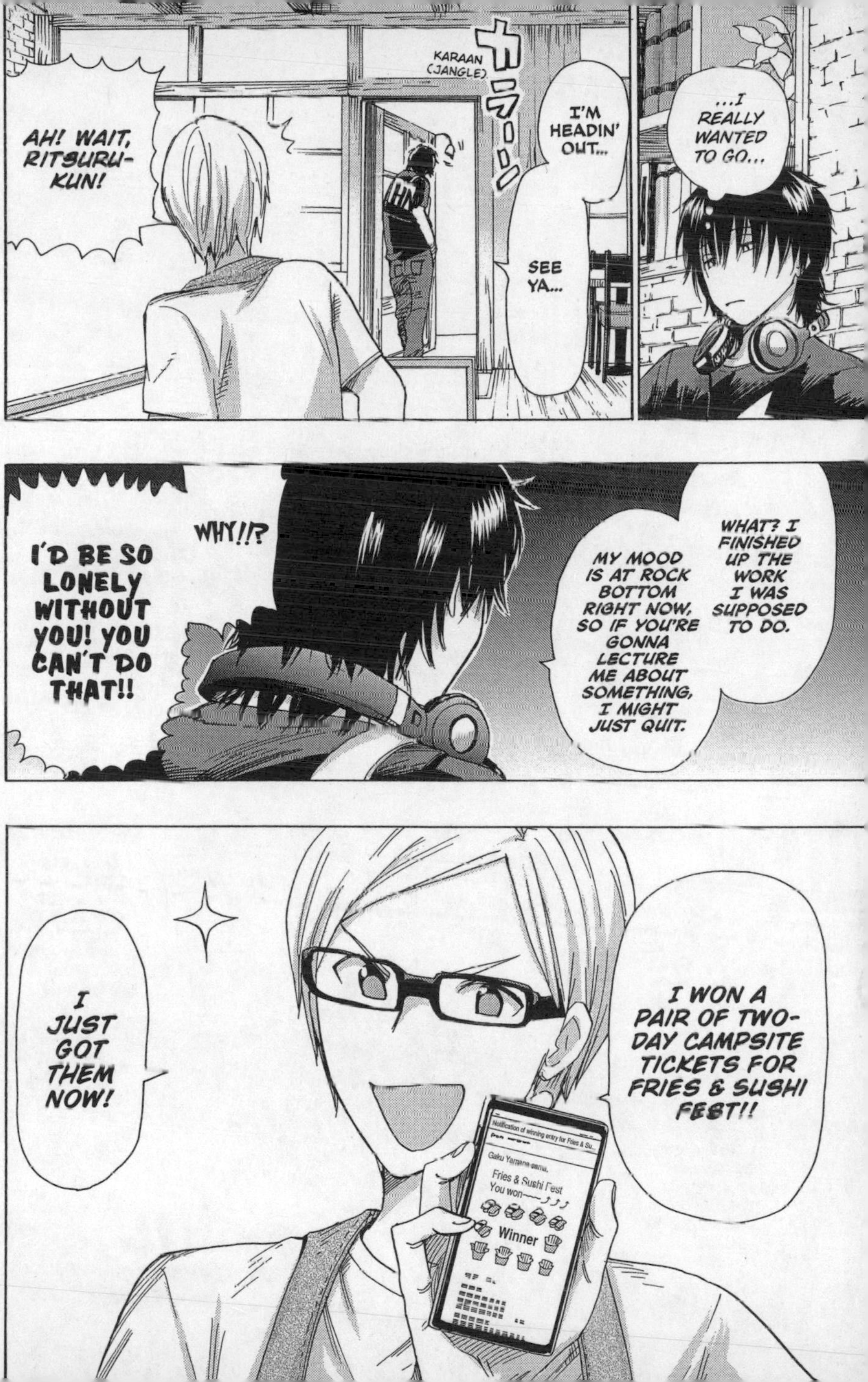
...I REALLY WANTED TO GO...
カラーン
KARAAN (JANGLE)
I'M HEADIN' OUT...
SEE YA...
AH! WAIT, RITSURU-KUN!
WHAT? I FINISHED UP THE WORK I WAS SUPPOSED TO DO.
MY MOOD IS AT ROCK BOTTOM RIGHT NOW, SO IF YOU'RE GONNA LECTURE ME ABOUT SOMETHING, I MIGHT JUST QUIT.
WHY!!?
I'D BE SO LONELY WITHOUT YOU! YOU CAN'T DO THAT!!
I WON A PAIR OF TWO-DAY CAMPSITE TICKETS FOR FRIES & SUSHI FEST!!
I JUST GOT THEM NOW!
Notification of winning entry for Fries & Su...
Gaku Yamana-sama,
Fries & Sushi Fest
You won~~~♪♪♪
Winner

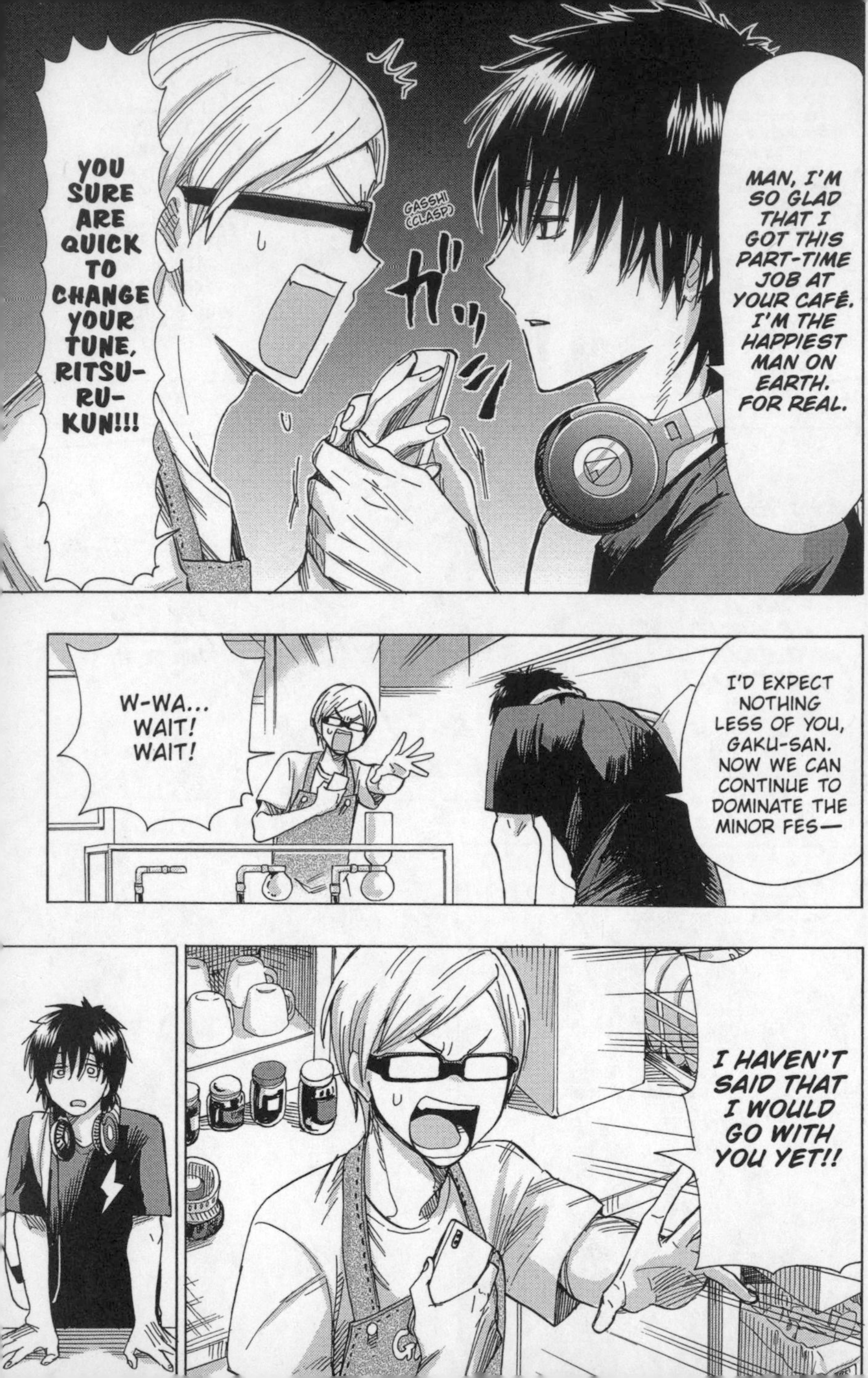
MAN, I'M SO GLAD THAT I GOT THIS PART-TIME JOB AT YOUR CAFÉ. I'M THE HAPPIEST MAN ON EARTH. FOR REAL.
GASSHI (CLASP)
YOU SURE ARE QUICK TO CHANGE YOUR TUNE, RITSU-RU-KUN!!!
I'D EXPECT NOTHING LESS OF YOU, GAKU-SAN. NOW WE CAN CONTINUE TO DOMINATE THE MINOR FES—
W-WA... WAIT! WAIT!
I HAVEN'T SAID THAT I WOULD GO WITH YOU YET!!

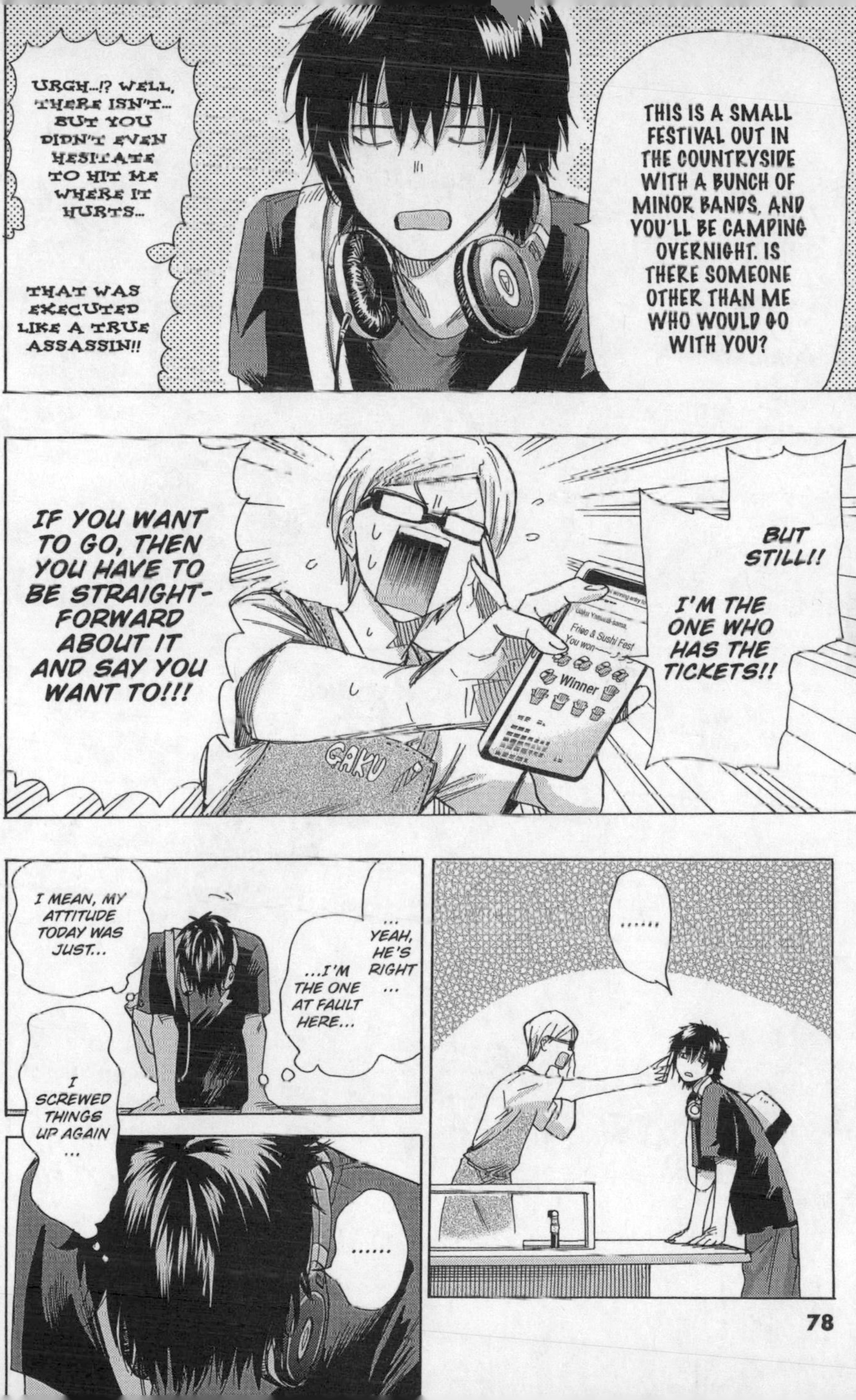
THIS IS A SMALL FESTIVAL OUT IN THE COUNTRYSIDE WITH A BUNCH OF MINOR BANDS, AND YOU'LL BE CAMPING OVERNIGHT. IS THERE SOMEONE OTHER THAN ME WHO WOULD GO WITH YOU?
URGH...!? WELL, THERE ISN'T... BUT YOU DIDN'T EVEN HESITATE TO HIT ME WHERE IT HURTS...
THAT WAS EXECUTED LIKE A TRUE ASSASSIN!!
BUT STILL!!
I'M THE ONE WHO HAS THE TICKETS!!
Fries & Sushi Fest
You won
Winner
GAKU
IF YOU WANT TO GO, THEN YOU HAVE TO BE STRAIGHT-FORWARD ABOUT IT AND SAY YOU WANT TO!!!
......
...YEAH, HE'S RIGHT...
...I'M THE ONE AT FAULT HERE...
I MEAN, MY ATTITUDE TODAY WAS JUST...
I SCREWED THINGS UP AGAIN...
......

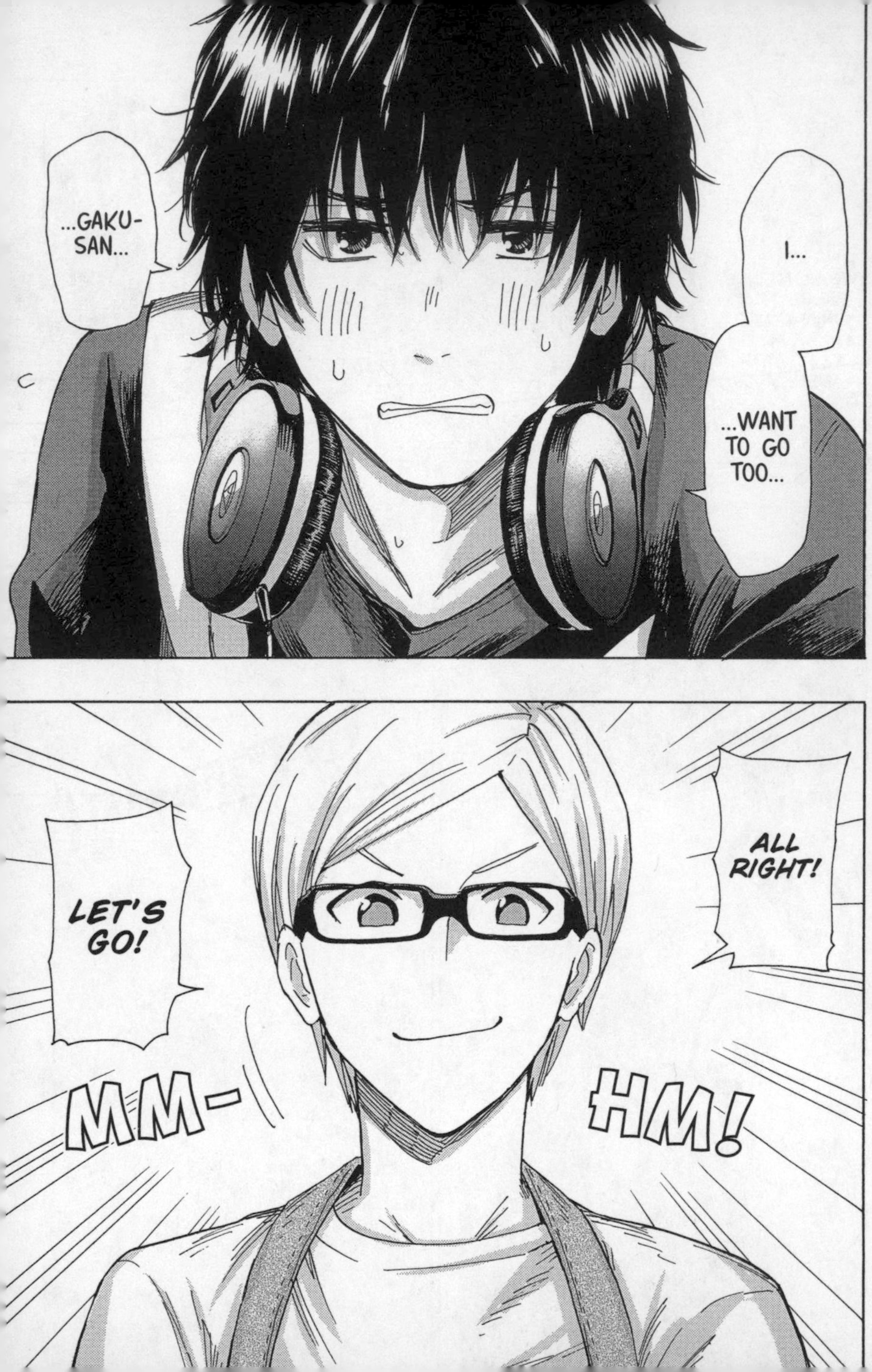
...GAKU-SAN...
I...
...WANT TO GO TOO...
ALL RIGHT!
LET'S GO!
MM-HM!

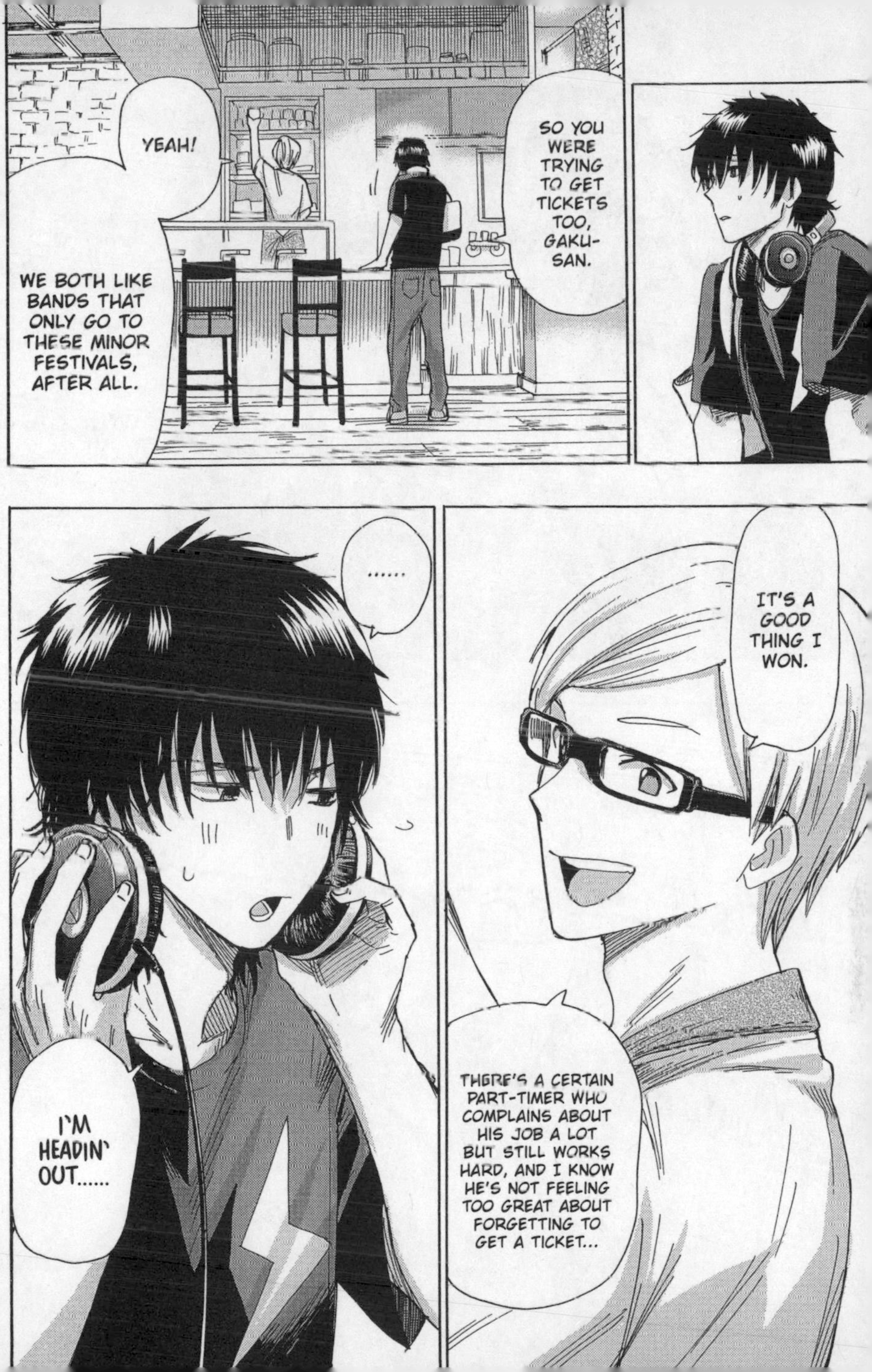
SO YOU WERE TRYING TO GET TICKETS TOO, GAKU-SAN.
YEAH!
WE BOTH LIKE BANDS THAT ONLY GO TO THESE MINOR FESTIVALS, AFTER ALL.
IT'S A GOOD THING I WON.
THERE'S A CERTAIN PART-TIMER WHO COMPLAINS ABOUT HIS JOB A LOT BUT STILL WORKS HARD, AND I KNOW HE'S NOT FEELING TOO GREAT ABOUT FORGETTING TO GET A TICKET...
......
I'M HEADIN' OUT......

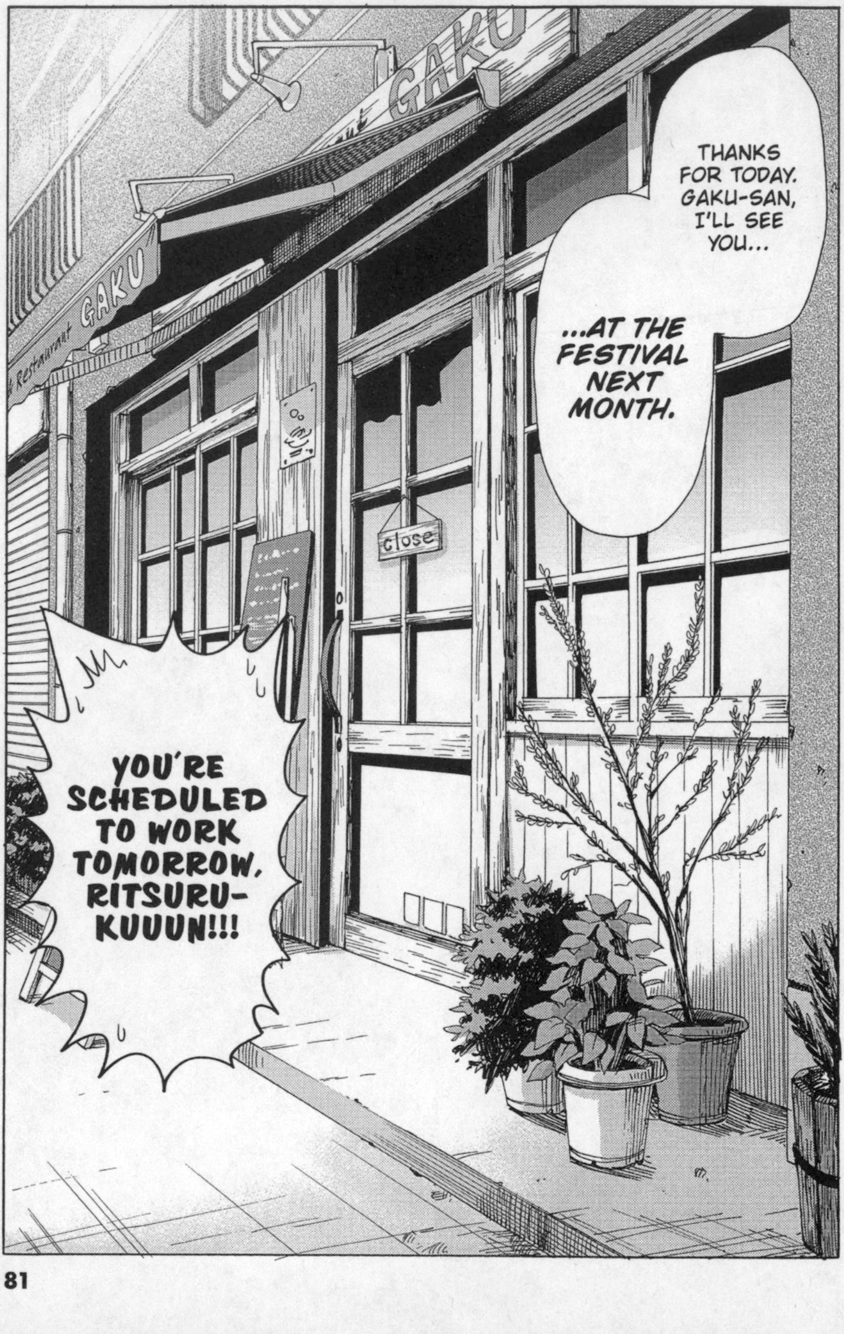
GAKU
GAKU
Restaurant GAKU
close
THANKS FOR TODAY. GAKU-SAN, I'LL SEE YOU...
...AT THE FESTIVAL NEXT MONTH.
YOU'RE SCHEDULED TO WORK TOMORROW, RITSURU-KUUUN!!!

Days on Fes

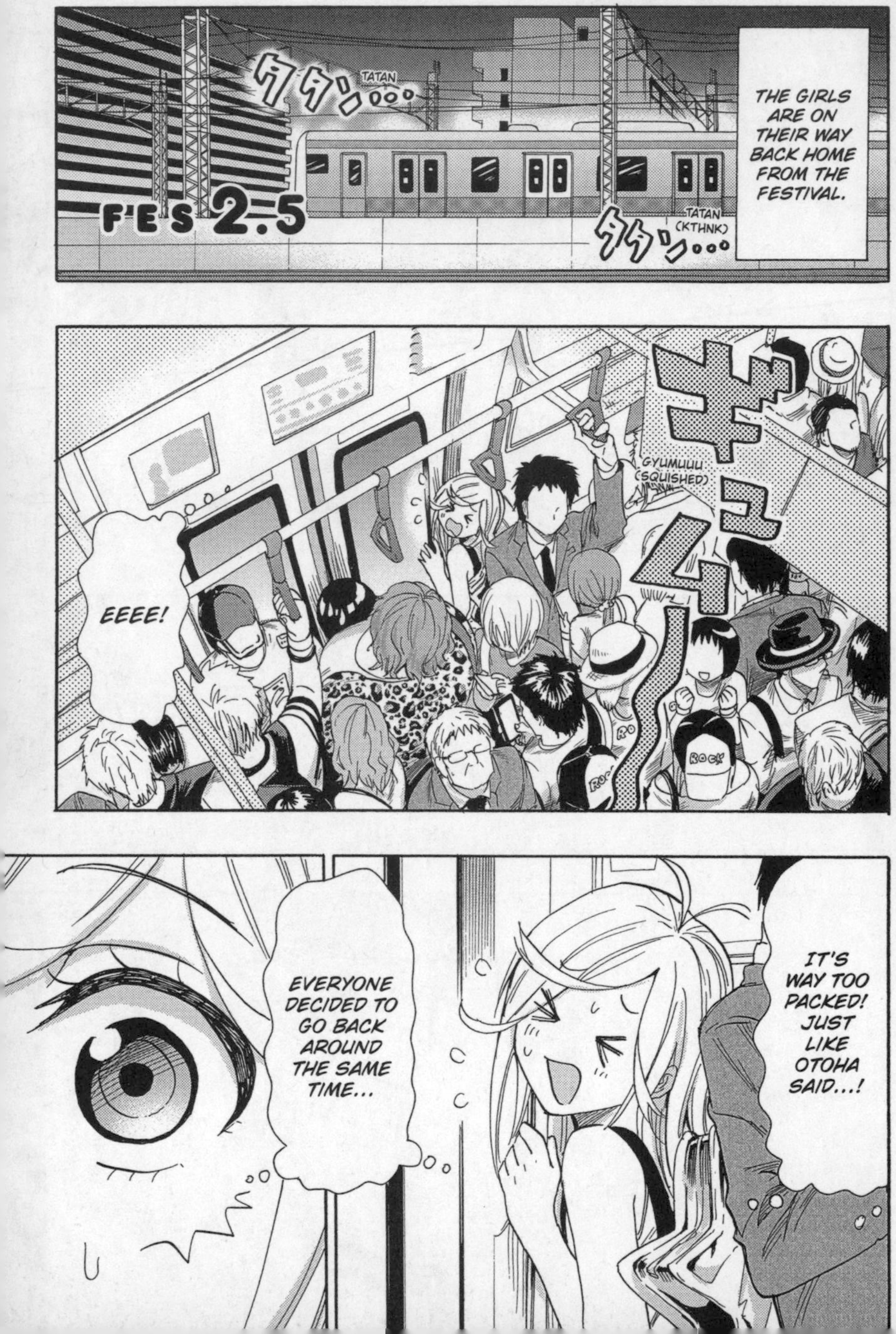
THE GIRLS ARE ON THEIR WAY BACK HOME FROM THE FESTIVAL.
TATAN
TATAN (KTHNK)
F'E'S 2.5
GYUMUUU (SQUISHED)
EEEE!
IT'S WAY TOO PACKED! JUST LIKE OTOHA SAID...!
EVERYONE DECIDED TO GO BACK AROUND THE SAME TIME...

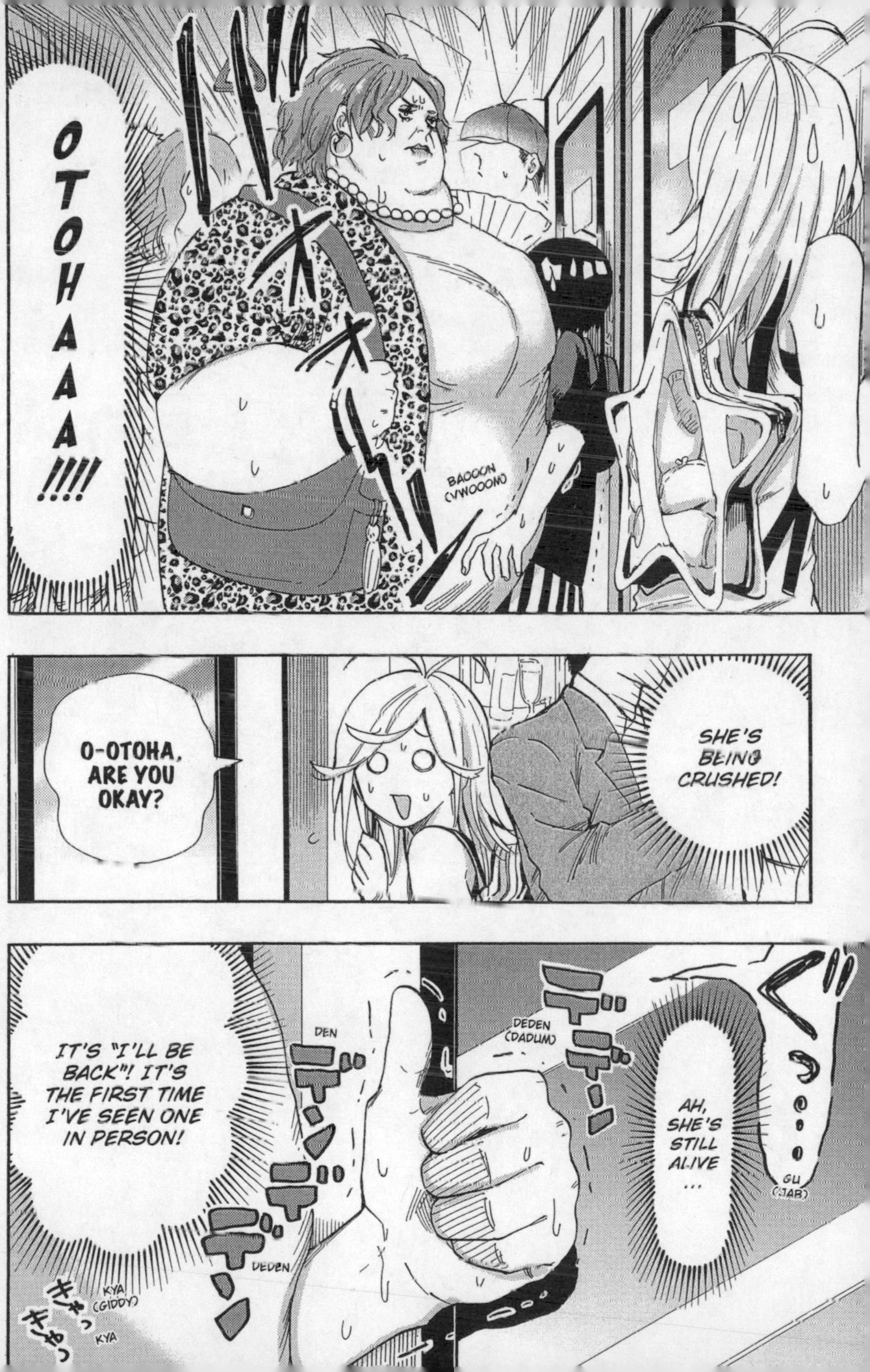
OTOHAAAA!!!!
BAOOON (VWOOOM)
SHE'S BEING CRUSHED!
O-OTOHA, ARE YOU OKAY?
GU (JAB)
AH, SHE'S STILL ALIVE ...
DEDEN (DADUM)
DEN
IT'S "I'LL BE BACK"! IT'S THE FIRST TIME I'VE SEEN ONE IN PERSON!
DEDEN
きゃっ KYA (GIDDY)
きゃっ KYA

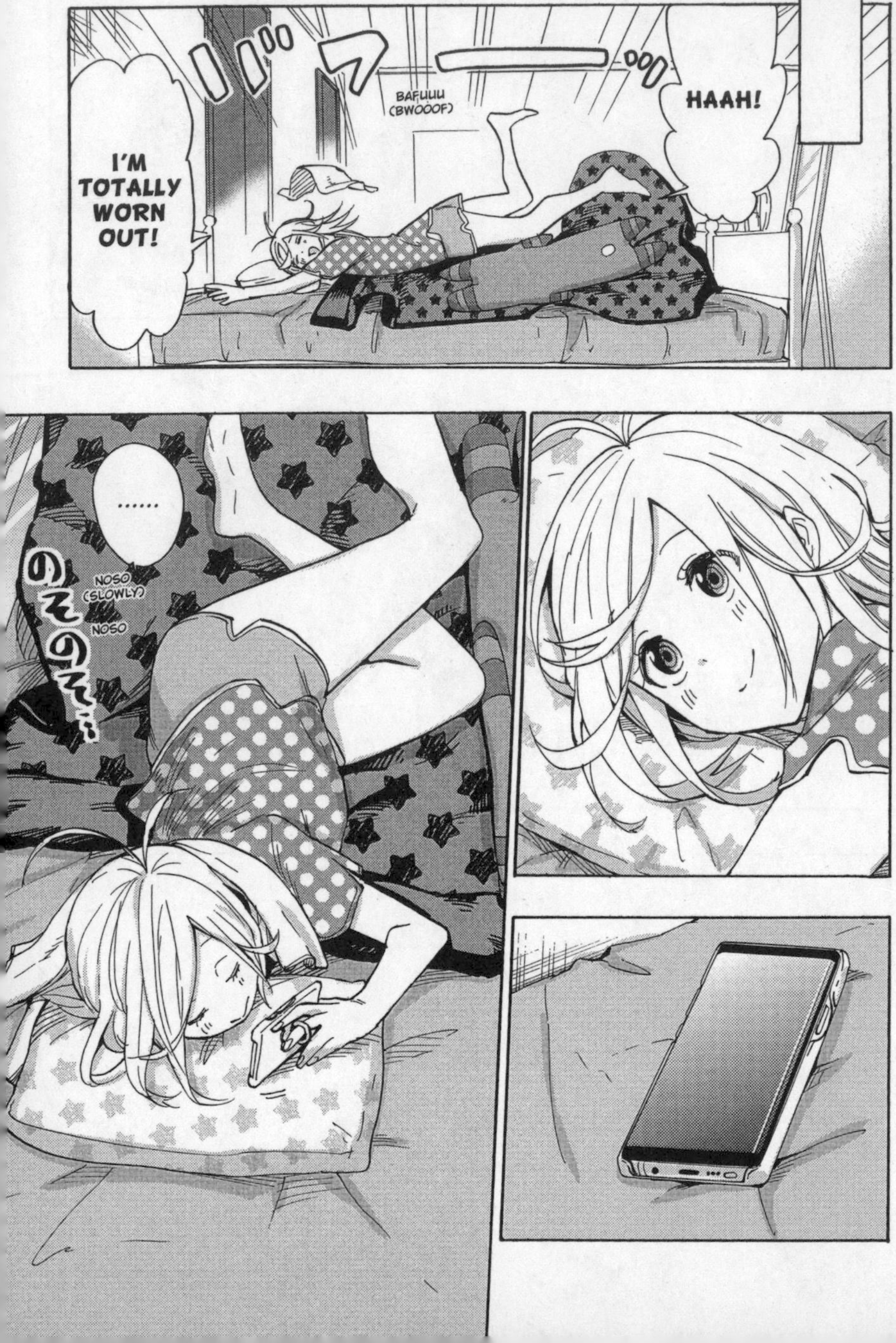
HAAH!
BAFUUU (BWOOOF)
I'M TOTALLY WORN OUT!
......
NOSO (SLOWLY) NOSO
のそのそ~

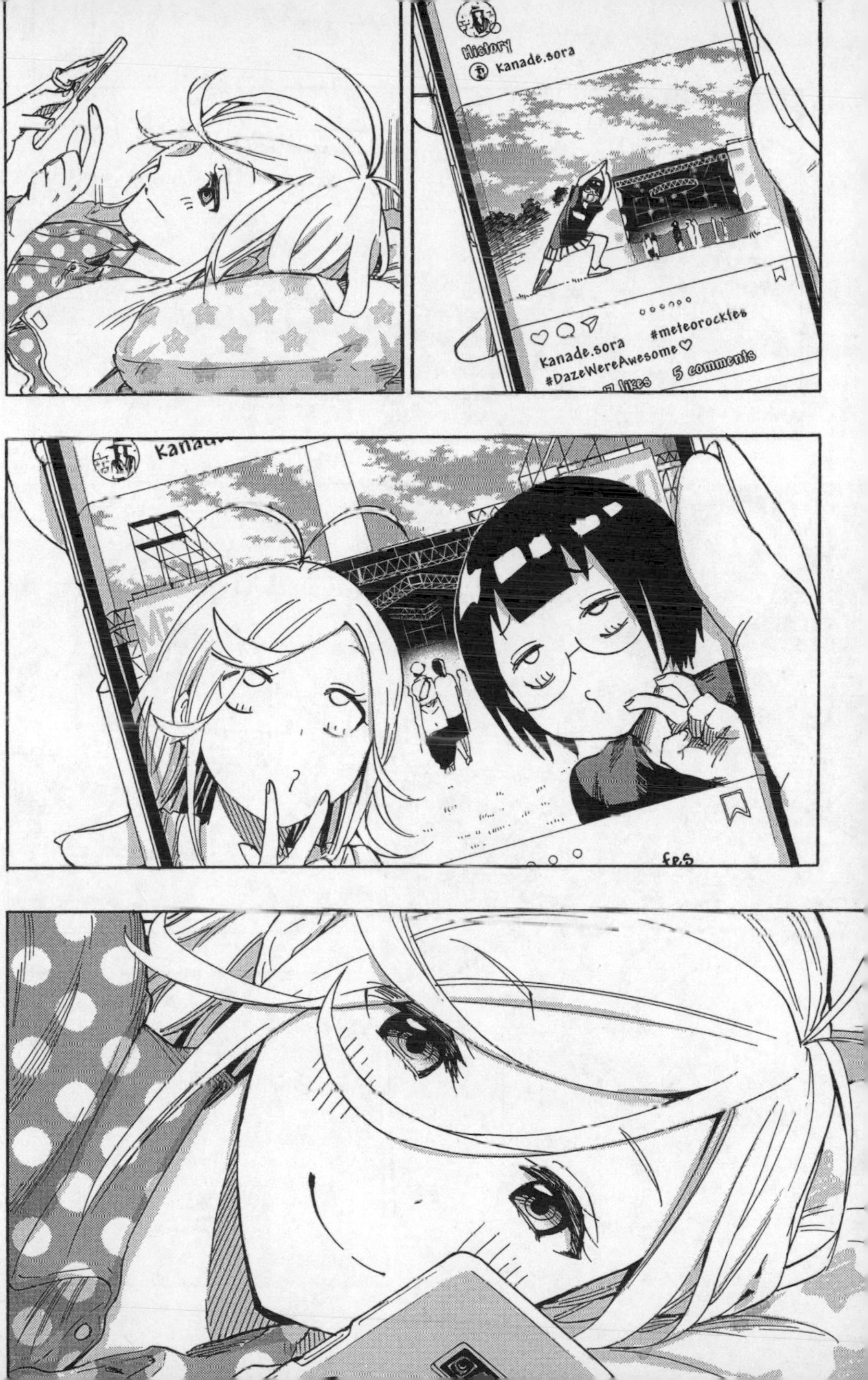
History
kanade.sora
#meteorockles
kanade.sora
#DazeWereAwesome♡
5 comments

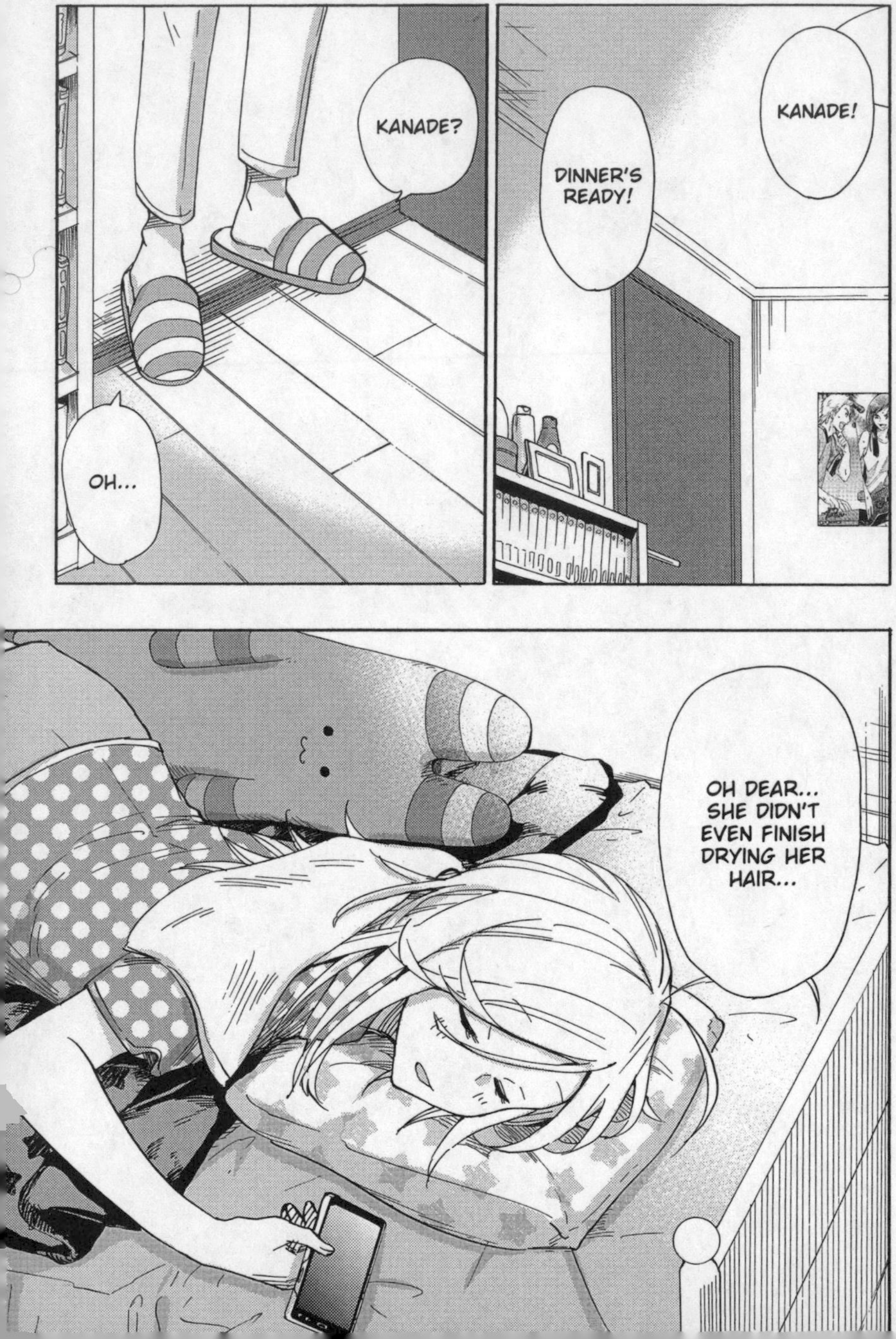
KANADE!
DINNER'S READY!
KANADE?
OH...
OH DEAR... SHE DIDN'T EVEN FINISH DRYING HER HAIR...

Days on Fes

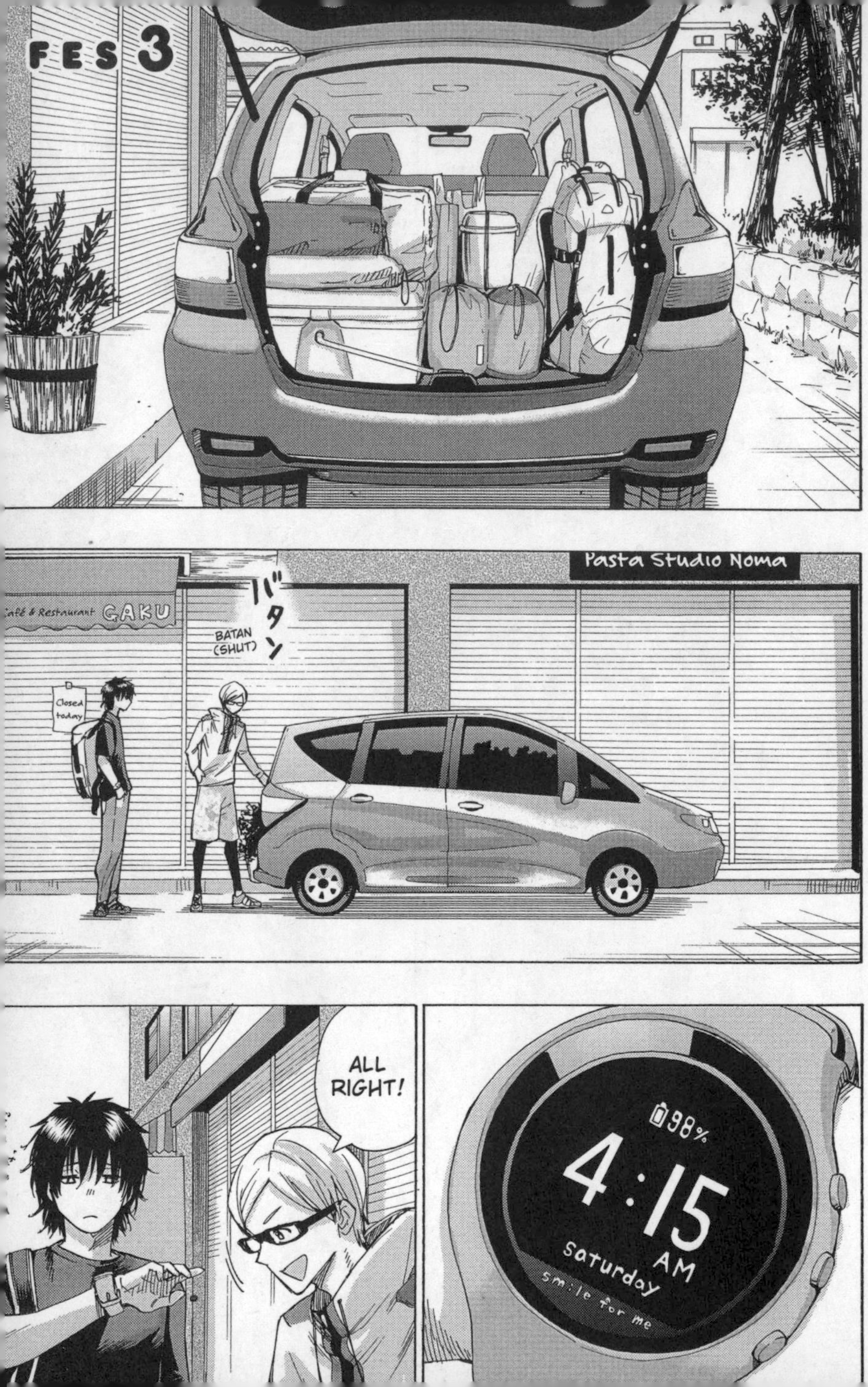
FES 3
Pasta Studio Noma
Café & Restaurant GAKU
バタン
BATAN (SHUT)
Closed today
98%
4:15
AM
Saturday
smile for me
ALL RIGHT!

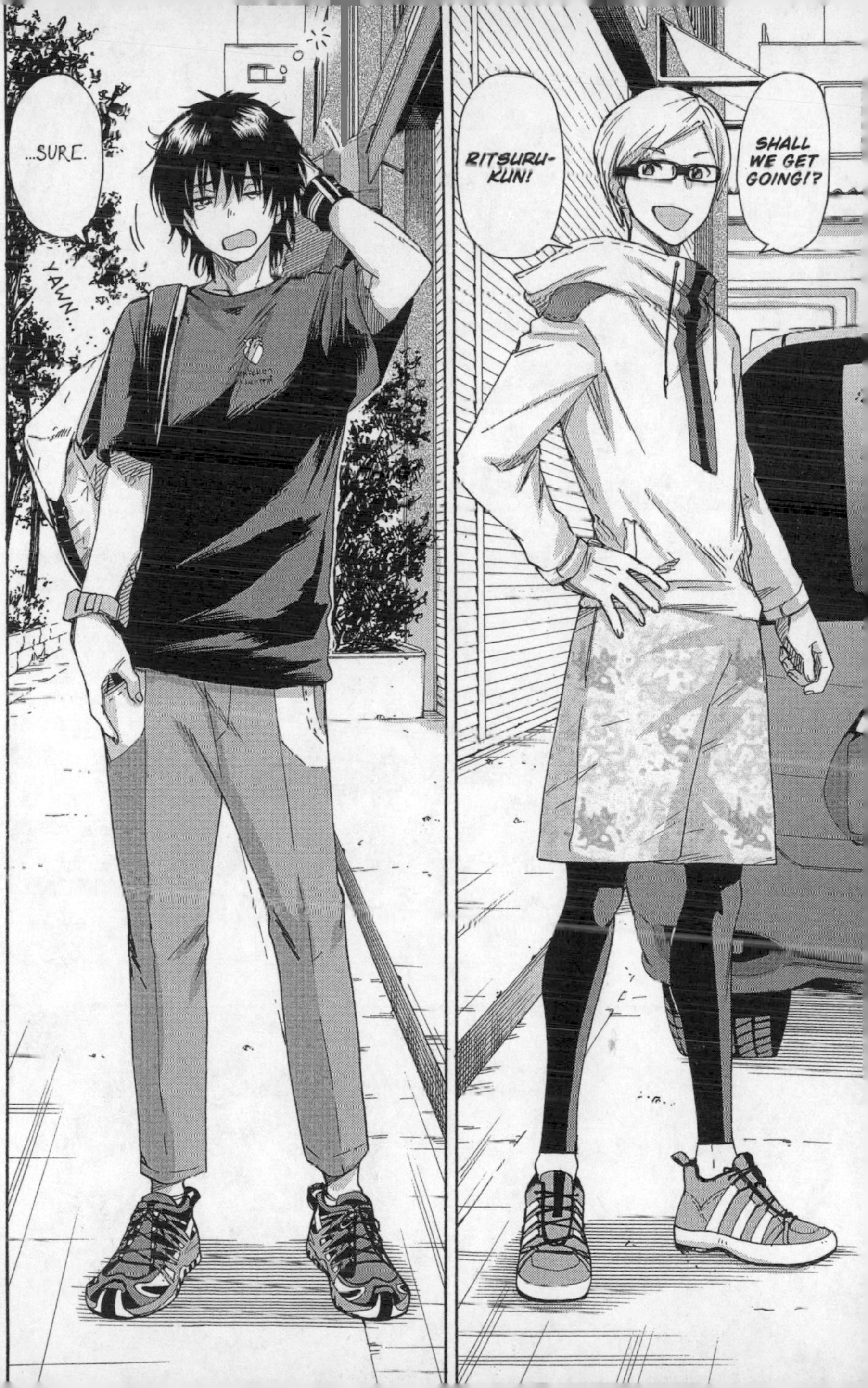
SHALL WE GET GOING!?
RITSURU-KUN!
...SURE.
YAWN...

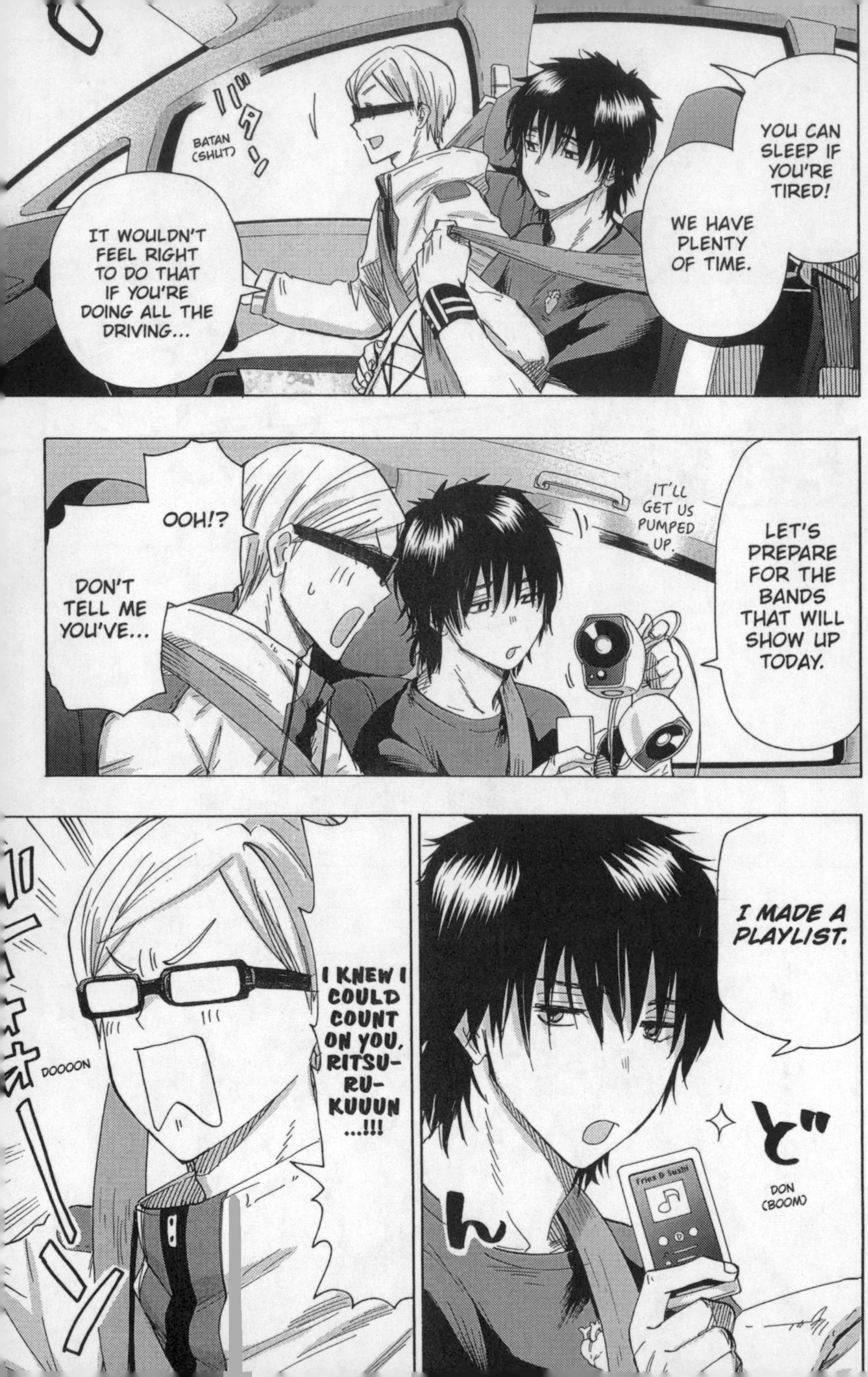
YOU CAN SLEEP IF YOU'RE TIRED!
WE HAVE PLENTY OF TIME.
BATAN (SHUT)
IT WOULDN'T FEEL RIGHT TO DO THAT IF YOU'RE DOING ALL THE DRIVING...
LET'S PREPARE FOR THE BANDS THAT WILL SHOW UP TODAY.
IT'LL GET US PUMPED UP.
OOH!?
DON'T TELL ME YOU'VE...
I MADE A PLAYLIST.
DON (BOOM)
I KNEW I COULD COUNT ON YOU, RITSU-RU-KUUUN ...!!!
DOOOON

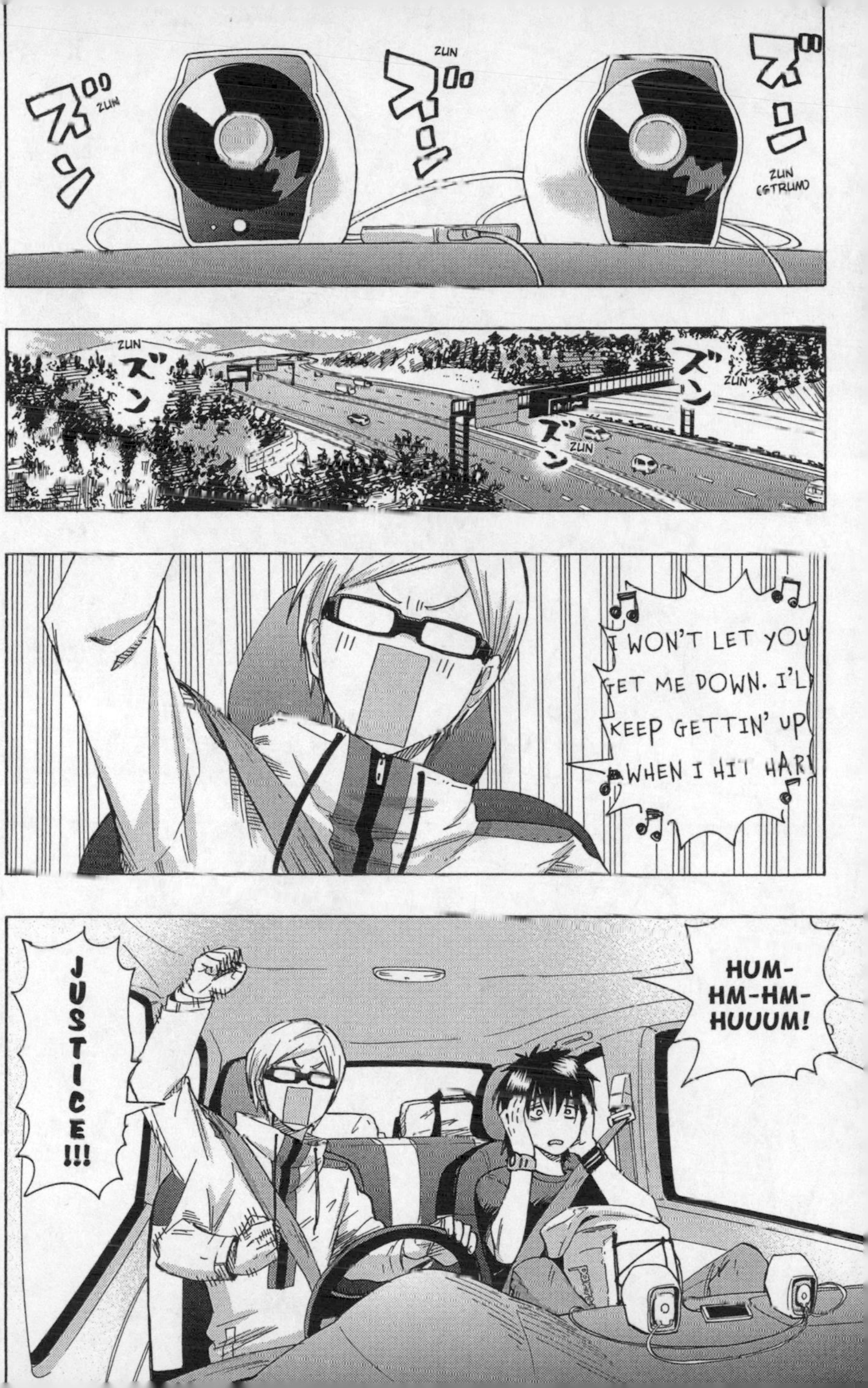
ZUN (STRUM)
ZUN
ZUN
ズン
ZUN
ズン
ZUN
ズン
ZUN
I WON'T LET YOU GET ME DOWN. I'L KEEP GETTIN' UP WHEN I HIT HAR
HUM-HM-HM-HUUUM!
JUSTICE!!!

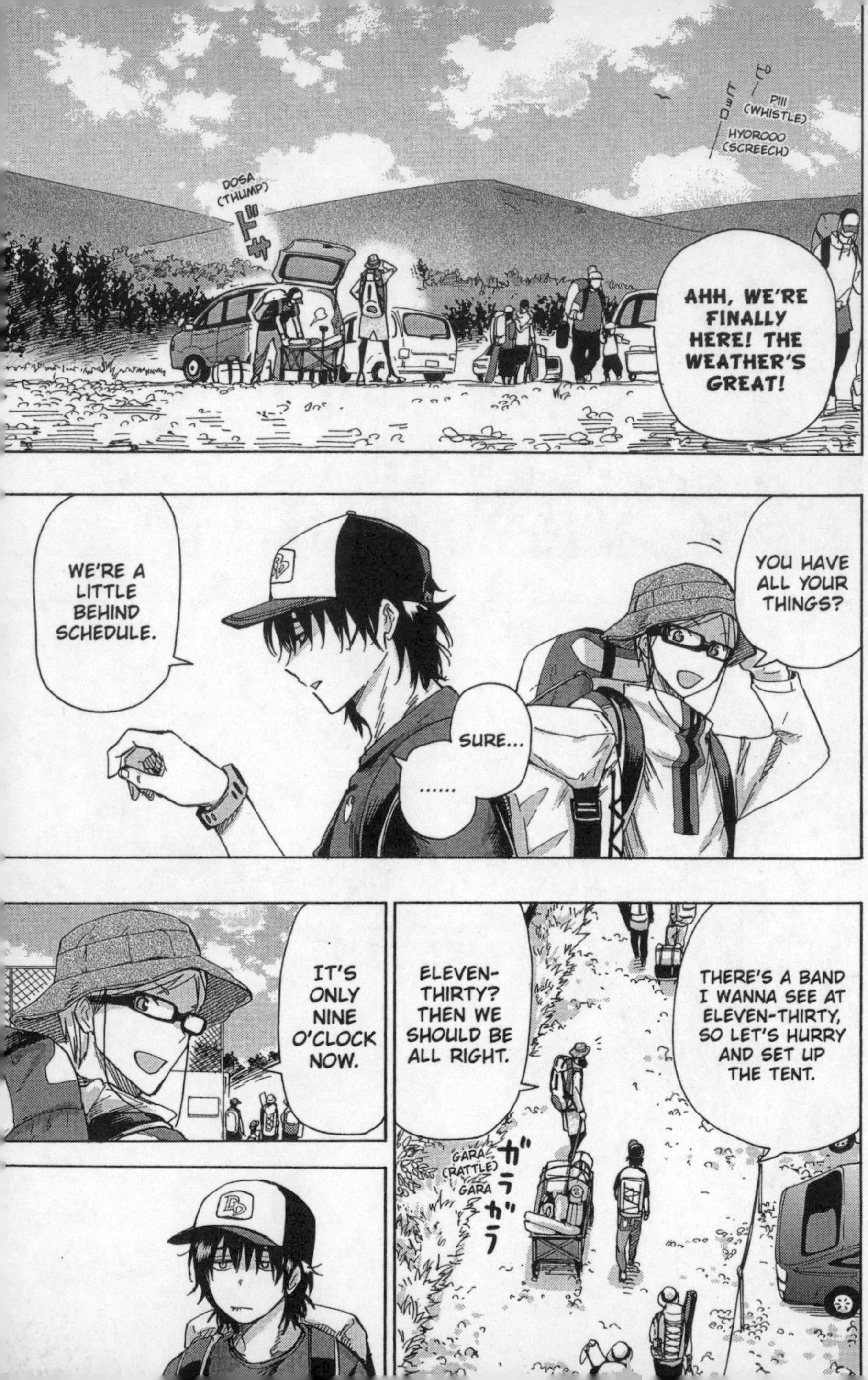
PIII (WHISTLE)
HYOROOO (SCREECH)
AHH, WE'RE FINALLY HERE! THE WEATHER'S GREAT!
DOSA (THUMP)
YOU HAVE ALL YOUR THINGS?
SURE...
......
WE'RE A LITTLE BEHIND SCHEDULE.
THERE'S A BAND I WANNA SEE AT ELEVEN-THIRTY, SO LET'S HURRY AND SET UP THE TENT.
ELEVEN-THIRTY? THEN WE SHOULD BE ALL RIGHT.
GARA (RATTLE) GARA
IT'S ONLY NINE O'CLOCK NOW.

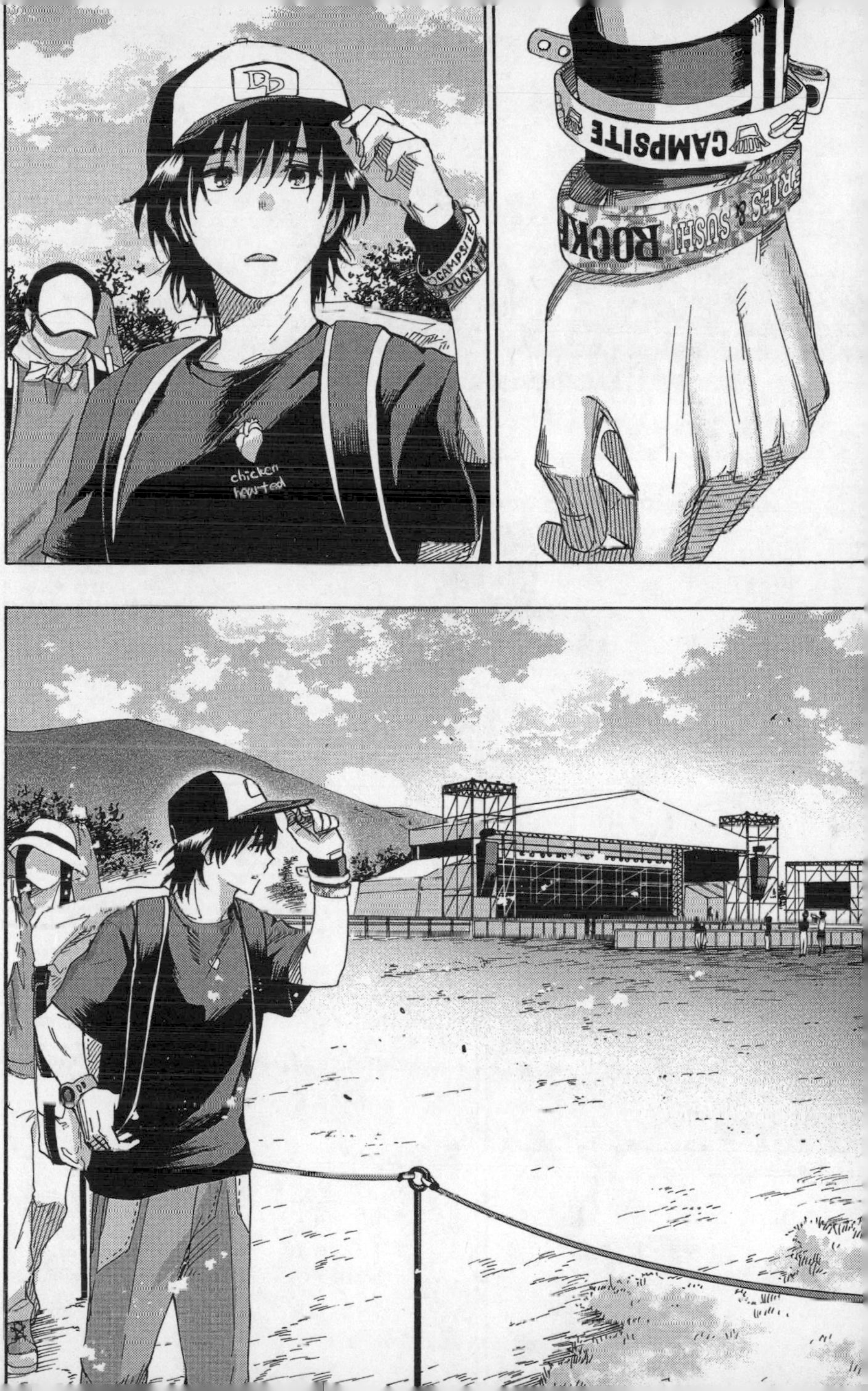
CAMPSITE
SUSHI
chicken
hearted
CAMPSITE

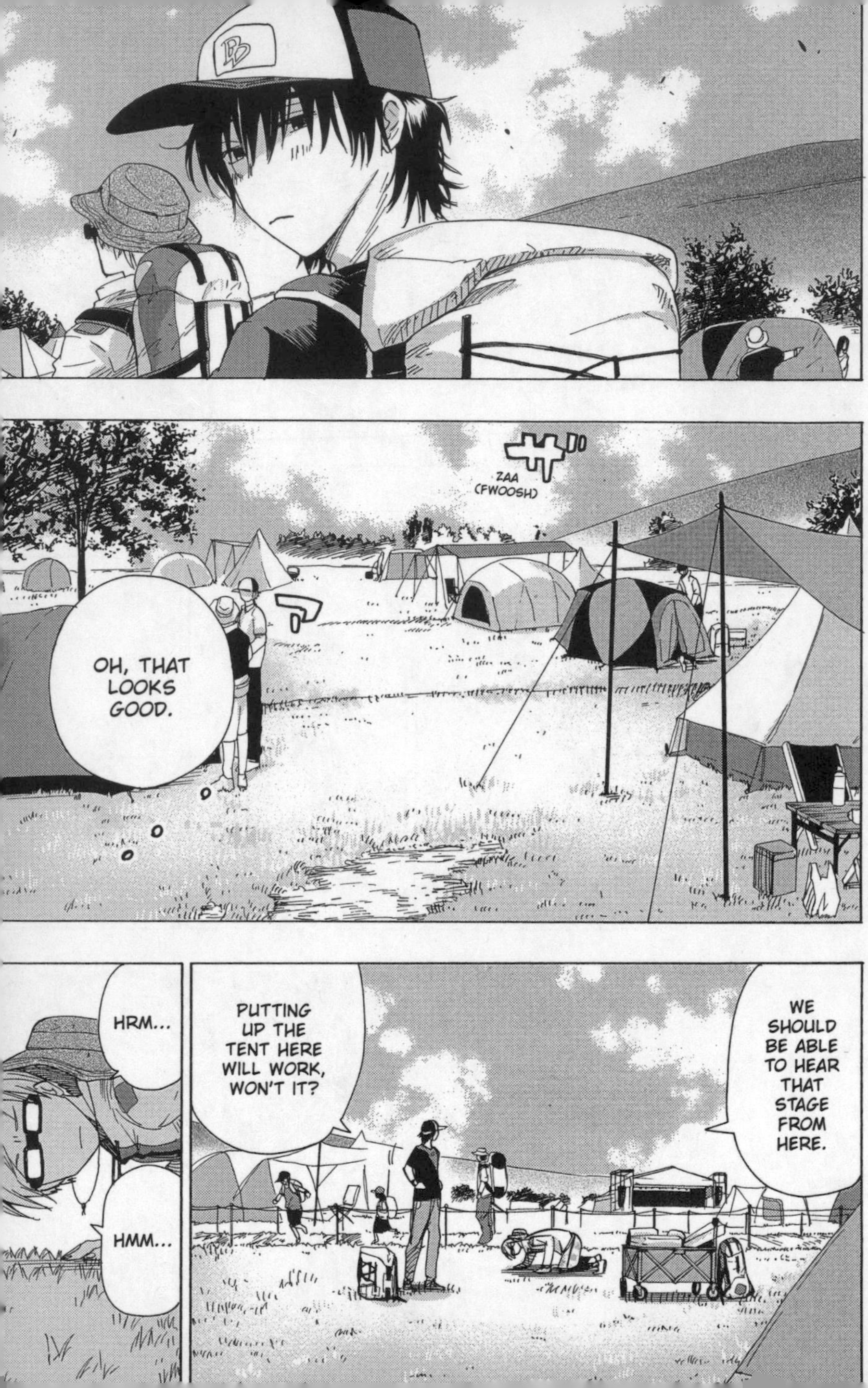
ZAA (FWOOSH)
OH, THAT LOOKS GOOD.
WE SHOULD BE ABLE TO HEAR THAT STAGE FROM HERE.
PUTTING UP THE TENT HERE WILL WORK, WON'T IT?
HRM...
HMM...

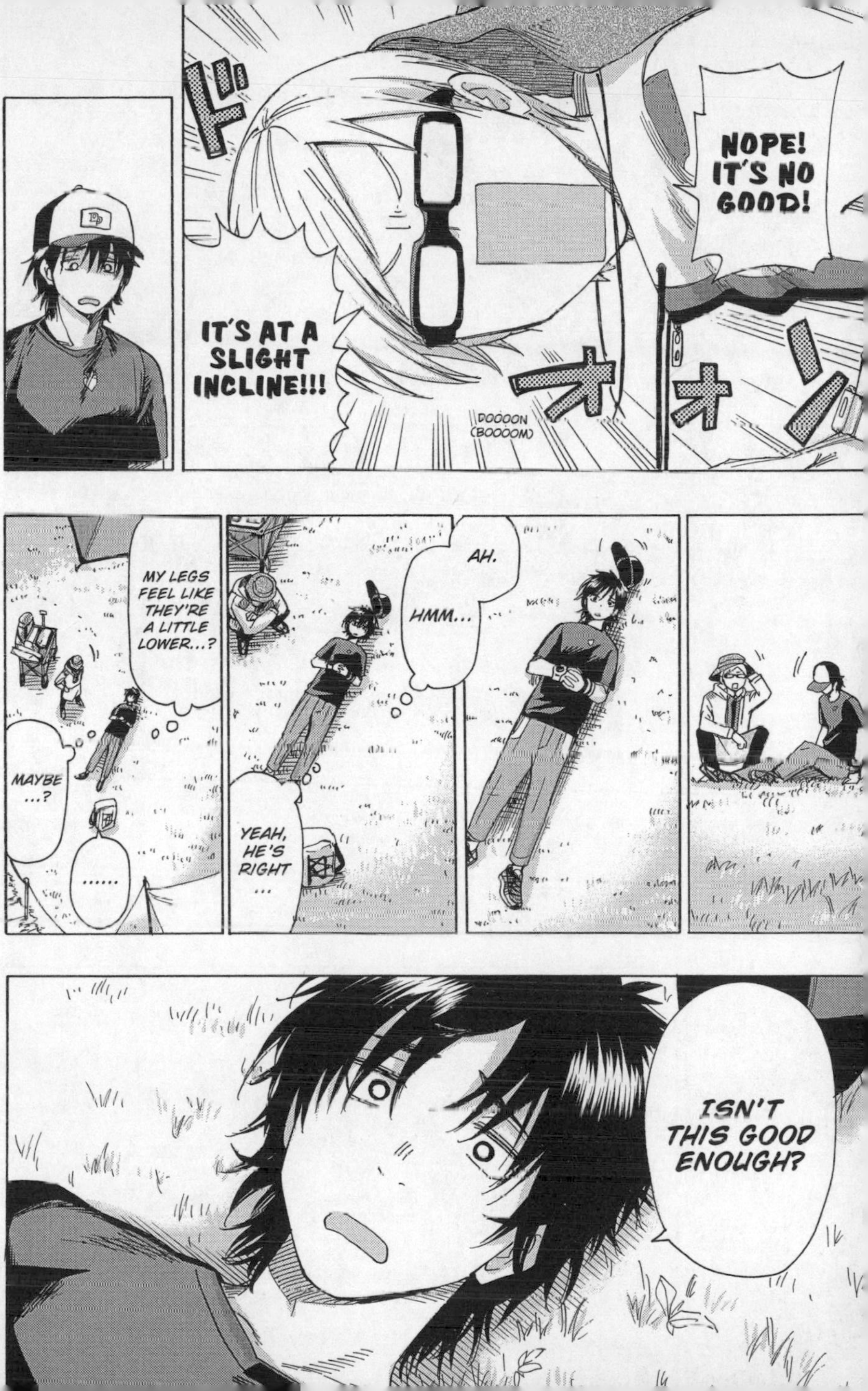
NOPE! IT'S NO GOOD!
IT'S AT A SLIGHT INCLINE!!!
ドオオン
DOOOON (BOOOOM)
AH.
HMM...
YEAH, HE'S RIGHT...
MY LEGS FEEL LIKE THEY'RE A LITTLE LOWER...?
MAYBE...?
....
ISN'T THIS GOOD ENOUGH?

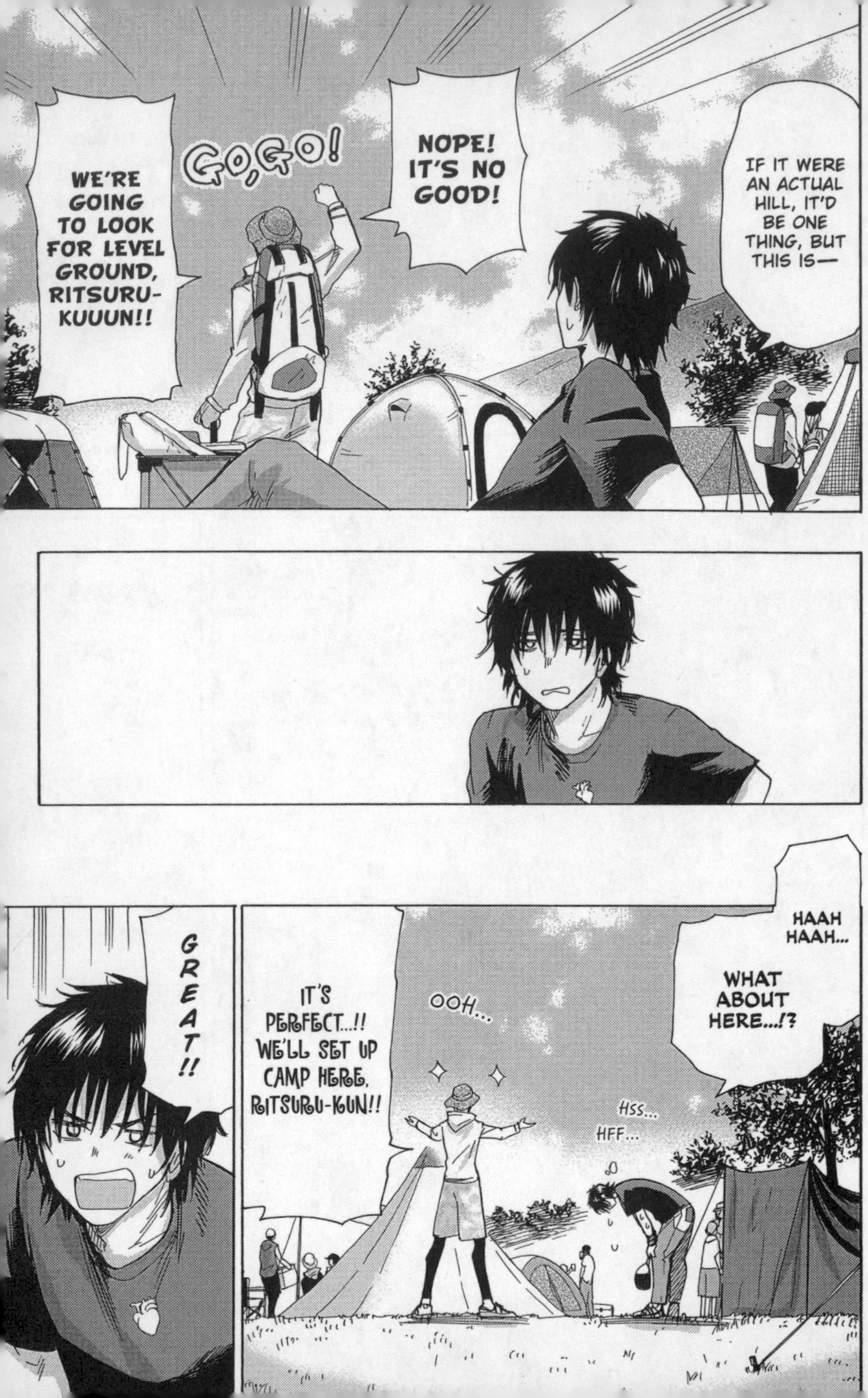
IF IT WERE AN ACTUAL HILL, IT'D BE ONE THING, BUT THIS IS—
NOPE! IT'S NO GOOD!
GO, GO!
WE'RE GOING TO LOOK FOR LEVEL GROUND, RITSURU-KUUUN!!
HAAH HAAH...
WHAT ABOUT HERE...!?
OOH...
IT'S PERFECT...!! WE'LL SET UP CAMP HERE, RITSURU-KUN!!
HSS...
HFF...
GREAT!!

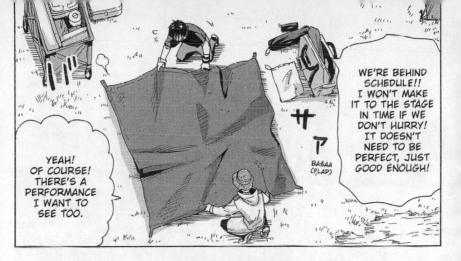

WE'RE BEHIND SCHEDULE!! I WON'T MAKE IT TO THE STAGE IN TIME IF WE DON'T HURRY! IT DOESN'T NEED TO BE PERFECT, JUST GOOD ENOUGH!

BASAA
(FLAP)

YEAH! OF COURSE! THERE'S A PERFORMANCE I WANT TO SEE TOO.

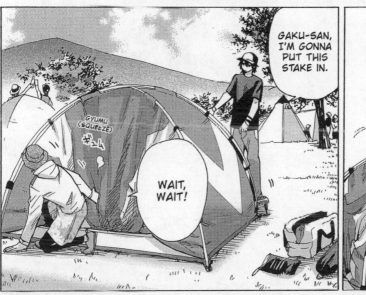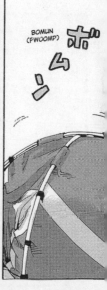

GAKU-SAN, I'M GONNA PUT THIS STAKE IN.

BOMUN
(FWOOMP)

GYUMU
(SQUEEZE)

WAIT, WAIT!

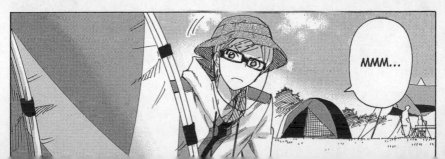

MMM...

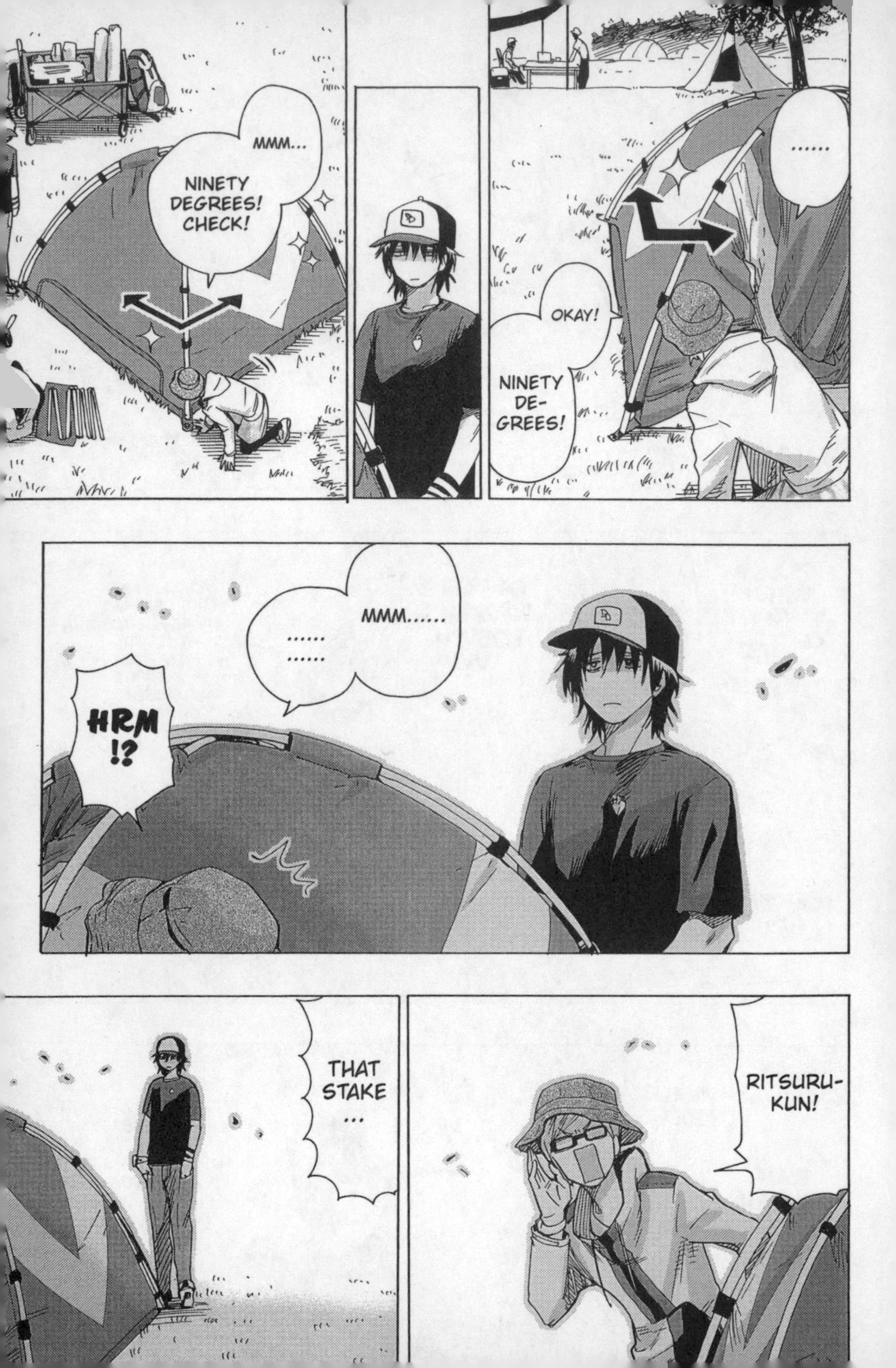
......
OKAY!
NINETY DE-GREES!
MMM...
NINETY DEGREES! CHECK!
MMM...... ....
HRM !?
RITSURU-KUN!
THAT STAKE ...

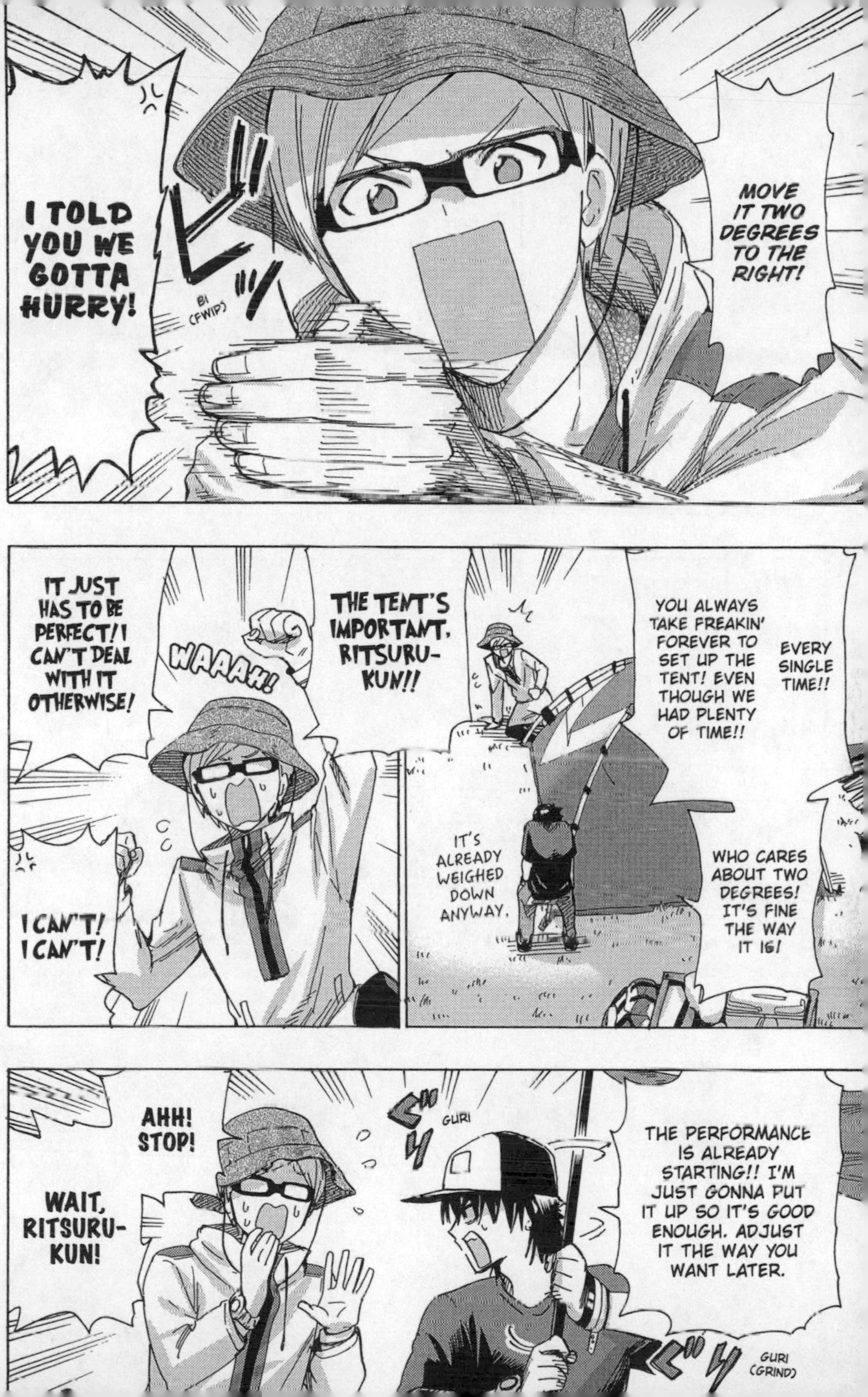
MOVE IT TWO DEGREES TO THE RIGHT!
BI (FWIP)
I TOLD YOU WE GOTTA HURRY!
YOU ALWAYS TAKE FREAKIN' FOREVER TO SET UP THE TENT! EVEN THOUGH WE HAD PLENTY OF TIME!!
EVERY SINGLE TIME!!
WHO CARES ABOUT TWO DEGREES! IT'S FINE THE WAY IT IS!
IT'S ALREADY WEIGHED DOWN ANYWAY.
THE TENT'S IMPORTANT, RITSURU-KUN!!
WAAAH!
IT JUST HAS TO BE PERFECT! I CAN'T DEAL WITH IT OTHERWISE!
I CAN'T! I CAN'T!
THE PERFORMANCE IS ALREADY STARTING!! I'M JUST GONNA PUT IT UP SO IT'S GOOD ENOUGH. ADJUST IT THE WAY YOU WANT LATER.
GURI
AHH! STOP!
WAIT, RITSURU-KUN!
GURI (GRIND)

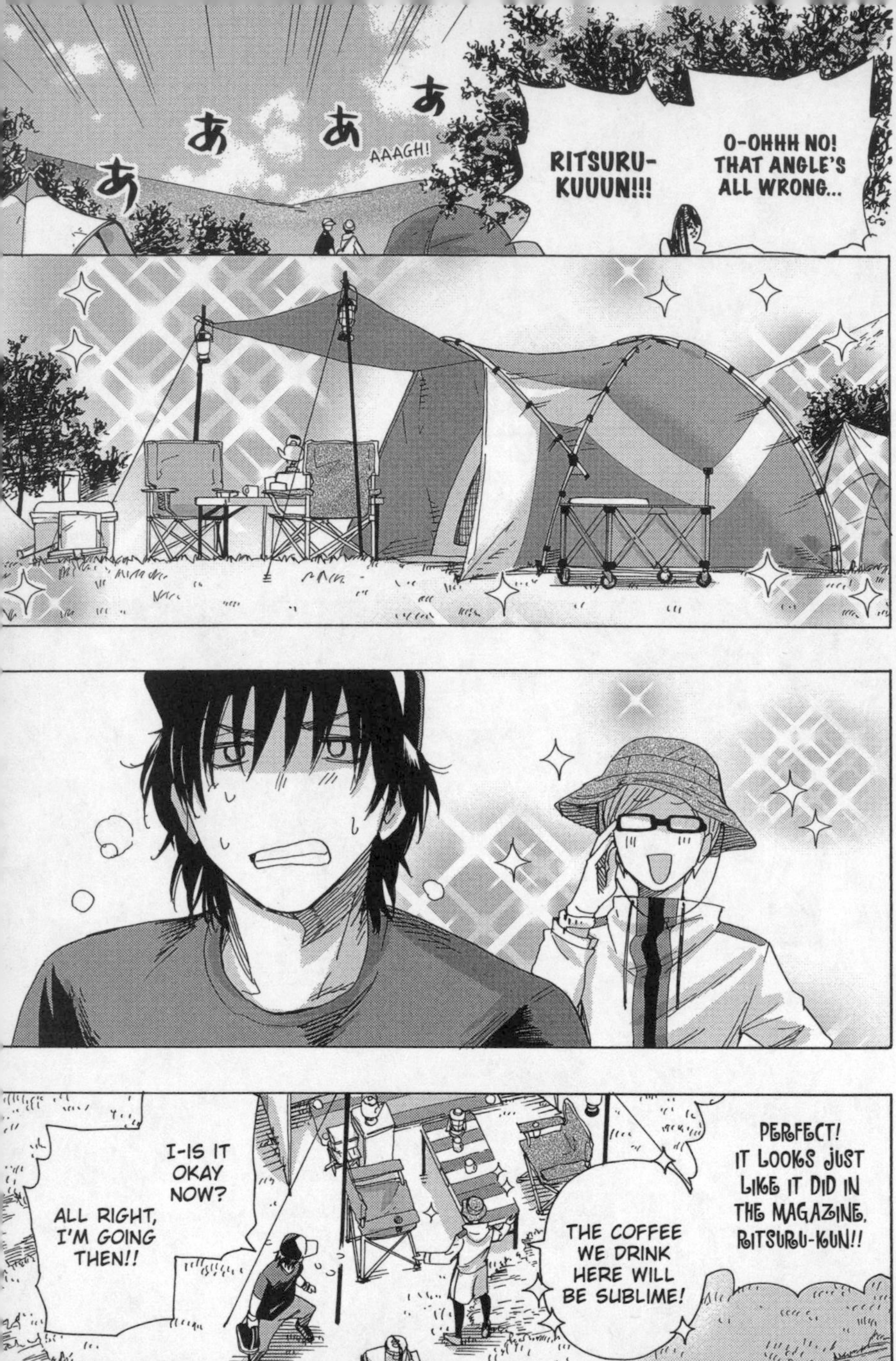
O-OHHH NO! THAT ANGLE'S ALL WRONG...
RITSURU-KUUUN!!!
あああ
AAAGH!
あ
PERFECT! IT LOOKS JUST LIKE IT DID IN THE MAGAZINE, RITSURU-KUN!!
THE COFFEE WE DRINK HERE WILL BE SUBLIME!
I-IS IT OKAY NOW?
ALL RIGHT, I'M GOING THEN!!

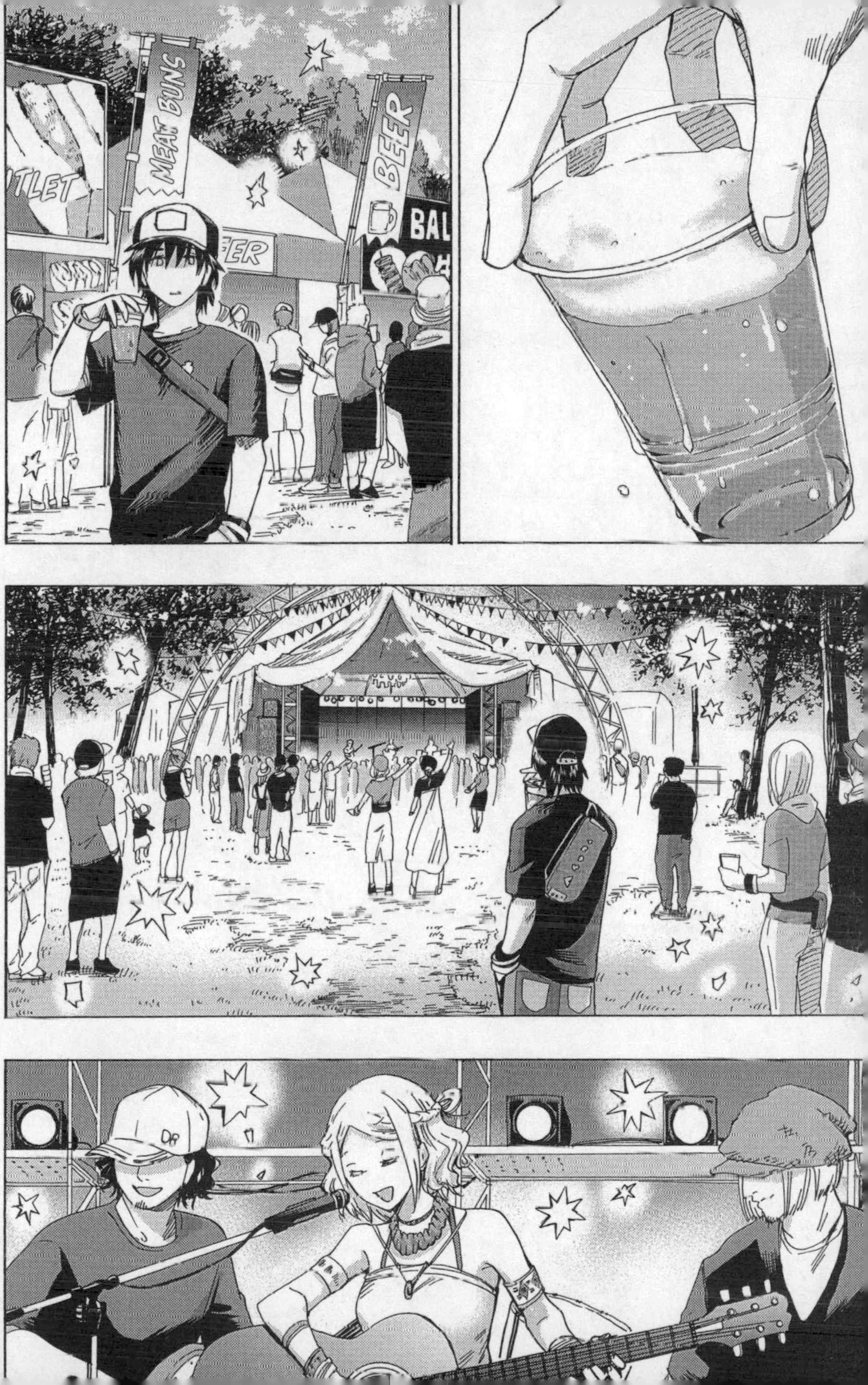
MEAT BUNS
BEER

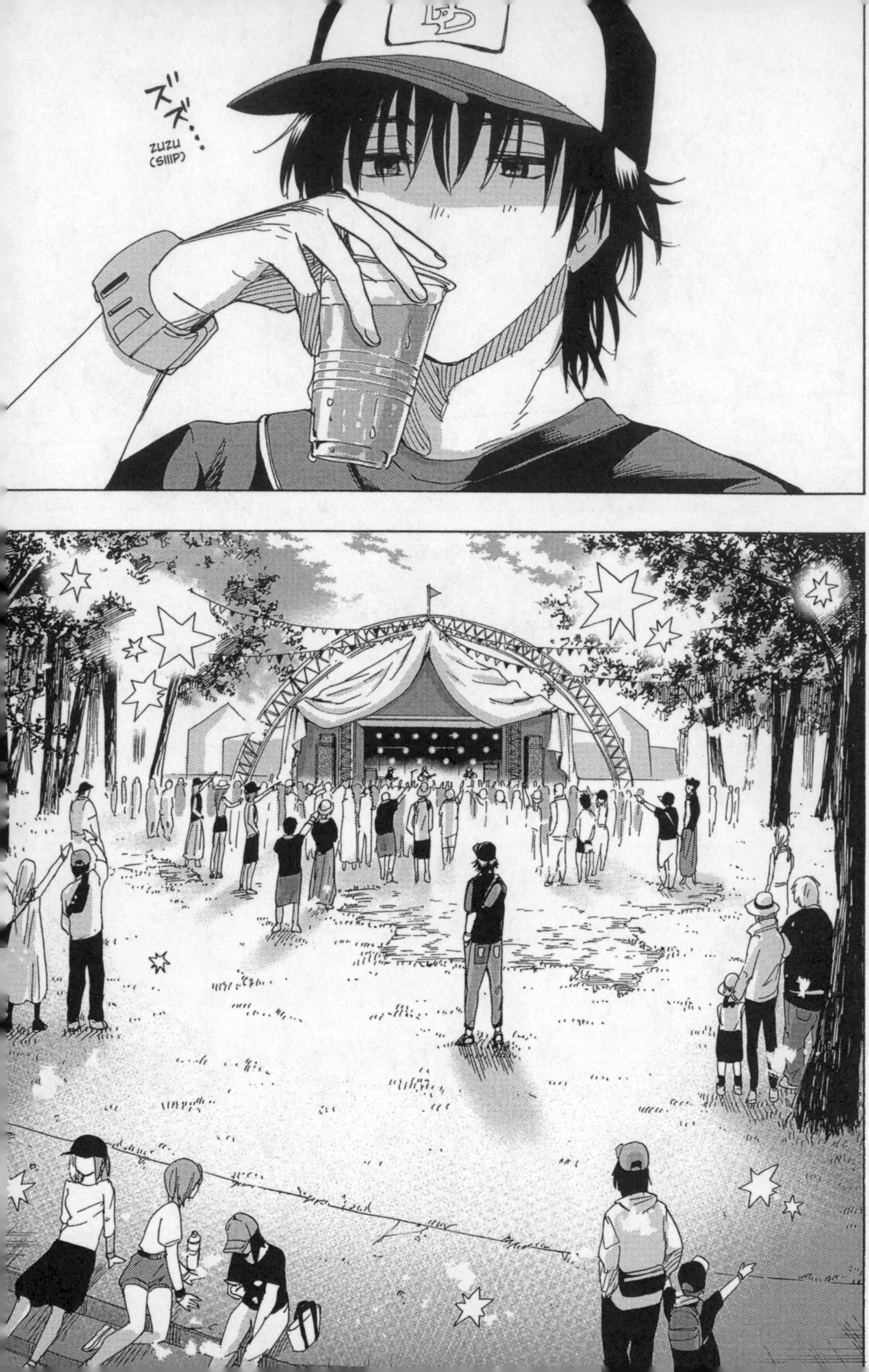
ズズ…
ZUZU
(SIIIP)

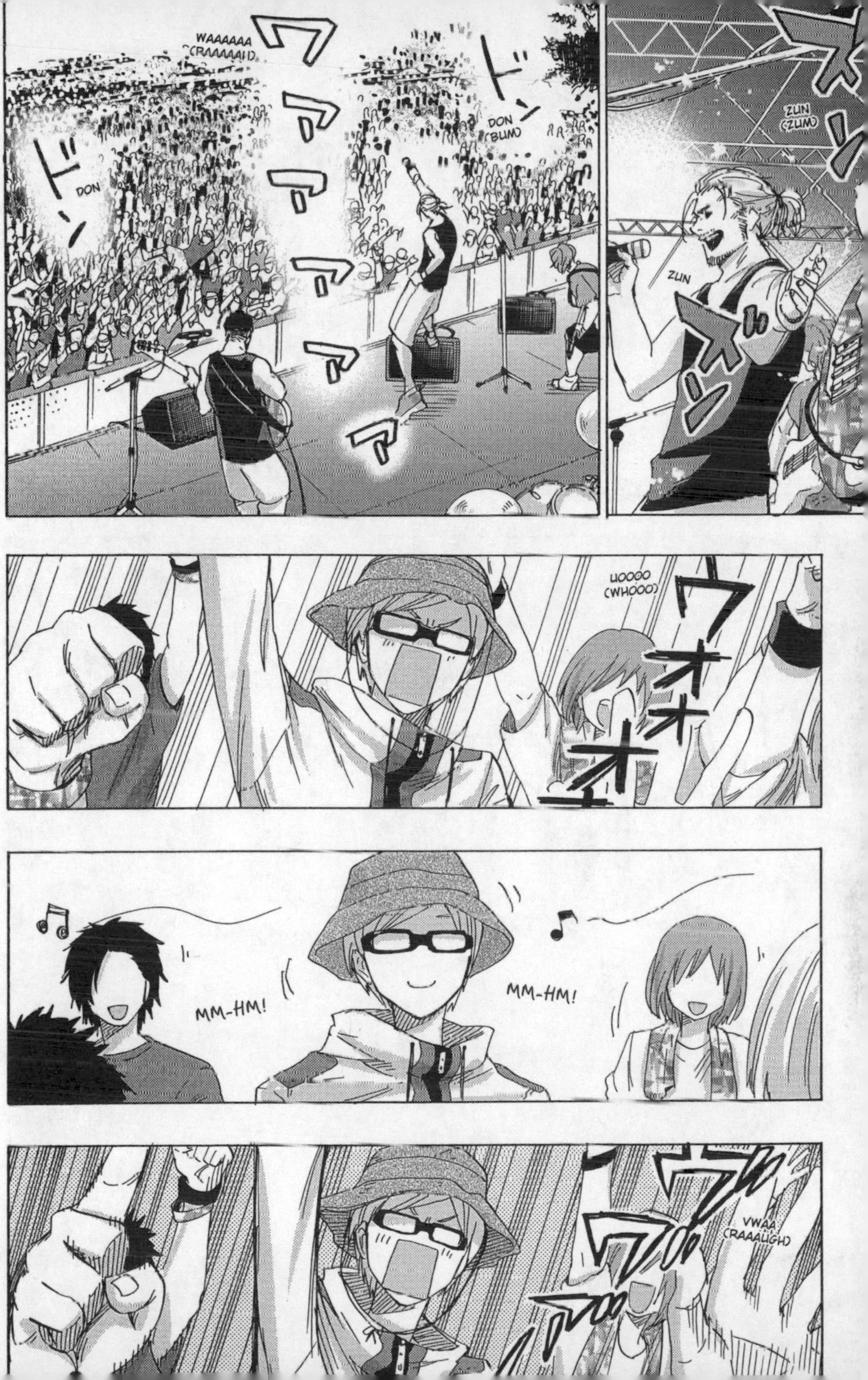
ZUN (ZUM)
ZUN
DON (BUM)
WAAAAAA (RAAAAAH)
DON
UOOOO (WHOOO)
MM-HM!
MM-HM!
VWAA (RAAAUGH)

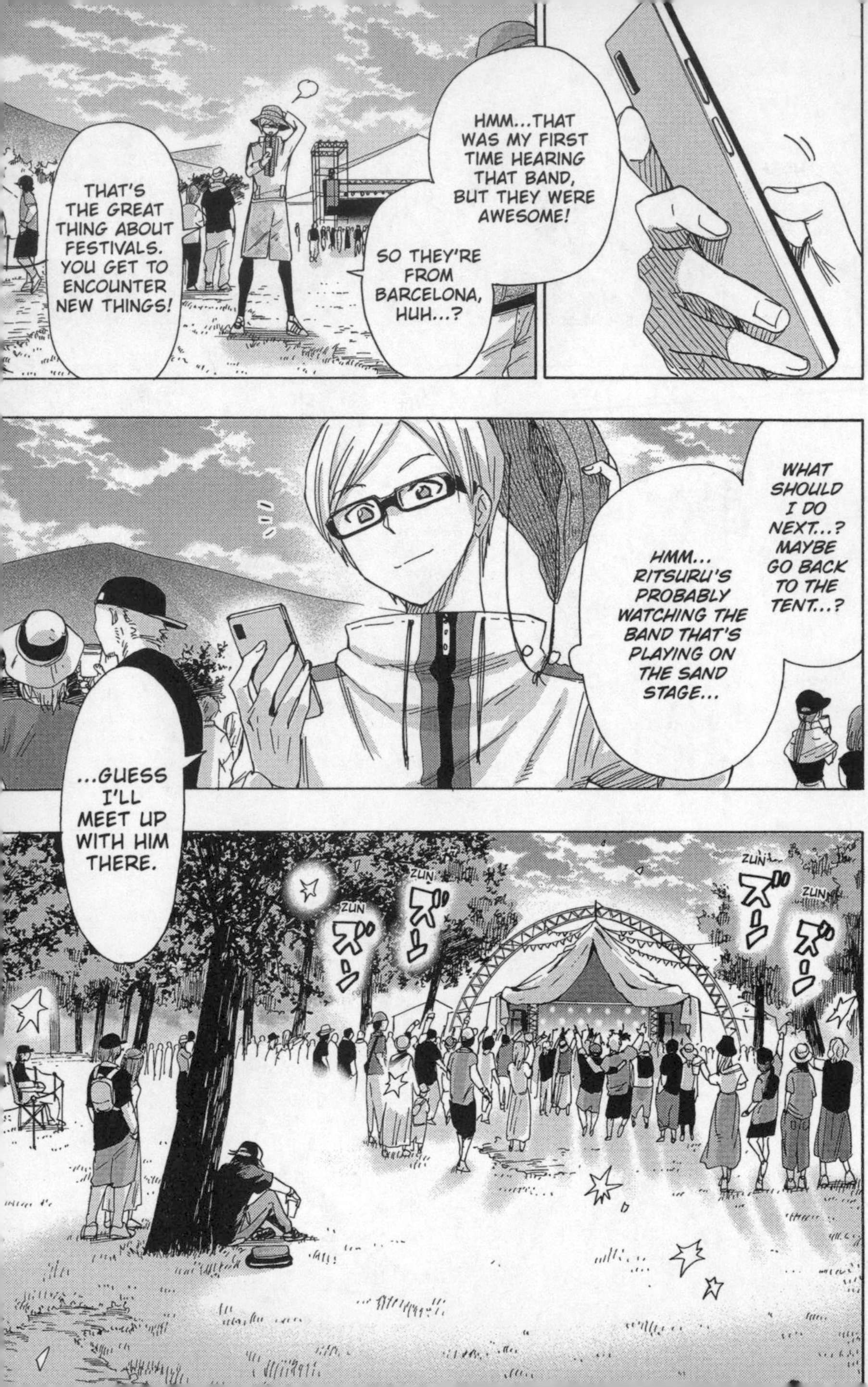
HMM...THAT WAS MY FIRST TIME HEARING THAT BAND, BUT THEY WERE AWESOME!
SO THEY'RE FROM BARCELONA, HUH...?
THAT'S THE GREAT THING ABOUT FESTIVALS. YOU GET TO ENCOUNTER NEW THINGS!
WHAT SHOULD I DO NEXT...? MAYBE GO BACK TO THE TENT...?
HMM... RITSURU'S PROBABLY WATCHING THE BAND THAT'S PLAYING ON THE SAND STAGE...
...GUESS I'LL MEET UP WITH HIM THERE.
ZUN
ZUN...
ZUN
ZUN

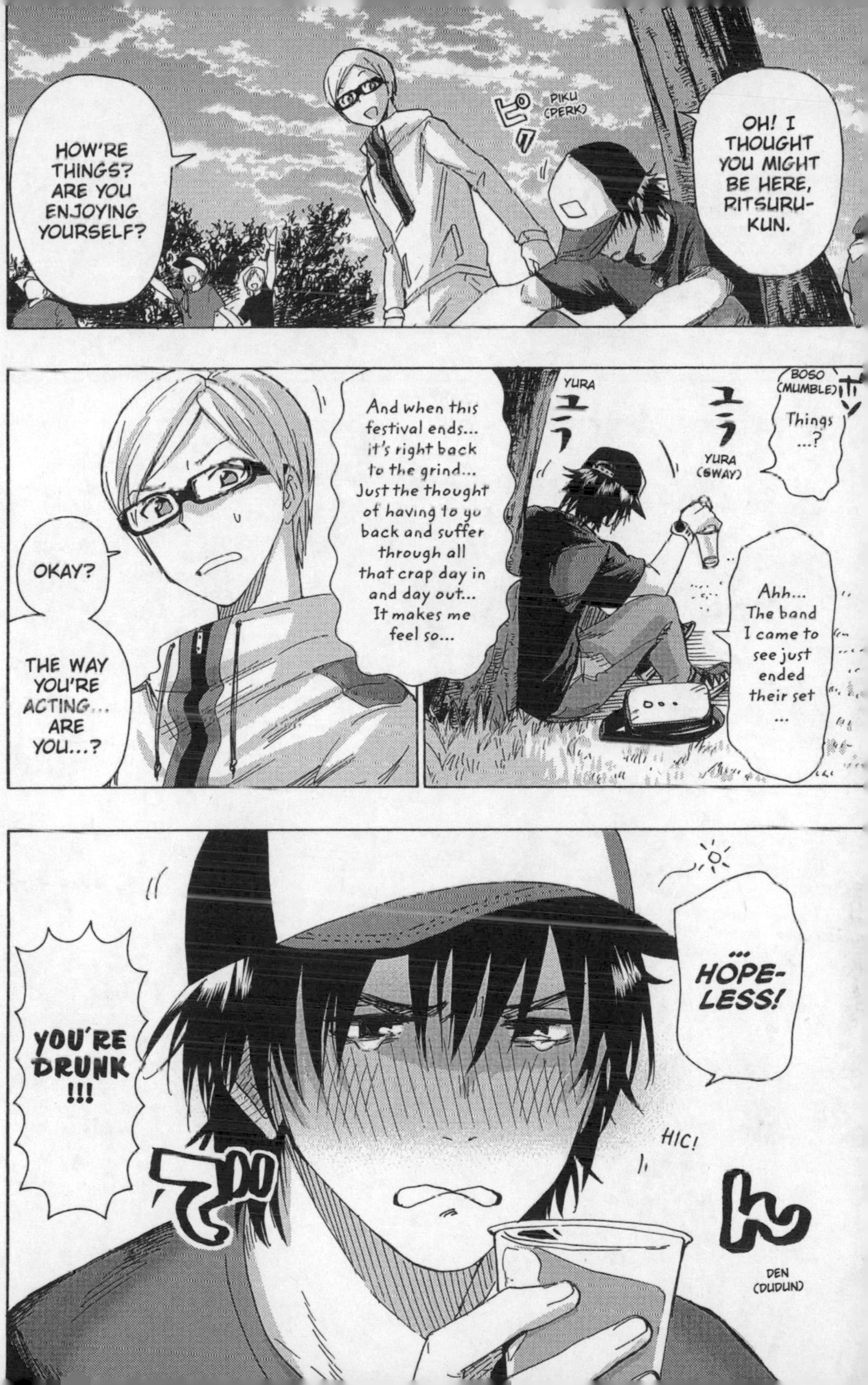
OH! I THOUGHT YOU MIGHT BE HERE, RITSURU-KUN.
PIKU (PERK)
HOW'RE THINGS? ARE YOU ENJOYING YOURSELF?
BOSO (MUMBLE)
Things...?
YURA
YURA (SWAY)
Ahh... The band I came to see just ended their set...
And when this festival ends... it's right back to the grind... Just the thought of having to go back and suffer through all that crap day in and day out... It makes me feel so...
OKAY?
THE WAY YOU'RE ACTING... ARE YOU...?
...HOPE-LESS!
HIC!
YOU'RE DRUNK!!!
DEN (DUDUN)

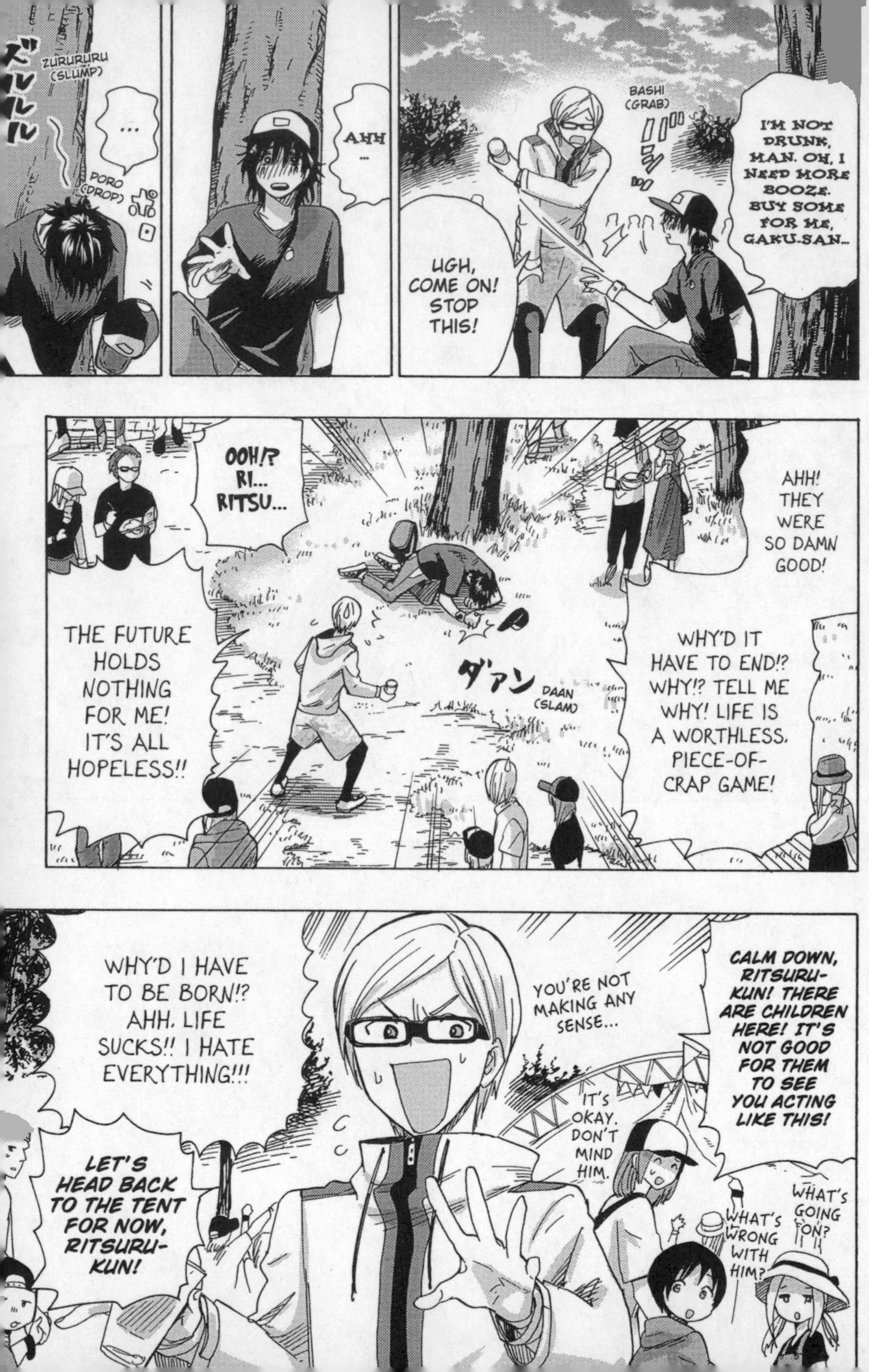
I'M NOT DRUNK, MAN. OH, I NEED MORE BOOZE. BUY SOME FOR ME, GAKU-SAN...
BASHI (GRAB)
UGH, COME ON! STOP THIS!
AHH ...
...
ズルルル
ZURURURU (SLUMP)
PORO (DROP)
AHH! THEY WERE SO DAMN GOOD!
WHY'D IT HAVE TO END!? WHY!? TELL ME WHY! LIFE IS A WORTHLESS, PIECE-OF-CRAP GAME!
ダアン
DAAN (SLAM)
OOH!? RI... RITSU...
THE FUTURE HOLDS NOTHING FOR ME! IT'S ALL HOPELESS!!
CALM DOWN, RITSURU-KUN! THERE ARE CHILDREN HERE! IT'S NOT GOOD FOR THEM TO SEE YOU ACTING LIKE THIS!
YOU'RE NOT MAKING ANY SENSE...
WHY'D I HAVE TO BE BORN!? AHH, LIFE SUCKS!! I HATE EVERYTHING!!!
WHAT'S GOING ON?
WHAT'S WRONG WITH HIM?
IT'S OKAY. DON'T MIND HIM.
LET'S HEAD BACK TO THE TENT FOR NOW, RITSURU-KUN!

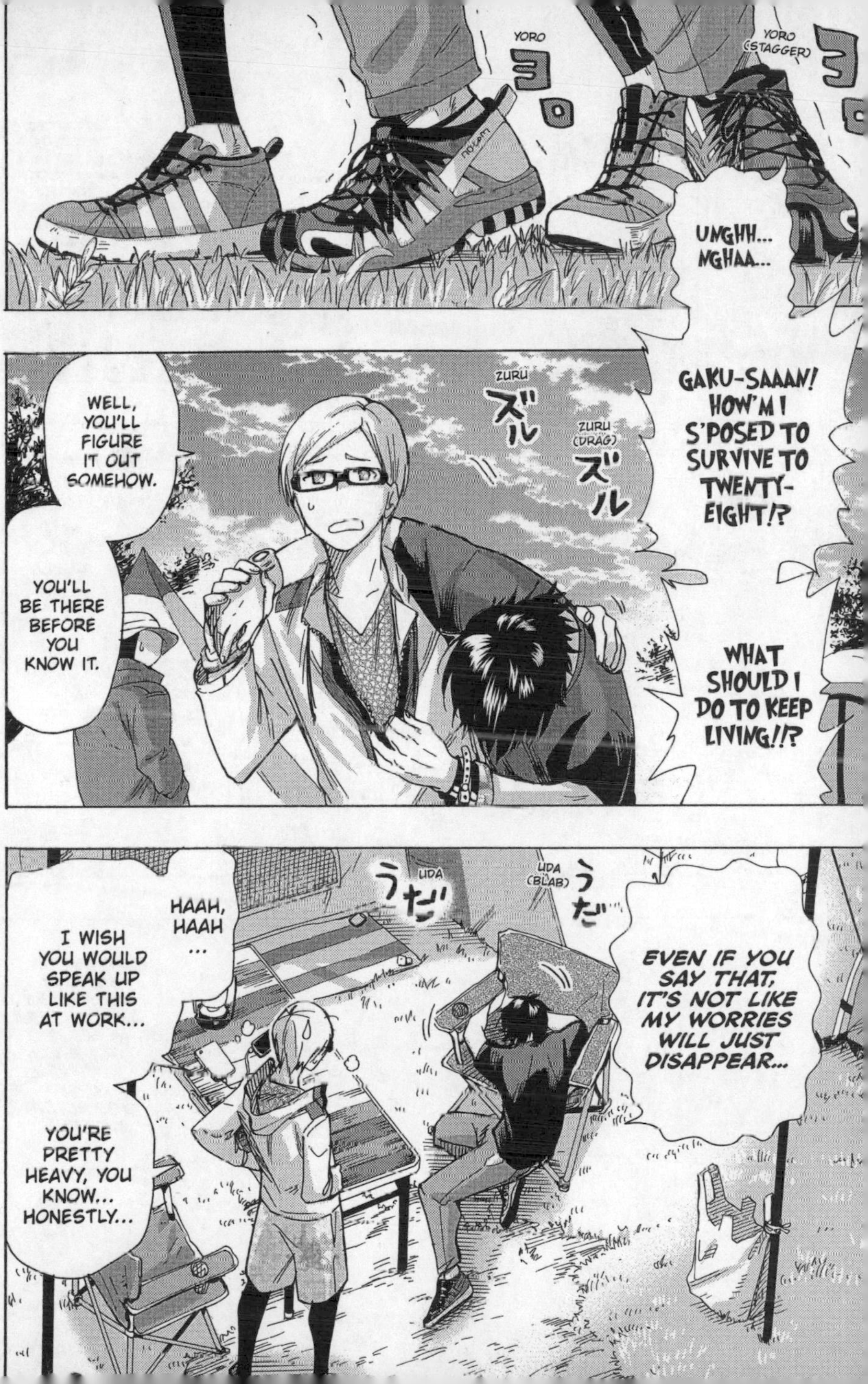
YORO (STAGGER) ヨロ
YORO ヨロ
UNGHH... NGHAA...
GAKU-SAAAN! HOW'M I S'POSED TO SURVIVE TO TWENTY-EIGHT!?
WHAT SHOULD I DO TO KEEP LIVING!!?
ZURU (DRAG) ズル
ZURU ズル
WELL, YOU'LL FIGURE IT OUT SOMEHOW.
YOU'LL BE THERE BEFORE YOU KNOW IT.
EVEN IF YOU SAY THAT, IT'S NOT LIKE MY WORRIES WILL JUST DISAPPEAR...
UDA (BLAB) うだ
UDA うだ
HAAH, HAAH ...
I WISH YOU WOULD SPEAK UP LIKE THIS AT WORK...
YOU'RE PRETTY HEAVY, YOU KNOW... HONESTLY...

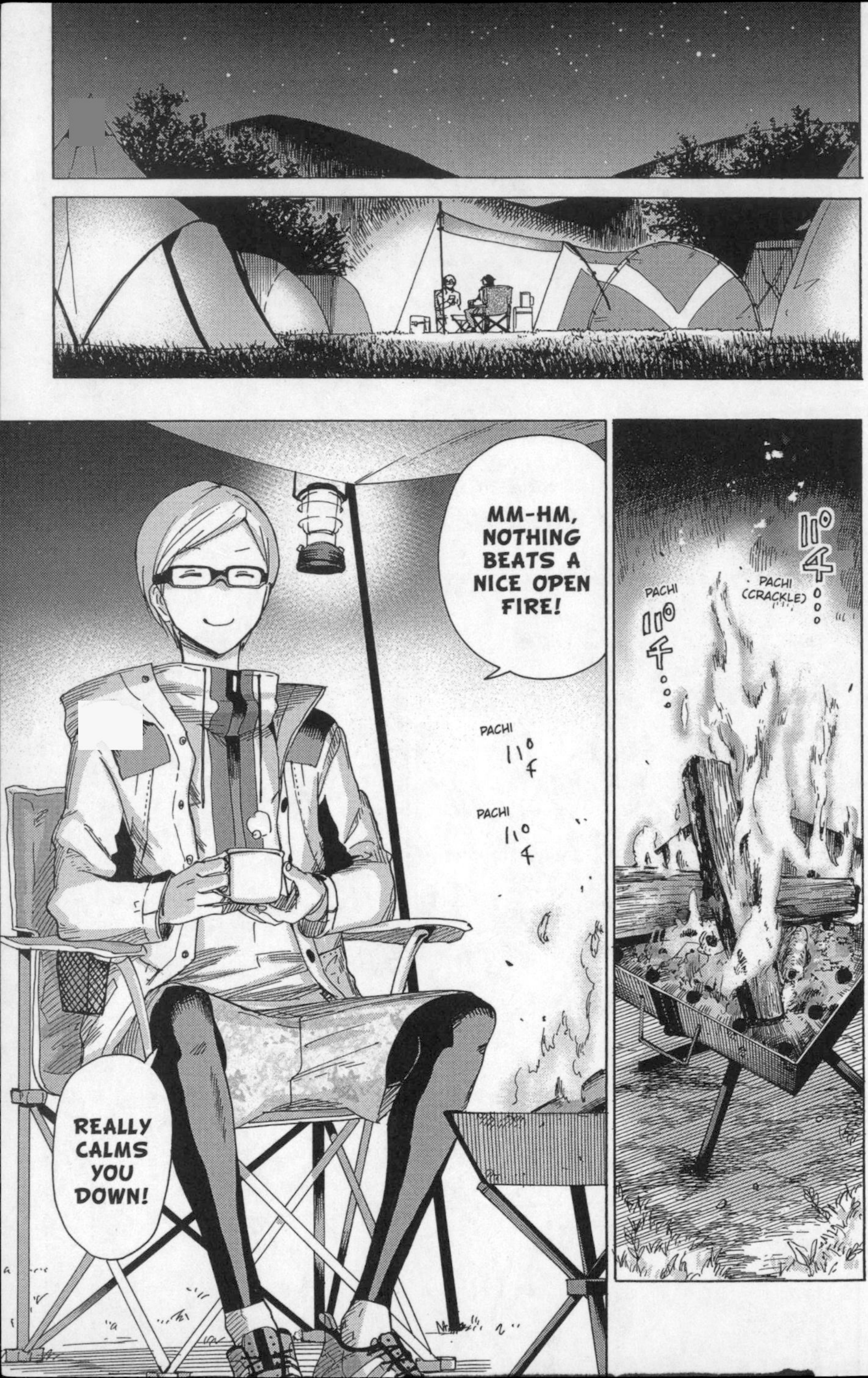
PACHI (CRACKLE)
PACHI
MM-HM, NOTHING BEATS A NICE OPEN FIRE!
PACHI
PACHI
REALLY CALMS YOU DOWN!

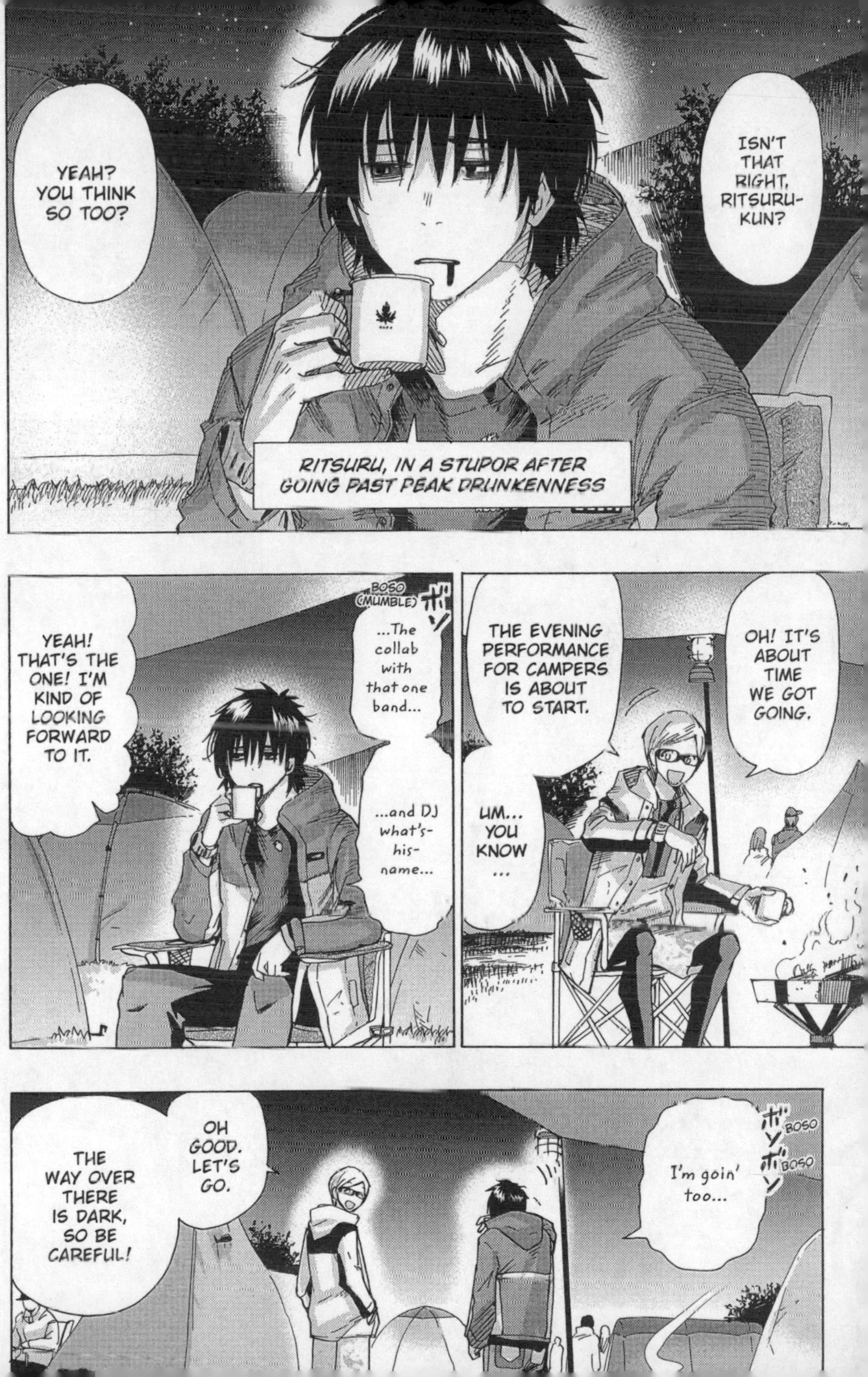
ISN'T THAT RIGHT, RITSURU-KUN?
YEAH? YOU THINK SO TOO?
RITSURU, IN A STUPOR AFTER GOING PAST PEAK DRUNKENNESS
OH! IT'S ABOUT TIME WE GOT GOING.
THE EVENING PERFORMANCE FOR CAMPERS IS ABOUT TO START.
UM... YOU KNOW ...
BOSO (MUMBLE)
...The collab with that one band...
...and DJ what's-his-name...
YEAH! THAT'S THE ONE! I'M KIND OF LOOKING FORWARD TO IT.
BOSO BOSO
I'm goin' too...
OH GOOD. LET'S GO.
THE WAY OVER THERE IS DARK, SO BE CAREFUL!

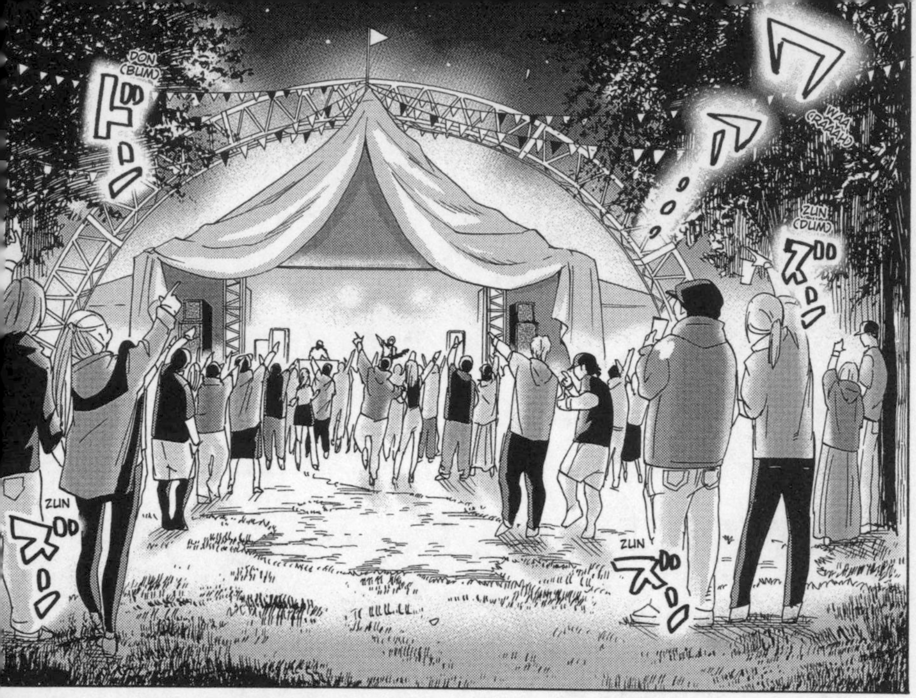
WAA (RAAAH)
ZUN (DUM)
DON (BUM)
ZUN
ZUN

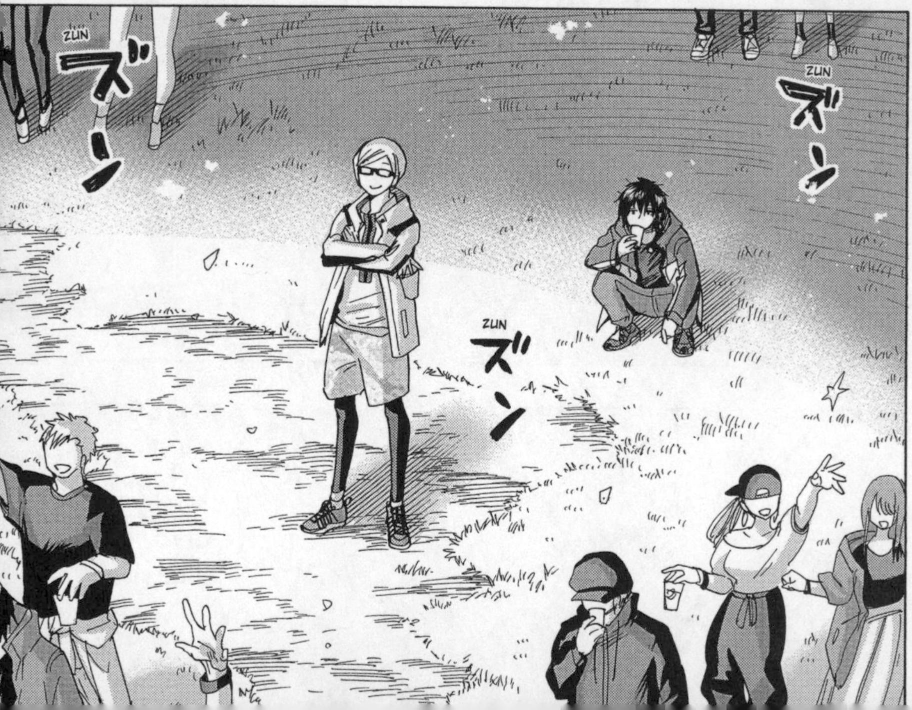
ZUN
ZUN
ZUN

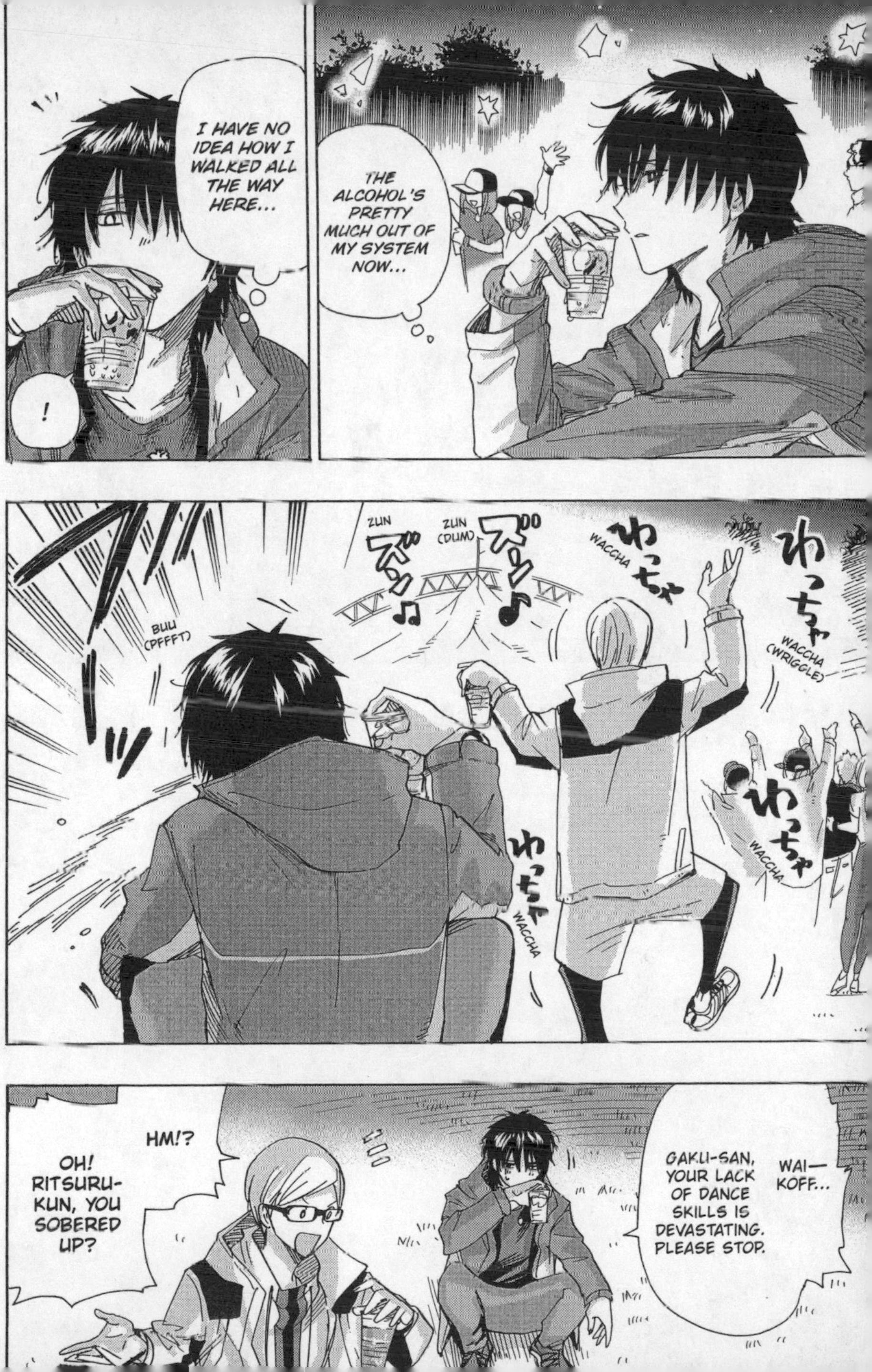
THE ALCOHOL'S PRETTY MUCH OUT OF MY SYSTEM NOW...
I HAVE NO IDEA HOW I WALKED ALL THE WAY HERE...
!
ZUN (DUM)
ZUN
WACCHA
WACCHA (WRIGGLE)
BUU (PFFFT)
WACCHA
WACCHA
WAI— KOFF...
GAKU-SAN, YOUR LACK OF DANCE SKILLS IS DEVASTATING. PLEASE STOP.
HM!?
OH! RITSURU-KUN, YOU SOBERED UP?

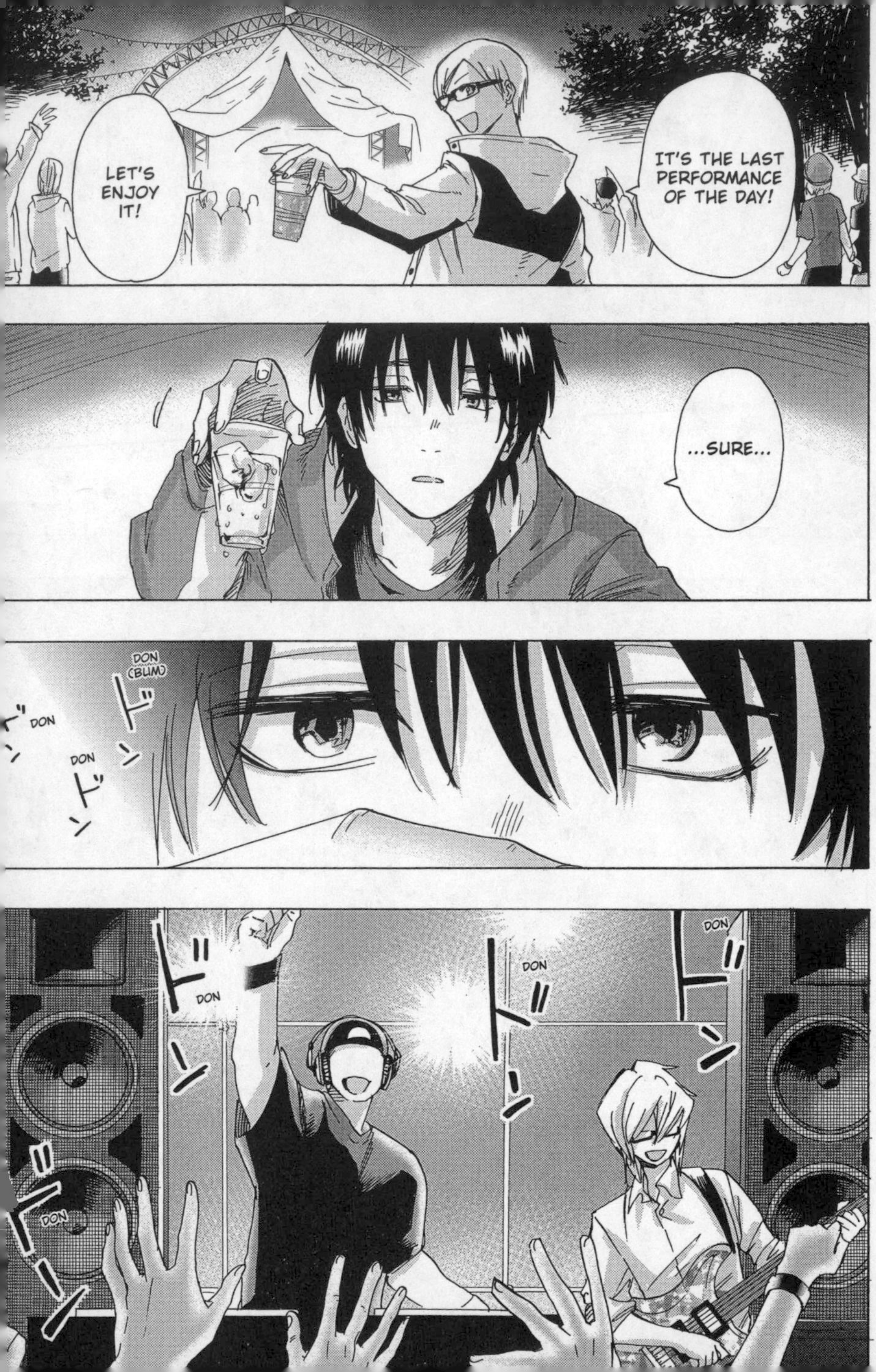
IT'S THE LAST PERFORMANCE OF THE DAY!
LET'S ENJOY IT!
...SURE...
DON (BUM)
DON
DON
DON
DON
DON
DON

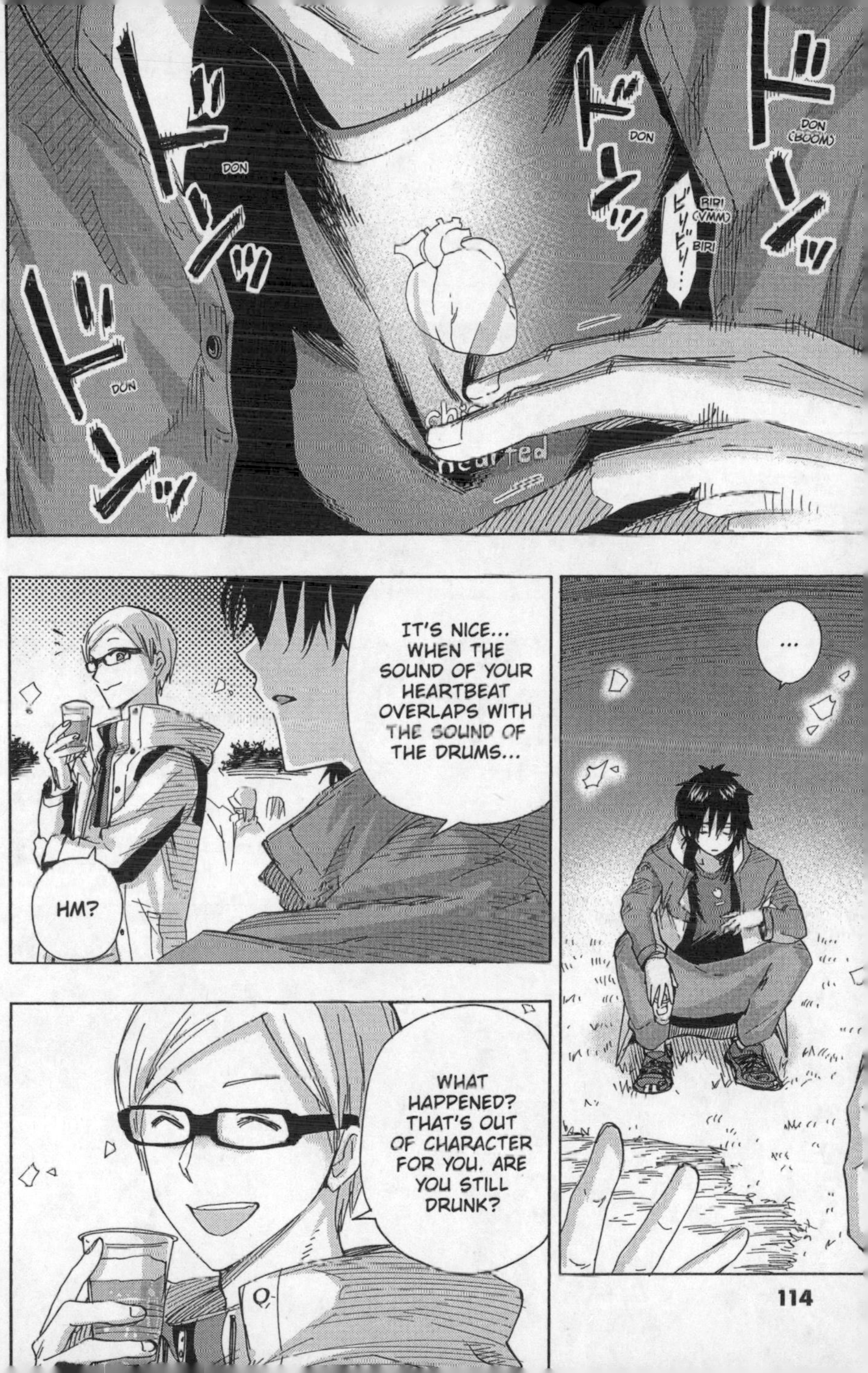
DON (BOOM)
BIRI (VMM) BIRI
DON
DON
DON
...
IT'S NICE... WHEN THE SOUND OF YOUR HEARTBEAT OVERLAPS WITH THE SOUND OF THE DRUMS...
HM?
WHAT HAPPENED? THAT'S OUT OF CHARACTER FOR YOU. ARE YOU STILL DRUNK?

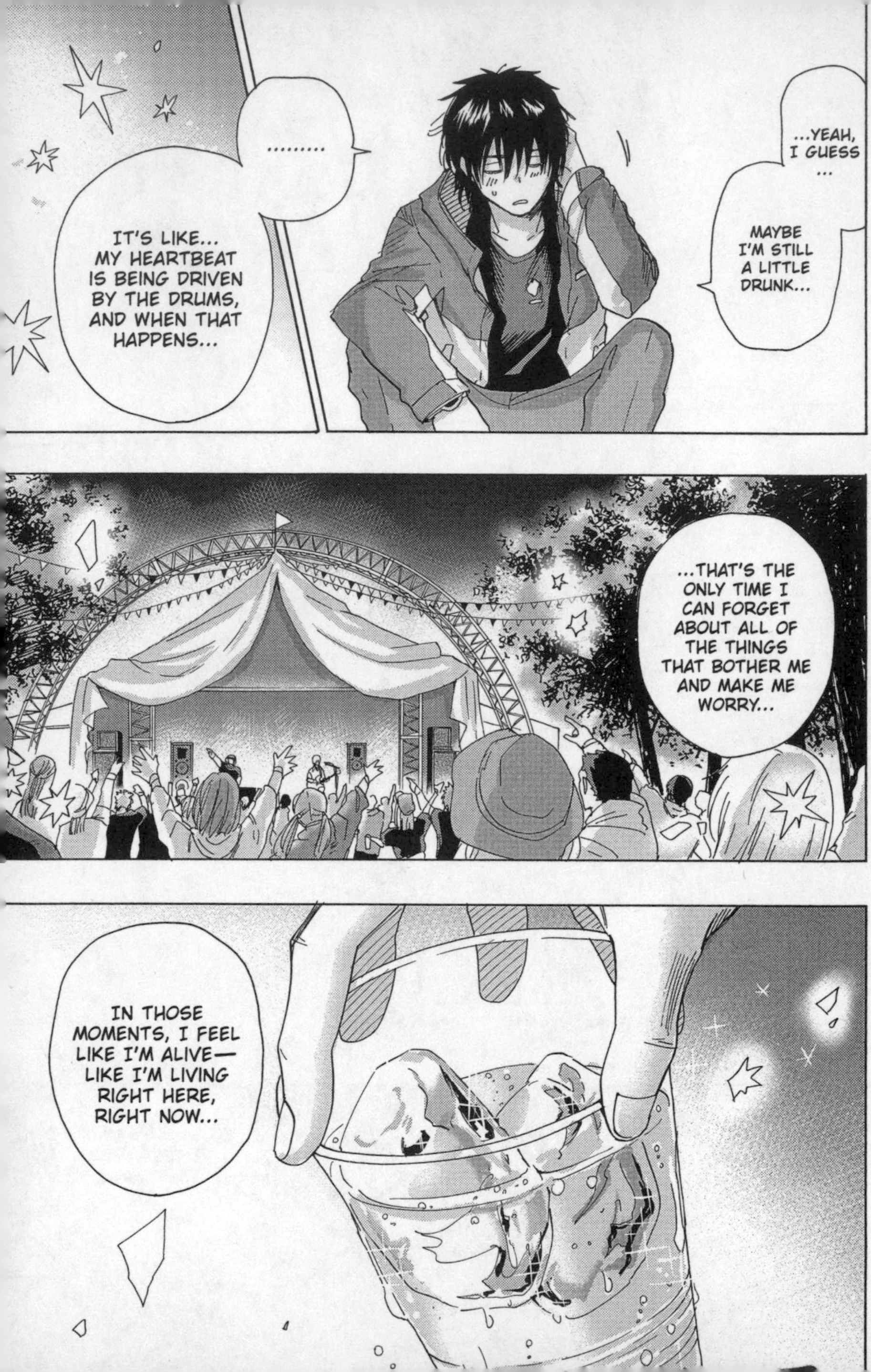
...YEAH, I GUESS...
MAYBE I'M STILL A LITTLE DRUNK...
....
IT'S LIKE... MY HEARTBEAT IS BEING DRIVEN BY THE DRUMS, AND WHEN THAT HAPPENS...
...THAT'S THE ONLY TIME I CAN FORGET ABOUT ALL OF THE THINGS THAT BOTHER ME AND MAKE ME WORRY...
IN THOSE MOMENTS, I FEEL LIKE I'M ALIVE—LIKE I'M LIVING RIGHT HERE, RIGHT NOW...

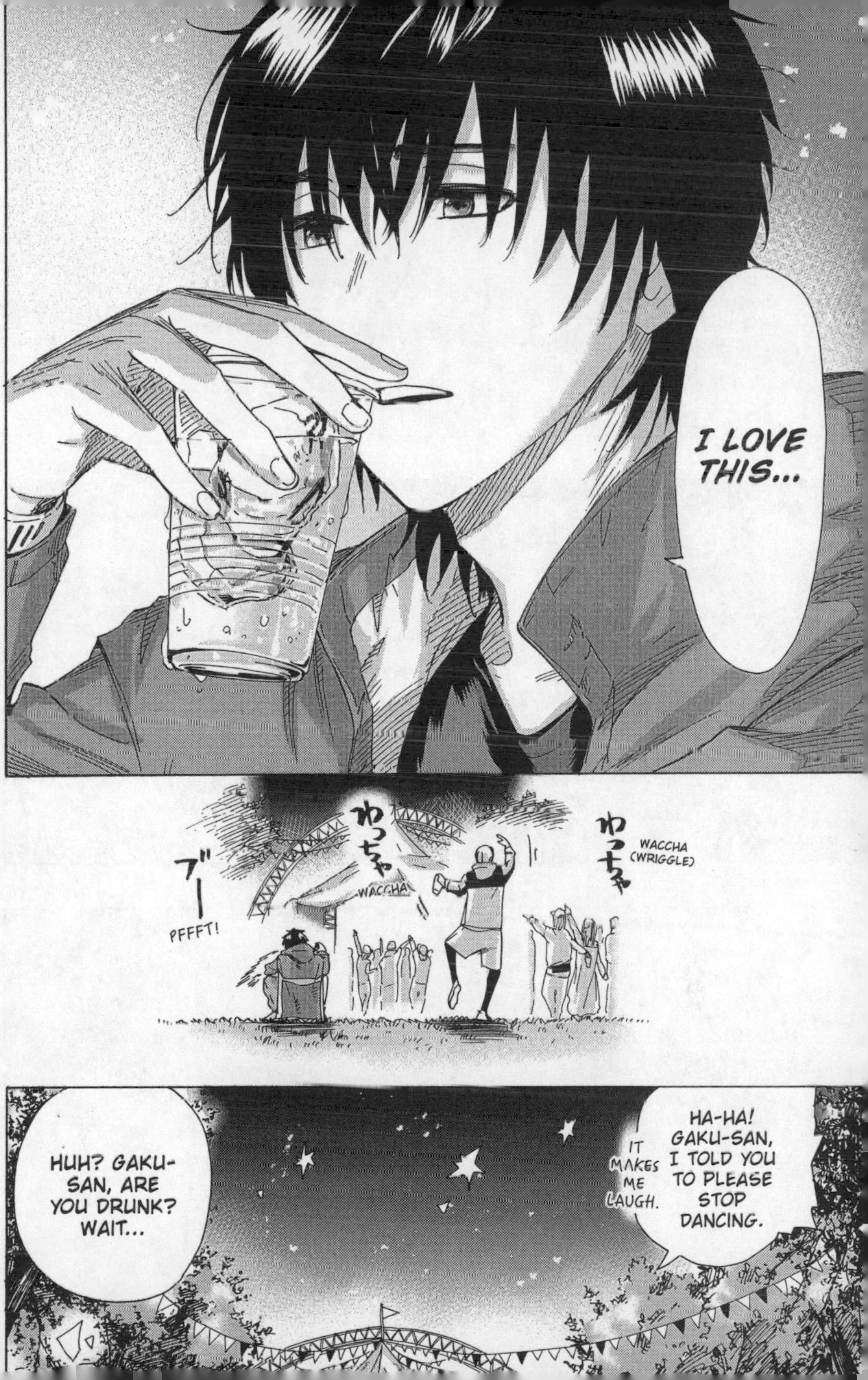
I LOVE THIS...
わっちゃ
WACCHA (WRIGGLE)
わっちゃ
WACCHA
ブー
PFFFT!
HA-HA! GAKU-SAN, I TOLD YOU TO PLEASE STOP DANCING.
IT MAKES ME LAUGH.
HUH? GAKU-SAN, ARE YOU DRUNK? WAIT...

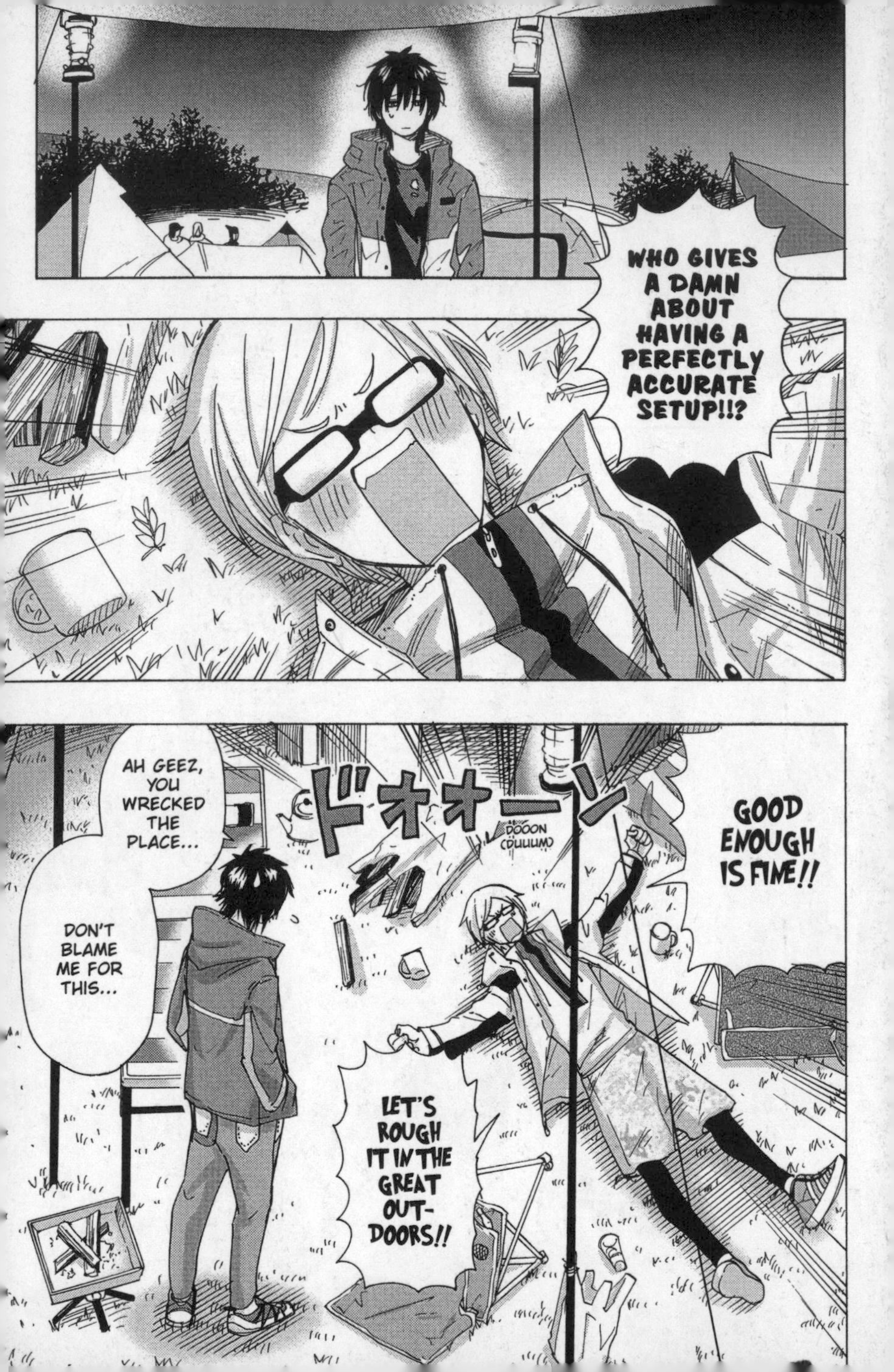
WHO GIVES A DAMN ABOUT HAVING A PERFECTLY ACCURATE SETUP!!?
GOOD ENOUGH IS FINE!!
ドオオーン
DOOON (DUUUM)
LET'S ROUGH IT IN THE GREAT OUT-DOORS!!
AH GEEZ, YOU WRECKED THE PLACE...
DON'T BLAME ME FOR THIS...

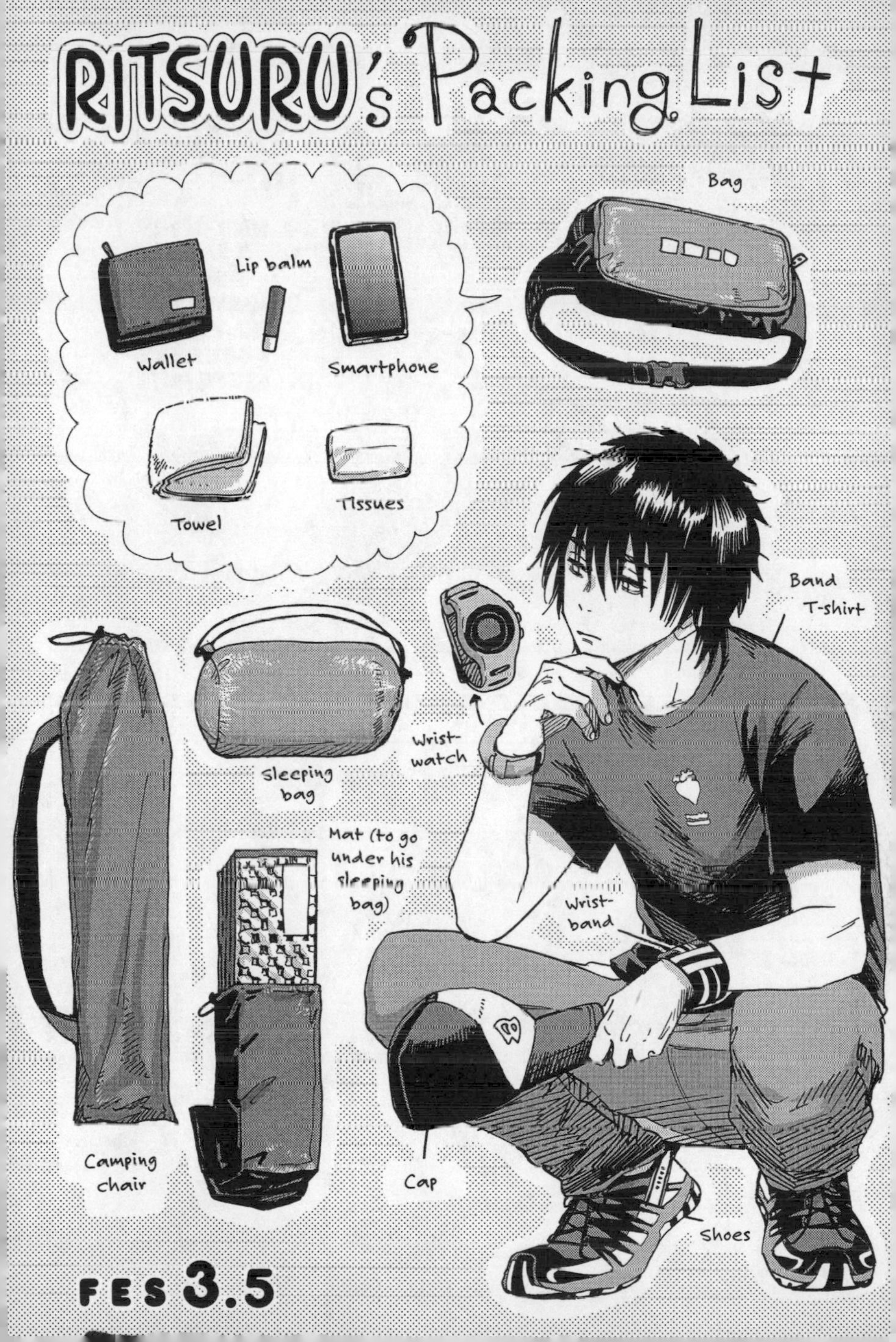
RITSURU's Packing List
Bag
Lip balm
Wallet
Smartphone
Towel
Tissues
Band T-shirt
Wrist-watch
Sleeping bag
Mat (to go under his sleeping bag)
Wrist-band
Camping chair
Cap
Shoes
FES 3.5

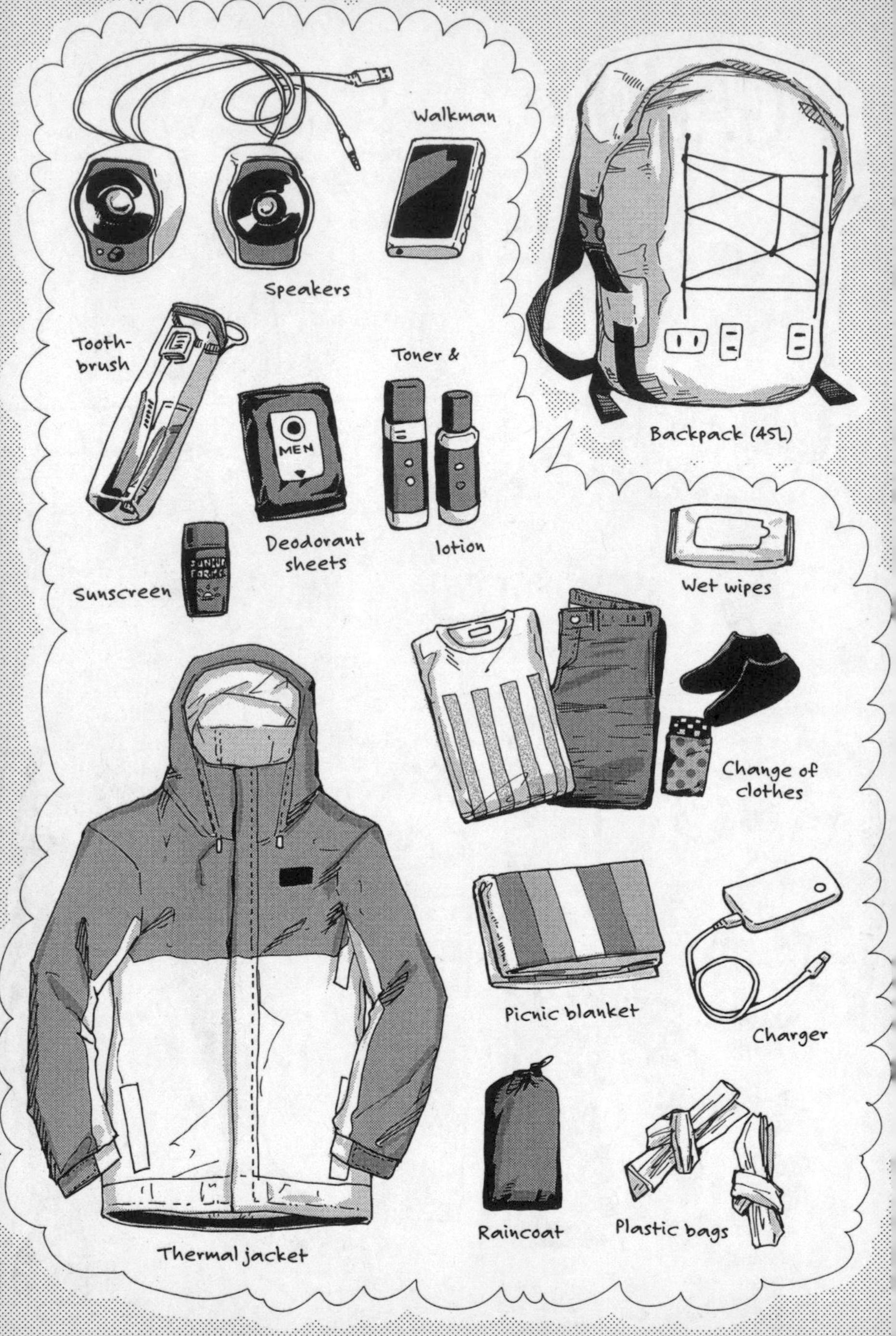
Backpack (45L)
Walkman
Speakers
Tooth-
brush
MEN
Deodorant
sheets
Toner &
lotion
Sunscreen
Wet wipes
Change of
clothes
Thermal jacket
Picnic blanket
Charger
Raincoat
Plastic bags

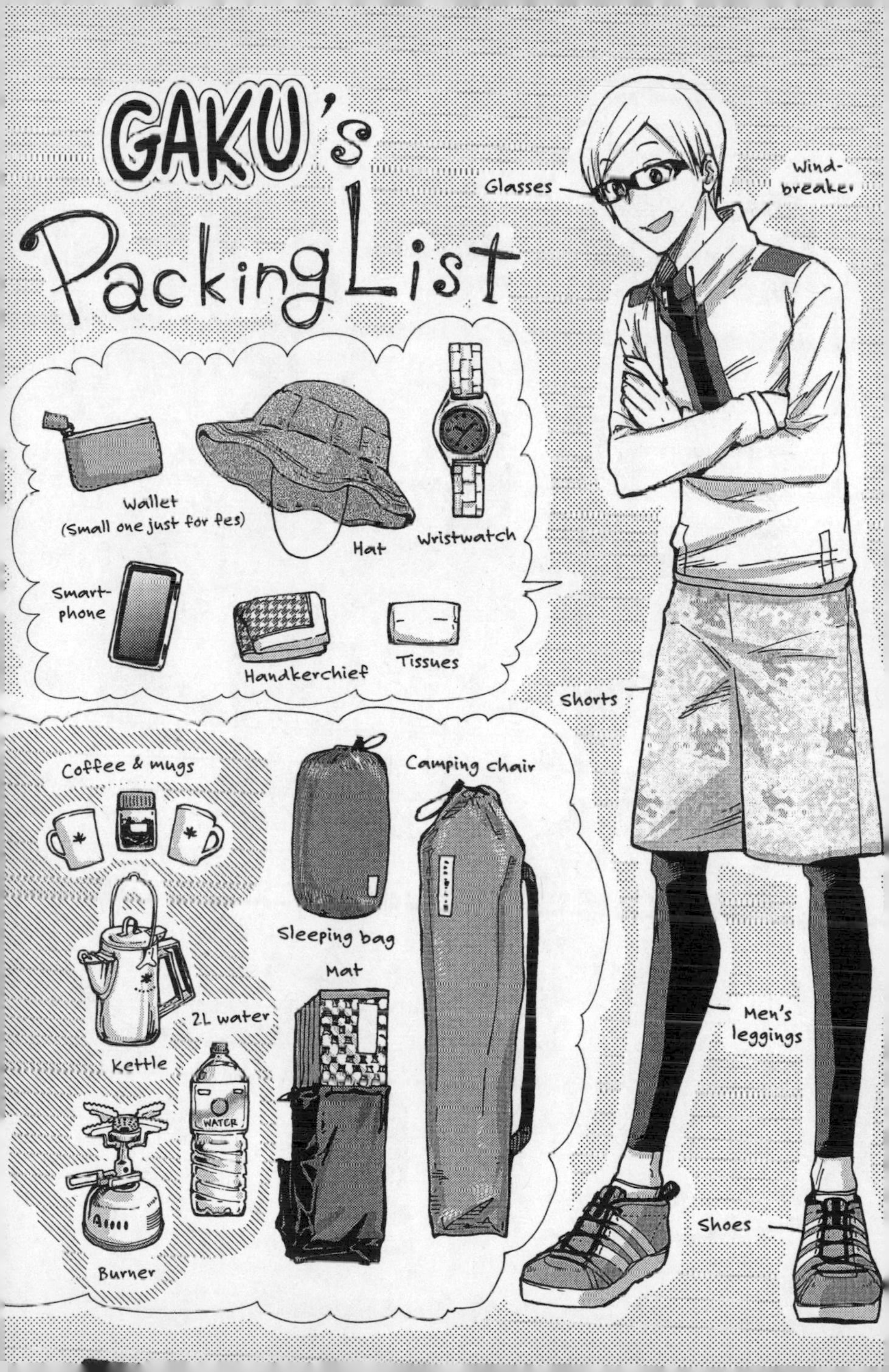
GAKU's Packing List
Glasses
Wind-
breake
Wallet
(Small one just for fes)
Hat
Wristwatch
Smart-
phone
Handkerchief
Tissues
Shorts
Coffee & mugs
Camping chair
Sleeping bag
Mat
2L water
WATER
Kettle
Burner
Men's
leggings
Shoes

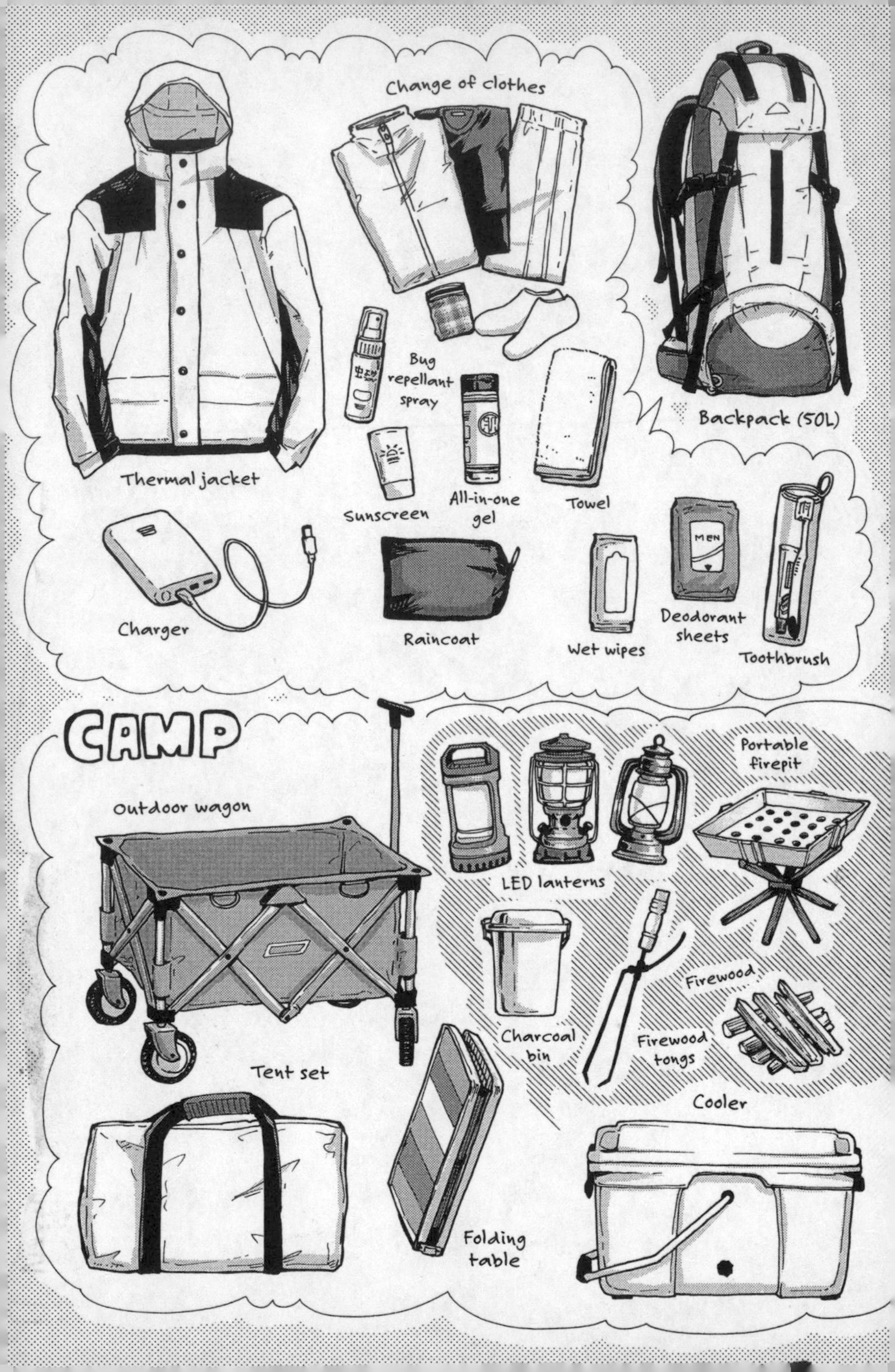
Backpack (50L)
Change of clothes
Thermal jacket
Bug repellant spray
Towel
All-in-one gel
Sunscreen
Toothbrush
MEN
Deodorant sheets
Wet wipes
Raincoat
Charger
CAMP
Portable firepit
LED lanterns
Outdoor wagon
Firewood
Firewood tongs
Charcoal bin
Cooler
Folding table
Tent set

Days on Fes

FES 4

ベ BE
ベ BE
ベ BE
ベ BE
ベ BE
ヴーッ VUUU
Alarm
07:00
Snooze
ヴーッ VUUU (BZZZ)
ベ BE (BIP)
ベ BE
ベ BE
ベ BE
ベ BE
ベベベ BE BE BE
ヴーッ VUUU
ヴーッ VUUU
07:00
ダスッ DASU (ZHF)
ダスッ DASU
SHU (SHWIP)
TSU (DRIP)
?...
FEELS COLD...
NOSO (SLOWLY)
のそ…
HAAH...

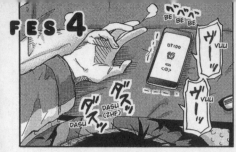

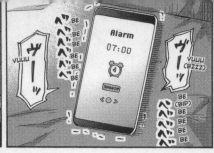

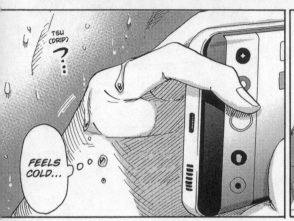

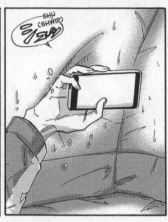

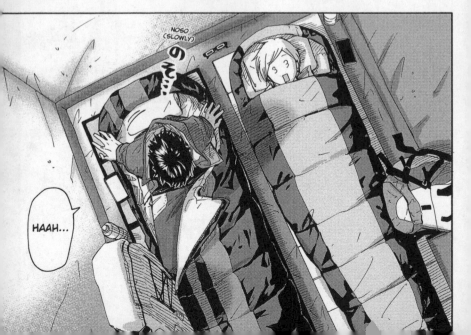

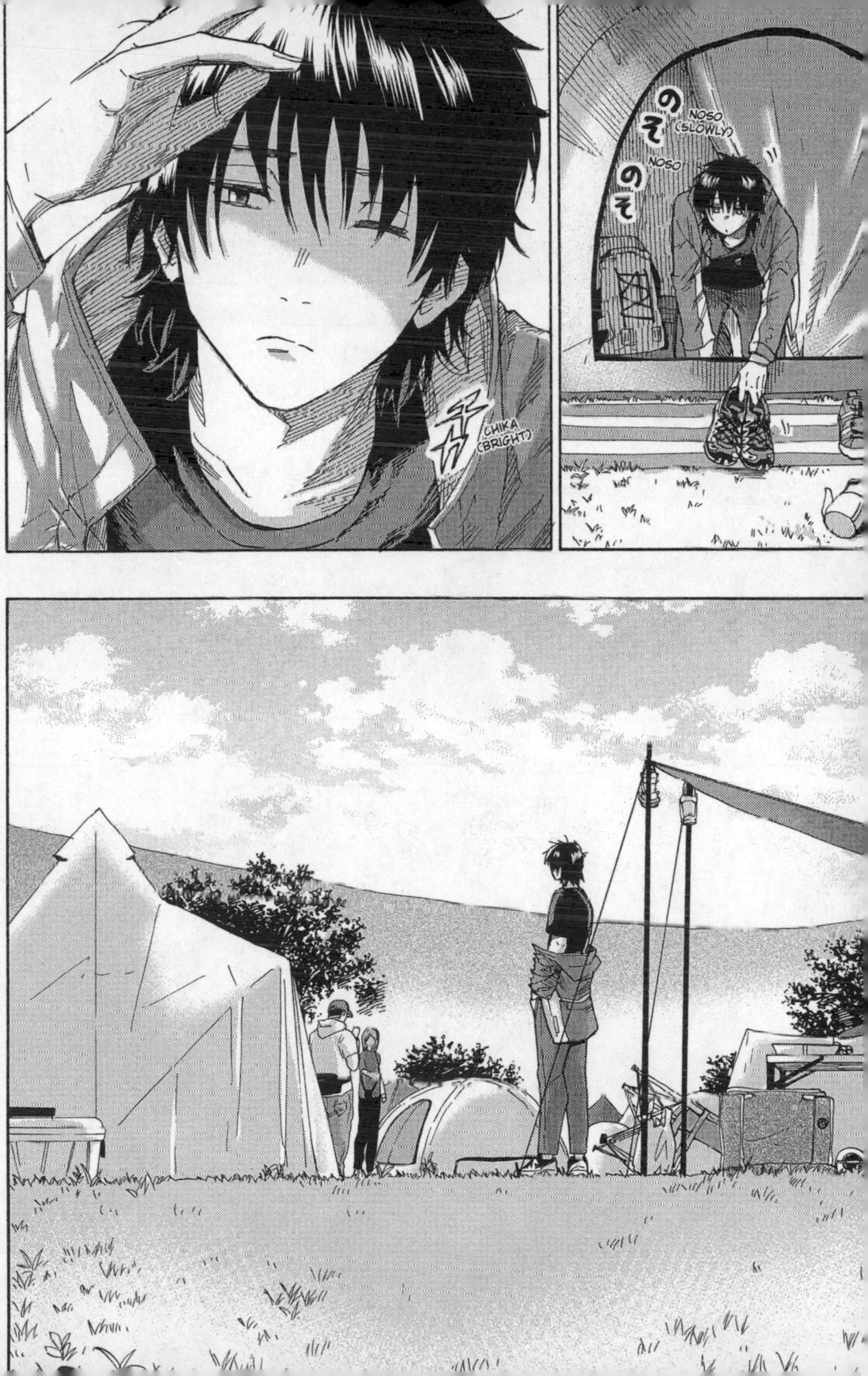
のそ
NOSO (SLOWLY)
のそ
NOSO
チカ
CHIKA (BRIGHT)

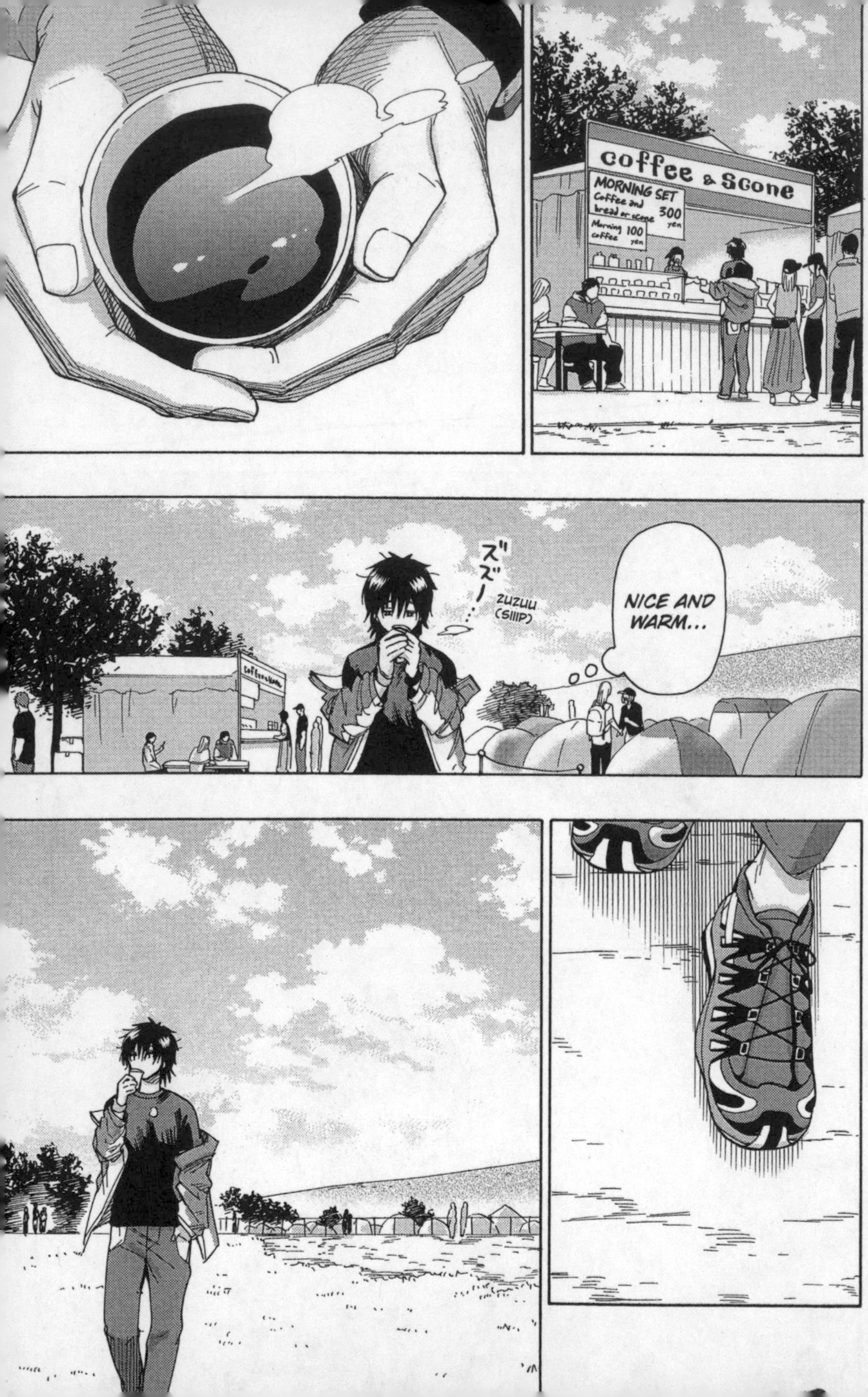
coffee & Scone
MORNING SET Coffee and bread or scone 300 yen
Morning coffee 100 yen
NICE AND WARM...
ズズー…
ZUZUU (SIIIP)

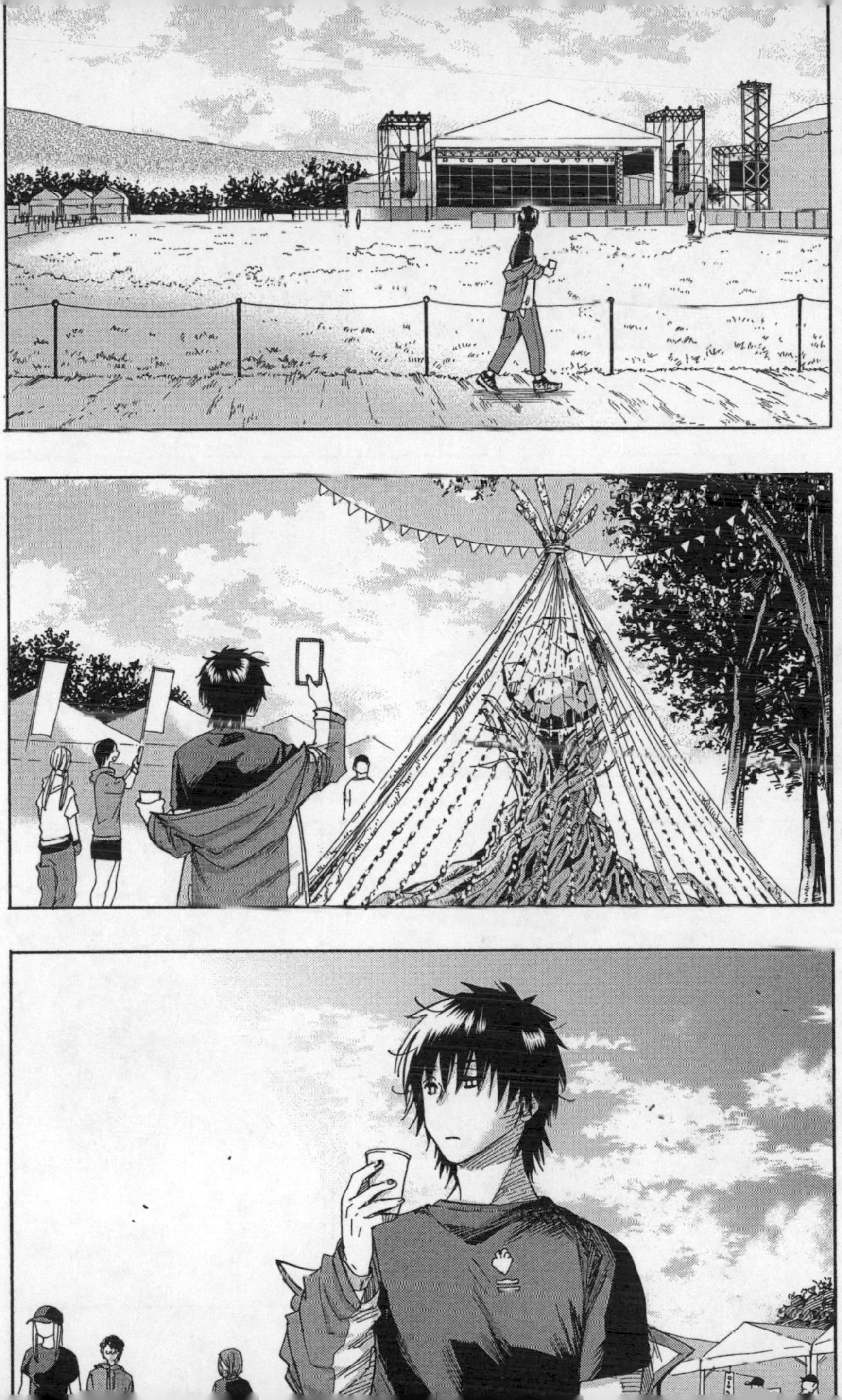

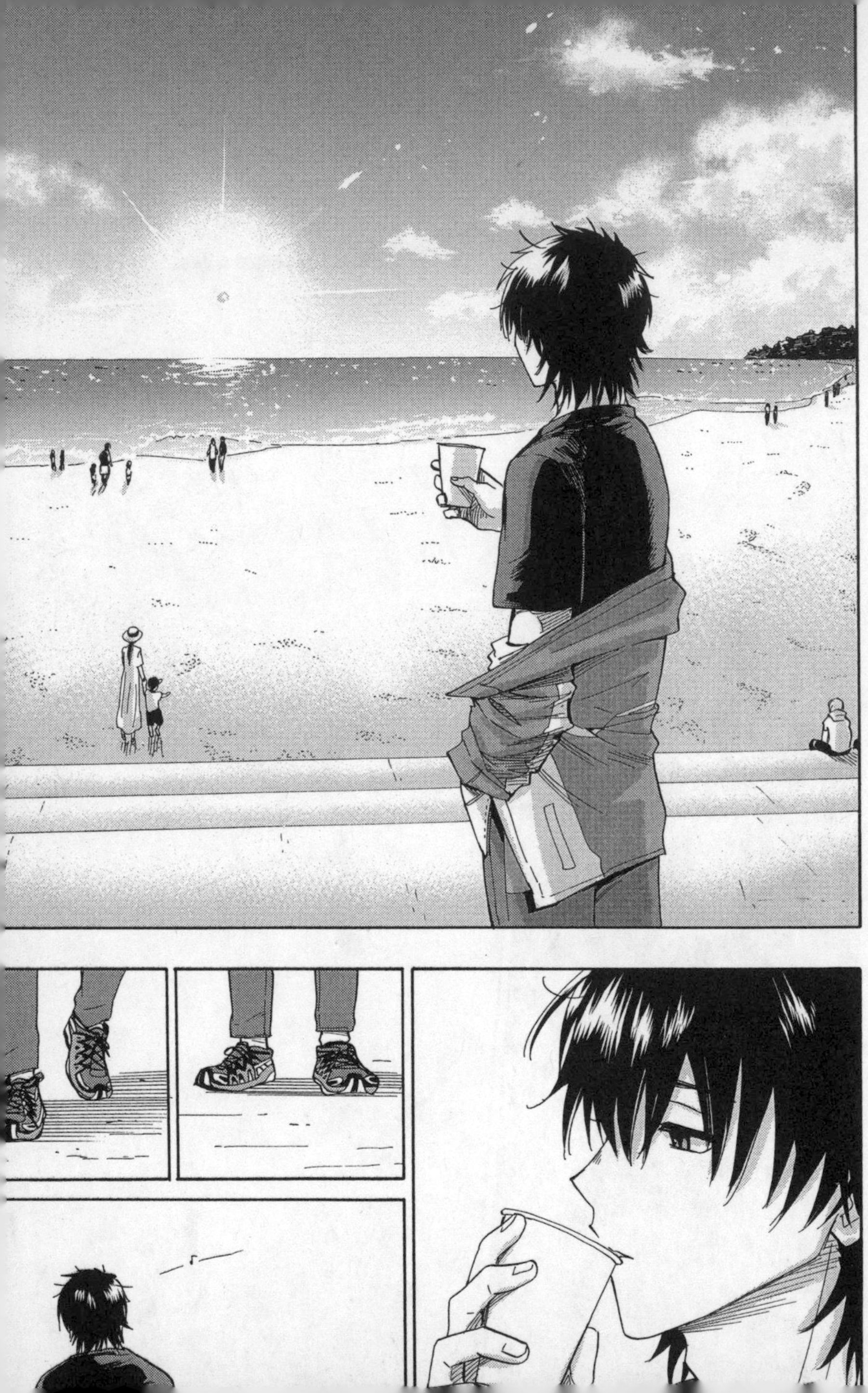

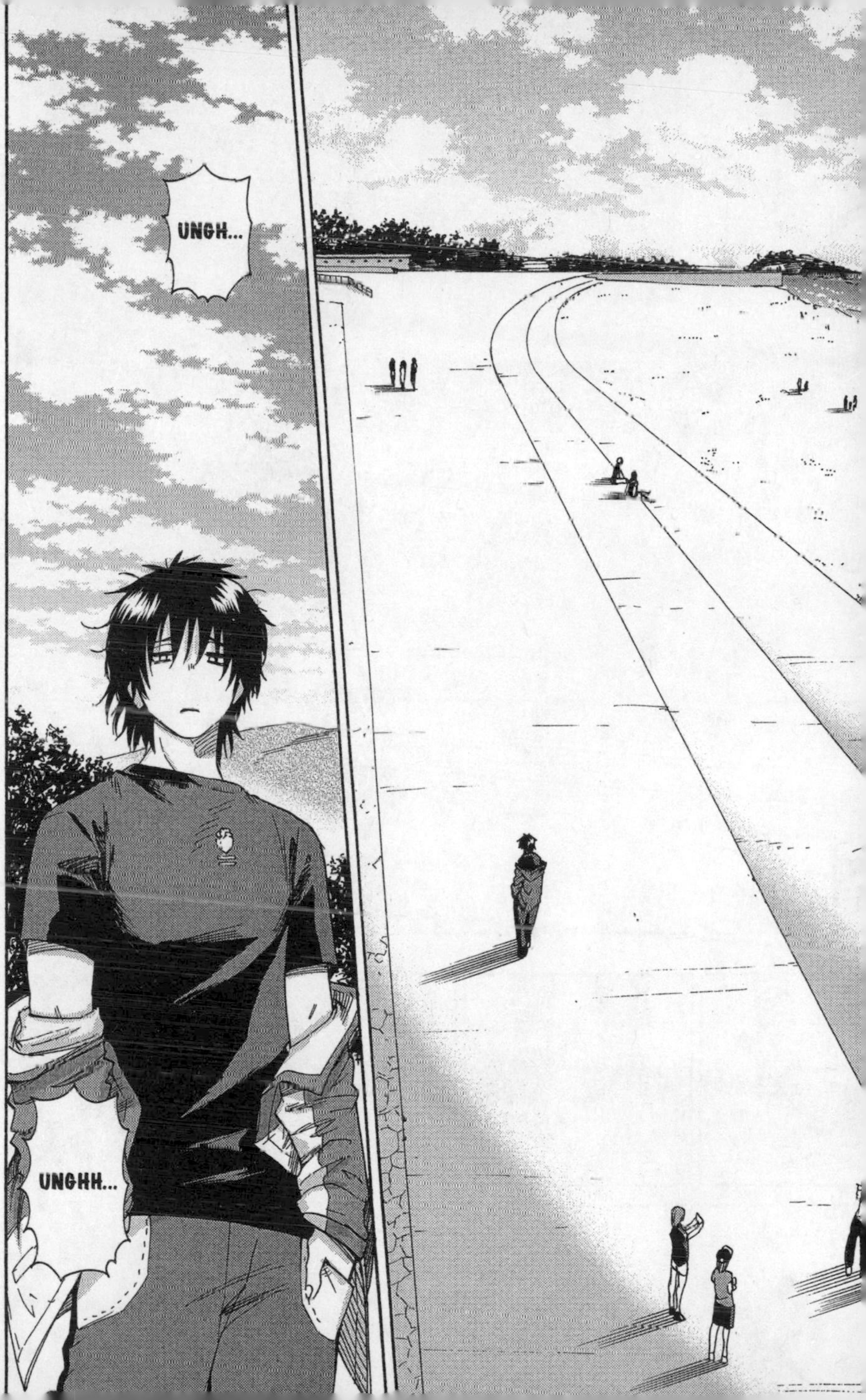
UNGH...
UNGHH...

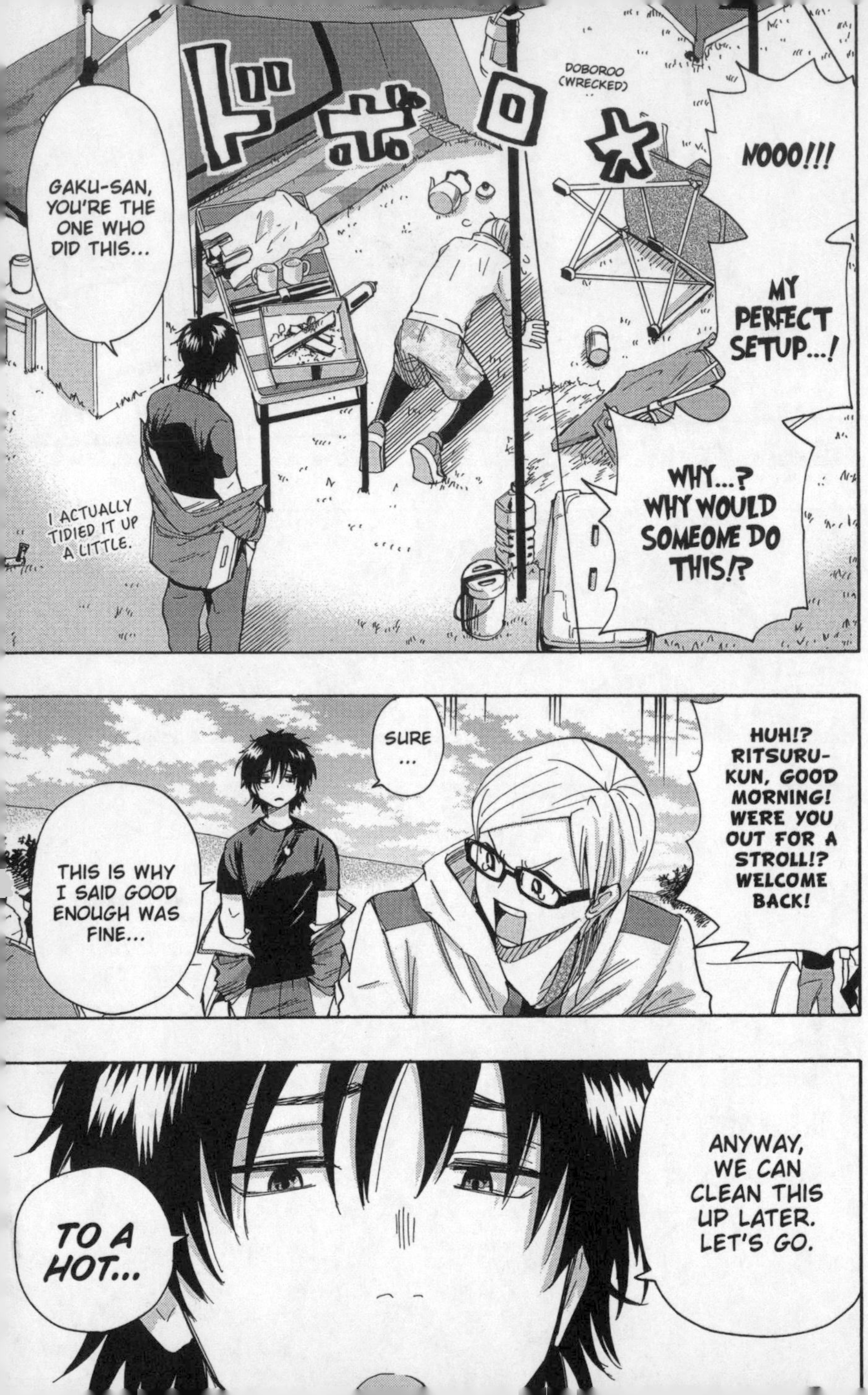
NOOO!!!
DOBOROO (WRECKED)
MY PERFECT SETUP...!
WHY...? WHY WOULD SOMEONE DO THIS!?
GAKU-SAN, YOU'RE THE ONE WHO DID THIS...
I ACTUALLY TIDIED IT UP A LITTLE.
HUH!? RITSURU-KUN, GOOD MORNING! WERE YOU OUT FOR A STROLL!? WELCOME BACK!
SURE ...
THIS IS WHY I SAID GOOD ENOUGH WAS FINE...
ANYWAY, WE CAN CLEAN THIS UP LATER. LET'S GO.
TO A HOT...

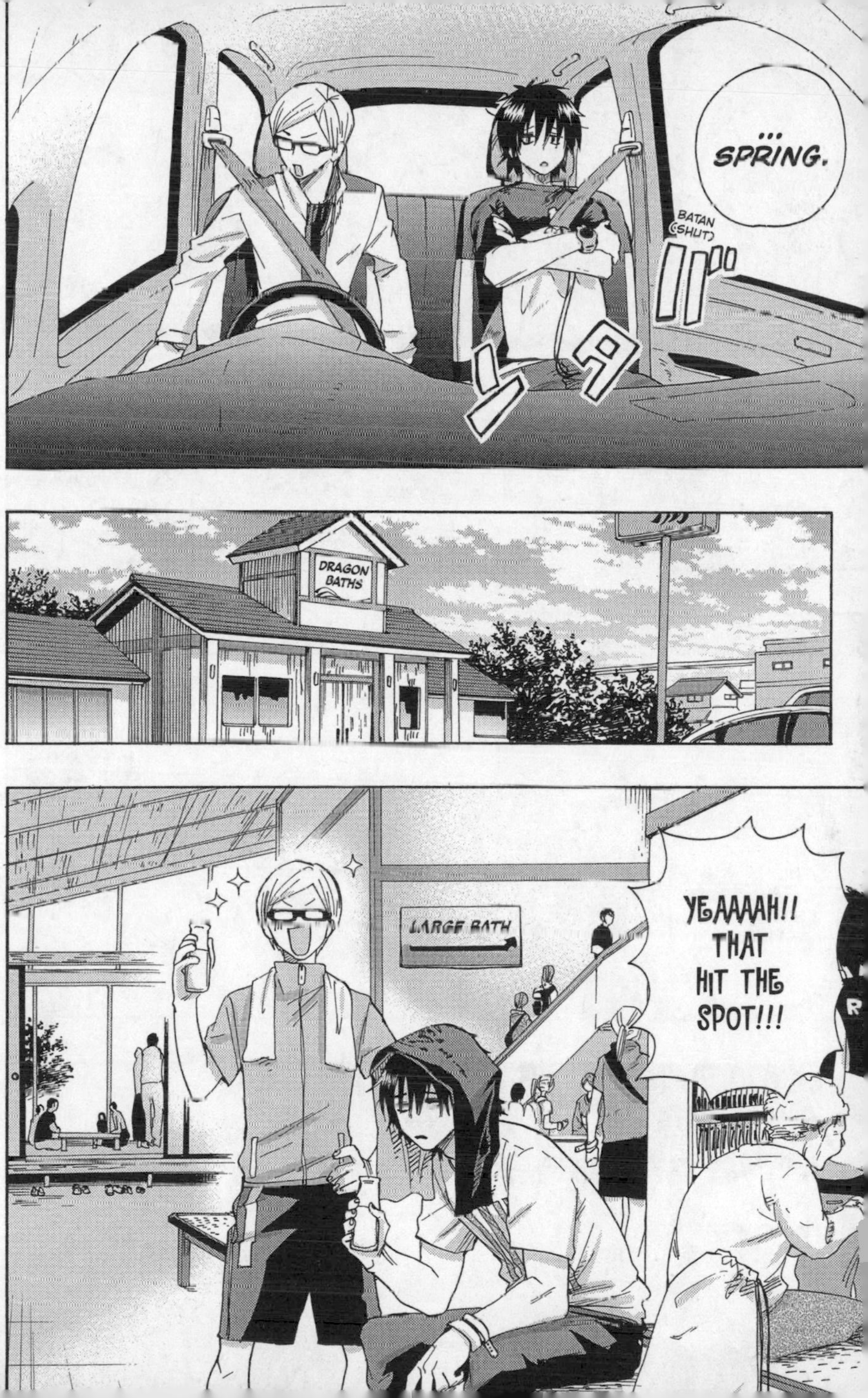

... SPRING.
BATAN (SHUT)
DRAGON BATHS
YEAAAAH!! THAT HIT THE SPOT!!!
LARGE BATH

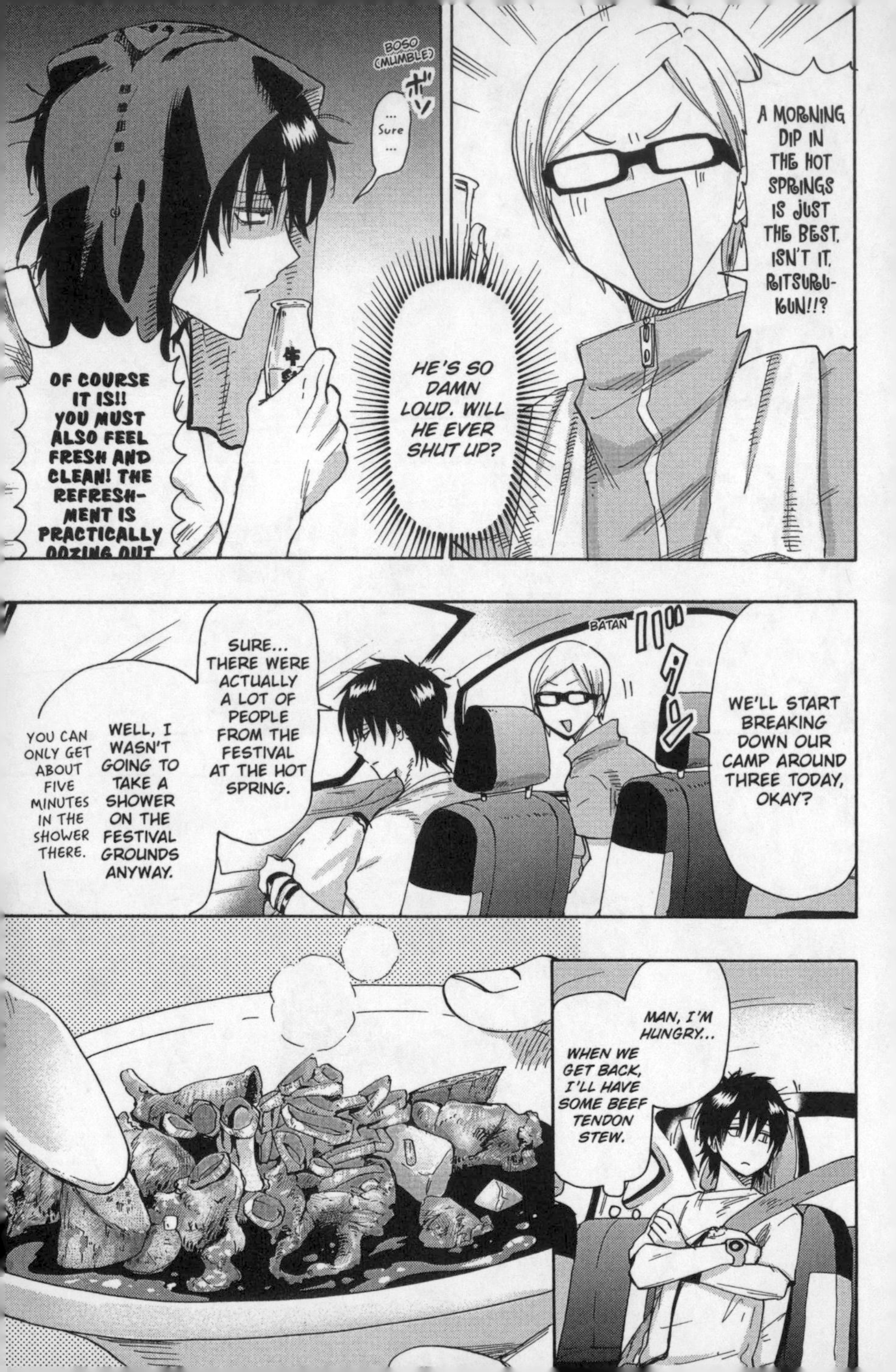
A MORNING DIP IN THE HOT SPRINGS IS JUST THE BEST, ISN'T IT, RITSURU-KUN!!?
BOSO (MUMBLE)
... Sure ...
HE'S SO DAMN LOUD. WILL HE EVER SHUT UP?
OF COURSE IT IS!! YOU MUST ALSO FEEL FRESH AND CLEAN! THE REFRESHMENT IS PRACTICALLY OOZING OUT
BATAN
WE'LL START BREAKING DOWN OUR CAMP AROUND THREE TODAY, OKAY?
SURE... THERE WERE ACTUALLY A LOT OF PEOPLE FROM THE FESTIVAL AT THE HOT SPRING.
WELL, I WASN'T GOING TO TAKE A SHOWER ON THE FESTIVAL GROUNDS ANYWAY.
YOU CAN ONLY GET ABOUT FIVE MINUTES IN THE SHOWER THERE.
MAN, I'M HUNGRY...
WHEN WE GET BACK, I'LL HAVE SOME BEEF TENDON STEW.

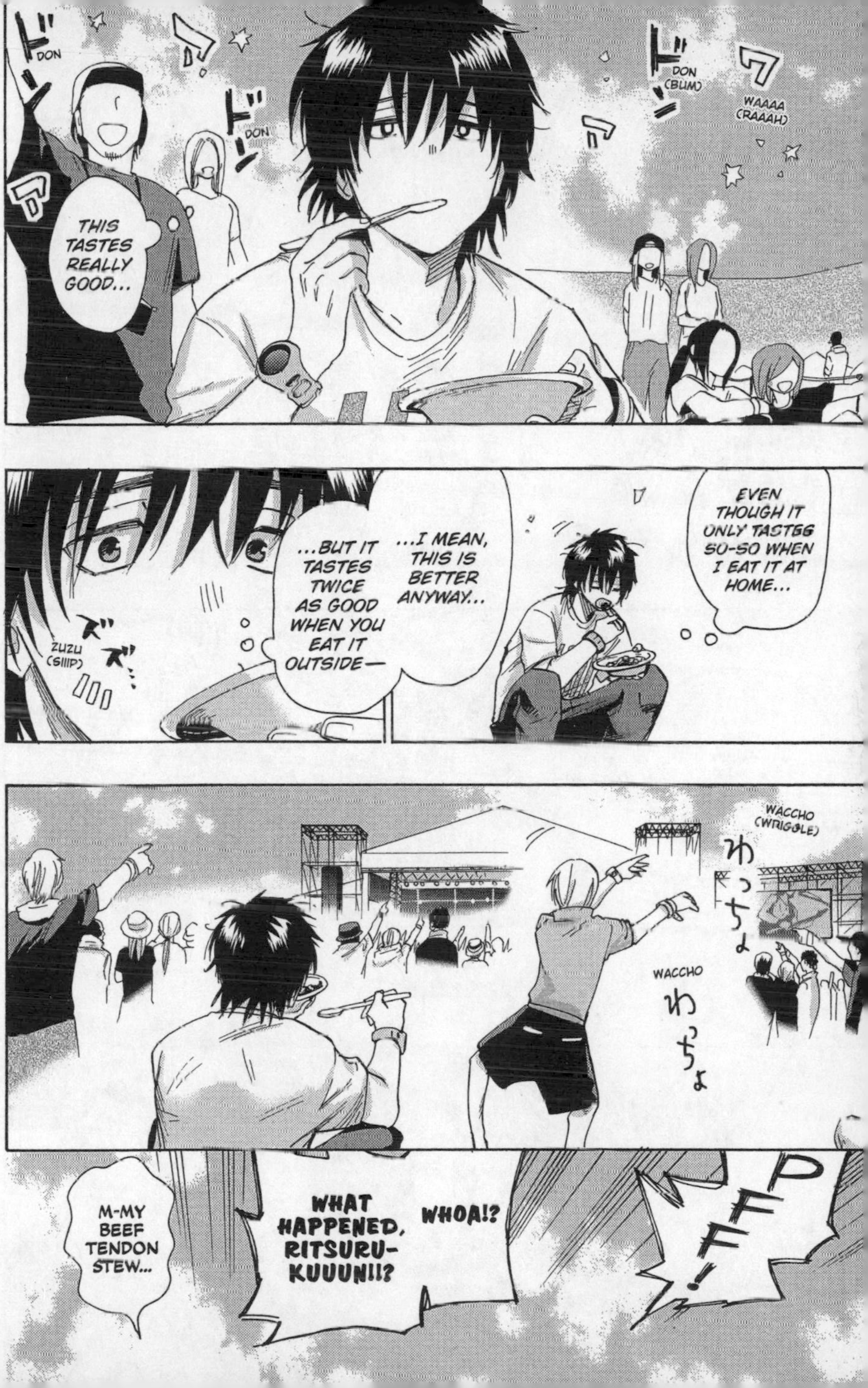

WAAAA (RAAAH)
DON (BUM)
DON
DON
THIS TASTES REALLY GOOD...
EVEN THOUGH IT ONLY TASTES SO-SO WHEN I EAT IT AT HOME...
...I MEAN, THIS IS BETTER ANYWAY...
...BUT IT TASTES TWICE AS GOOD WHEN YOU EAT IT OUTSIDE—
ZUZU (SIIIP)
わっちょ
WACCHO (WRIGGLE)
わっちょ
WACCHO
PFFF!
WHOA!?
WHAT HAPPENED, RITSURU-KUUUN!!?
M-MY BEEF TENDON STEW...

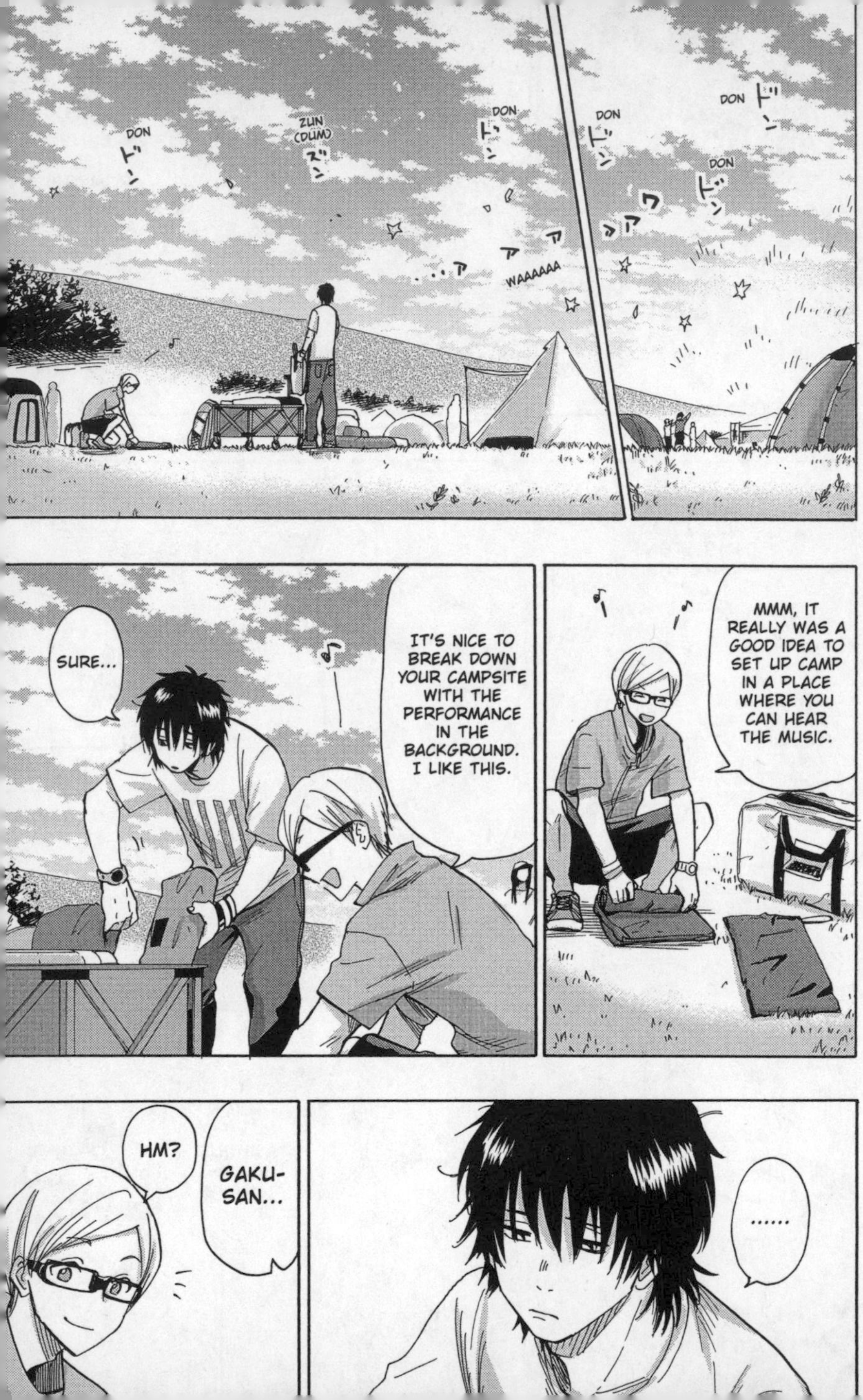
DON ドン
DON ドン
DON ドン
WAAAAAA ワアアア
DON ドン
ZUN (DUM) ズン
DON ドン
MMM, IT REALLY WAS A GOOD IDEA TO SET UP CAMP IN A PLACE WHERE YOU CAN HEAR THE MUSIC.
IT'S NICE TO BREAK DOWN YOUR CAMPSITE WITH THE PERFORMANCE IN THE BACKGROUND. I LIKE THIS.
SURE...
......
GAKU-SAN...
HM?

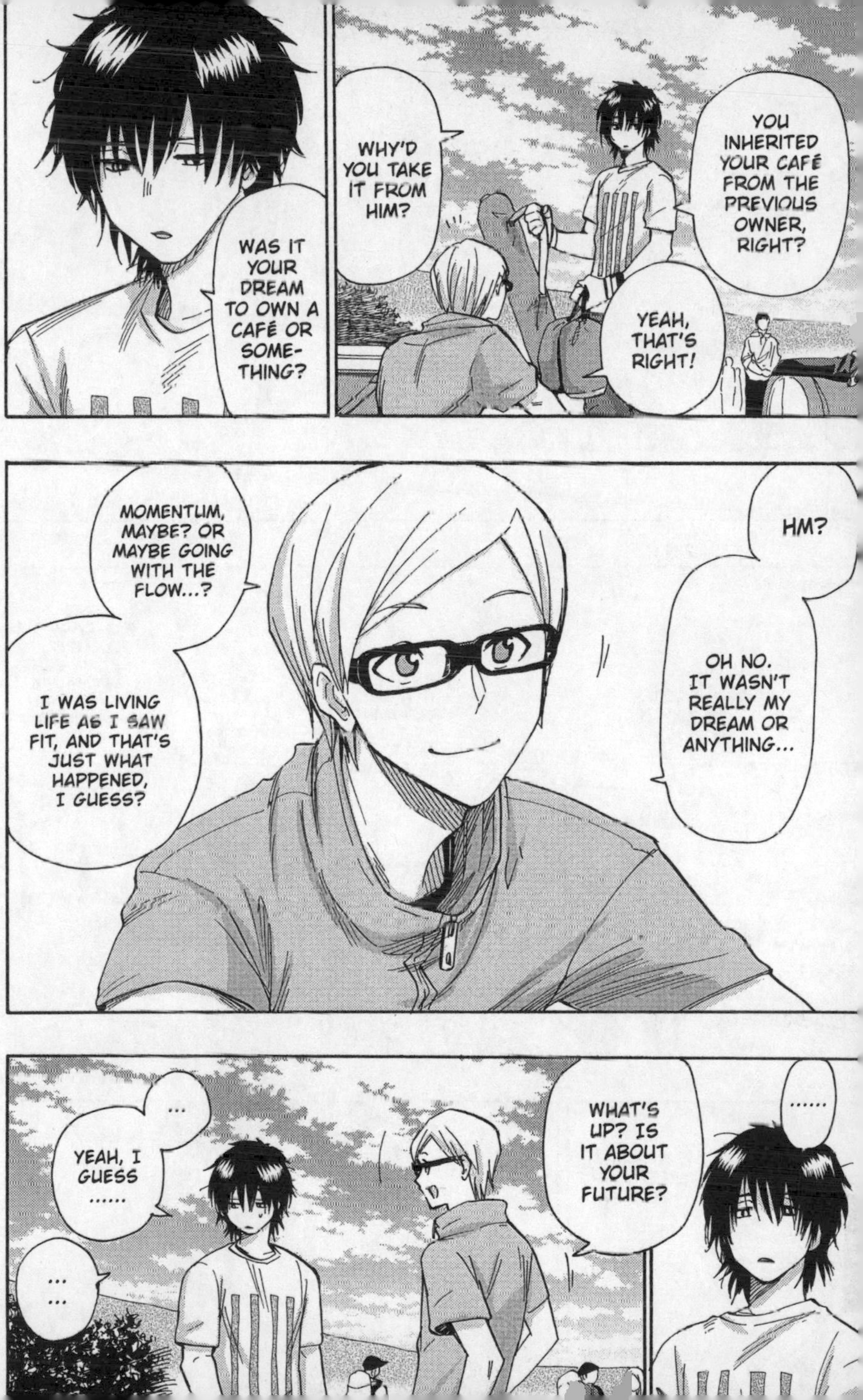
YOU INHERITED YOUR CAFÉ FROM THE PREVIOUS OWNER, RIGHT?
YEAH, THAT'S RIGHT!
WHY'D YOU TAKE IT FROM HIM?
WAS IT YOUR DREAM TO OWN A CAFÉ OR SOME-THING?
HM?
OH NO. IT WASN'T REALLY MY DREAM OR ANYTHING...
MOMENTUM, MAYBE? OR MAYBE GOING WITH THE FLOW...?
I WAS LIVING LIFE AS I SAW FIT, AND THAT'S JUST WHAT HAPPENED, I GUESS?
......
WHAT'S UP? IS IT ABOUT YOUR FUTURE?
...
YEAH, I GUESS ......
... ...

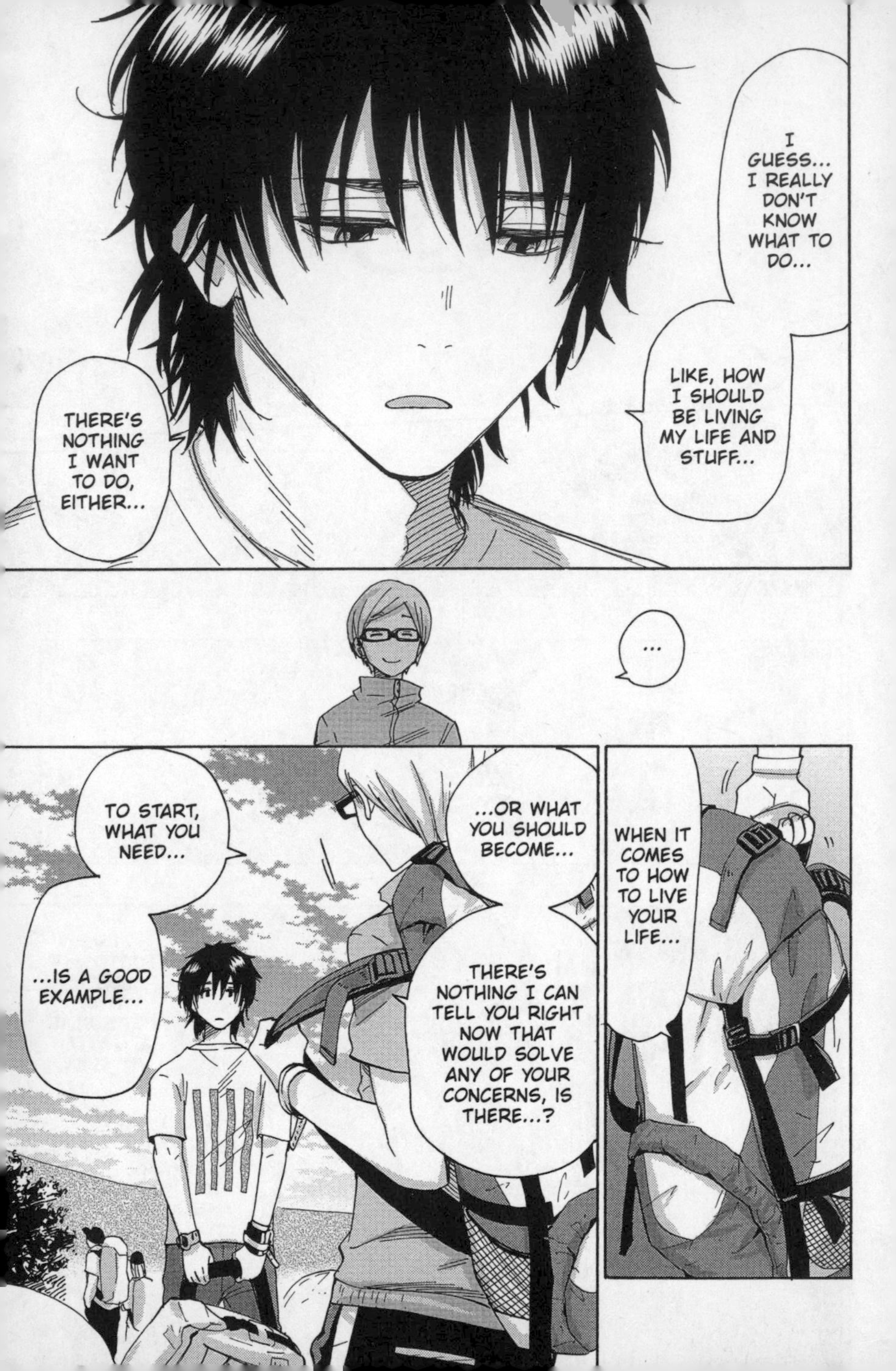
I GUESS... I REALLY DON'T KNOW WHAT TO DO...
LIKE, HOW I SHOULD BE LIVING MY LIFE AND STUFF...
THERE'S NOTHING I WANT TO DO, EITHER...
...
WHEN IT COMES TO HOW TO LIVE YOUR LIFE...
...OR WHAT YOU SHOULD BECOME...
THERE'S NOTHING I CAN TELL YOU RIGHT NOW THAT WOULD SOLVE ANY OF YOUR CONCERNS, IS THERE...?
TO START, WHAT YOU NEED...
...IS A GOOD EXAMPLE...

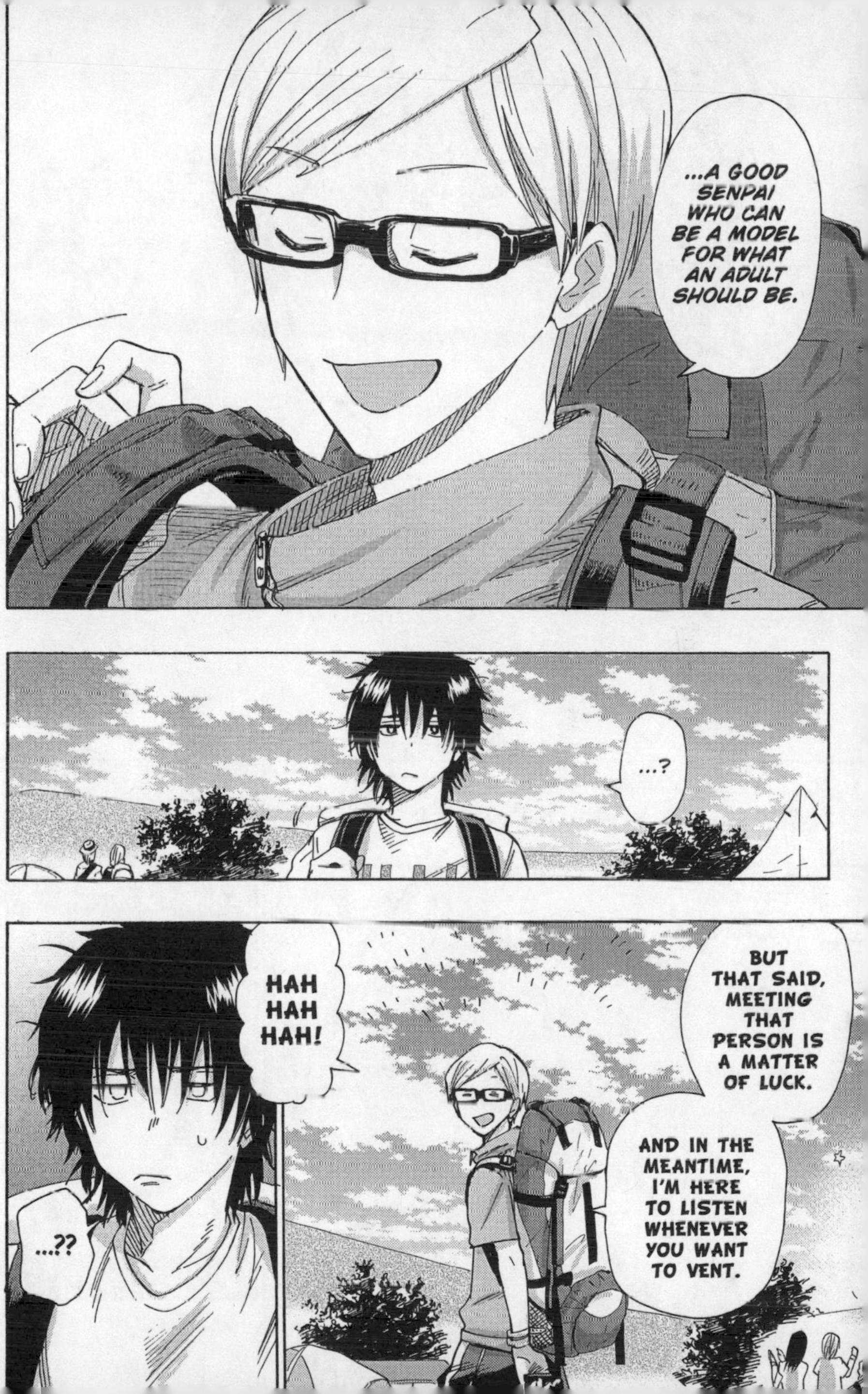
...A GOOD SENPAI WHO CAN BE A MODEL FOR WHAT AN ADULT SHOULD BE.
...?
BUT THAT SAID, MEETING THAT PERSON IS A MATTER OF LUCK.
AND IN THE MEANTIME, I'M HERE TO LISTEN WHENEVER YOU WANT TO VENT.
HAH HAH HAH!
...??

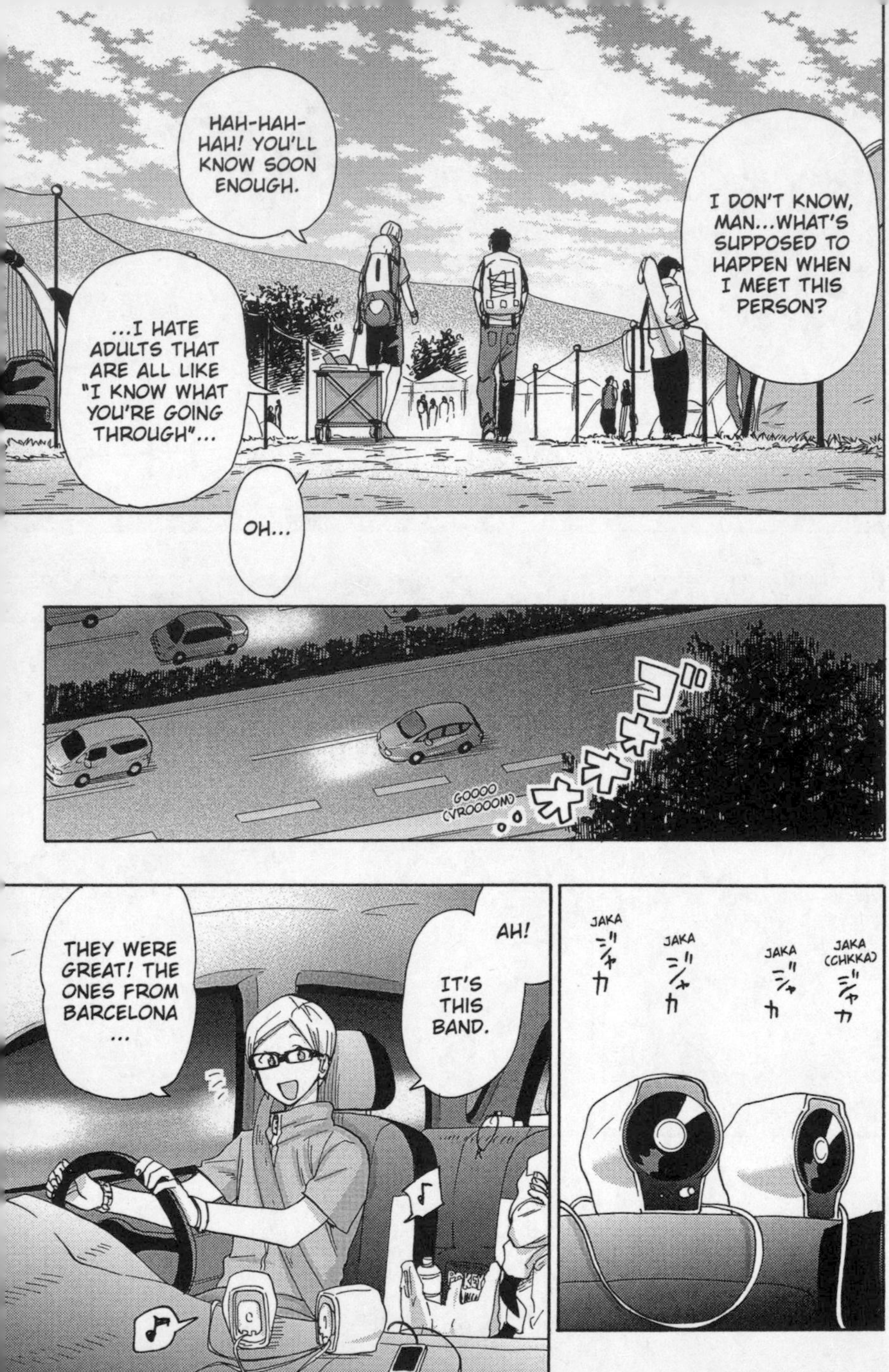
I DON'T KNOW, MAN...WHAT'S SUPPOSED TO HAPPEN WHEN I MEET THIS PERSON?
HAH-HAH-HAH! YOU'LL KNOW SOON ENOUGH.
...I HATE ADULTS THAT ARE ALL LIKE "I KNOW WHAT YOU'RE GOING THROUGH"...
OH...
ゴオオオ
GOOOO (VROOOOM)
JAKA (CHKKA)
ジャカ
JAKA
ジャカ
JAKA
ジャカ
JAKA
ジャカ
AH!
IT'S THIS BAND.
THEY WERE GREAT! THE ONES FROM BARCELONA ...

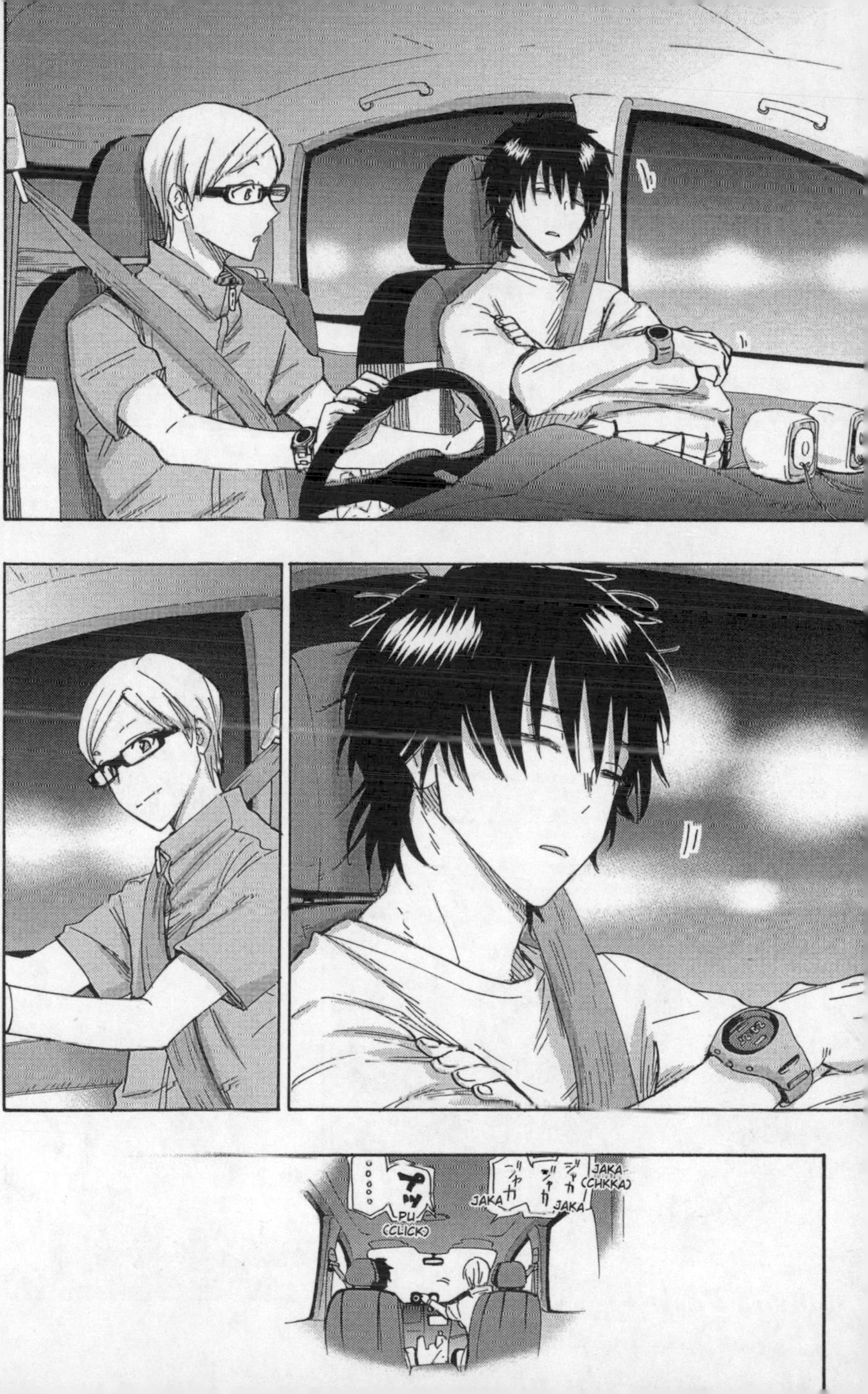
JAKA-
(CHKKA)
JAKA
JAKA
PU
(CLICK)

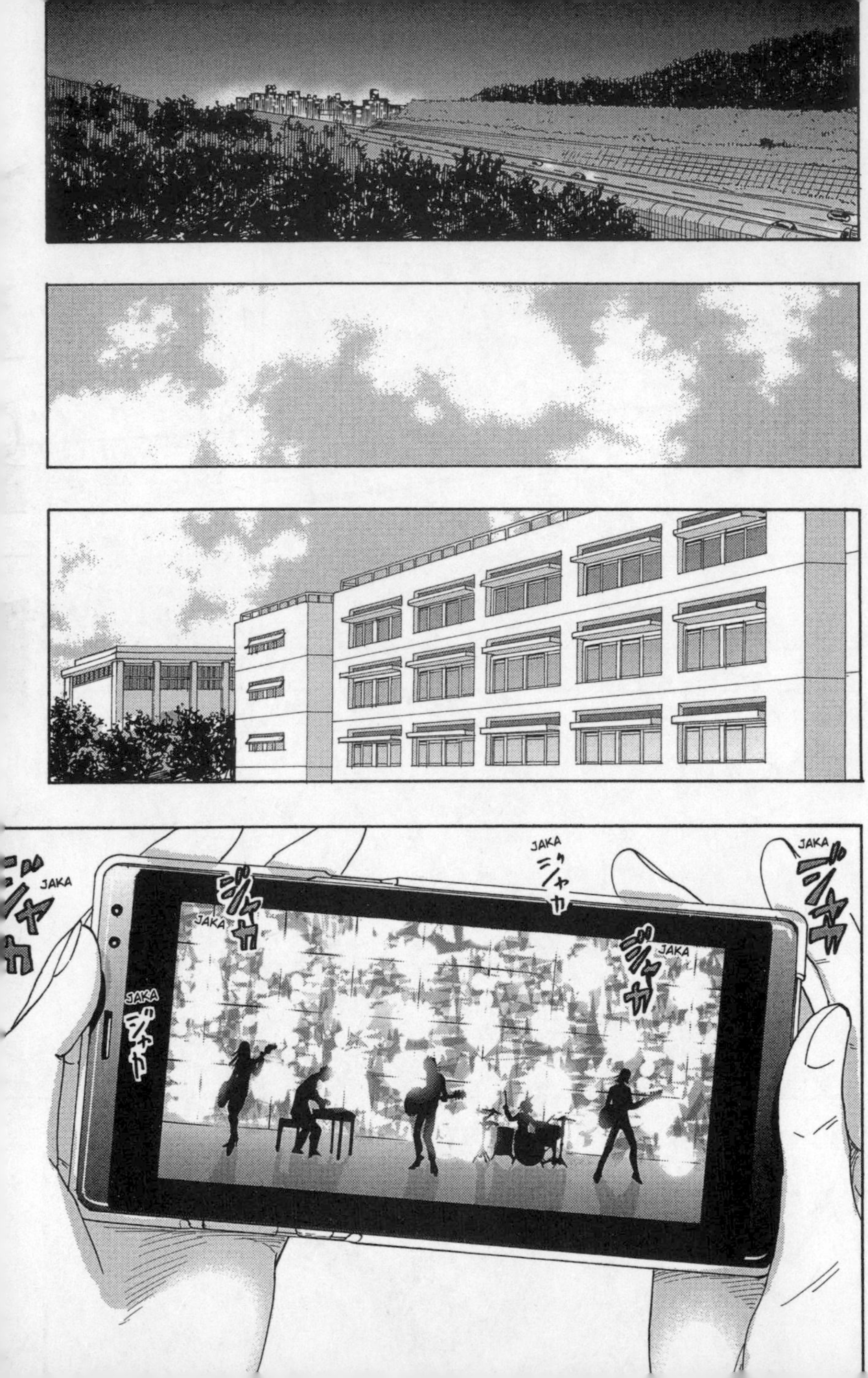
JAKA
ジャカ
JAKA
ジャカ
JAKA
ジャカ
JAKA
ジャカ
JAKA
ジャカ
JAKA
ジャカ

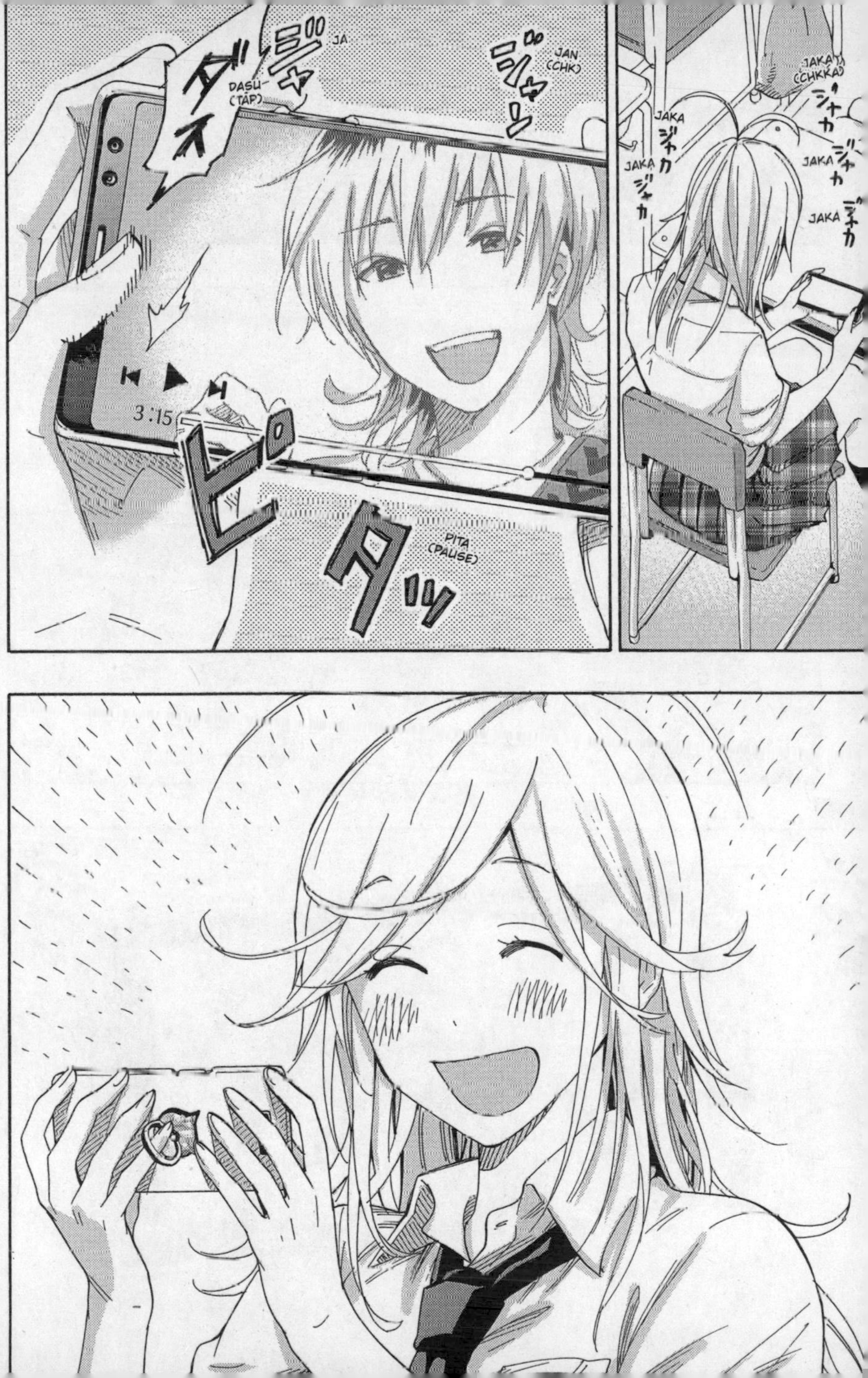
JAKA (CHKKA)
JAKA
JAKA
JAKA
JAKA
JAN (CHK)
JA
DASU (TAP)
3:15
PITA (PAUSE)

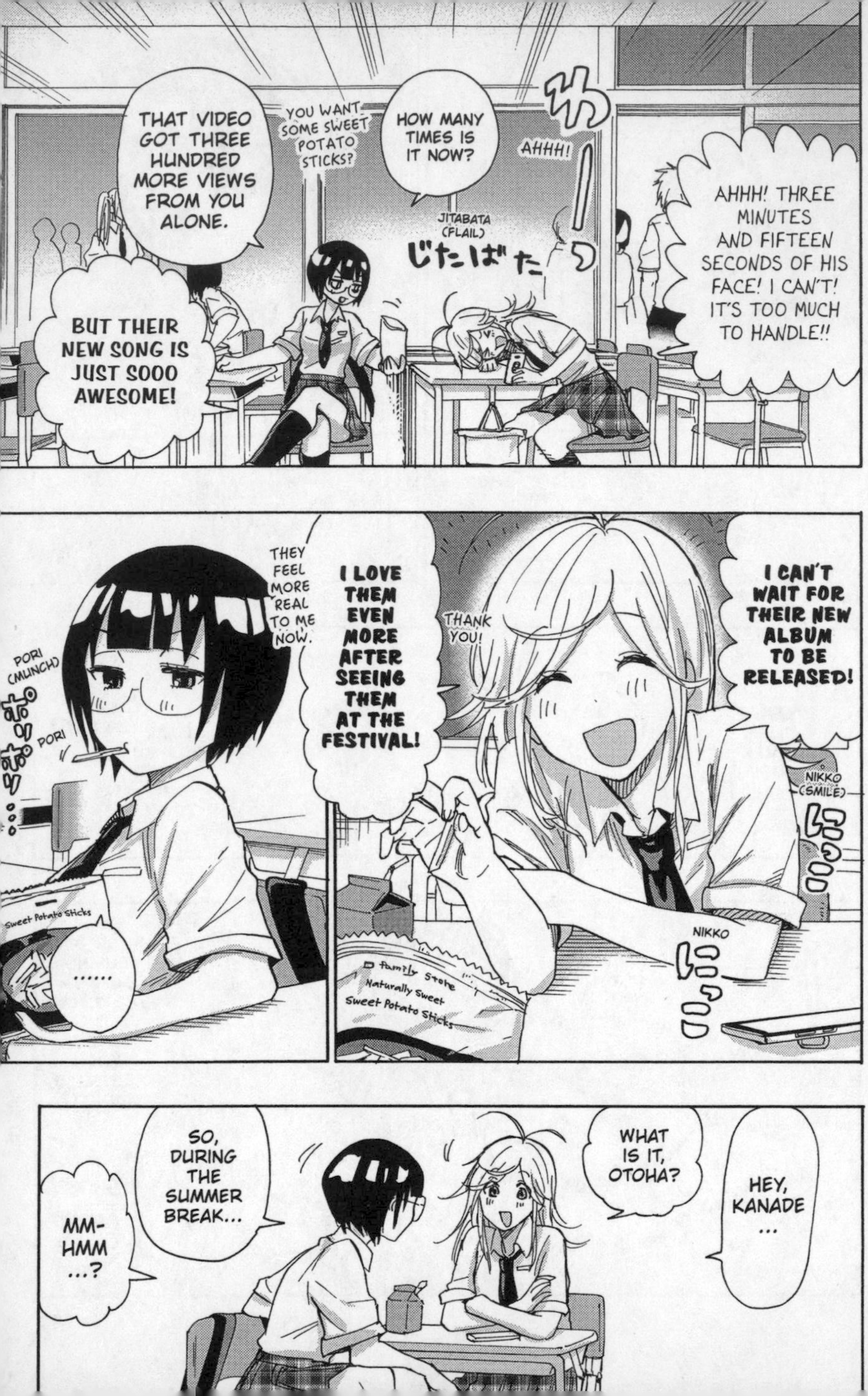
AHHH! THREE MINUTES AND FIFTEEN SECONDS OF HIS FACE! I CAN'T! IT'S TOO MUCH TO HANDLE!!
AHHH!
JITABATA (FLAIL)
じたばた
HOW MANY TIMES IS IT NOW?
YOU WANT SOME SWEET POTATO STICKS?
THAT VIDEO GOT THREE HUNDRED MORE VIEWS FROM YOU ALONE.
BUT THEIR NEW SONG IS JUST SOOO AWESOME!
I CAN'T WAIT FOR THEIR NEW ALBUM TO BE RELEASED!
NIKKO (SMILE)
NIKKO
I LOVE THEM EVEN MORE AFTER SEEING THEM AT THE FESTIVAL!
THANK YOU!
D family Store
Naturally Sweet
Sweet Potato Sticks
THEY FEEL MORE REAL TO ME NOW.
PORI (MUNCH)
PORI
Sweet Potato Sticks
......
HEY, KANADE...
WHAT IS IT, OTOHA?
SO, DURING THE SUMMER BREAK...
MM-HMM...?

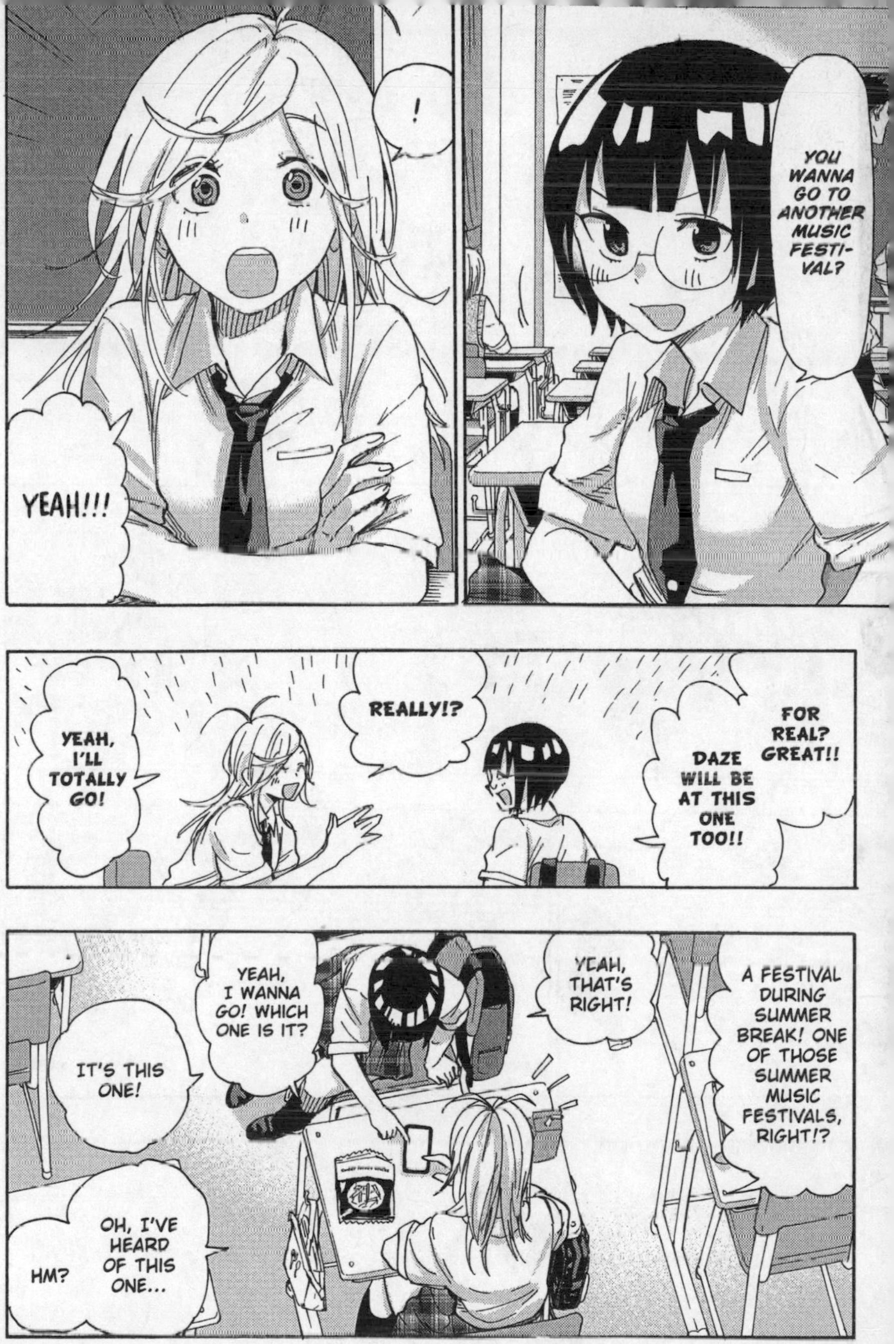
YOU WANNA GO TO ANOTHER MUSIC FESTIVAL?
!
YEAH!!!
FOR REAL? GREAT!!
DAZE WILL BE AT THIS ONE TOO!!
REALLY!?
YEAH, I'LL TOTALLY GO!
A FESTIVAL DURING SUMMER BREAK! ONE OF THOSE SUMMER MUSIC FESTIVALS, RIGHT!?
YEAH, THAT'S RIGHT!
YEAH, I WANNA GO! WHICH ONE IS IT?
IT'S THIS ONE!
OH, I'VE HEARD OF THIS ONE...
HM?

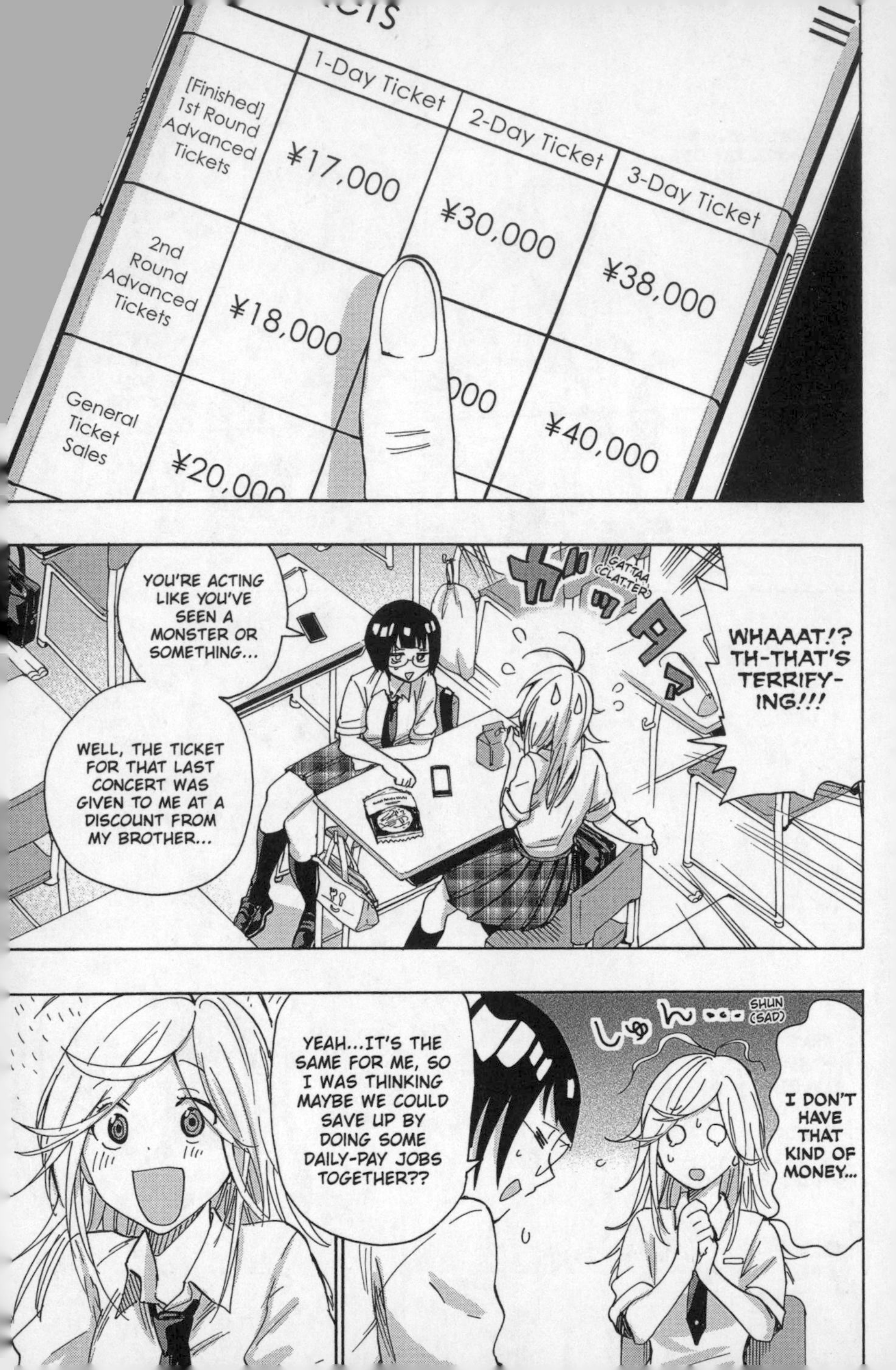

1-Day Ticket
2-Day Ticket
3-Day Ticket
[Finished] 1st Round Advanced Tickets
¥17,000
¥30,000
¥38,000
2nd Round Advanced Tickets
¥18,000
000
General Ticket Sales
¥20,000
¥40,000
WHAAAT!? TH-THAT'S TERRIFYING!!!
GATTAA (CLATTER)
YOU'RE ACTING LIKE YOU'VE SEEN A MONSTER OR SOMETHING...
WELL, THE TICKET FOR THAT LAST CONCERT WAS GIVEN TO ME AT A DISCOUNT FROM MY BROTHER...
SHUN (SAD)
I DON'T HAVE THAT KIND OF MONEY...
YEAH...IT'S THE SAME FOR ME, SO I WAS THINKING MAYBE WE COULD SAVE UP BY DOING SOME DAILY-PAY JOBS TOGETHER??

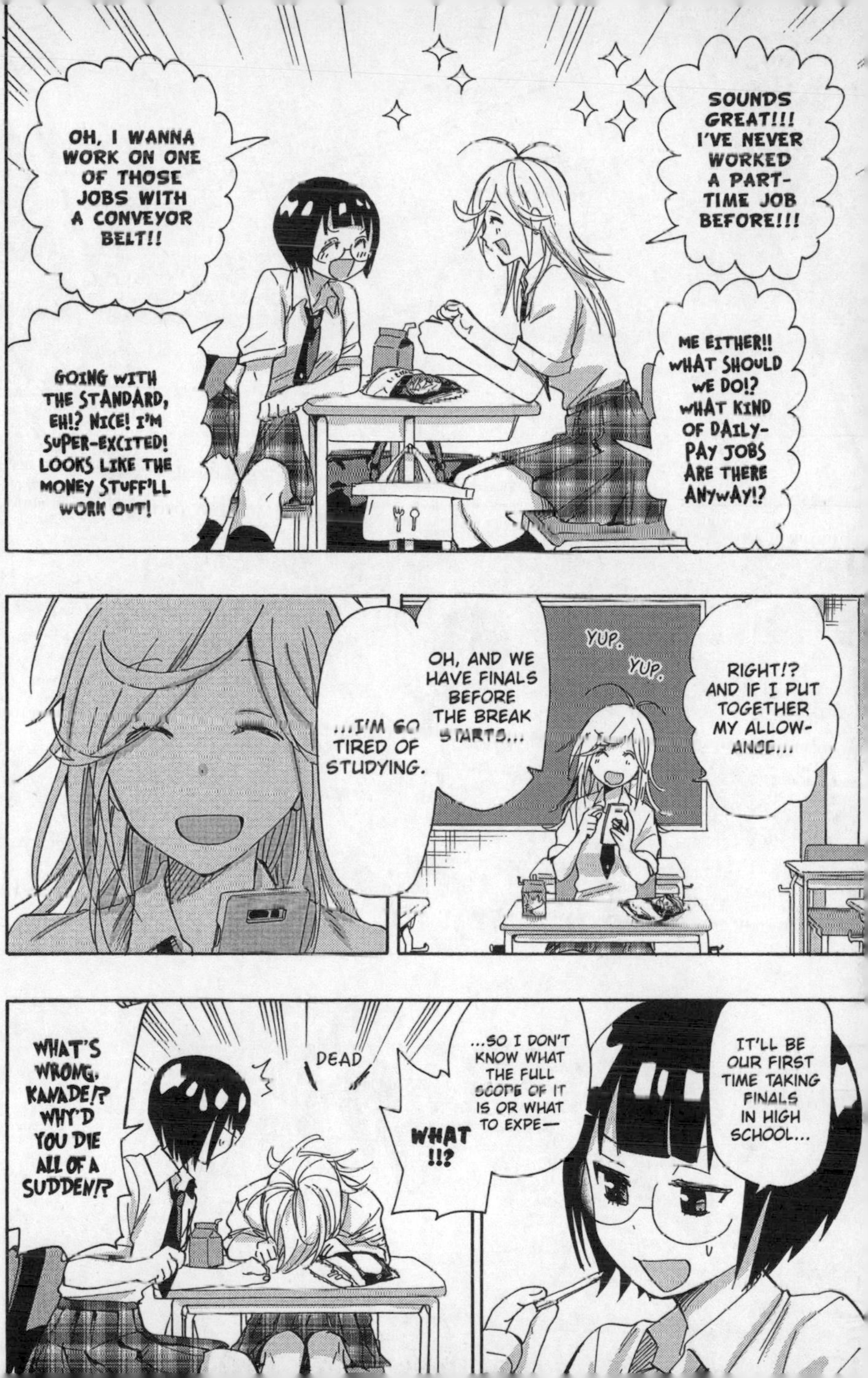
SOUNDS GREAT!!! I'VE NEVER WORKED A PART-TIME JOB BEFORE!!!
OH, I WANNA WORK ON ONE OF THOSE JOBS WITH A CONVEYOR BELT!!
ME EITHER!! WHAT SHOULD WE DO!? WHAT KIND OF DAILY-PAY JOBS ARE THERE ANYWAY!?
GOING WITH THE STANDARD, EH!? NICE! I'M SUPER-EXCITED! LOOKS LIKE THE MONEY STUFF'LL WORK OUT!
RIGHT!? AND IF I PUT TOGETHER MY ALLOW-ANCE...
YUP. YUP.
OH, AND WE HAVE FINALS BEFORE THE BREAK STARTS...
...I'M SO TIRED OF STUDYING.
IT'LL BE OUR FIRST TIME TAKING FINALS IN HIGH SCHOOL...
...SO I DON'T KNOW WHAT THE FULL SCOPE OF IT IS OR WHAT TO EXPE—
WHAT !!?
DEAD
WHAT'S WRONG, KANADE!? WHY'D YOU DIE ALL OF A SUDDEN!?

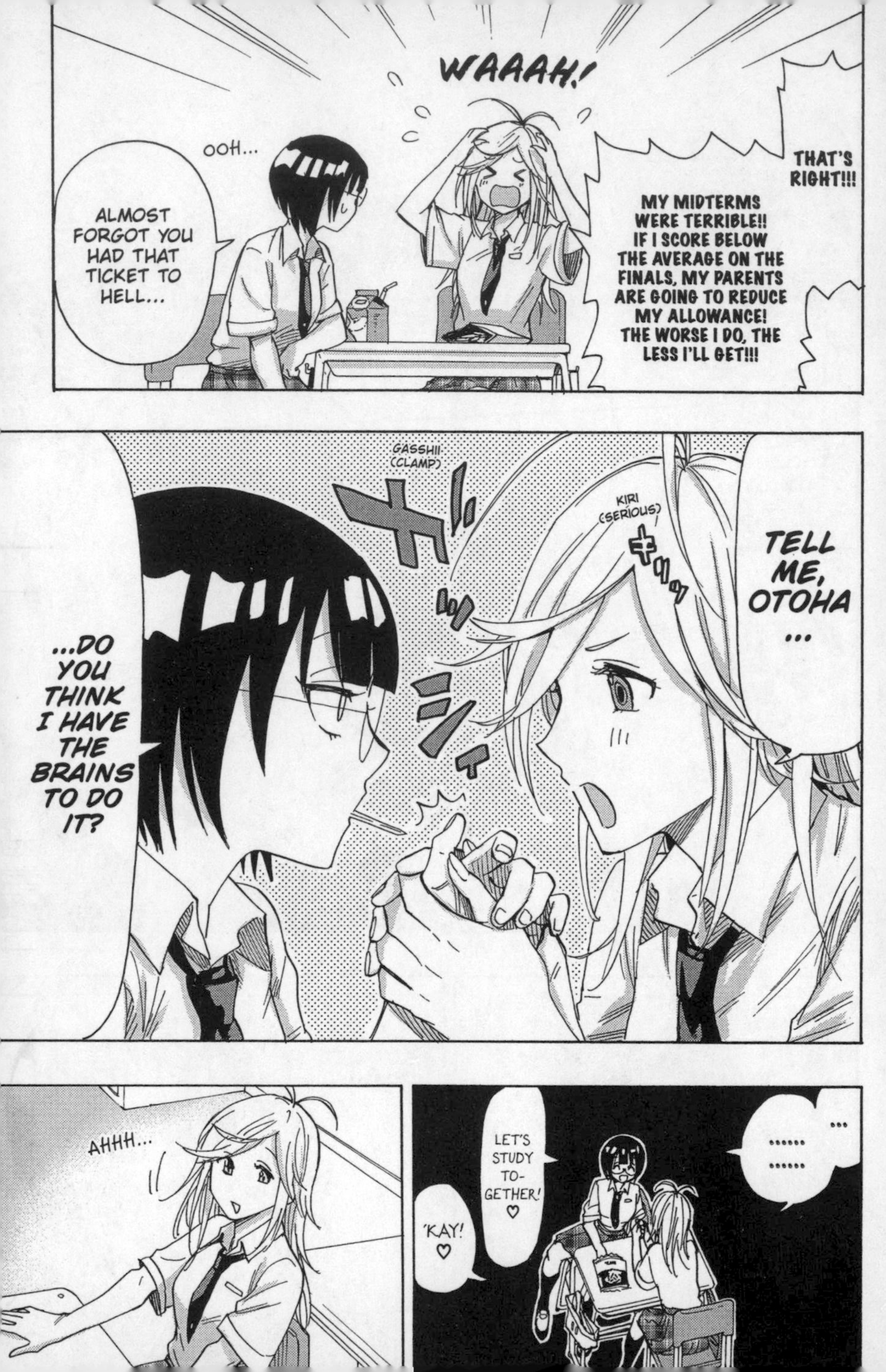
WAAAH!
THAT'S RIGHT!!!
MY MIDTERMS WERE TERRIBLE!! IF I SCORE BELOW THE AVERAGE ON THE FINALS, MY PARENTS ARE GOING TO REDUCE MY ALLOWANCE! THE WORSE I DO, THE LESS I'LL GET!!!
OOH...
ALMOST FORGOT YOU HAD THAT TICKET TO HELL...
TELL ME, OTOHA...
KIRI (SERIOUS)
GASSHI (CLAMP)
...DO YOU THINK I HAVE THE BRAINS TO DO IT?
... .
LET'S STUDY TO-GETHER! ♡
'KAY! ♡
AHHH...

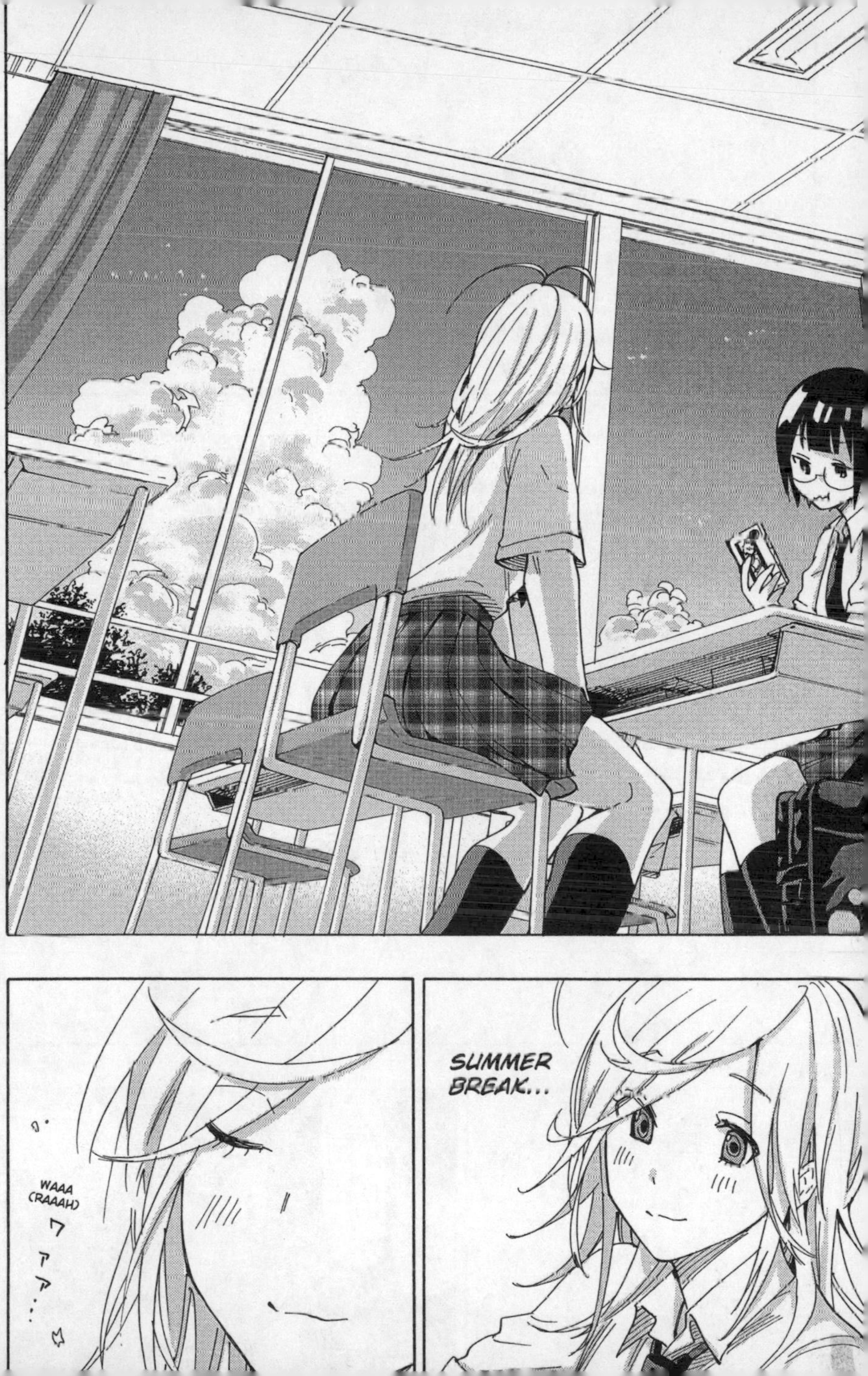
SUMMER BREAK...
WAAA (RAAAH)
ワァァ...

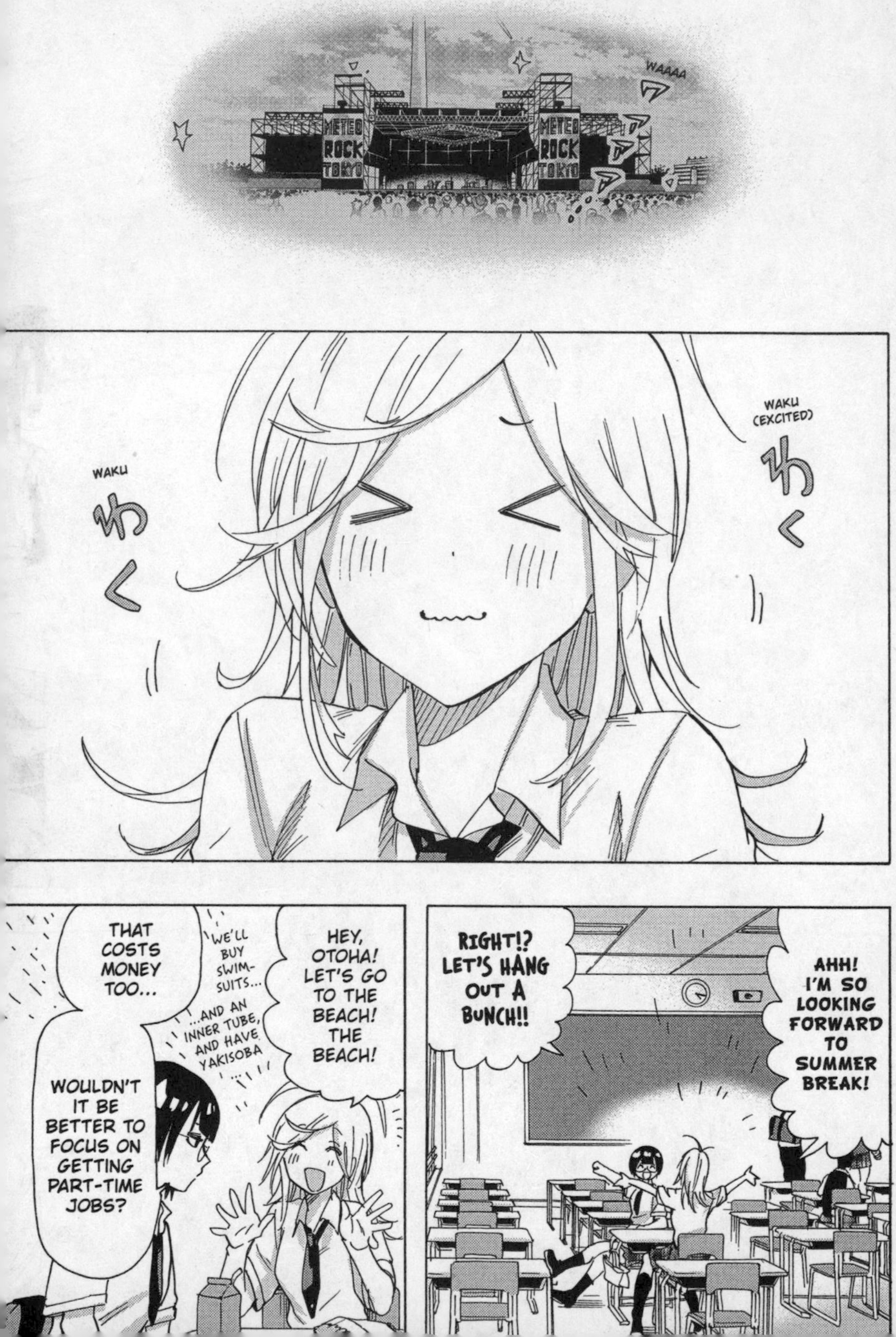
METEO ROCK TOKYO
METEO ROCK TOKYO
WAAAA
WAKU (EXCITED)
WAKU
AHH! I'M SO LOOKING FORWARD TO SUMMER BREAK!
RIGHT!? LET'S HANG OUT A BUNCH!!
HEY, OTOHA! LET'S GO TO THE BEACH! THE BEACH!
WE'LL BUY SWIM-SUITS...
...AND AN INNER TUBE, AND HAVE YAKISOBA...
THAT COSTS MONEY TOO...
WOULDN'T IT BE BETTER TO FOCUS ON GETTING PART-TIME JOBS?

Days on Fes

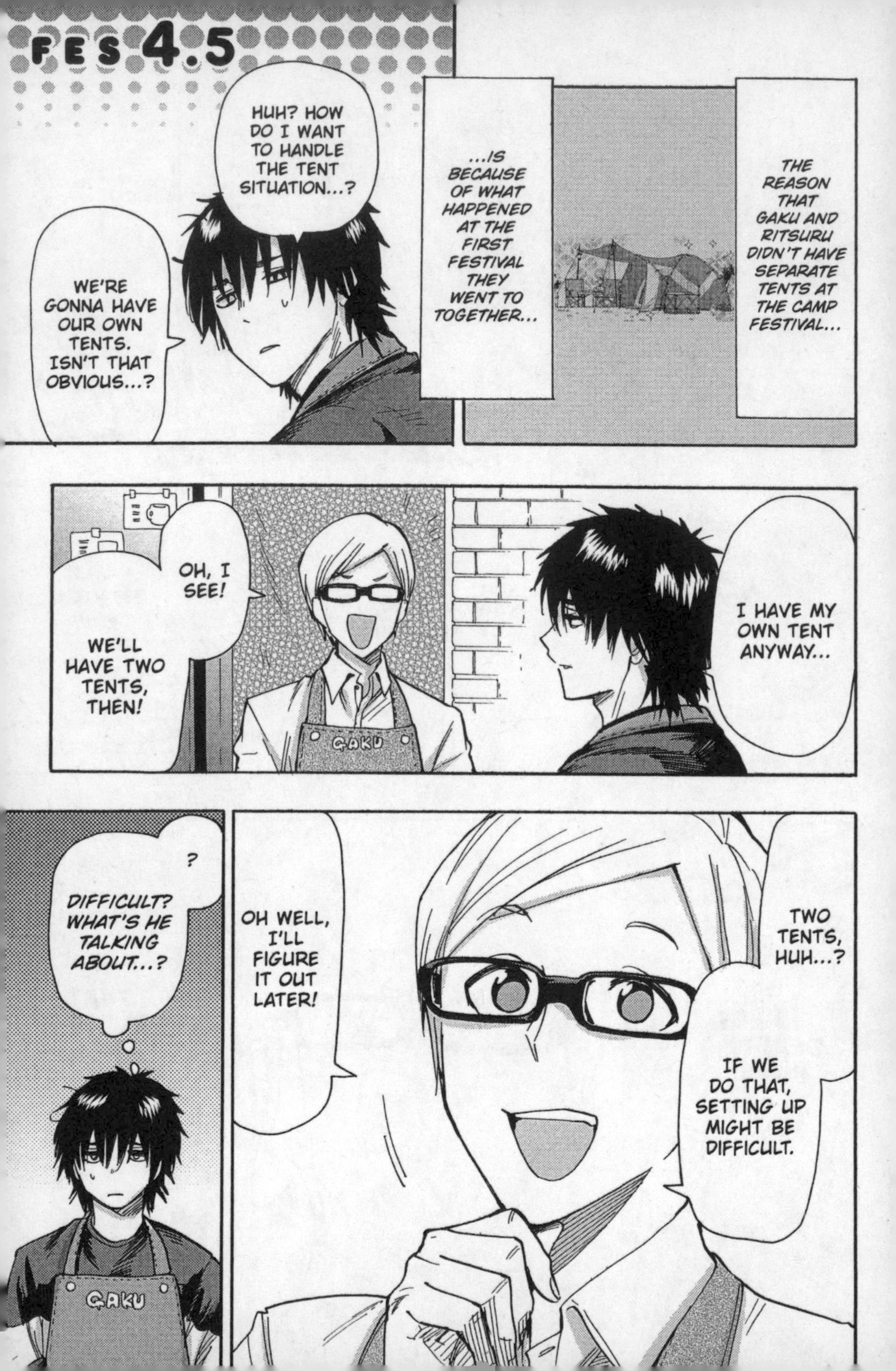
FES 4.5
THE REASON THAT GAKU AND RITSURU DIDN'T HAVE SEPARATE TENTS AT THE CAMP FESTIVAL...
...IS BECAUSE OF WHAT HAPPENED AT THE FIRST FESTIVAL THEY WENT TO TOGETHER...
HUH? HOW DO I WANT TO HANDLE THE TENT SITUATION...?
WE'RE GONNA HAVE OUR OWN TENTS. ISN'T THAT OBVIOUS...?
I HAVE MY OWN TENT ANYWAY...
OH, I SEE!
WE'LL HAVE TWO TENTS, THEN!
GAKU
TWO TENTS, HUH...?
IF WE DO THAT, SETTING UP MIGHT BE DIFFICULT.
OH WELL, I'LL FIGURE IT OUT LATER!
?
DIFFICULT? WHAT'S HE TALKING ABOUT...?
GAKU

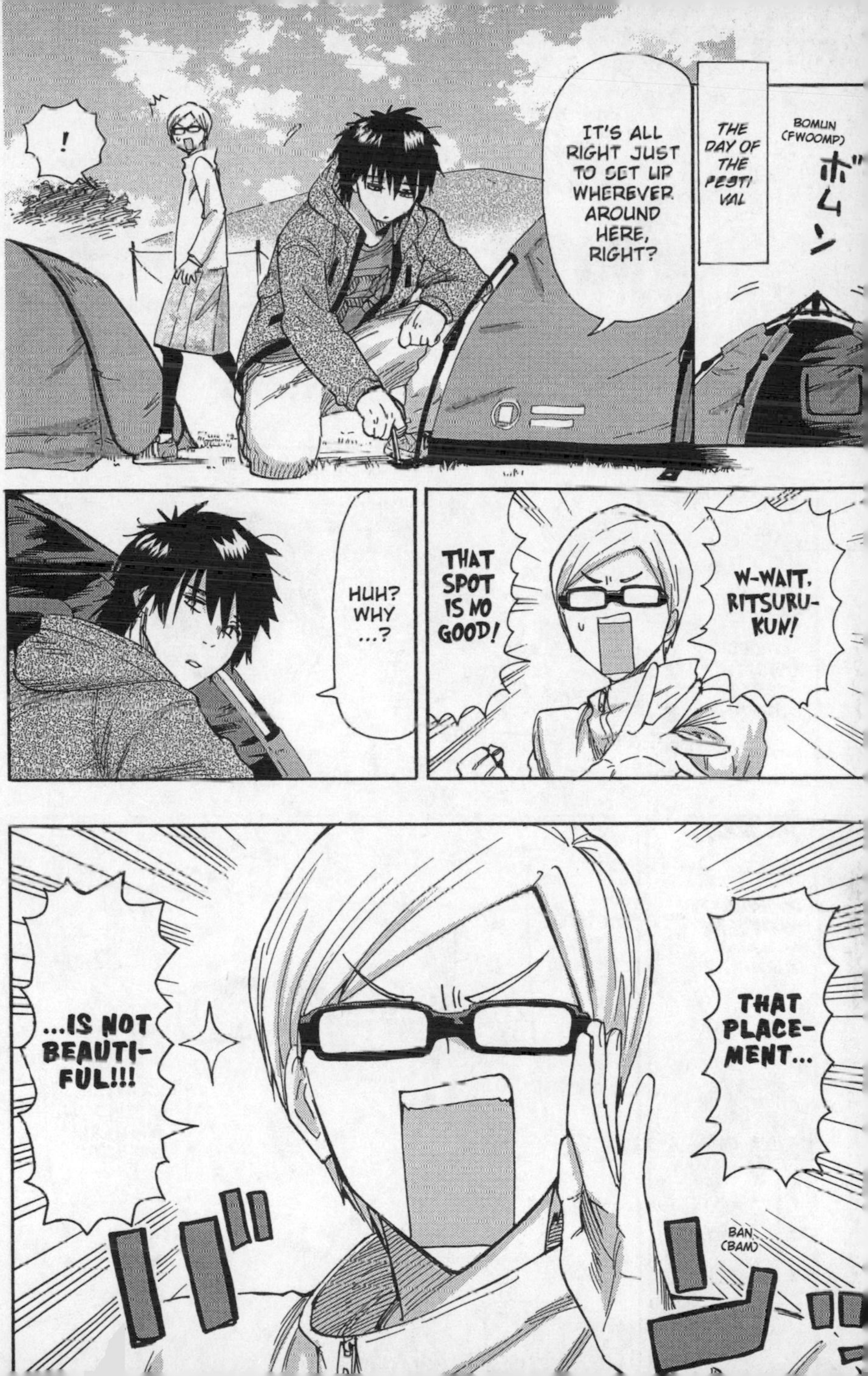
THE DAY OF THE FESTIVAL
BOMUN (FWOOMP)
ボムン
IT'S ALL RIGHT JUST TO SET UP WHEREVER AROUND HERE, RIGHT?
!
W-WAIT, RITSURU-KUN!
THAT SPOT IS NO GOOD!
HUH? WHY ...?
THAT PLACEMENT...
BAN (BAM)
...IS NOT BEAUTIFUL!!!

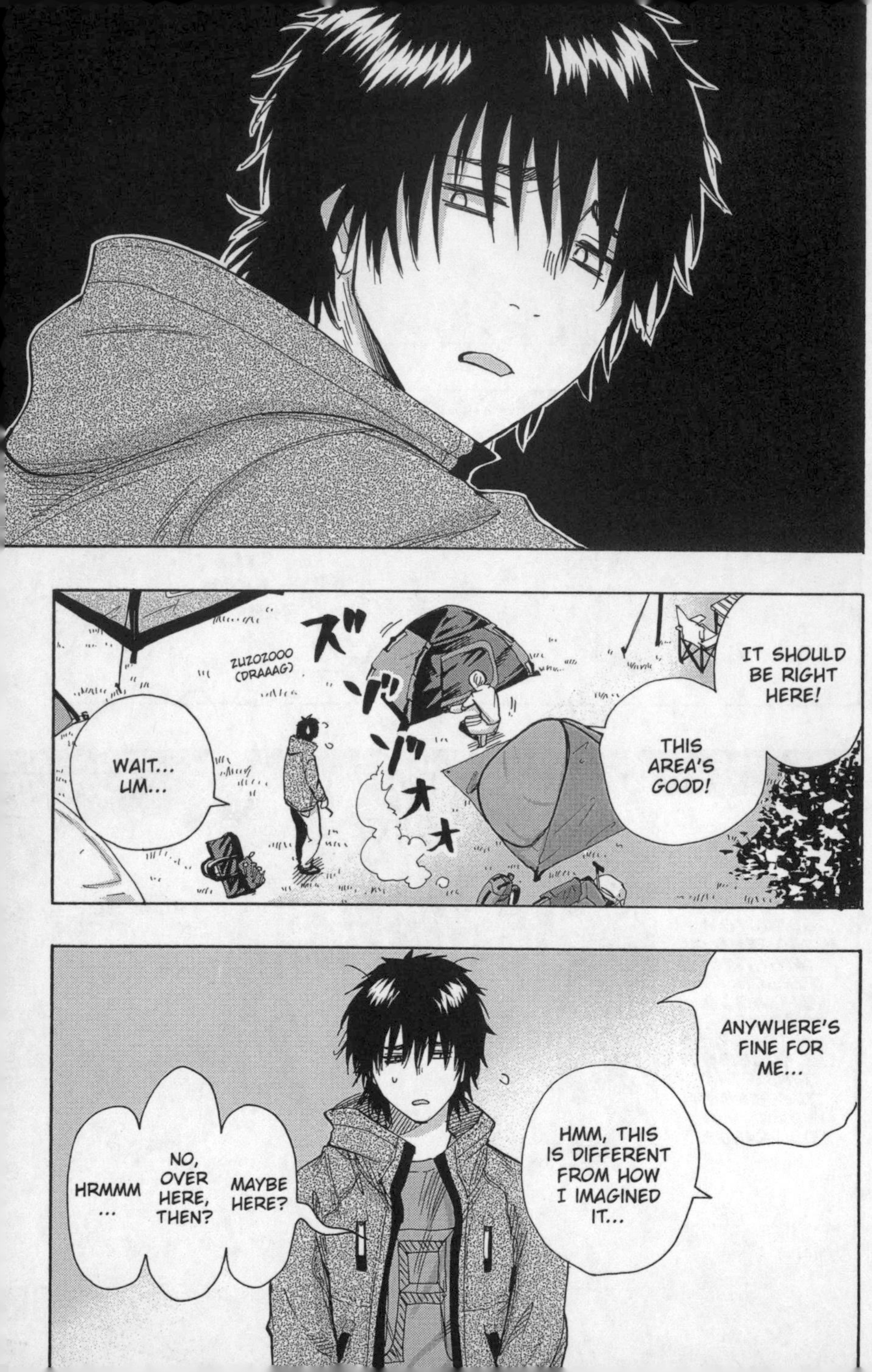
IT SHOULD BE RIGHT HERE!
THIS AREA'S GOOD!
ZUZOZOOO (DRAAAG)
WAIT... UM...
ANYWHERE'S FINE FOR ME...
HMM, THIS IS DIFFERENT FROM HOW I IMAGINED IT...
MAYBE HERE?
NO, OVER HERE, THEN?
HRMMM ...

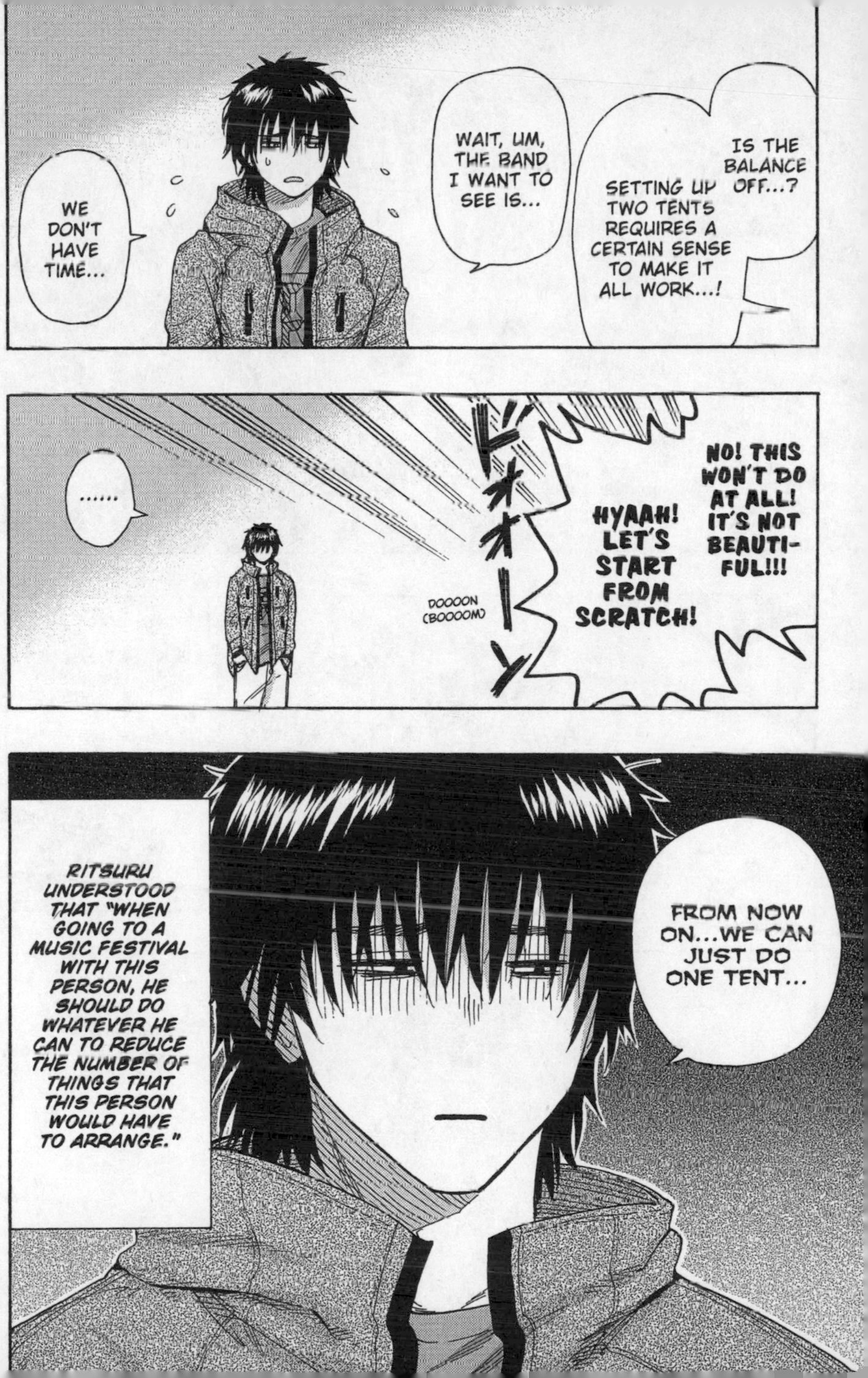
IS THE BALANCE OFF...?
SETTING UP TWO TENTS REQUIRES A CERTAIN SENSE TO MAKE IT ALL WORK...!
WAIT, UM, THE BAND I WANT TO SEE IS...
WE DON'T HAVE TIME...
NO! THIS WON'T DO AT ALL! IT'S NOT BEAUTI-FUL!!!
HYAAH! LET'S START FROM SCRATCH!
DOOOON (BOOOOM)
......
FROM NOW ON...WE CAN JUST DO ONE TENT...
RITSURU UNDERSTOOD THAT "WHEN GOING TO A MUSIC FESTIVAL WITH THIS PERSON, HE SHOULD DO WHATEVER HE CAN TO REDUCE THE NUMBER OF THINGS THAT THIS PERSON WOULD HAVE TO ARRANGE."

Days on Fes

Days on Fes

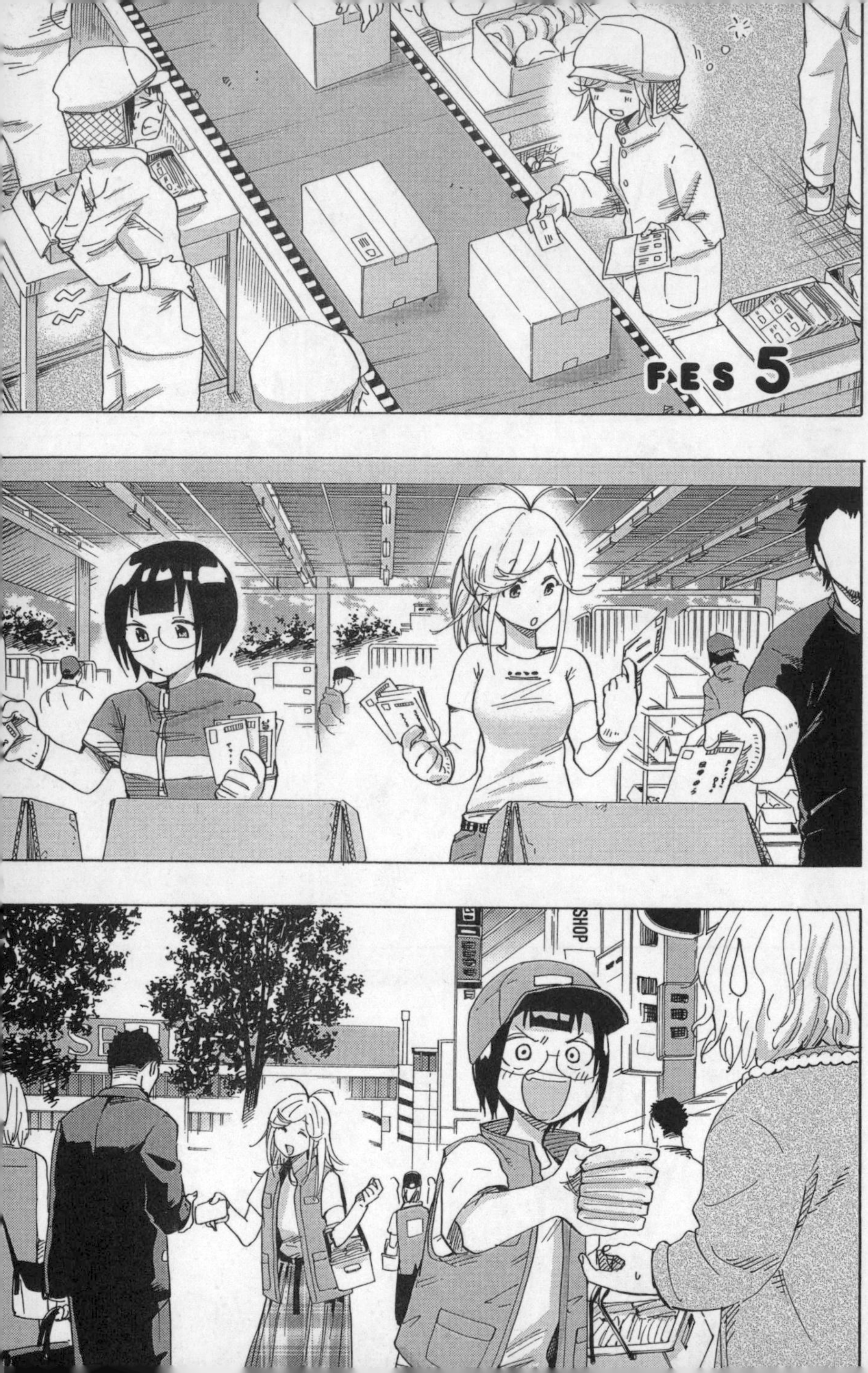
FES 5
SHOP

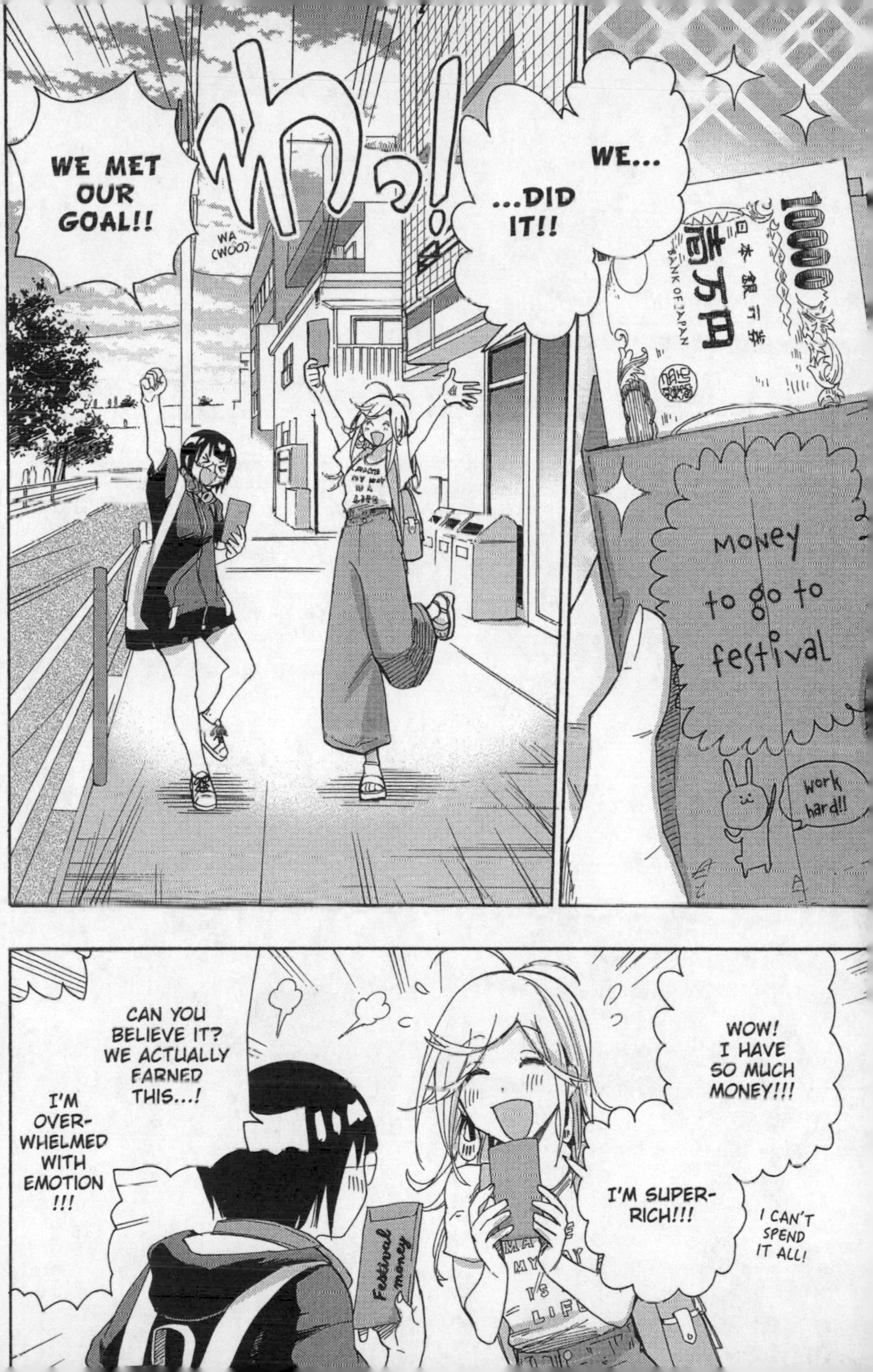

10000
BANK OF JAPAN
money to go to festival
work hard!!
WE...
...DID IT!!
わっ!
WA (WOO)
WE MET OUR GOAL!!
WOW! I HAVE SO MUCH MONEY!!!
I'M SUPER-RICH!!!
I CAN'T SPEND IT ALL!
CAN YOU BELIEVE IT? WE ACTUALLY EARNED THIS...!
I'M OVER-WHELMED WITH EMOTION!!!
Festival money

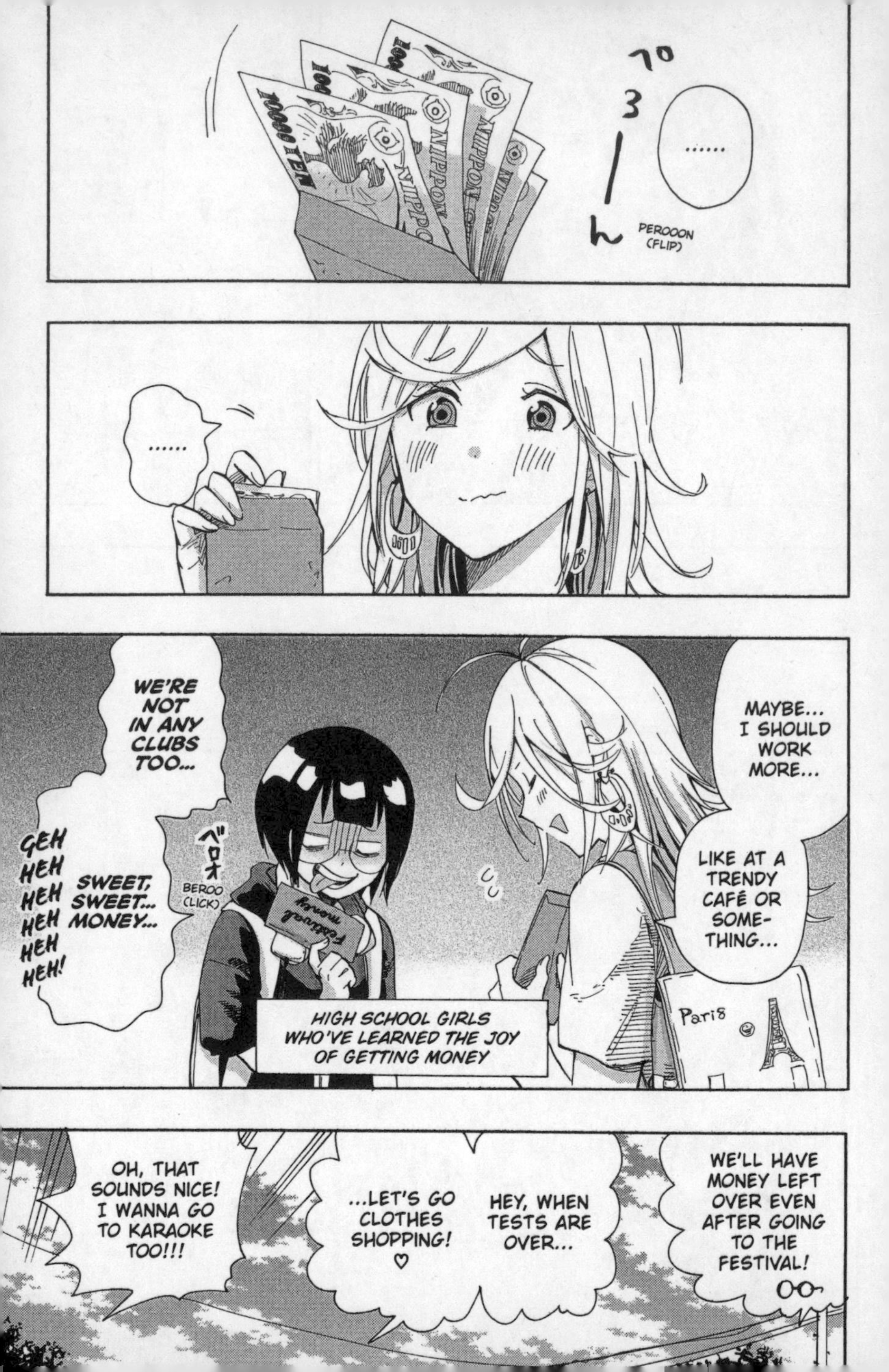
......
PEROOON (FLIP)
......
MAYBE... I SHOULD WORK MORE...
LIKE AT A TRENDY CAFÉ OR SOME-THING...
WE'RE NOT IN ANY CLUBS TOO...
ベロォ BEROO (LICK)
SWEET, SWEET... MONEY...
GEH HEH HEH HEH HEH HEH!
Festival money
Paris
HIGH SCHOOL GIRLS WHO'VE LEARNED THE JOY OF GETTING MONEY
WE'LL HAVE MONEY LEFT OVER EVEN AFTER GOING TO THE FESTIVAL!
HEY, WHEN TESTS ARE OVER...
...LET'S GO CLOTHES SHOPPING! ♡
OH, THAT SOUNDS NICE! I WANNA GO TO KARAOKE TOO!!!

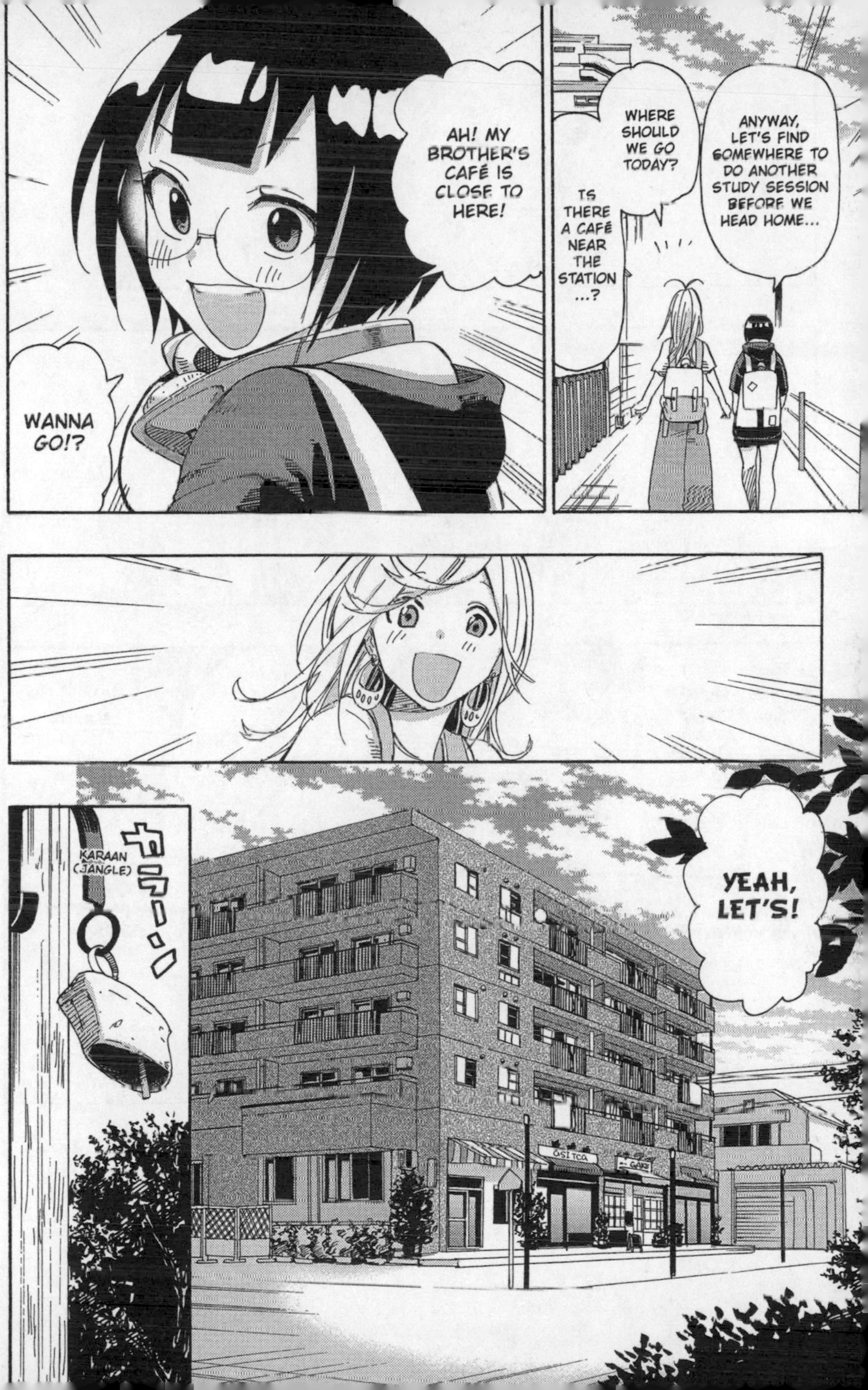
ANYWAY, LET'S FIND SOMEWHERE TO DO ANOTHER STUDY SESSION BEFORE WE HEAD HOME...
WHERE SHOULD WE GO TODAY?
IS THERE A CAFÉ NEAR THE STATION ...?
AH! MY BROTHER'S CAFÉ IS CLOSE TO HERE!
WANNA GO!?
YEAH, LET'S!
KARAAN (JANGLE)

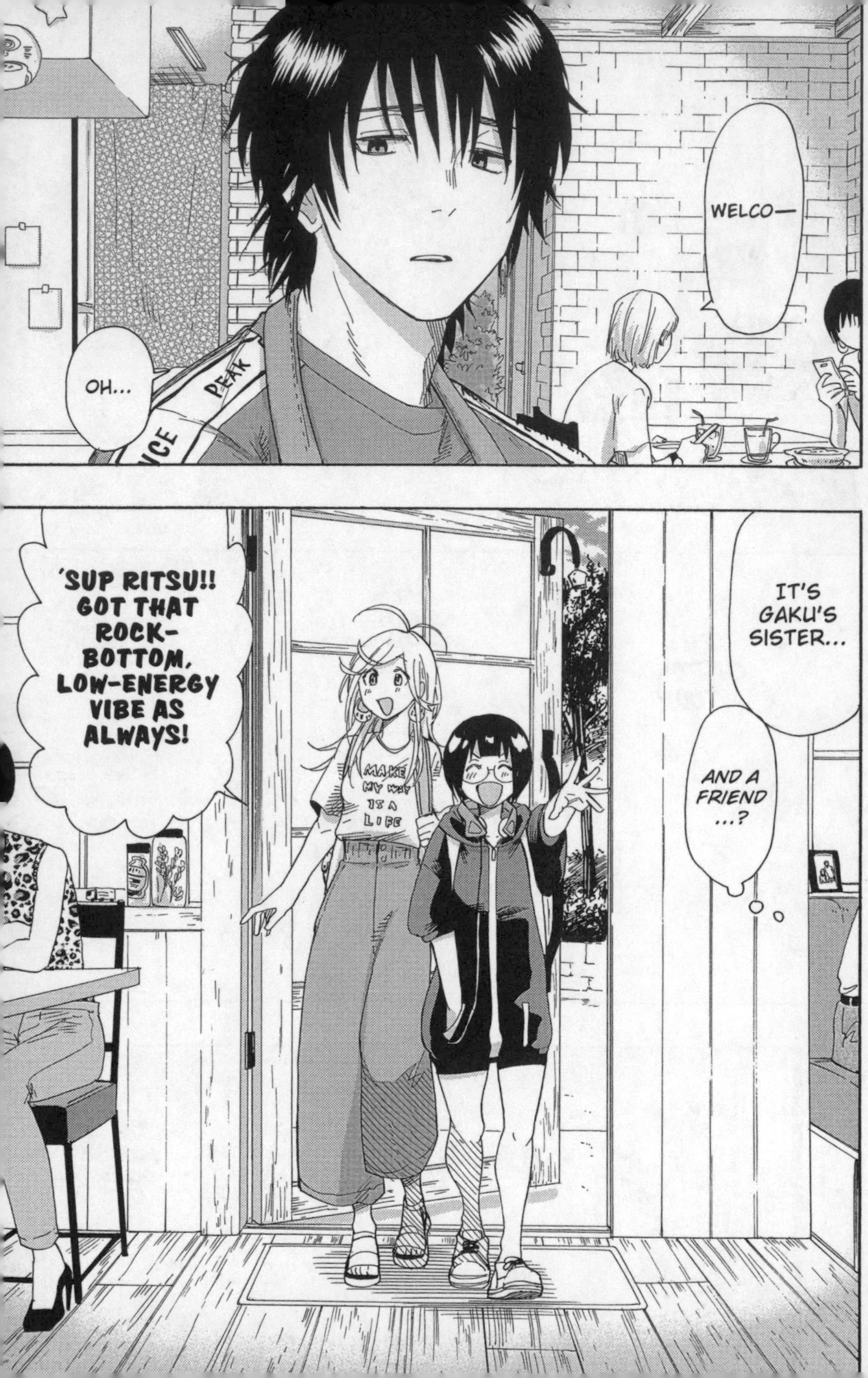
WELCO—
OH...
PEAK
IT'S GAKU'S SISTER...
AND A FRIEND ...?
'SUP RITSU!! GOT THAT ROCK-BOTTOM, LOW-ENERGY VIBE AS ALWAYS!
MAKE MY WAY IS A LIFE

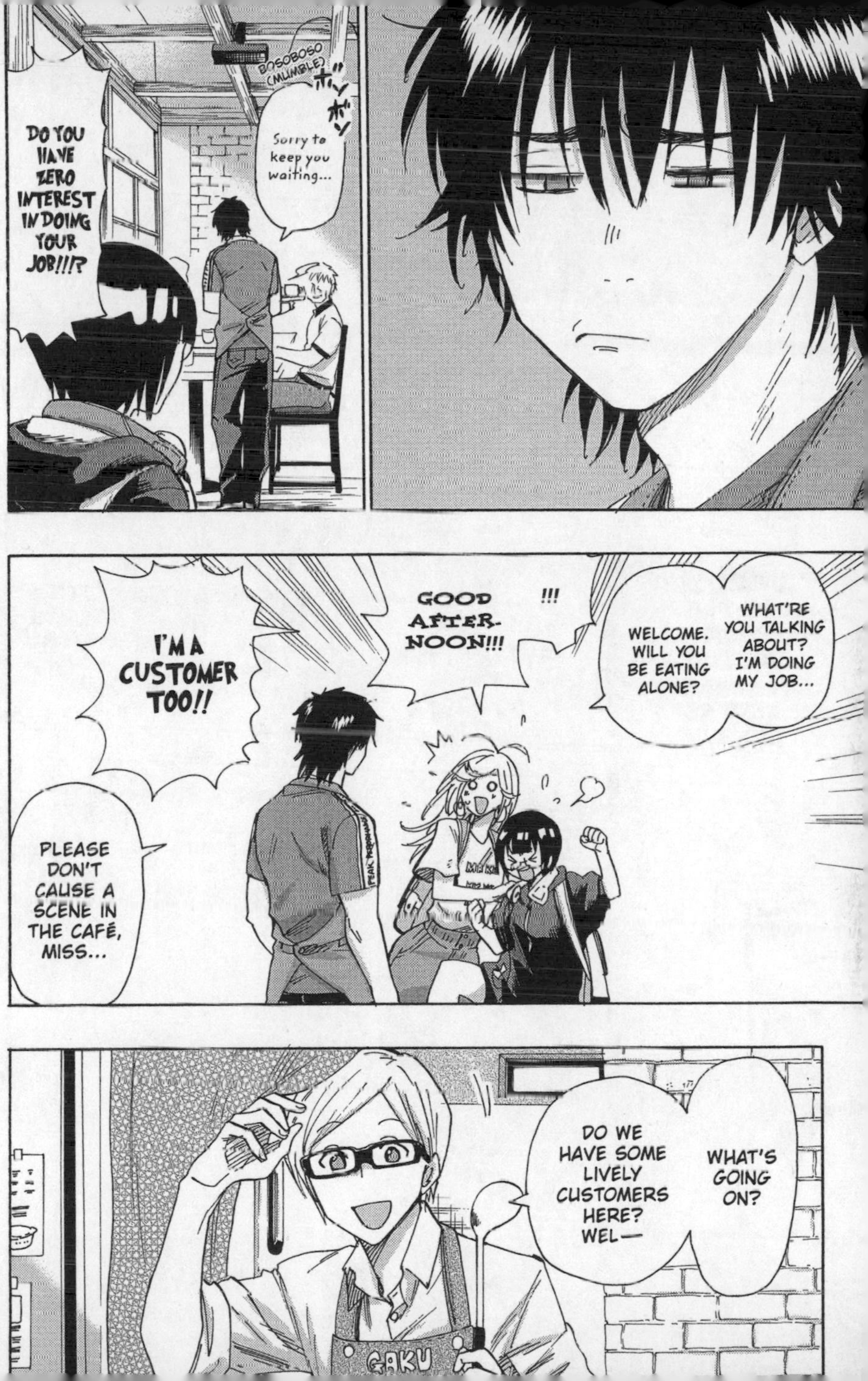
BOSOBOSO (MUMBLE)
Sorry to keep you waiting...
DO YOU HAVE ZERO INTEREST IN DOING YOUR JOB!!!?
WHAT'RE YOU TALKING ABOUT? I'M DOING MY JOB...
WELCOME. WILL YOU BE EATING ALONE?
!!!
GOOD AFTER-NOON!!!
I'M A CUSTOMER TOO!!
PLEASE DON'T CAUSE A SCENE IN THE CAFÉ, MISS...
WHAT'S GOING ON?
DO WE HAVE SOME LIVELY CUSTOMERS HERE? WEL—
GAKU

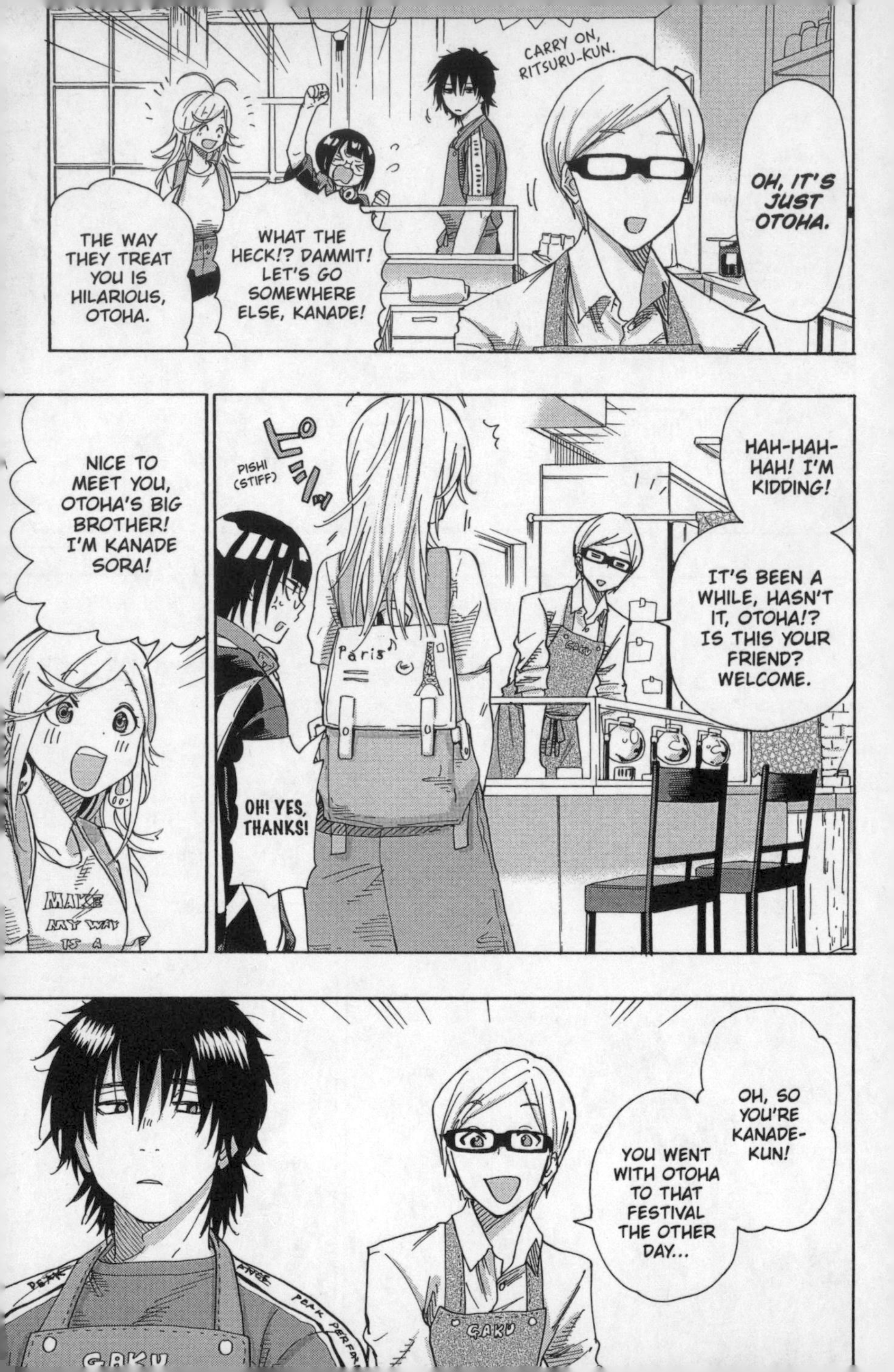
OH, IT'S JUST OTOHA.
CARRY ON, RITSURU-KUN.
WHAT THE HECK!? DAMMIT! LET'S GO SOMEWHERE ELSE, KANADE!
THE WAY THEY TREAT YOU IS HILARIOUS, OTOHA.
HAH-HAH-HAH! I'M KIDDING!
IT'S BEEN A WHILE, HASN'T IT, OTOHA!? IS THIS YOUR FRIEND? WELCOME.
PISHI (STIFF)
OH! YES, THANKS!
NICE TO MEET YOU, OTOHA'S BIG BROTHER! I'M KANADE SORA!
OH, SO YOU'RE KANADE-KUN!
YOU WENT WITH OTOHA TO THAT FESTIVAL THE OTHER DAY...

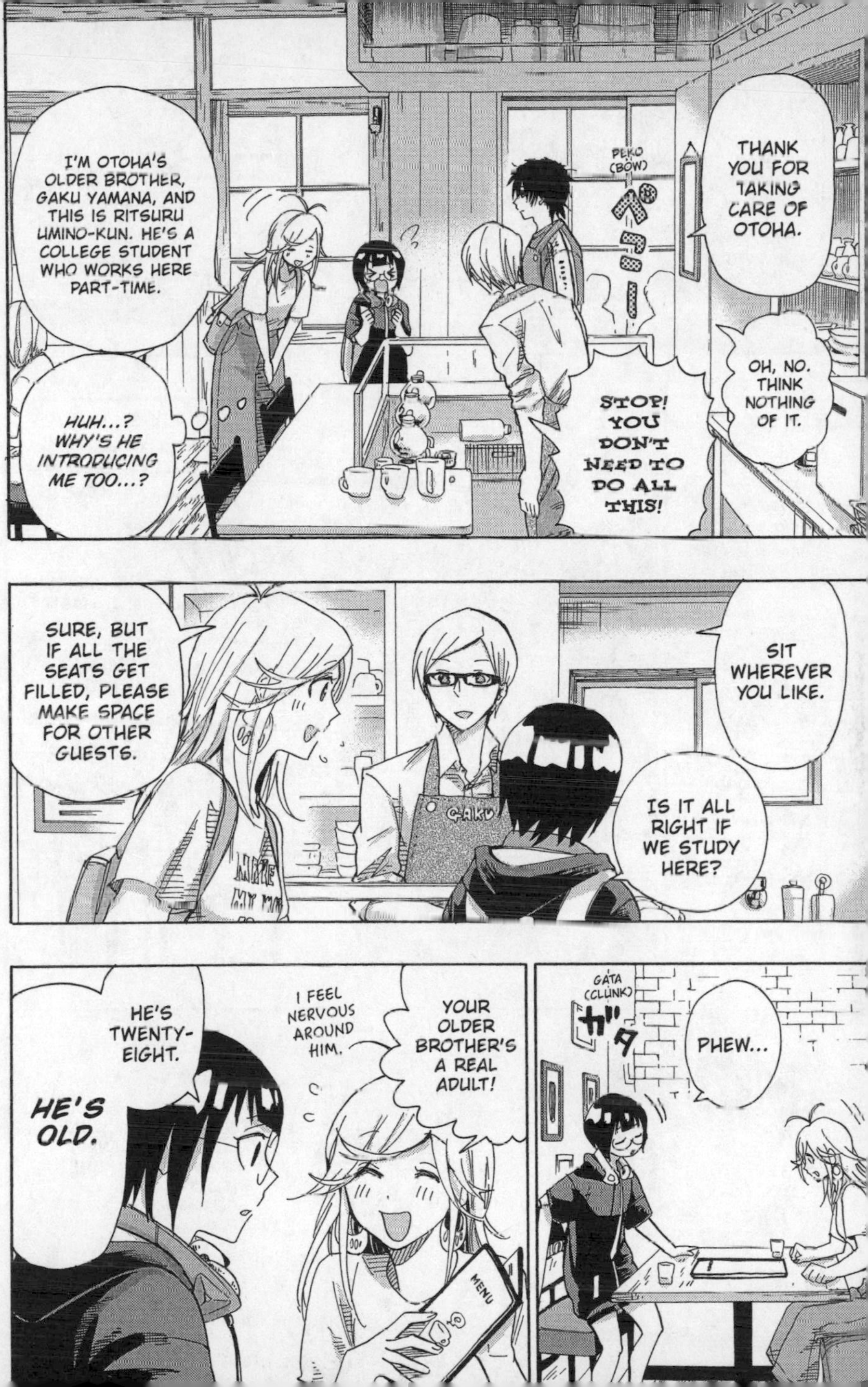
THANK YOU FOR TAKING CARE OF OTOHA.
PEKO (BOW)
OH, NO. THINK NOTHING OF IT.
STOP! YOU DON'T NEED TO DO ALL THIS!
I'M OTOHA'S OLDER BROTHER, GAKU YAMANA, AND THIS IS RITSURU UMINO-KUN. HE'S A COLLEGE STUDENT WHO WORKS HERE PART-TIME.
HUH...? WHY'S HE INTRODUCING ME TOO...?
SIT WHEREVER YOU LIKE.
IS IT ALL RIGHT IF WE STUDY HERE?
GAKU
SURE, BUT IF ALL THE SEATS GET FILLED, PLEASE MAKE SPACE FOR OTHER GUESTS.
GATA (CLUNK)
PHEW...
YOUR OLDER BROTHER'S A REAL ADULT!
I FEEL NERVOUS AROUND HIM.
MENU
HE'S TWENTY-EIGHT.
HE'S OLD.

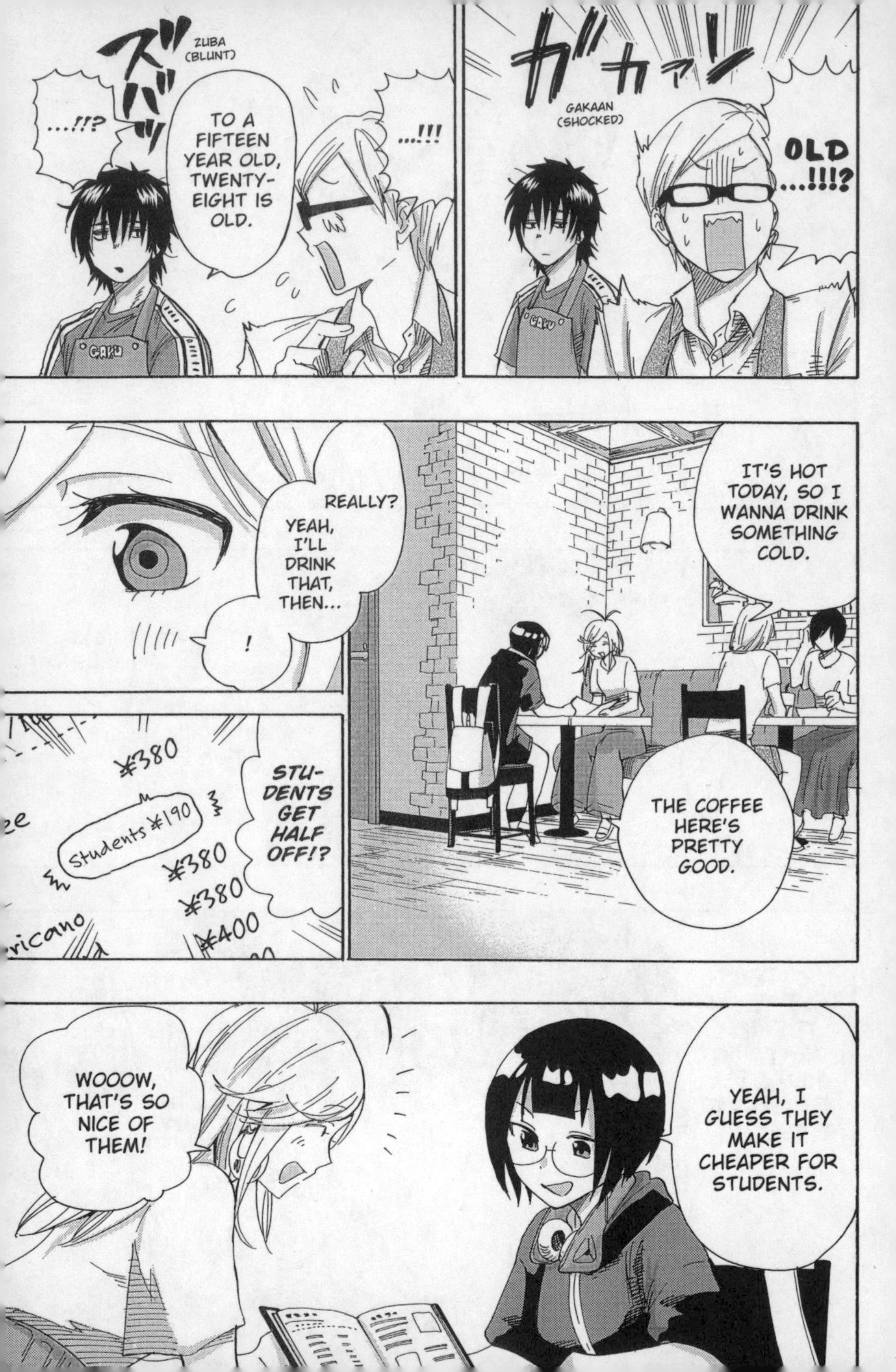
GAKAAN (SHOCKED)
OLD ...!!!?
ZUBA (BLUNT)
...!!!
TO A FIFTEEN YEAR OLD, TWENTY-EIGHT IS OLD.
...!!?
IT'S HOT TODAY, SO I WANNA DRINK SOMETHING COLD.
THE COFFEE HERE'S PRETTY GOOD.
REALLY?
YEAH, I'LL DRINK THAT, THEN...
!
STU-DENTS GET HALF OFF!?
¥380
Students ¥190
¥380
¥380
¥400
YEAH, I GUESS THEY MAKE IT CHEAPER FOR STUDENTS.
WOOOW, THAT'S SO NICE OF THEM!

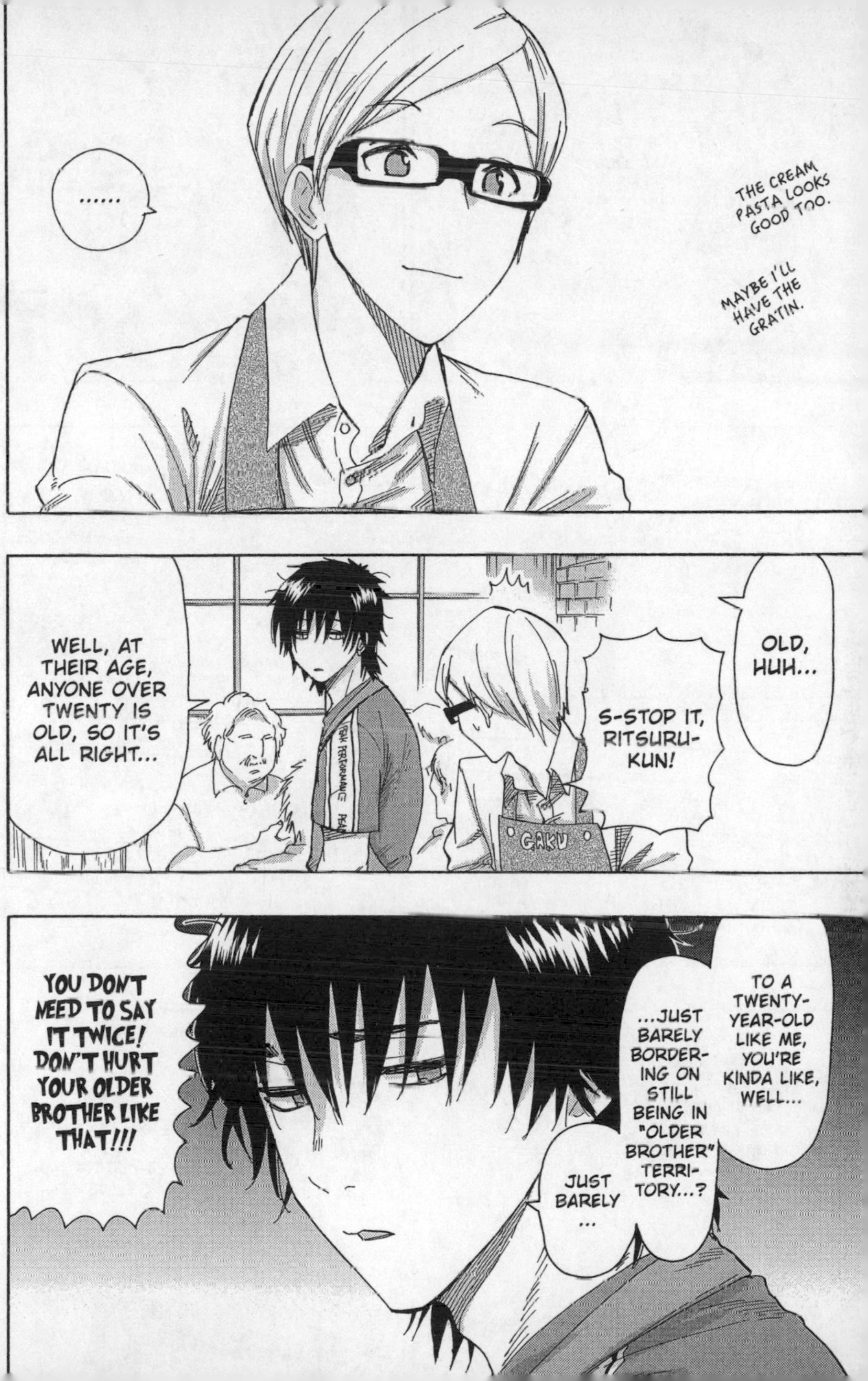
THE CREAM PASTA LOOKS GOOD TOO.
MAYBE I'LL HAVE THE GRATIN.
......
OLD, HUH...
S-STOP IT, RITSURU-KUN!
GAKU
WELL, AT THEIR AGE, ANYONE OVER TWENTY IS OLD, SO IT'S ALL RIGHT...
TO A TWENTY-YEAR-OLD LIKE ME, YOU'RE KINDA LIKE, WELL...
...JUST BARELY BORDERING ON STILL BEING IN "OLDER BROTHER" TERRITORY...?
JUST BARELY ...
YOU DON'T NEED TO SAY IT TWICE! DON'T HURT YOUR OLDER BROTHER LIKE THAT!!!

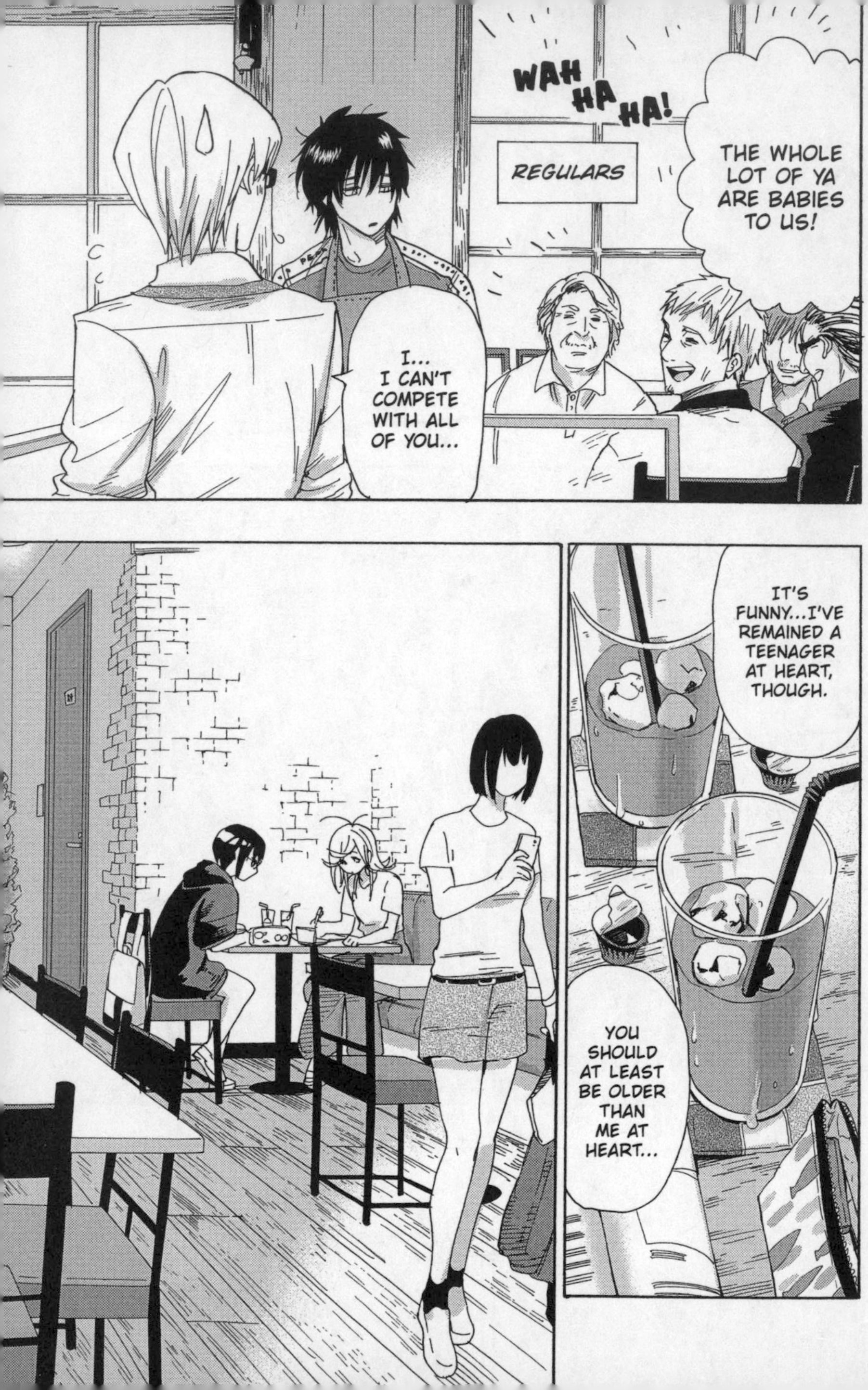
THE WHOLE LOT OF YA ARE BABIES TO US!
WAH HA HA!
REGULARS
I... I CAN'T COMPETE WITH ALL OF YOU...
IT'S FUNNY...I'VE REMAINED A TEENAGER AT HEART, THOUGH.
YOU SHOULD AT LEAST BE OLDER THAN ME AT HEART...

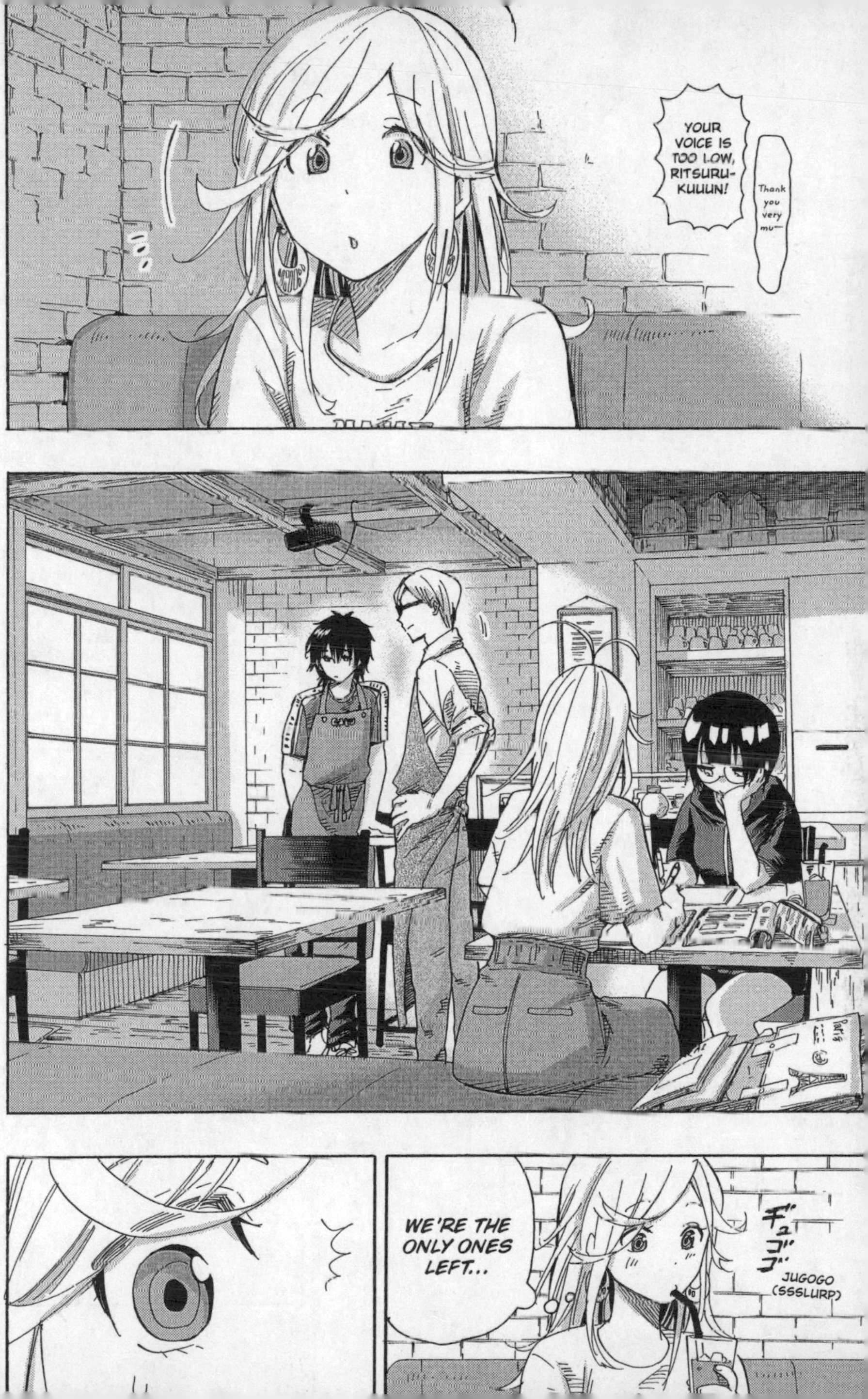

Thank you very mu—
YOUR VOICE IS TOO LOW, RITSURU-KUUUN!
ギュゴゴ
JUGOGO (SSSLURP)
WE'RE THE ONLY ONES LEFT...

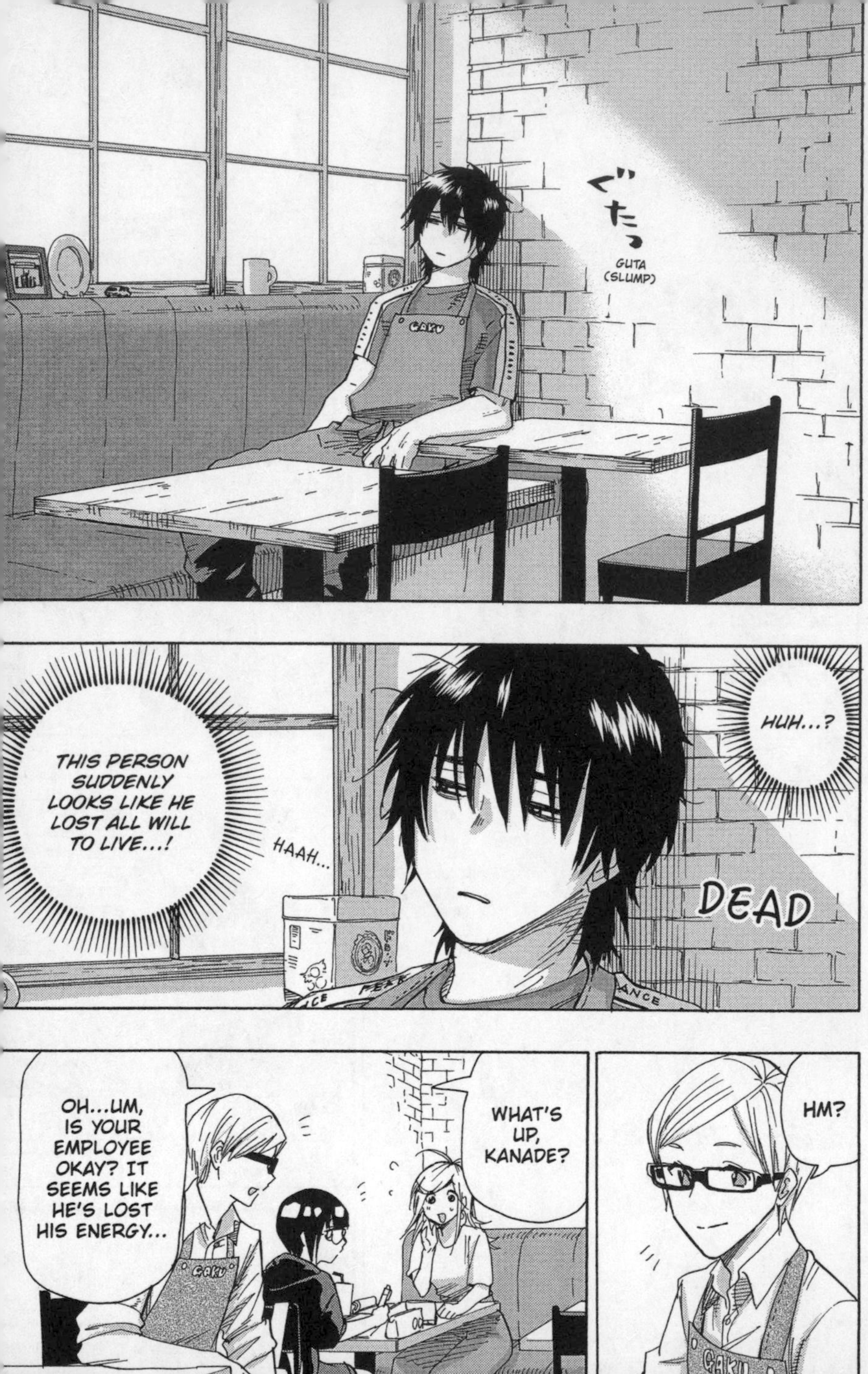
ぐたっ
GUTA (SLUMP)
HUH...?
THIS PERSON SUDDENLY LOOKS LIKE HE LOST ALL WILL TO LIVE...!
HAAH...
DEAD
HM?
WHAT'S UP, KANADE?
OH...UM, IS YOUR EMPLOYEE OKAY? IT SEEMS LIKE HE'S LOST HIS ENERGY...

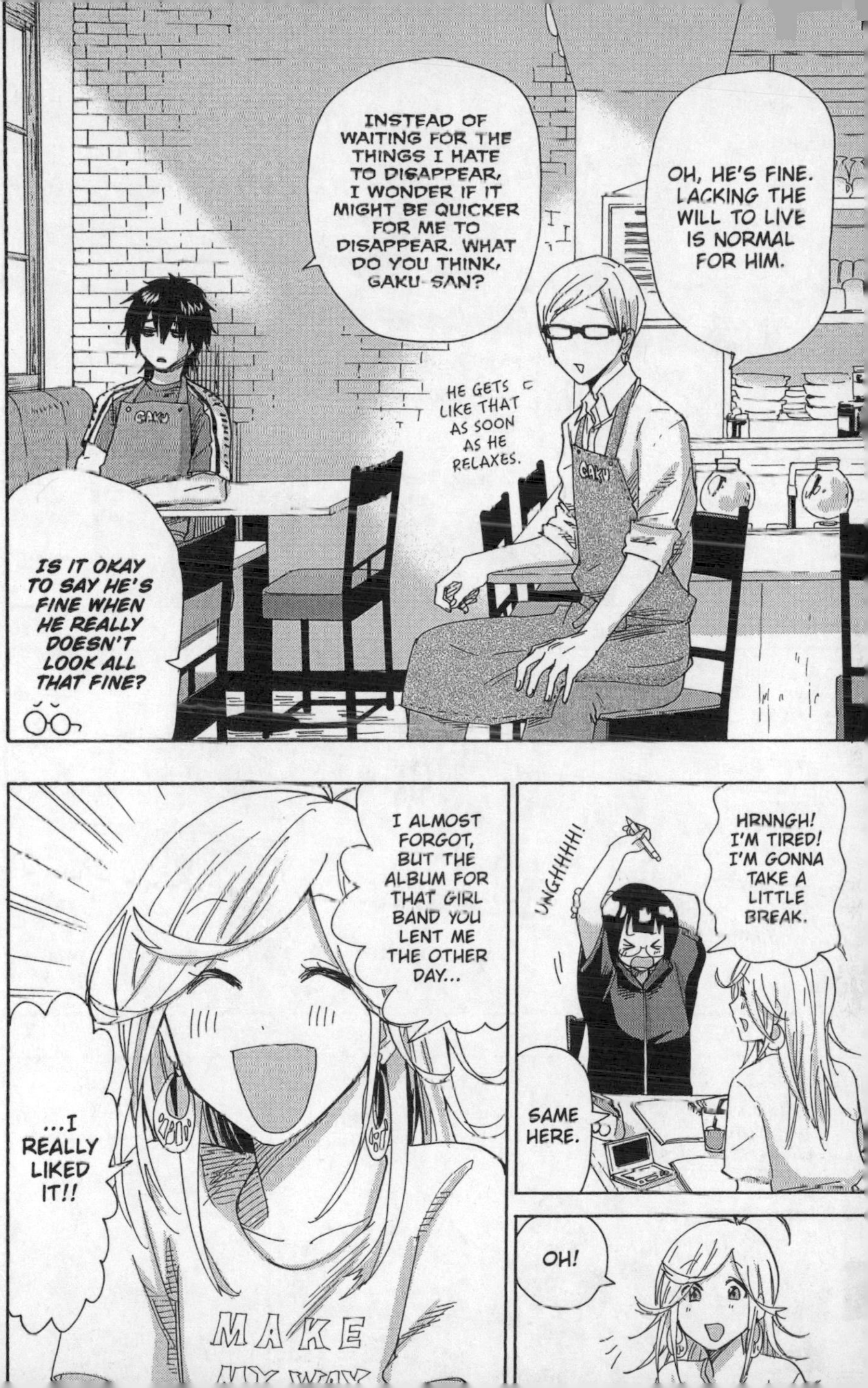
OH, HE'S FINE. LACKING THE WILL TO LIVE IS NORMAL FOR HIM.
INSTEAD OF WAITING FOR THE THINGS I HATE TO DISAPPEAR, I WONDER IF IT MIGHT BE QUICKER FOR ME TO DISAPPEAR. WHAT DO YOU THINK, GAKU-SAN?
HE GETS LIKE THAT AS SOON AS HE RELAXES.
GAKU
GAKU
IS IT OKAY TO SAY HE'S FINE WHEN HE REALLY DOESN'T LOOK ALL THAT FINE?
HRNNGH! I'M TIRED! I'M GONNA TAKE A LITTLE BREAK.
UNGHHHH!
SAME HERE.
OH!
I ALMOST FORGOT, BUT THE ALBUM FOR THAT GIRL BAND YOU LENT ME THE OTHER DAY...
...I REALLY LIKED IT!!
MAKE

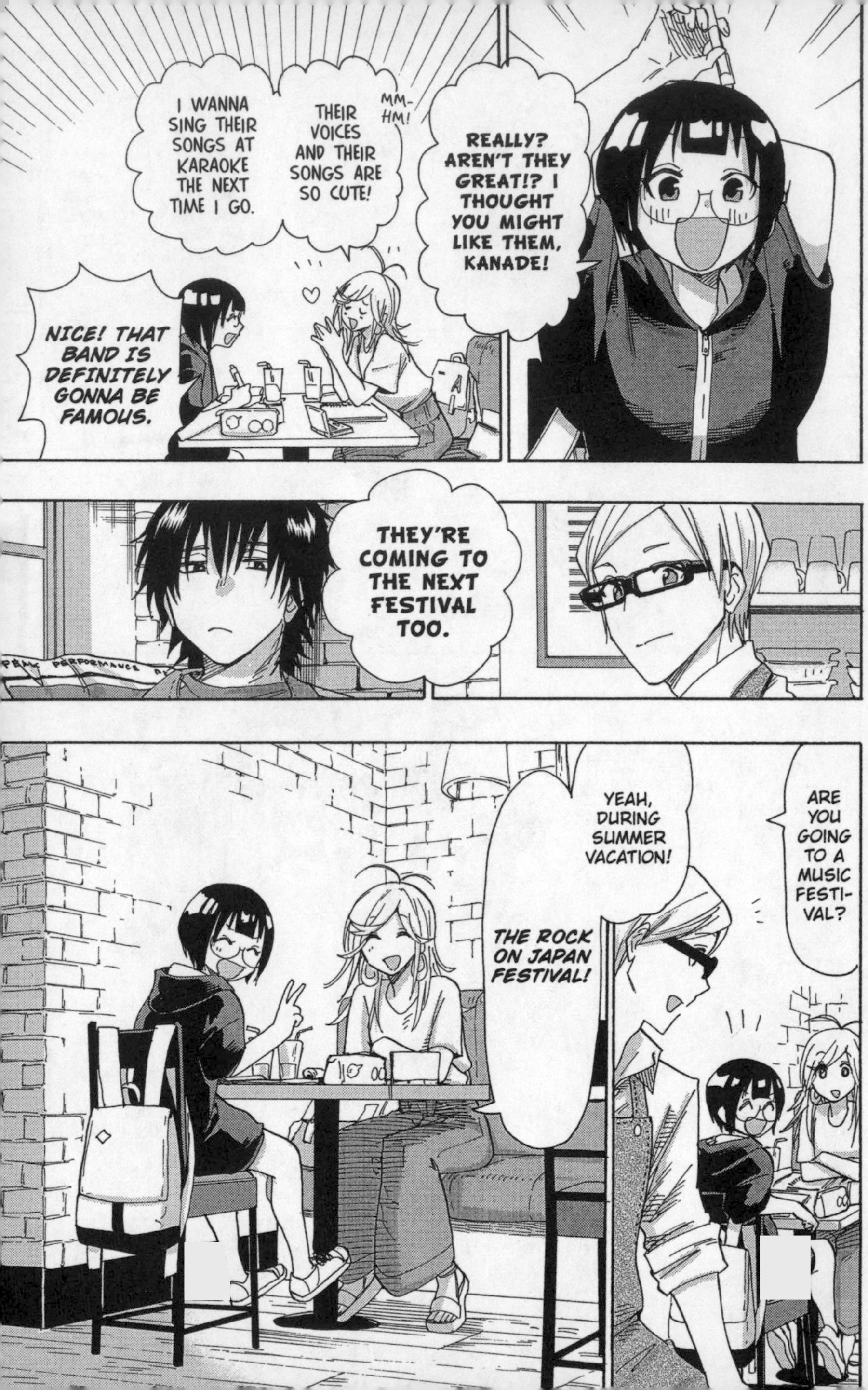
REALLY? AREN'T THEY GREAT!? I THOUGHT YOU MIGHT LIKE THEM, KANADE!
MM-HM!
THEIR VOICES AND THEIR SONGS ARE SO CUTE!
I WANNA SING THEIR SONGS AT KARAOKE THE NEXT TIME I GO.
NICE! THAT BAND IS DEFINITELY GONNA BE FAMOUS.
THEY'RE COMING TO THE NEXT FESTIVAL TOO.
PEAK PERFORMANCE
ARE YOU GOING TO A MUSIC FESTI-VAL?
YEAH, DURING SUMMER VACATION!
THE ROCK ON JAPAN FESTIVAL!

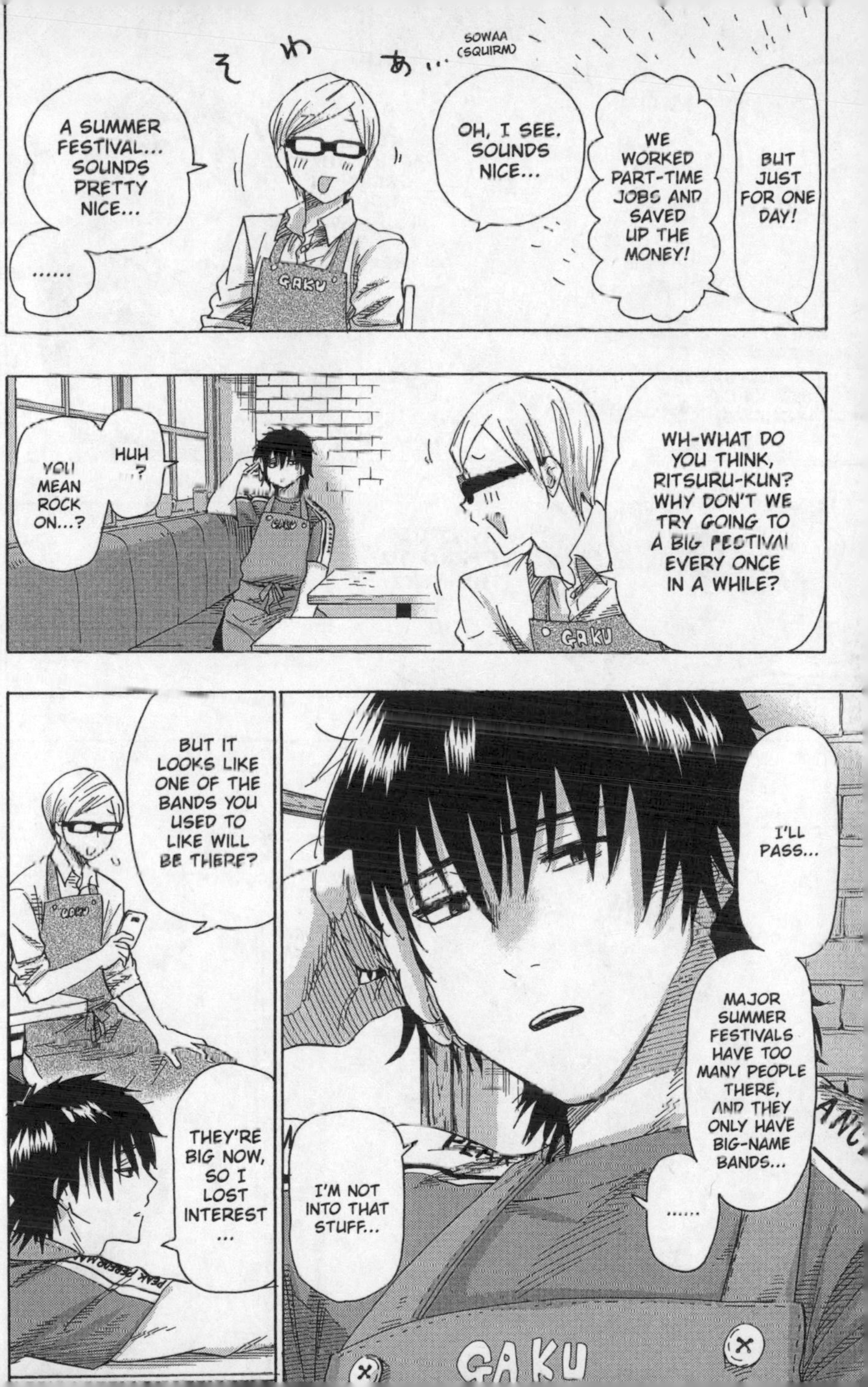
BUT JUST FOR ONE DAY!
WE WORKED PART-TIME JOBS AND SAVED UP THE MONEY!
OH, I SEE. SOUNDS NICE...
そわぁ...
SOWAA (SQUIRM)
A SUMMER FESTIVAL... SOUNDS PRETTY NICE...
......
WH-WHAT DO YOU THINK, RITSURU-KUN? WHY DON'T WE TRY GOING TO A BIG FESTIVAL EVERY ONCE IN A WHILE?
HUH?
YOU MEAN ROCK ON...?
I'LL PASS...
MAJOR SUMMER FESTIVALS HAVE TOO MANY PEOPLE THERE, AND THEY ONLY HAVE BIG-NAME BANDS...
......
I'M NOT INTO THAT STUFF...
GAKU
BUT IT LOOKS LIKE ONE OF THE BANDS YOU USED TO LIKE WILL BE THERE?
THEY'RE BIG NOW, SO I LOST INTEREST...

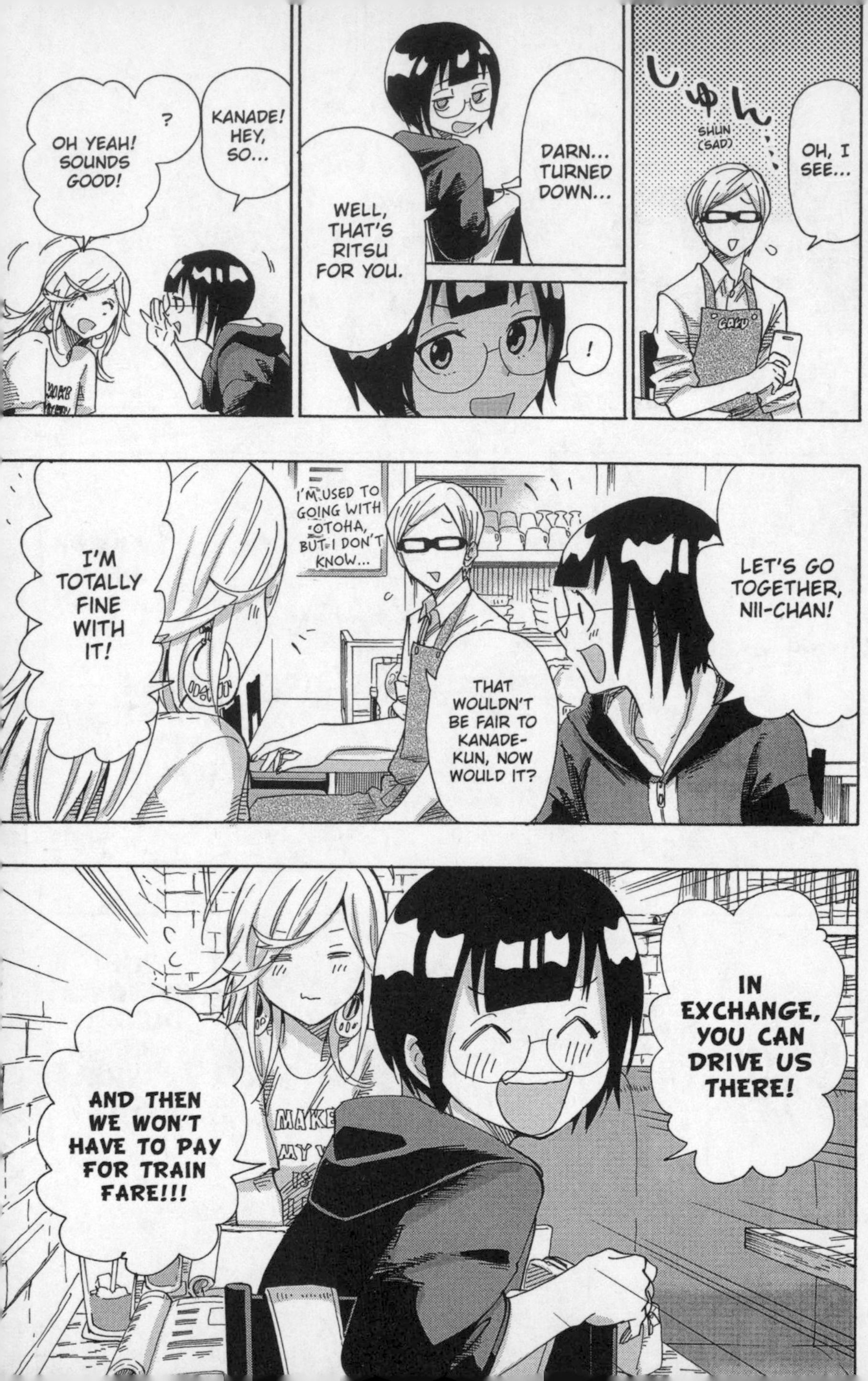

しゅん
SHUN (SAD)
OH, I SEE...
DARN... TURNED DOWN...
WELL, THAT'S RITSU FOR YOU.
!
KANADE! HEY, SO...
?
OH YEAH! SOUNDS GOOD!
LET'S GO TOGETHER, NII-CHAN!
THAT WOULDN'T BE FAIR TO KANADE-KUN, NOW WOULD IT?
I'M USED TO GOING WITH OTOHA, BUT I DON'T KNOW...
I'M TOTALLY FINE WITH IT!
IN EXCHANGE, YOU CAN DRIVE US THERE!
AND THEN WE WON'T HAVE TO PAY FOR TRAIN FARE!!!

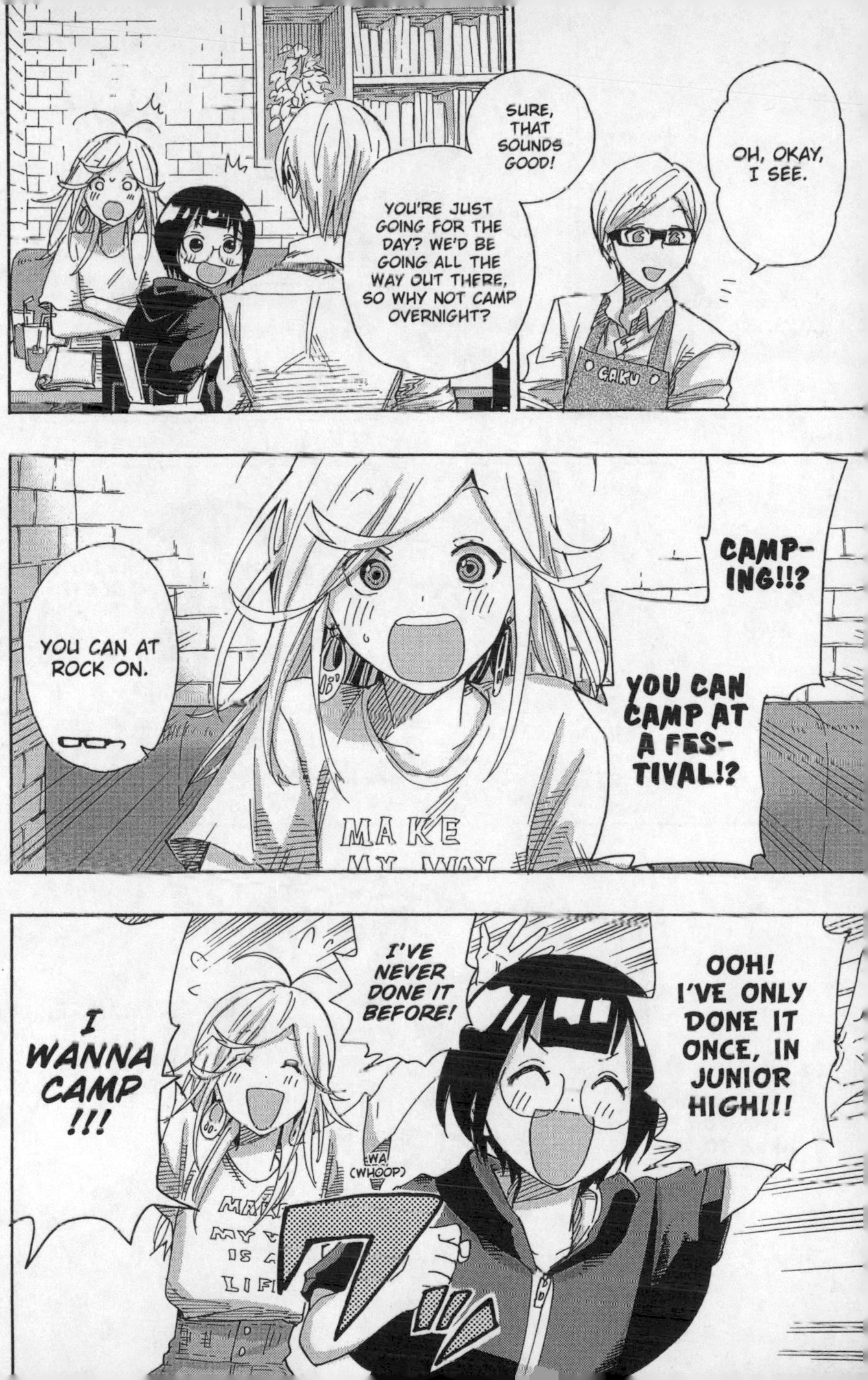
OH, OKAY, I SEE.
SURE, THAT SOUNDS GOOD!
YOU'RE JUST GOING FOR THE DAY? WE'D BE GOING ALL THE WAY OUT THERE, SO WHY NOT CAMP OVERNIGHT?
GAKU
CAMPING!!?
YOU CAN CAMP AT A FESTIVAL!?
YOU CAN AT ROCK ON.
OOH! I'VE ONLY DONE IT ONCE, IN JUNIOR HIGH!!!
I'VE NEVER DONE IT BEFORE!
WA (WHOOP)
I WANNA CAMP!!!

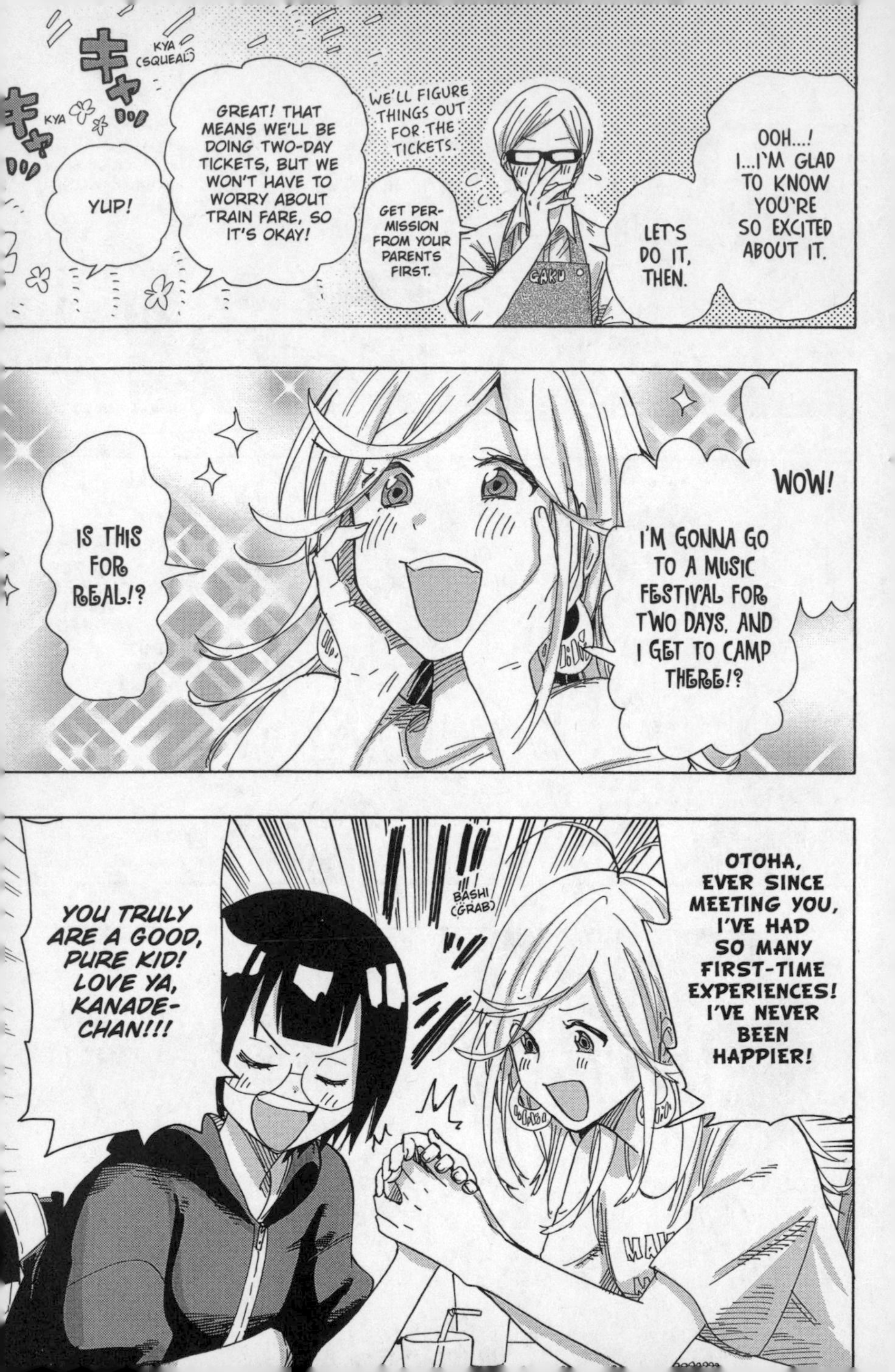
OOH...! I...I'M GLAD TO KNOW YOU'RE SO EXCITED ABOUT IT.
LET'S DO IT, THEN.
WE'LL FIGURE THINGS OUT FOR THE TICKETS.
GET PERMISSION FROM YOUR PARENTS FIRST.
GAKU
KYA (SQUEAL)
GREAT! THAT MEANS WE'LL BE DOING TWO-DAY TICKETS, BUT WE WON'T HAVE TO WORRY ABOUT TRAIN FARE, SO IT'S OKAY!
KYA
YUP!
WOW!
I'M GONNA GO TO A MUSIC FESTIVAL FOR TWO DAYS, AND I GET TO CAMP THERE!?
IS THIS FOR REAL!?
OTOHA, EVER SINCE MEETING YOU, I'VE HAD SO MANY FIRST-TIME EXPERIENCES! I'VE NEVER BEEN HAPPIER!
BASHI (GRAB)
YOU TRULY ARE A GOOD, PURE KID! LOVE YA, KANADE-CHAN!!!

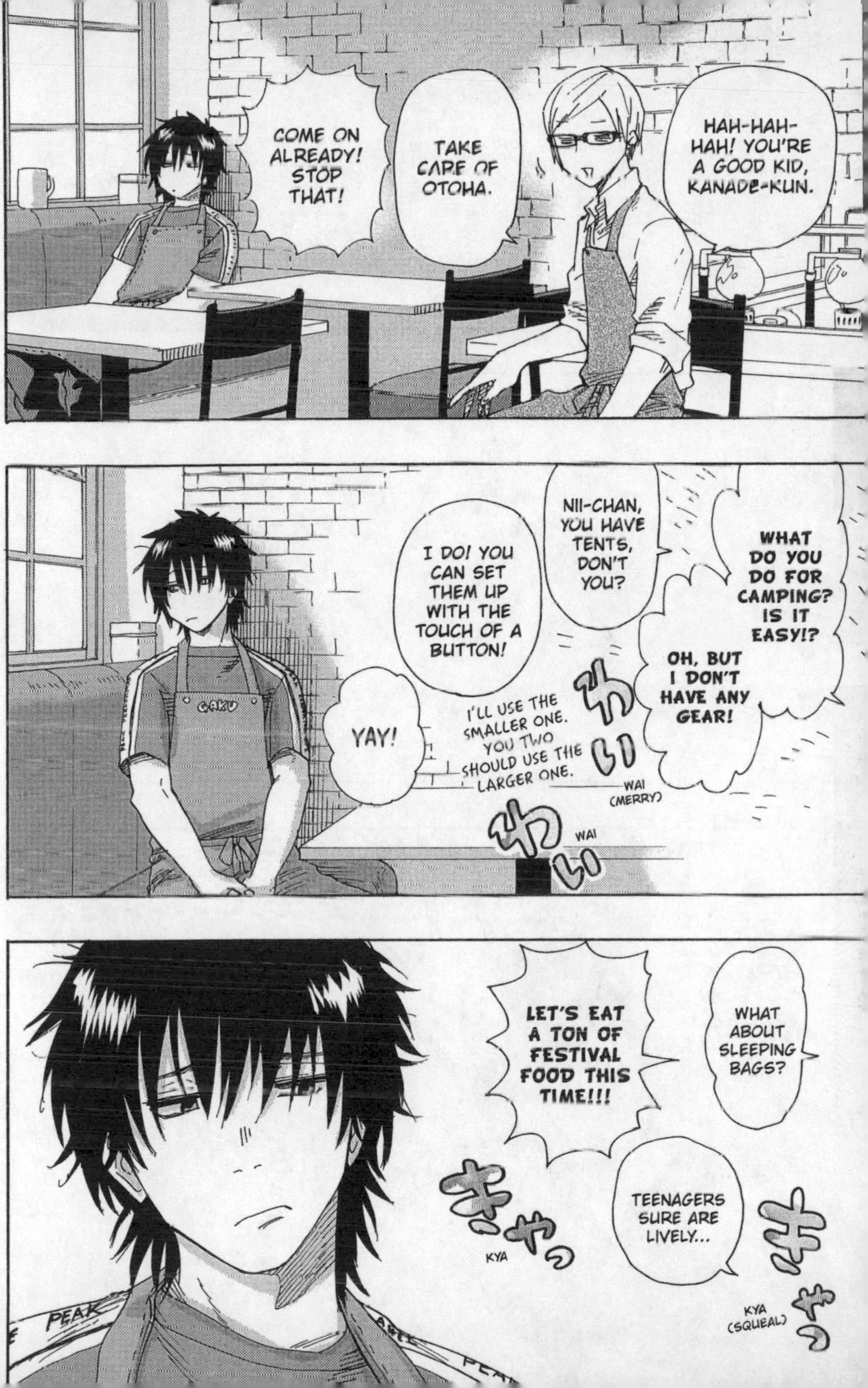
HAH-HAH-HAH! YOU'RE A GOOD KID, KANADE-KUN.
TAKE CARE OF OTOHA.
COME ON ALREADY! STOP THAT!
WHAT DO YOU DO FOR CAMPING? IS IT EASY!?
OH, BUT I DON'T HAVE ANY GEAR!
NII-CHAN, YOU HAVE TENTS, DON'T YOU?
I DO! YOU CAN SET THEM UP WITH THE TOUCH OF A BUTTON!
I'LL USE THE SMALLER ONE. YOU TWO SHOULD USE THE LARGER ONE.
WAI (MERRY)
GAKU
YAY!
WAI
WHAT ABOUT SLEEPING BAGS?
LET'S EAT A TON OF FESTIVAL FOOD THIS TIME!!!
KYA (SQUEAL)
TEENAGERS SURE ARE LIVELY...
KYA
PEAK

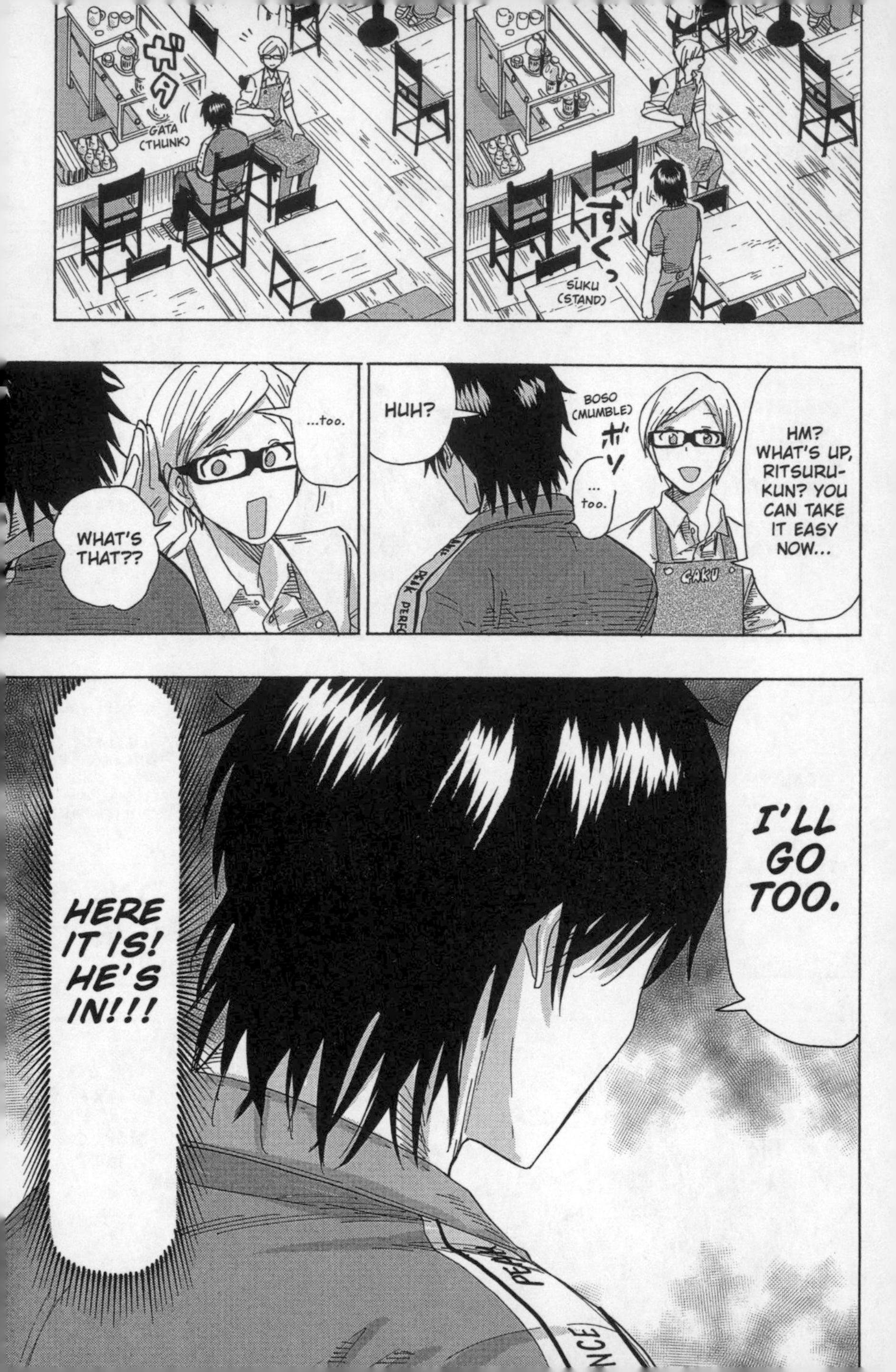
すくっ
SUKU (STAND)
ガタ
GATA (THUNK)
HM? WHAT'S UP, RITSURU-KUN? YOU CAN TAKE IT EASY NOW...
BOSO (MUMBLE)
ボソ
... too.
HUH?
...too.
WHAT'S THAT??
I'LL GO TOO.
HERE IT IS! HE'S IN!!!

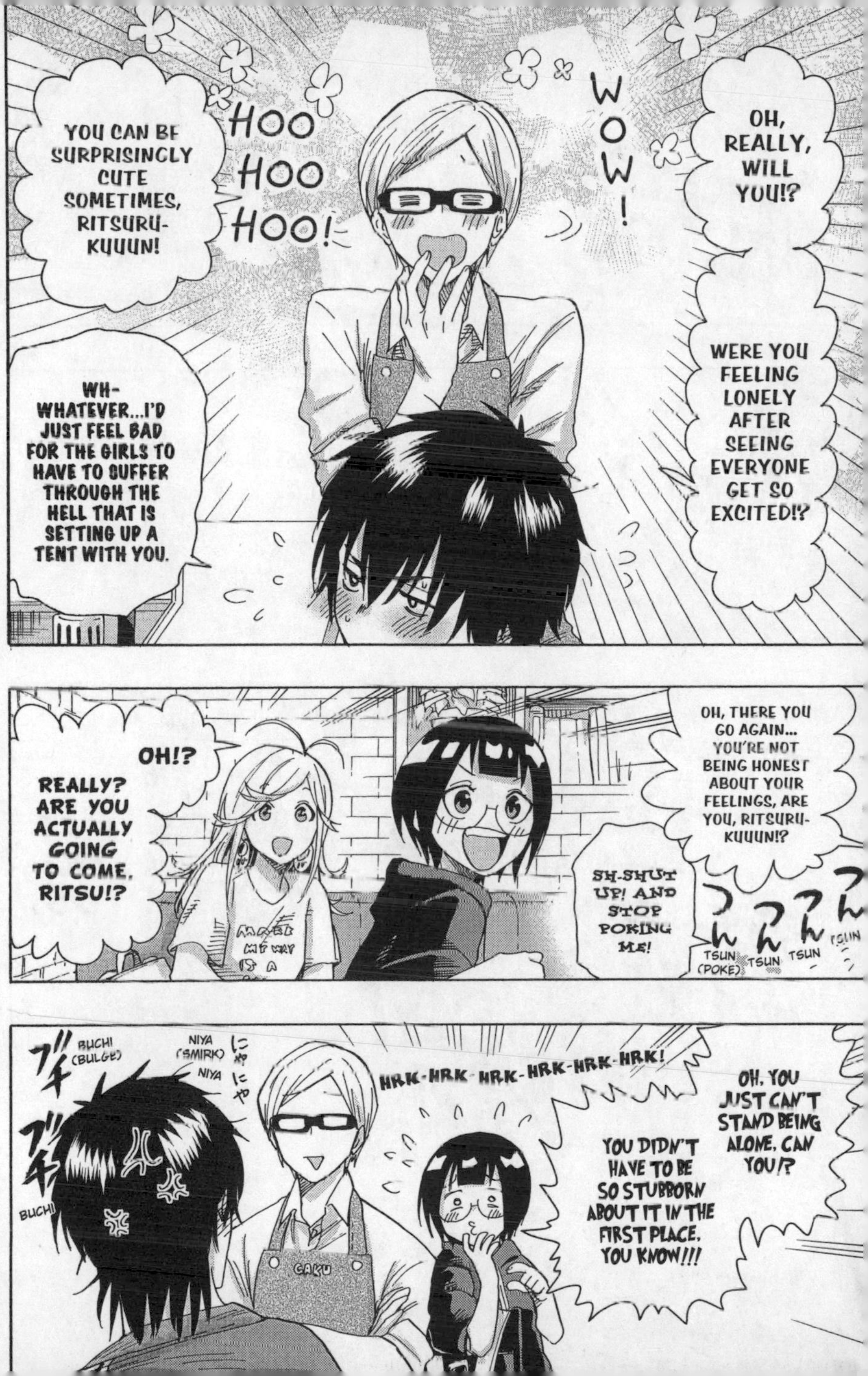
OH, REALLY, WILL YOU!?
WOW!
HOO HOO HOO!
YOU CAN BE SURPRISINGLY CUTE SOMETIMES, RITSURU-KUUUN!
WERE YOU FEELING LONELY AFTER SEEING EVERYONE GET SO EXCITED!?
WH-WHATEVER...I'D JUST FEEL BAD FOR THE GIRLS TO HAVE TO SUFFER THROUGH THE HELL THAT IS SETTING UP A TENT WITH YOU.
OH, THERE YOU GO AGAIN... YOU'RE NOT BEING HONEST ABOUT YOUR FEELINGS, ARE YOU, RITSURU-KUUUN!?
TSUN (POKE) TSUN TSUN TSUN
SH-SHUT UP! AND STOP POKING ME!
OH!?
REALLY? ARE YOU ACTUALLY GOING TO COME, RITSU!?
OH, YOU JUST CAN'T STAND BEING ALONE, CAN YOU!?
HRK-HRK-HRK-HRK-HRK-HRK!
YOU DIDN'T HAVE TO BE SO STUBBORN ABOUT IT IN THE FIRST PLACE, YOU KNOW!!!
GAKU
NIYA (SMIRK) NIYA
BUCHI (BULGE) BUCHI

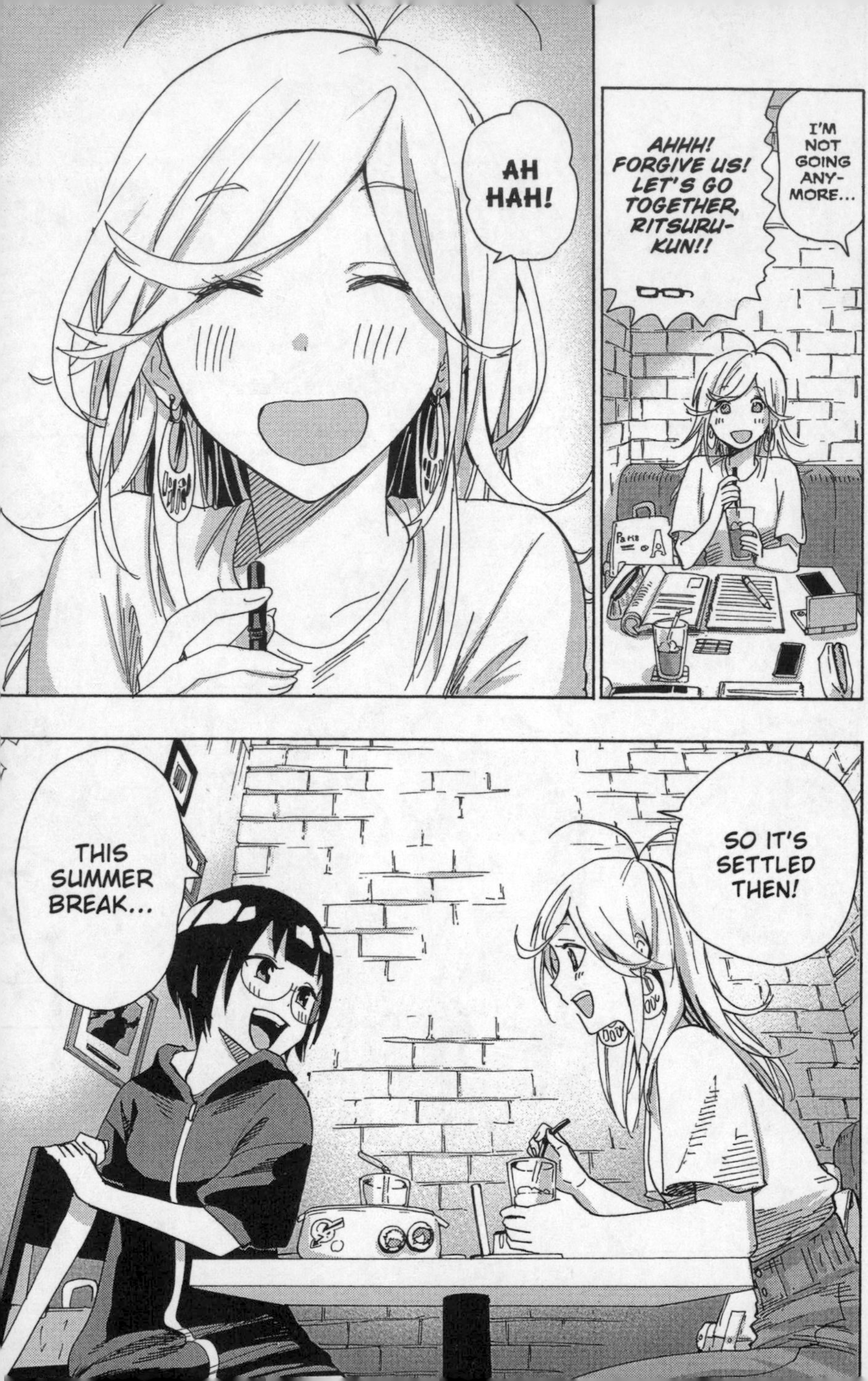
I'M NOT GOING ANY-MORE...
AHHH! FORGIVE US! LET'S GO TOGETHER, RITSURU-KUN!!
AH HAH!
SO IT'S SETTLED THEN!
THIS SUMMER BREAK...

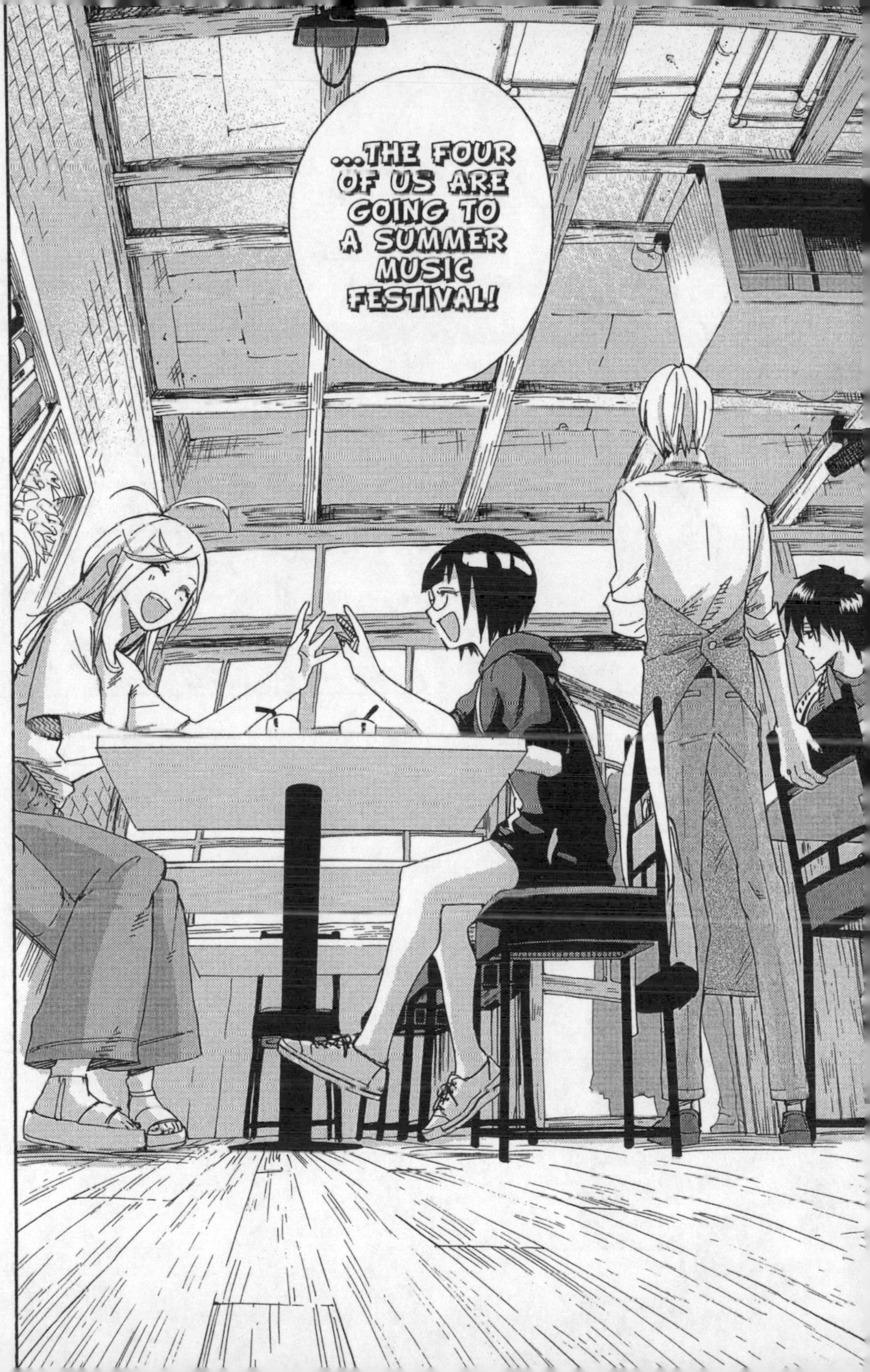
...THE FOUR OF US ARE GOING TO A SUMMER MUSIC FESTIVAL!

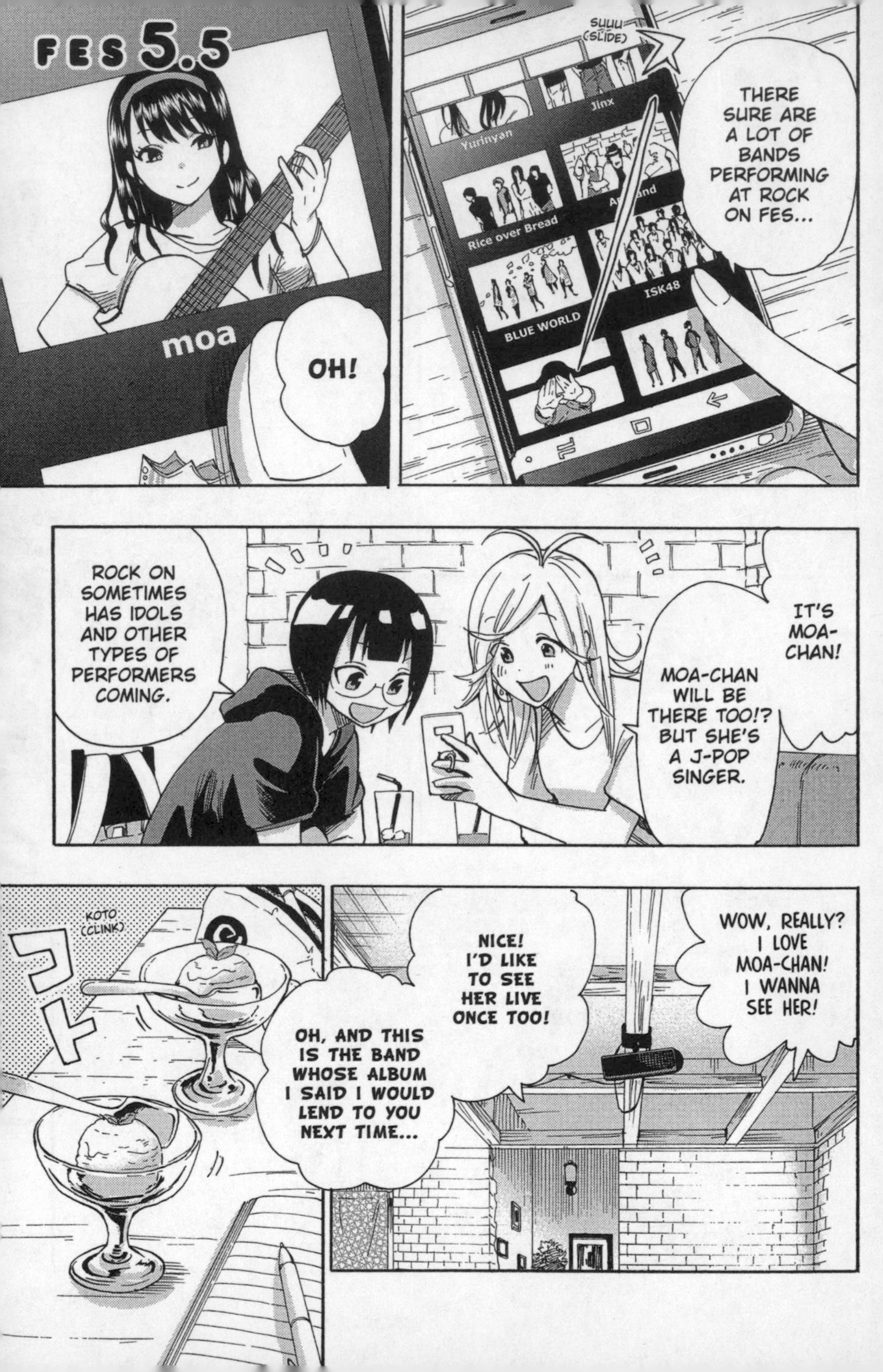
FES 5.5
SUUU (SLIDE)
THERE SURE ARE A LOT OF BANDS PERFORMING AT ROCK ON FES...
Yurinyan
Jinx
Rice over Bread
ISK48
BLUE WORLD
moa
OH!
IT'S MOA-CHAN!
MOA-CHAN WILL BE THERE TOO!? BUT SHE'S A J-POP SINGER.
ROCK ON SOMETIMES HAS IDOLS AND OTHER TYPES OF PERFORMERS COMING.
WOW, REALLY? I LOVE MOA-CHAN! I WANNA SEE HER!
NICE! I'D LIKE TO SEE HER LIVE ONCE TOO!
OH, AND THIS IS THE BAND WHOSE ALBUM I SAID I WOULD LEND TO YOU NEXT TIME...
KOTO (CLINK)

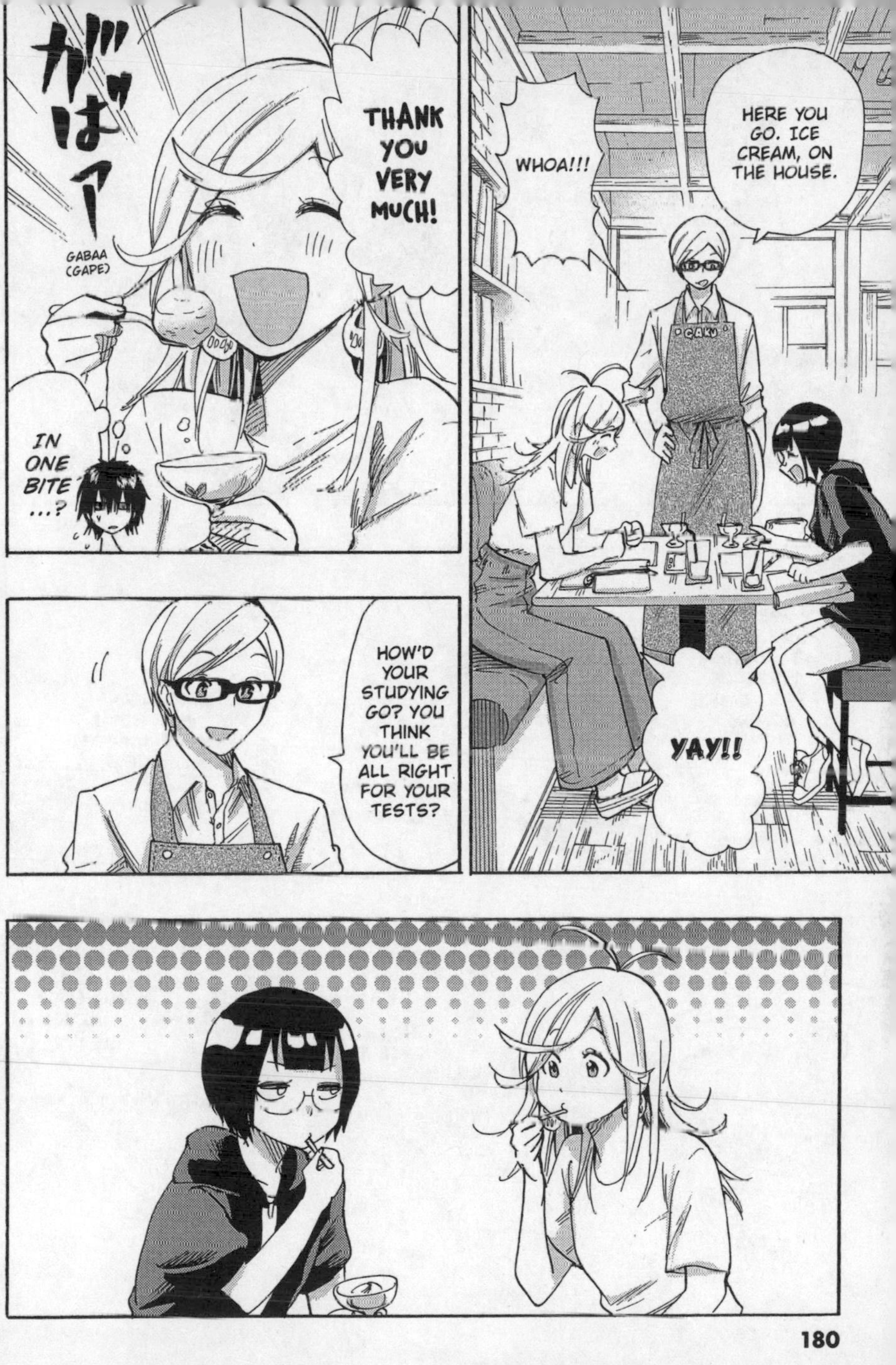
HERE YOU GO. ICE CREAM, ON THE HOUSE.
WHOA!!!
YAY!!
THANK YOU VERY MUCH!
がばァ
GABAA (GAPE)
IN ONE BITE ...?
HOW'D YOUR STUDYING GO? YOU THINK YOU'LL BE ALL RIGHT FOR YOUR TESTS?

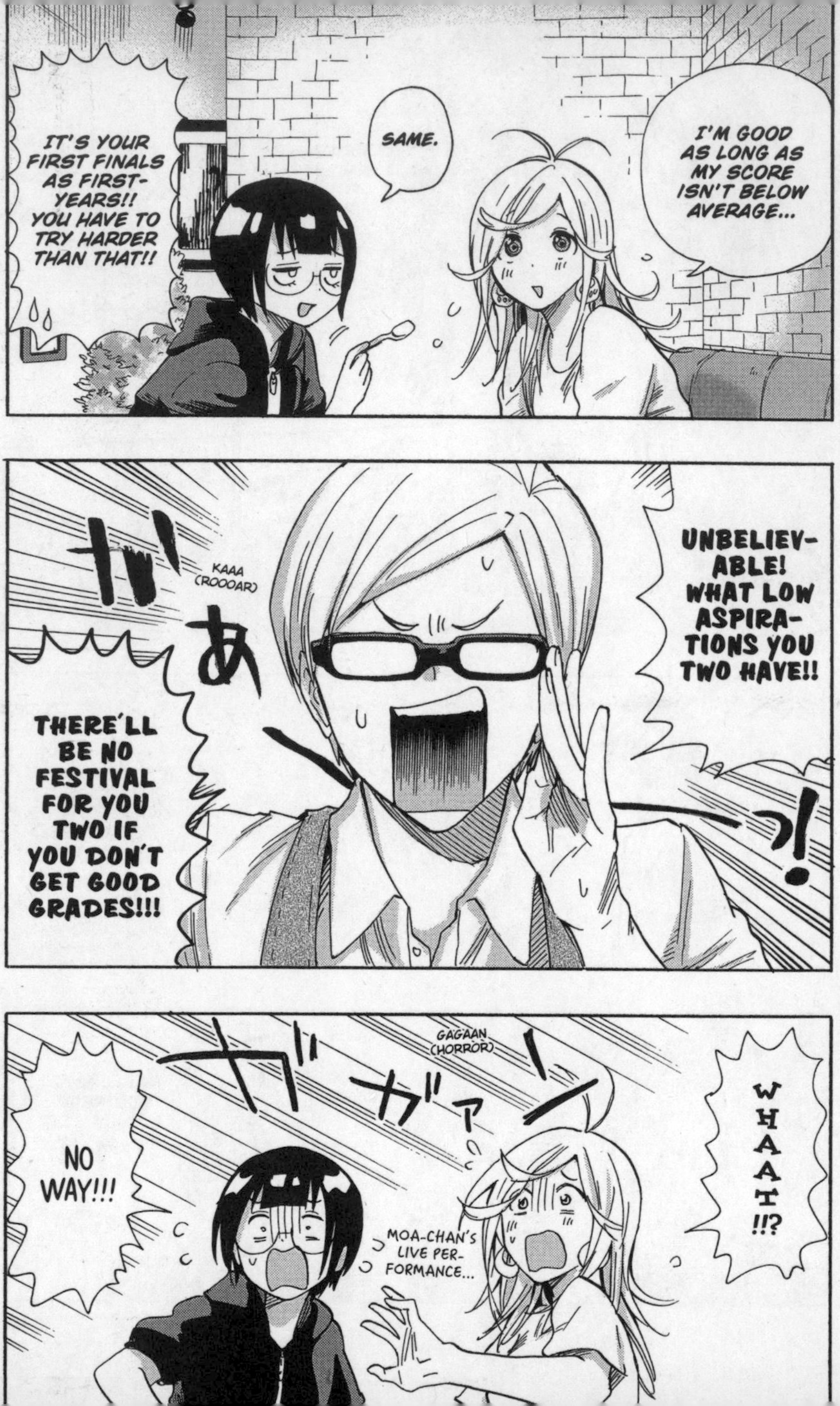
I'M GOOD AS LONG AS MY SCORE ISN'T BELOW AVERAGE...
SAME.
IT'S YOUR FIRST FINALS AS FIRST-YEARS!! YOU HAVE TO TRY HARDER THAN THAT!!
UNBELIEV-ABLE! WHAT LOW ASPIRA-TIONS YOU TWO HAVE!!
がぁーっ!
KAAA (ROOOAR)
THERE'LL BE NO FESTIVAL FOR YOU TWO IF YOU DON'T GET GOOD GRADES!!!
WHAAAT!!?
ガガァーン
GAGAAN (HORROR)
MOA-CHAN'S LIVE PER-FORMANCE...
NO WAY!!!

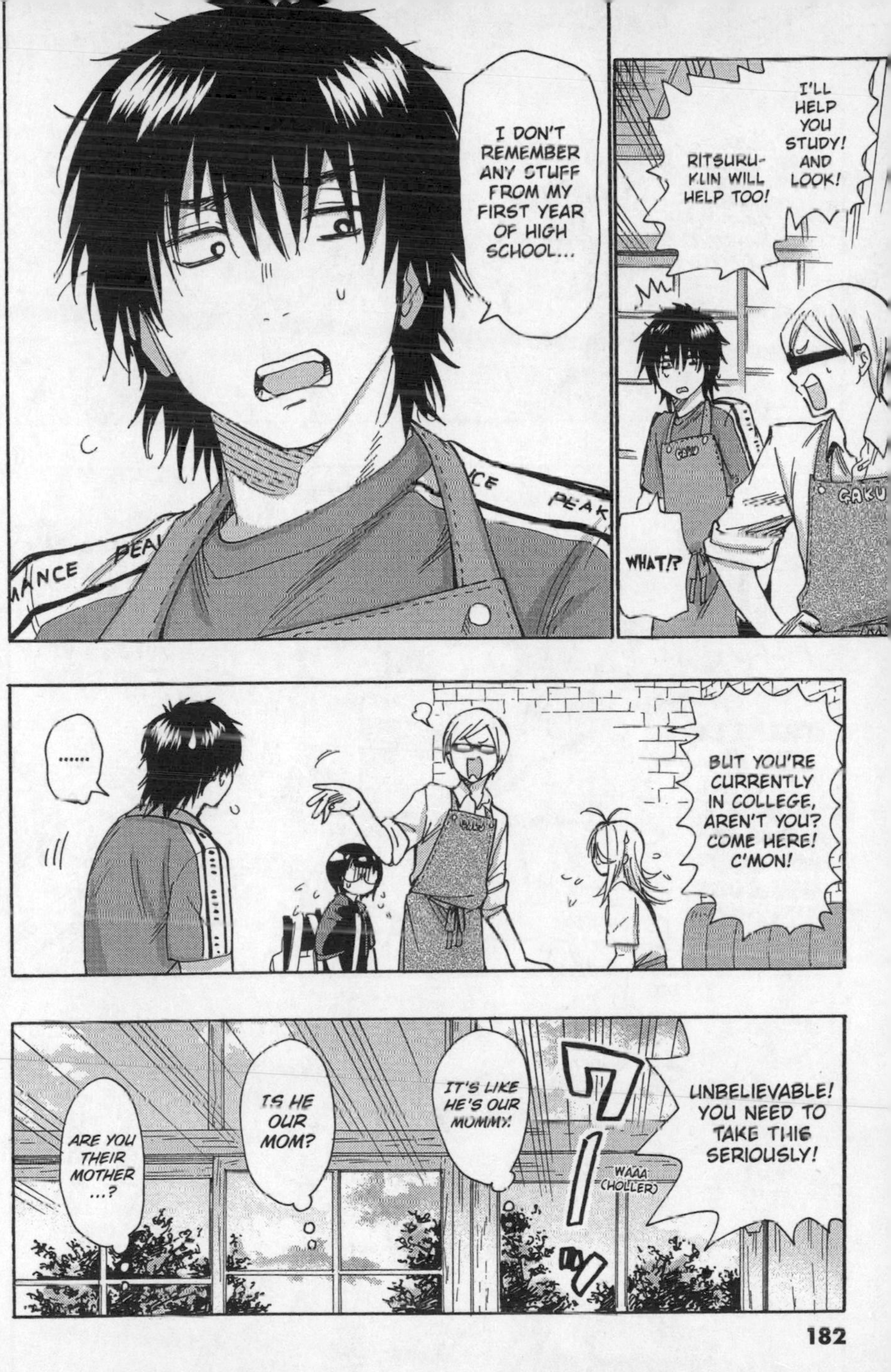
I'LL HELP YOU STUDY! AND LOOK!
RITSURU-KUN WILL HELP TOO!
WHAT!?
I DON'T REMEMBER ANY STUFF FROM MY FIRST YEAR OF HIGH SCHOOL...
BUT YOU'RE CURRENTLY IN COLLEGE, AREN'T YOU? COME HERE! C'MON!
......
UNBELIEVABLE! YOU NEED TO TAKE THIS SERIOUSLY!
WAAA (HOLLER)
IT'S LIKE HE'S OUR MOMMY.
IS HE OUR MOM?
ARE YOU THEIR MOTHER ...?
PEAK
GAKU

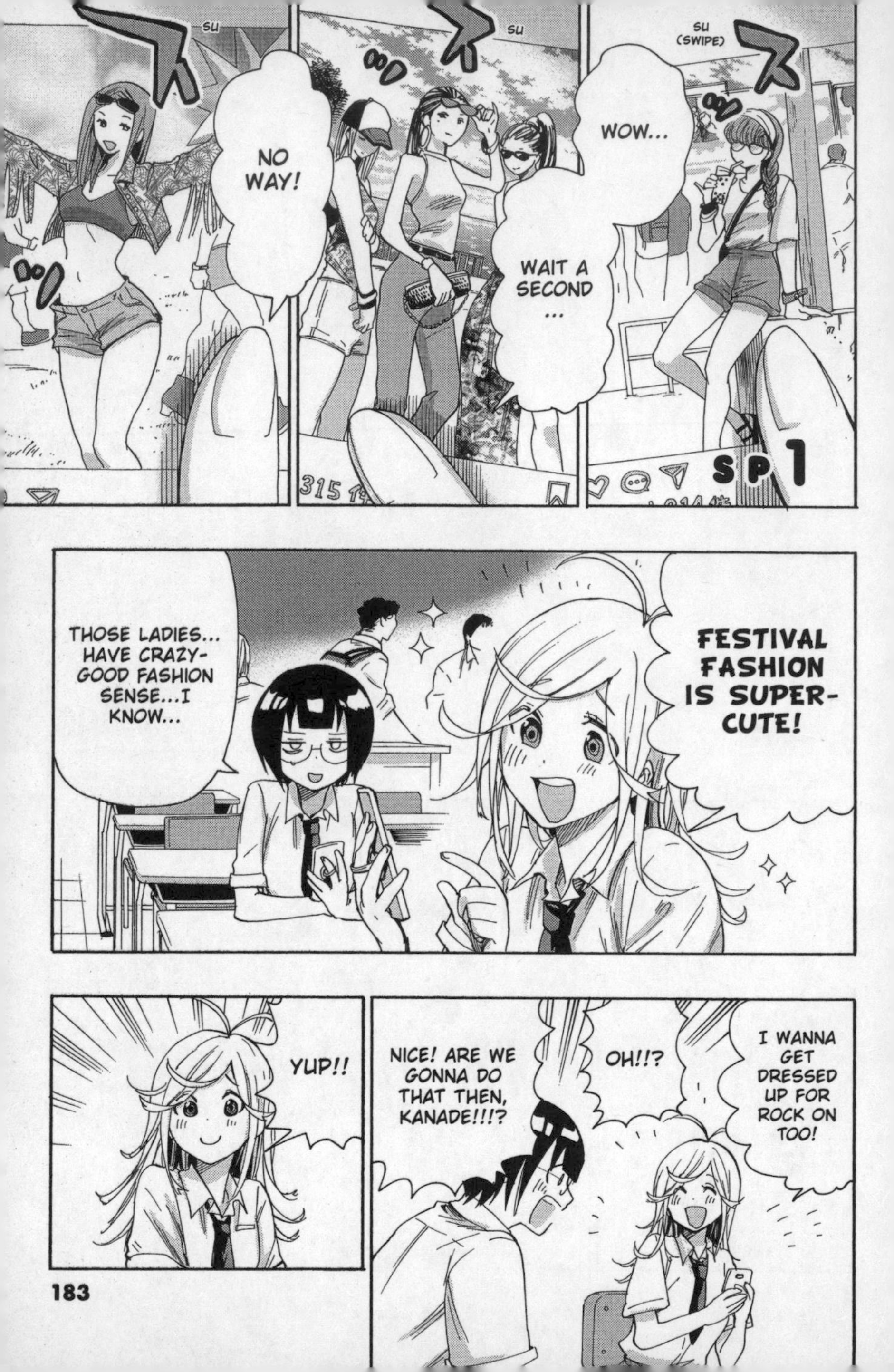

SU (SWIPE)
WOW...
WAIT A SECOND ...
SU
NO WAY!
SU
FESTIVAL FASHION IS SUPER-CUTE!
THOSE LADIES... HAVE CRAZY-GOOD FASHION SENSE...I KNOW...
I WANNA GET DRESSED UP FOR ROCK ON TOO!
OH!!?
NICE! ARE WE GONNA DO THAT THEN, KANADE!!!?
YUP!!

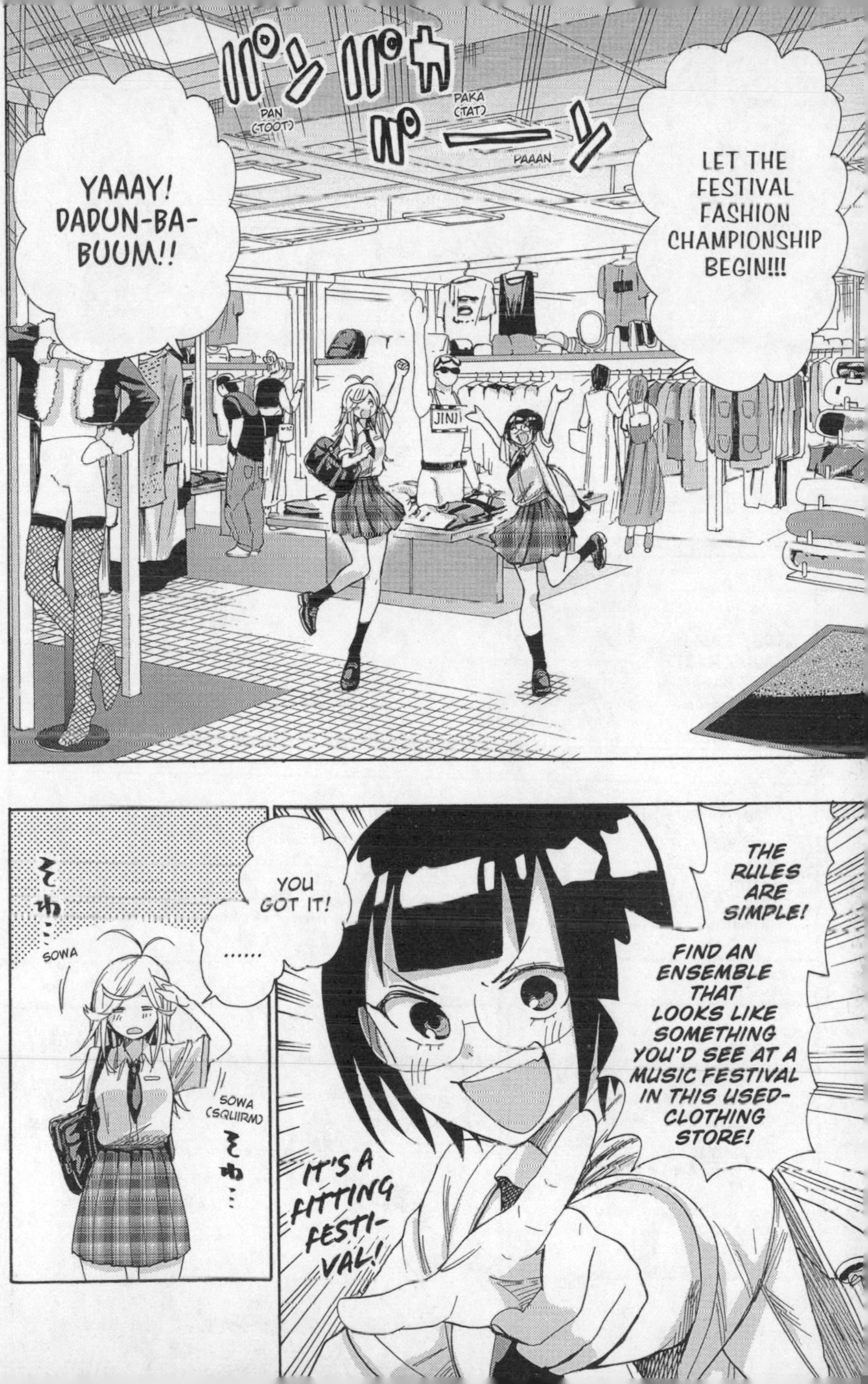
LET THE FESTIVAL FASHION CHAMPIONSHIP BEGIN!!!
PAN (TOOT)
PAKA (TAT)
PAAAN
YAAAY! DADUN-BA-BUUM!!
JINJ
THE RULES ARE SIMPLE!
FIND AN ENSEMBLE THAT LOOKS LIKE SOMETHING YOU'D SEE AT A MUSIC FESTIVAL IN THIS USED-CLOTHING STORE!
IT'S A FITTING FESTI-VAL!
YOU GOT IT!
......
SOWA
SOWA (SQUIRM)

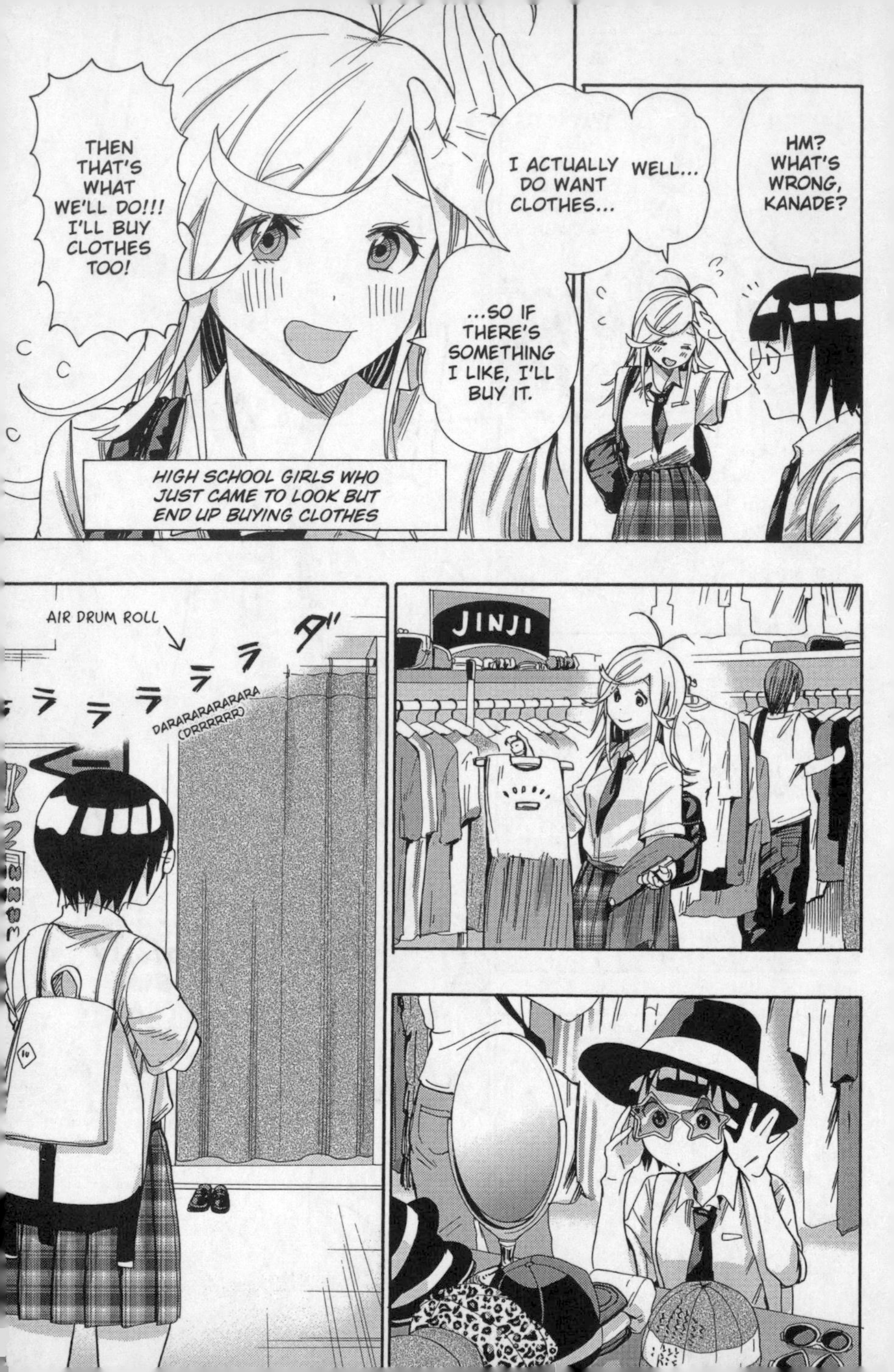
HM? WHAT'S WRONG, KANADE?
WELL...
I ACTUALLY DO WANT CLOTHES...
...SO IF THERE'S SOMETHING I LIKE, I'LL BUY IT.
THEN THAT'S WHAT WE'LL DO!!! I'LL BUY CLOTHES TOO!
HIGH SCHOOL GIRLS WHO JUST CAME TO LOOK BUT END UP BUYING CLOTHES
JINJI
AIR DRUM ROLL
DARARARARARA (DRRRRRR)

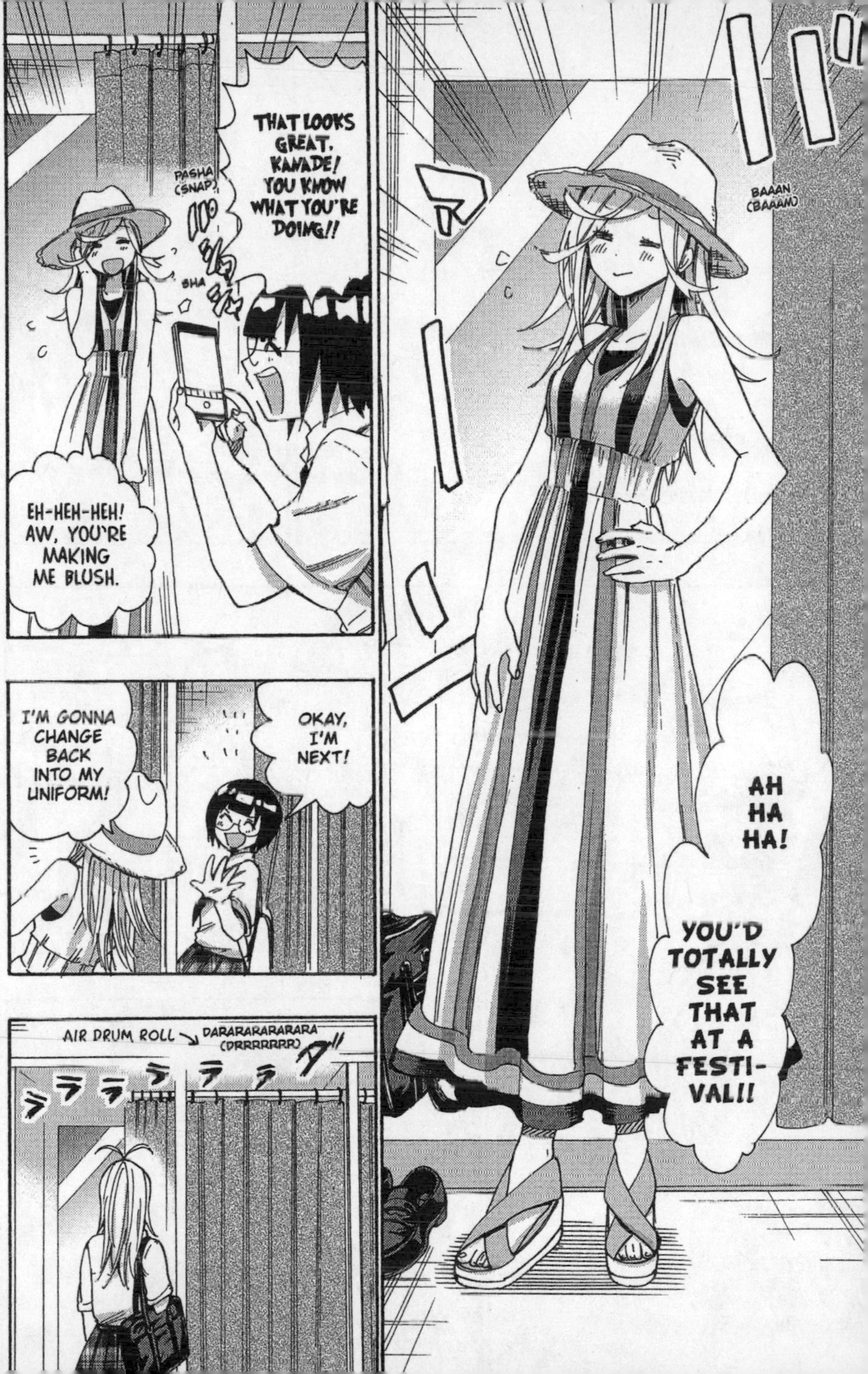
BAAAN (BAAAM)
AH HA HA!
YOU'D TOTALLY SEE THAT AT A FESTIVAL!!
THAT LOOKS GREAT, KANADE! YOU KNOW WHAT YOU'RE DOING!!
PASHA (SNAP)
BHA
EH-HEH-HEH! AW, YOU'RE MAKING ME BLUSH.
OKAY, I'M NEXT!
I'M GONNA CHANGE BACK INTO MY UNIFORM!
AIR DRUM ROLL
DARARARARARARA (DRRRRRRR)

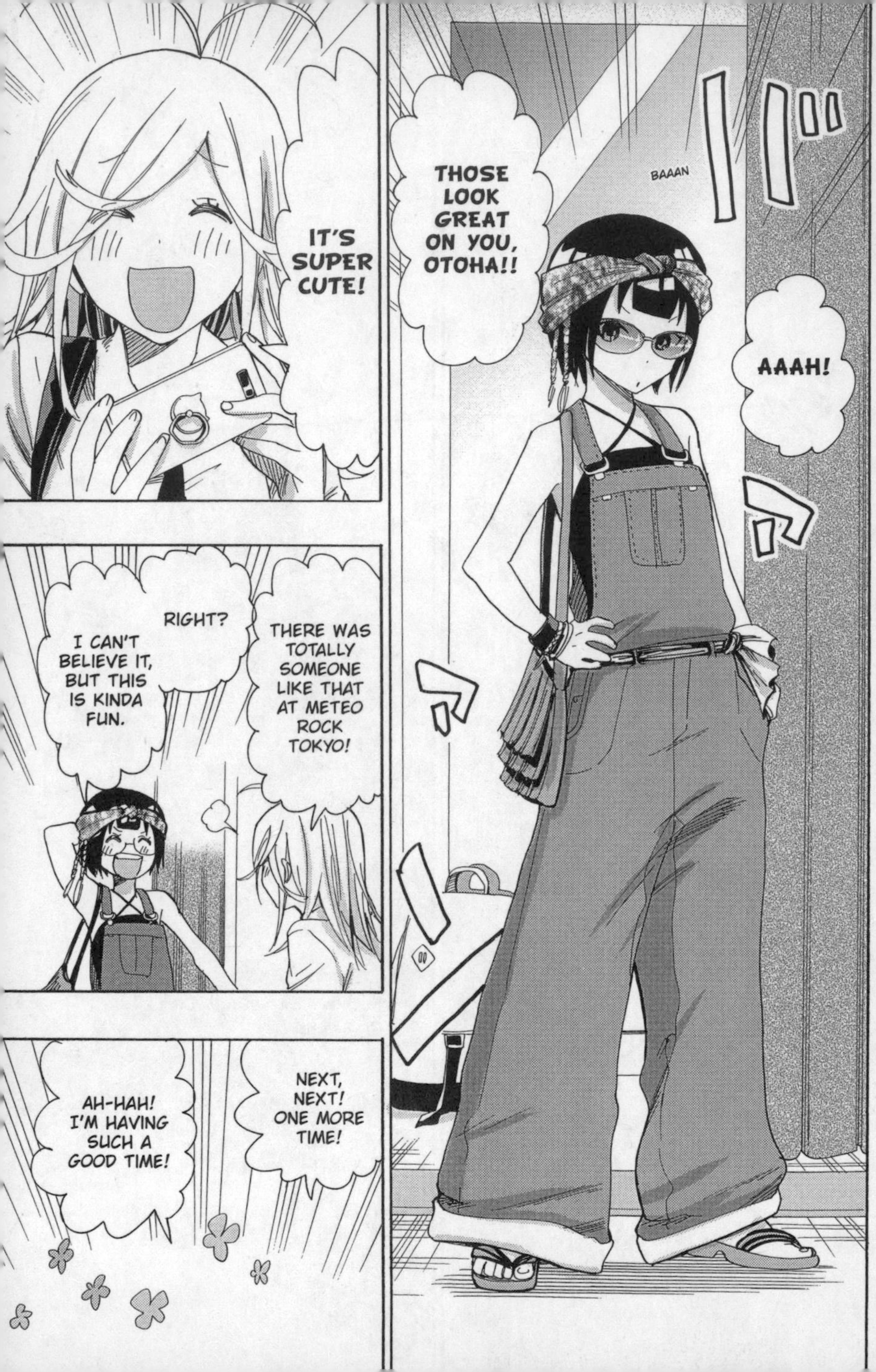
BAAAN
THOSE LOOK GREAT ON YOU, OTOHA!!
AAAH!
IT'S SUPER CUTE!
THERE WAS TOTALLY SOMEONE LIKE THAT AT METEO ROCK TOKYO!
RIGHT?
I CAN'T BELIEVE IT, BUT THIS IS KINDA FUN.
NEXT, NEXT! ONE MORE TIME!
AH-HAH! I'M HAVING SUCH A GOOD TIME!

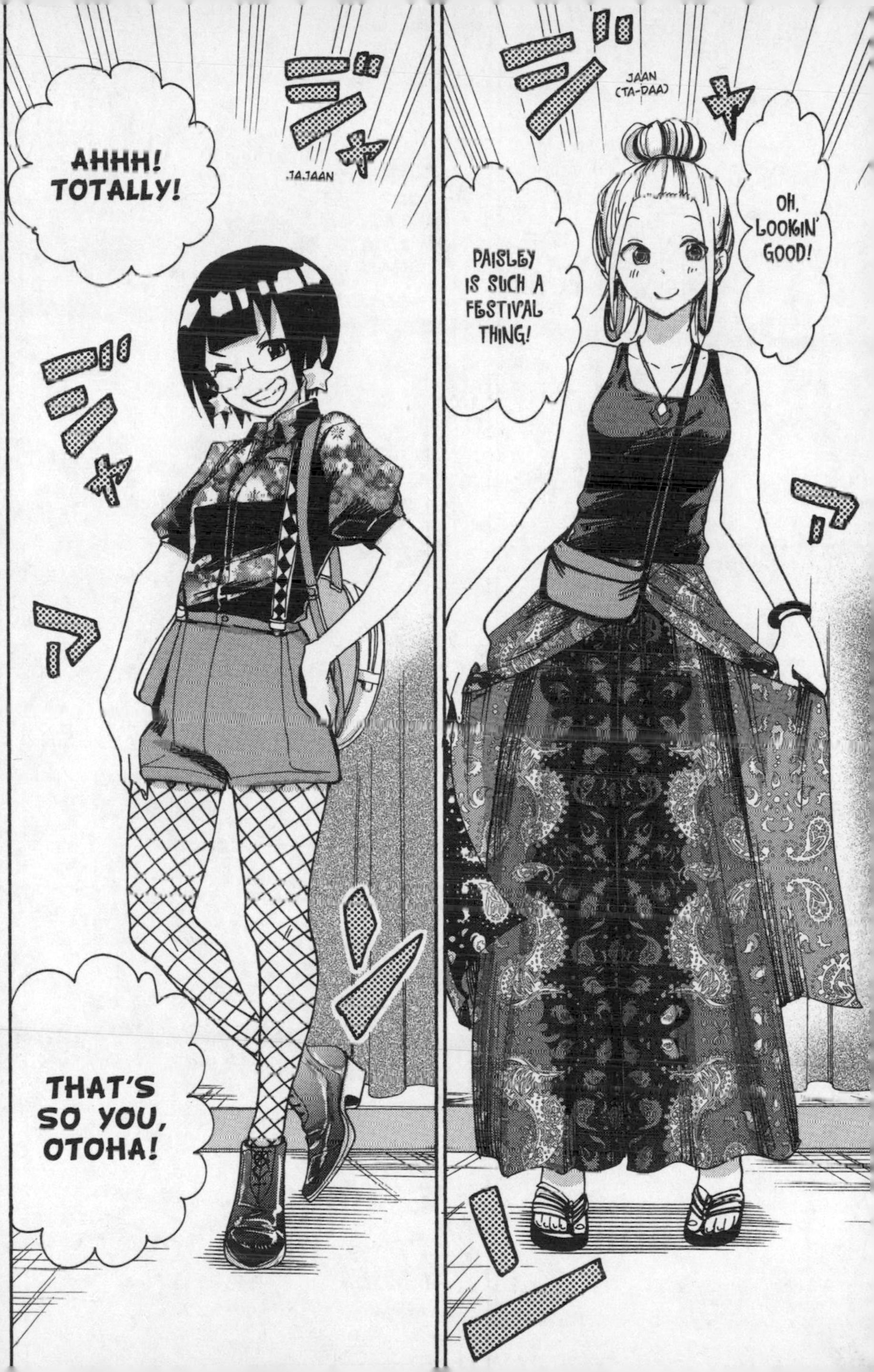

JAAN (TA-DAA)
OH, LOOKIN' GOOD!
PAISLEY IS SUCH A FESTIVAL THING!
JAJAAN
AHHH! TOTALLY!
THAT'S SO YOU, OTOHA!

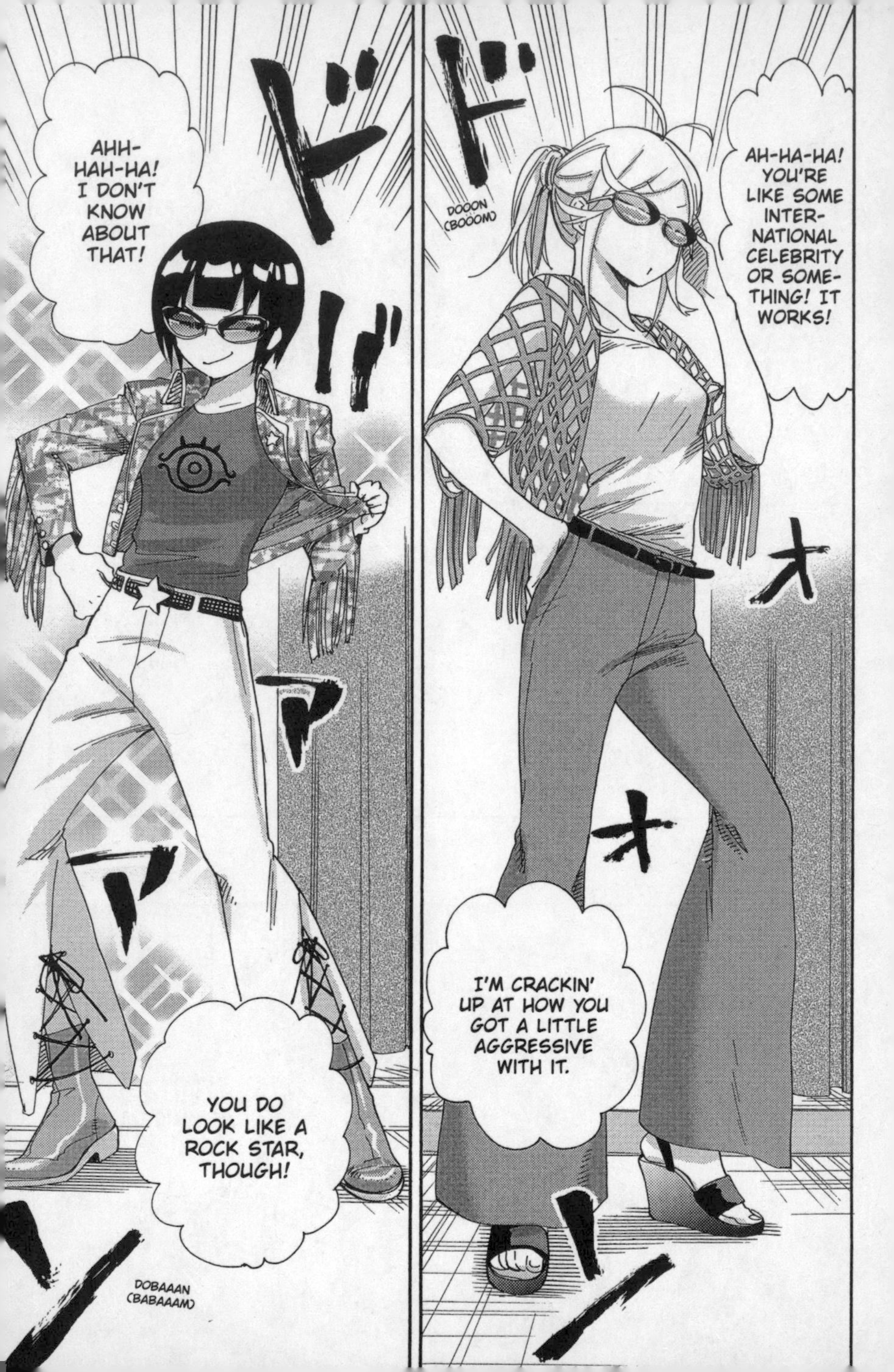
AH-HA-HA! YOU'RE LIKE SOME INTER-NATIONAL CELEBRITY OR SOME-THING! IT WORKS!
DOOON (BOOOM)
I'M CRACKIN' UP AT HOW YOU GOT A LITTLE AGGRESSIVE WITH IT.
AHH-HAH-HA! I DON'T KNOW ABOUT THAT!
YOU DO LOOK LIKE A ROCK STAR, THOUGH!
DOBAAAN (BABAAAM)

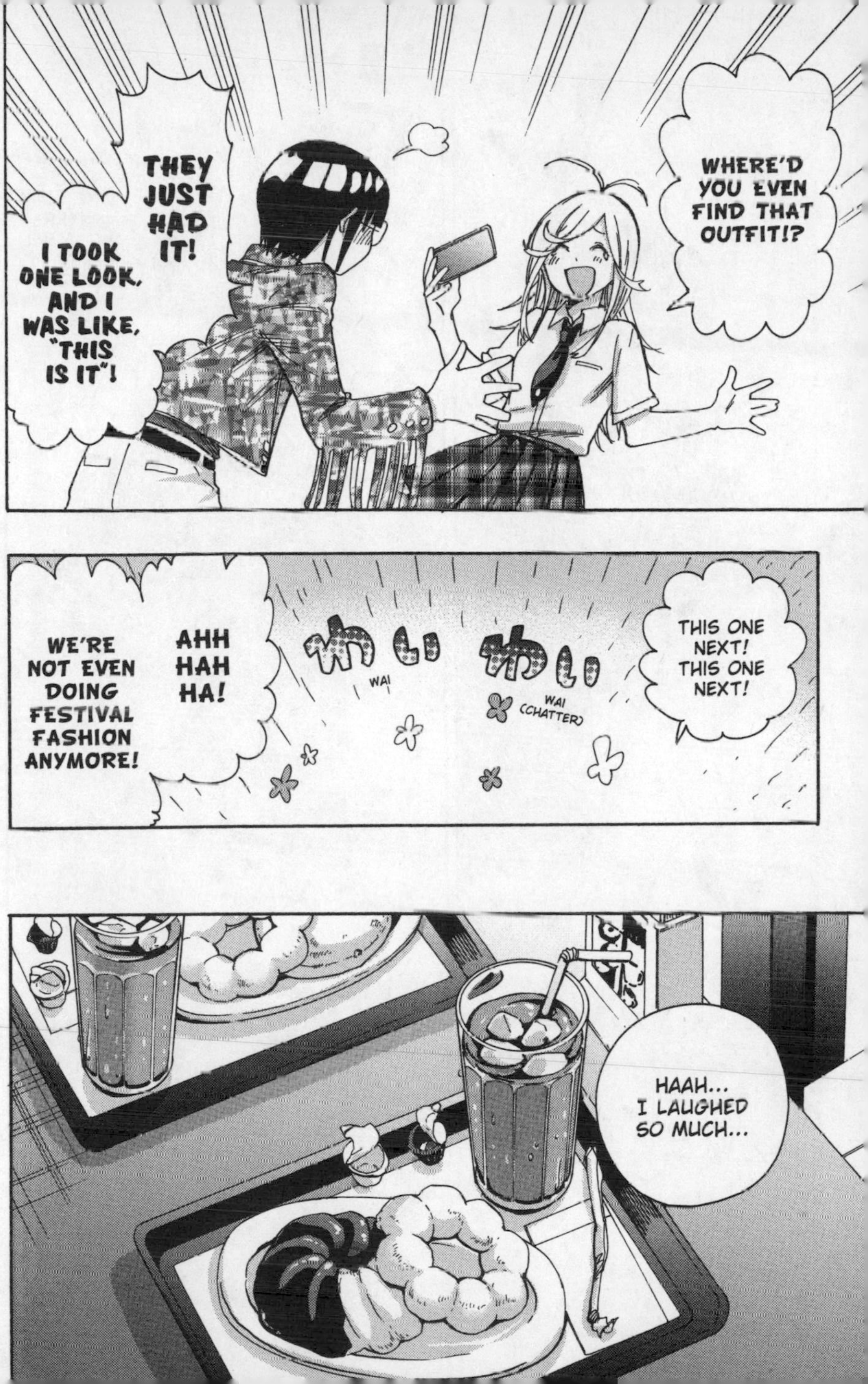
WHERE'D YOU EVEN FIND THAT OUTFIT!?
THEY JUST HAD IT!
I TOOK ONE LOOK, AND I WAS LIKE, "THIS IS IT"!
THIS ONE NEXT! THIS ONE NEXT!
わい わい
WAI
WAI (CHATTER)
AHH HAH HA!
WE'RE NOT EVEN DOING FESTIVAL FASHION ANYMORE!
HAAH... I LAUGHED SO MUCH...

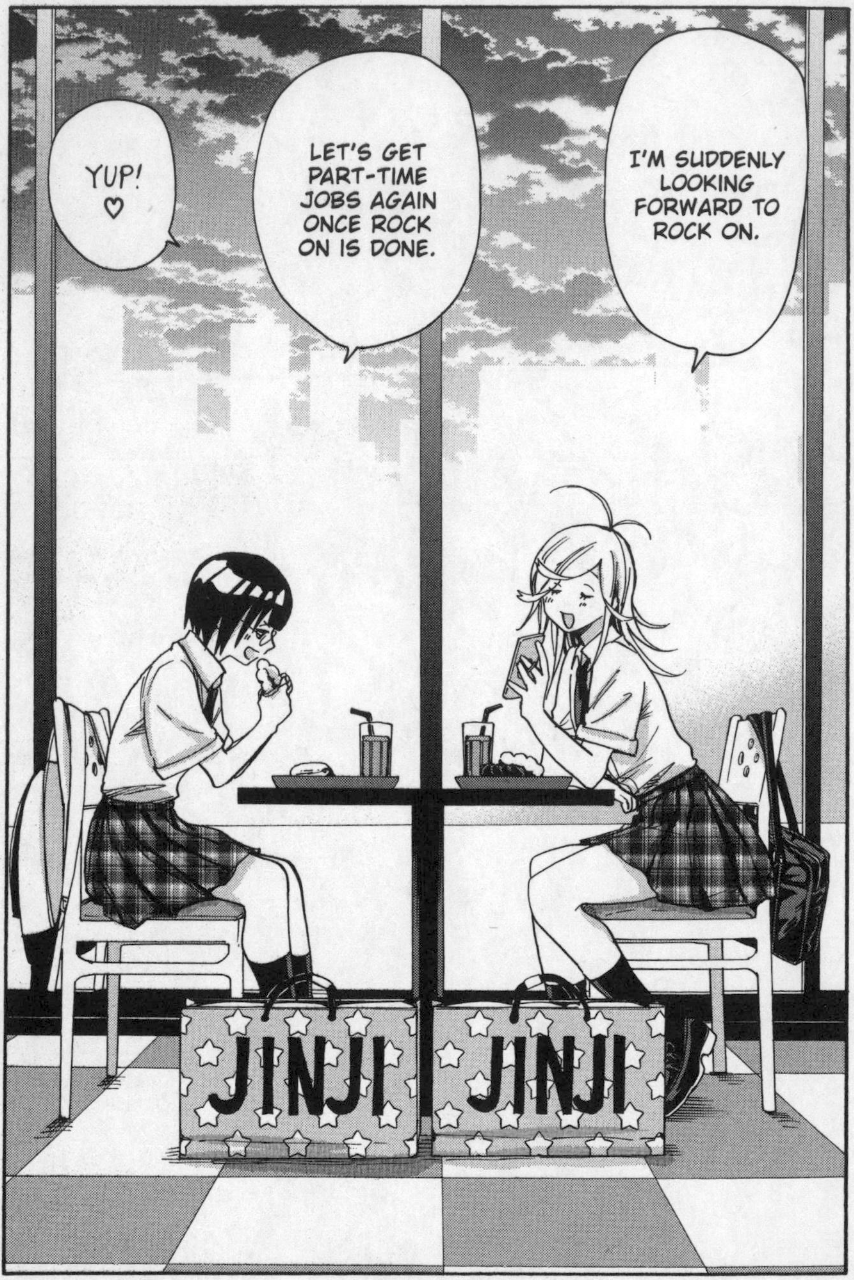
I'M SUDDENLY LOOKING FORWARD TO ROCK ON.
LET'S GET PART-TIME JOBS AGAIN ONCE ROCK ON IS DONE.
YUP! ♡
JINJI
JINJI

Days on Fes

SP 2

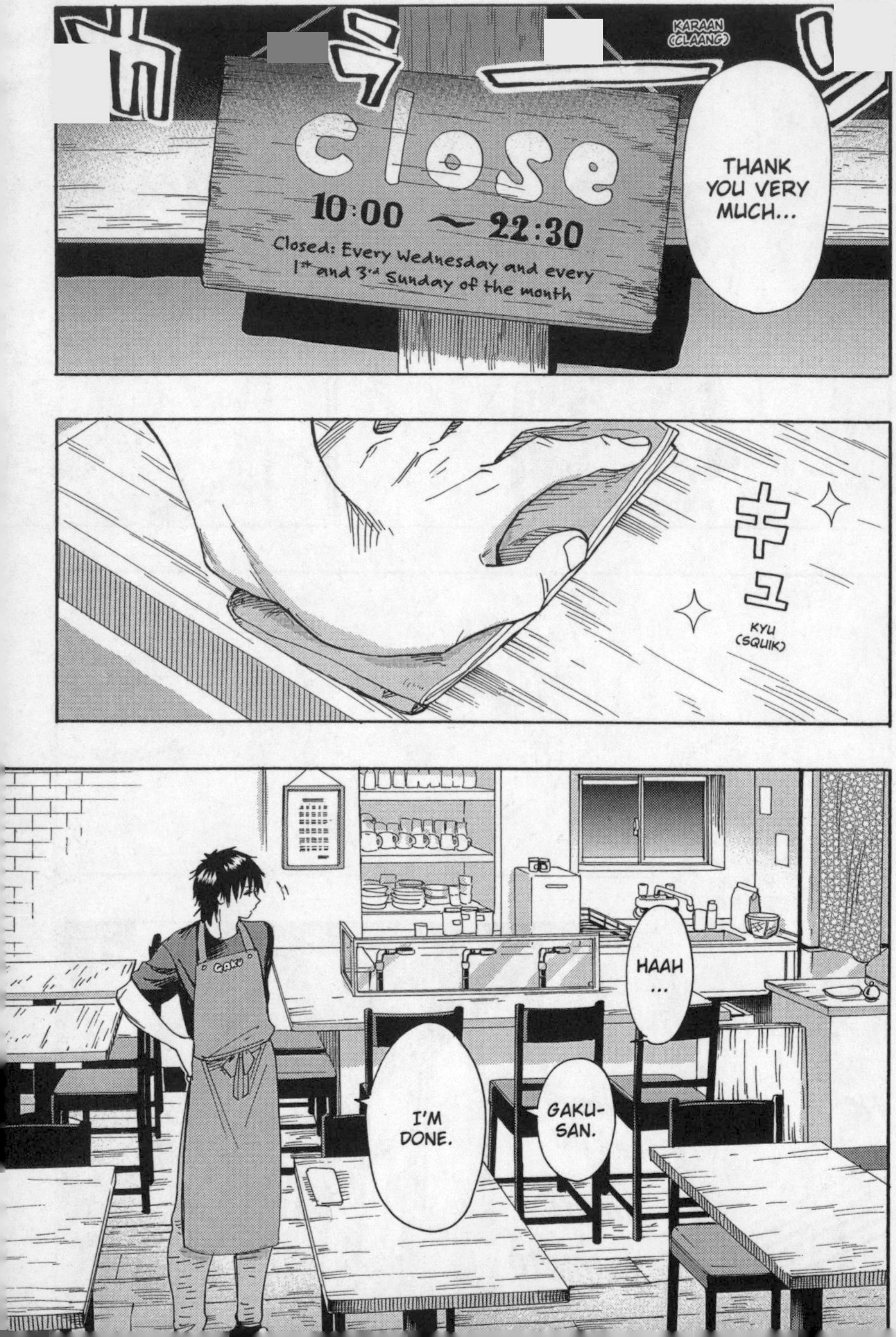
KARAAN
(CLAANG)
THANK YOU VERY MUCH...
close
10:00 ~ 22:30
Closed: Every Wednesday and every 1st and 3rd Sunday of the month
KYU
(SQUIK)
HAAH ...
GAKU-SAN.
I'M DONE.

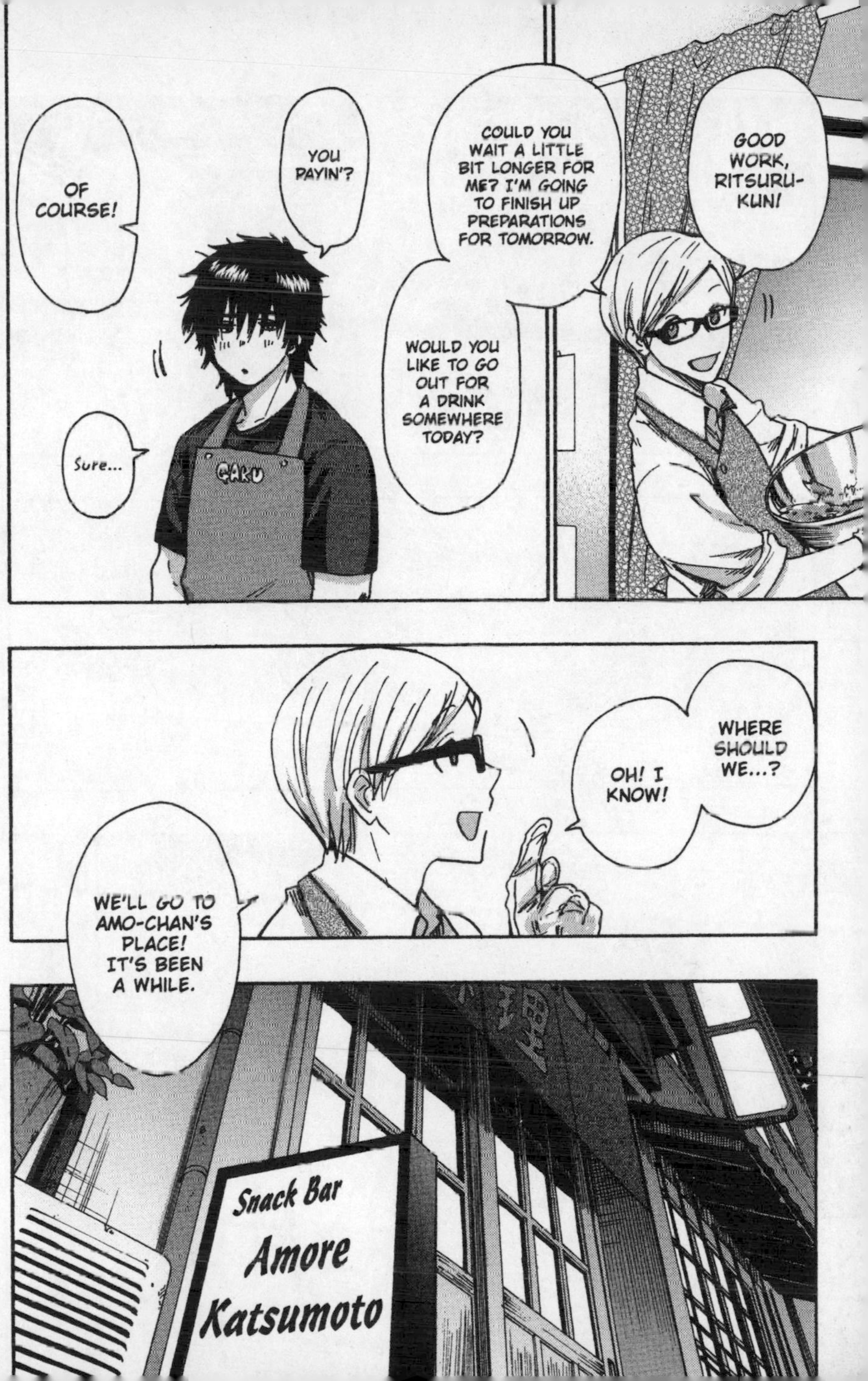
GOOD WORK, RITSURU-KUN!
COULD YOU WAIT A LITTLE BIT LONGER FOR ME? I'M GOING TO FINISH UP PREPARATIONS FOR TOMORROW.
WOULD YOU LIKE TO GO OUT FOR A DRINK SOMEWHERE TODAY?
YOU PAYIN'?
OF COURSE!
GAKU
Sure...
WHERE SHOULD WE...?
OH! I KNOW!
WE'LL GO TO AMO-CHAN'S PLACE! IT'S BEEN A WHILE.
Snack Bar
Amore
Katsumoto

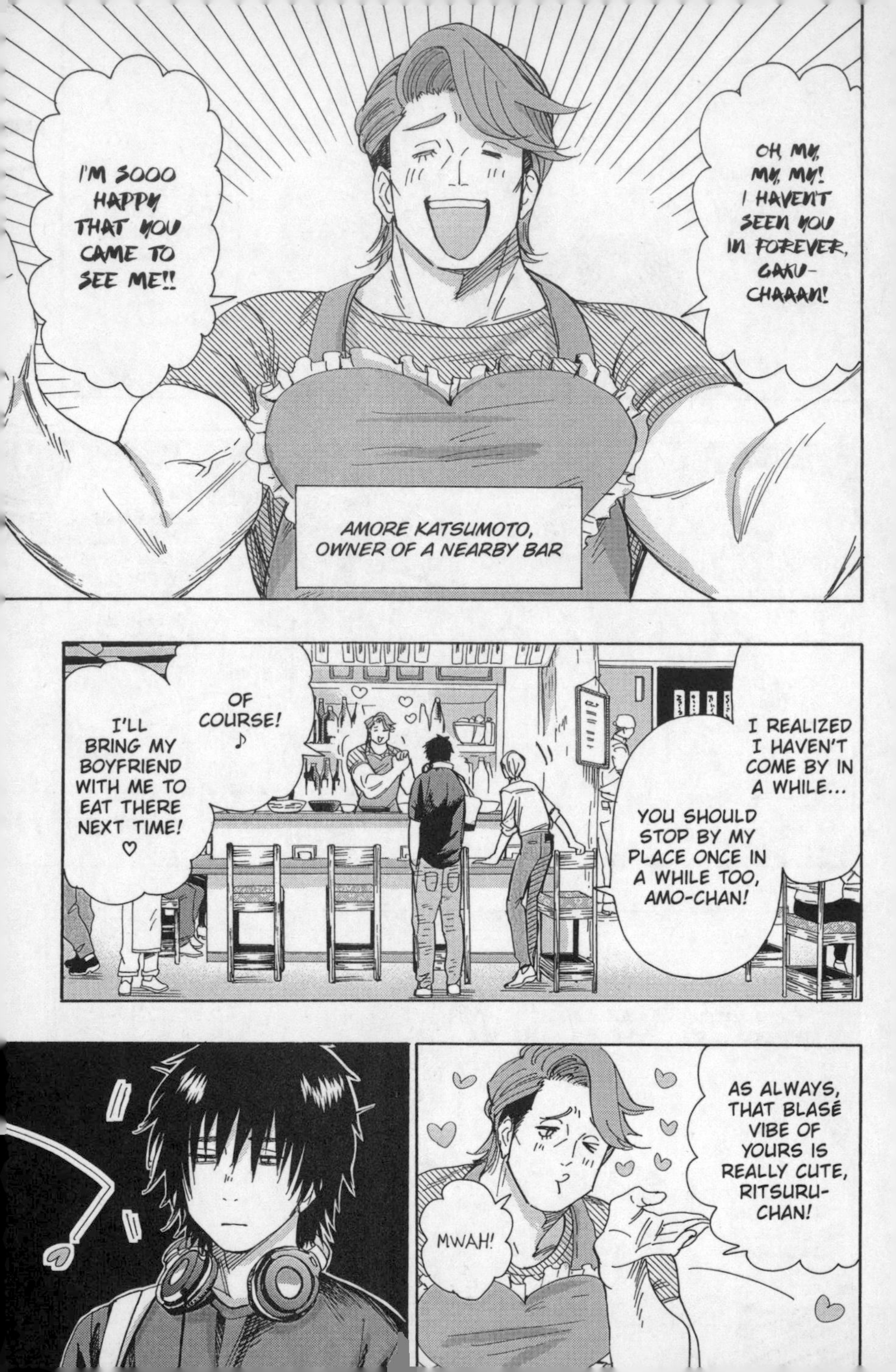
OH, MY, MY, MY! I HAVEN'T SEEN YOU IN FOREVER, GAKU-CHAAAN!
I'M SOOO HAPPY THAT YOU CAME TO SEE ME!!
AMORE KATSUMOTO, OWNER OF A NEARBY BAR
I REALIZED I HAVEN'T COME BY IN A WHILE...
YOU SHOULD STOP BY MY PLACE ONCE IN A WHILE TOO, AMO-CHAN!
OF COURSE! ♪
I'LL BRING MY BOYFRIEND WITH ME TO EAT THERE NEXT TIME! ♡
AS ALWAYS, THAT BLASÉ VIBE OF YOURS IS REALLY CUTE, RITSURU-CHAN!
MWAH!

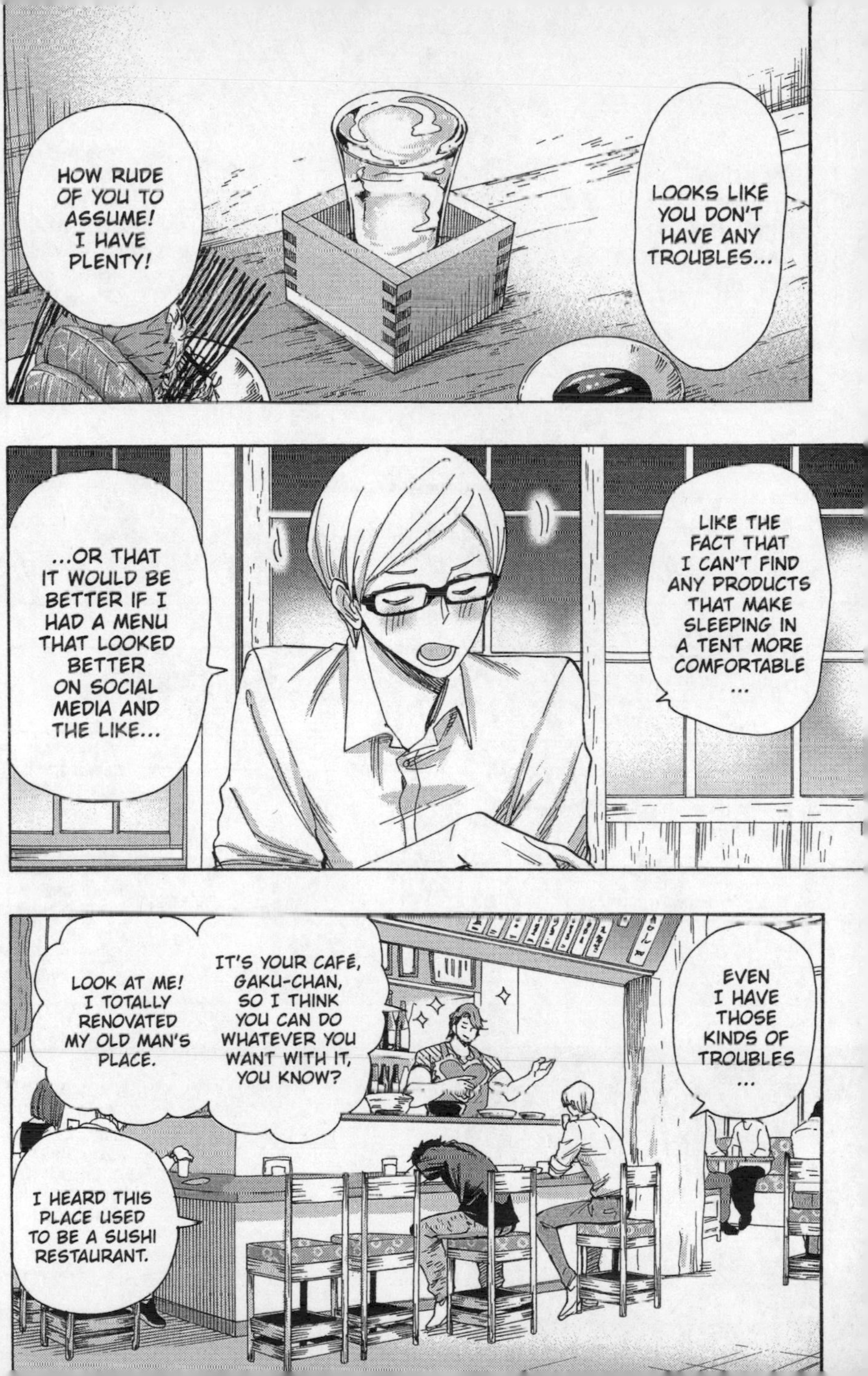
LOOKS LIKE YOU DON'T HAVE ANY TROUBLES...
HOW RUDE OF YOU TO ASSUME! I HAVE PLENTY!
LIKE THE FACT THAT I CAN'T FIND ANY PRODUCTS THAT MAKE SLEEPING IN A TENT MORE COMFORTABLE...
...OR THAT IT WOULD BE BETTER IF I HAD A MENU THAT LOOKED BETTER ON SOCIAL MEDIA AND THE LIKE...
EVEN I HAVE THOSE KINDS OF TROUBLES...
IT'S YOUR CAFÉ, GAKU-CHAN, SO I THINK YOU CAN DO WHATEVER YOU WANT WITH IT, YOU KNOW?
LOOK AT ME! I TOTALLY RENOVATED MY OLD MAN'S PLACE.
I HEARD THIS PLACE USED TO BE A SUSHI RESTAURANT.

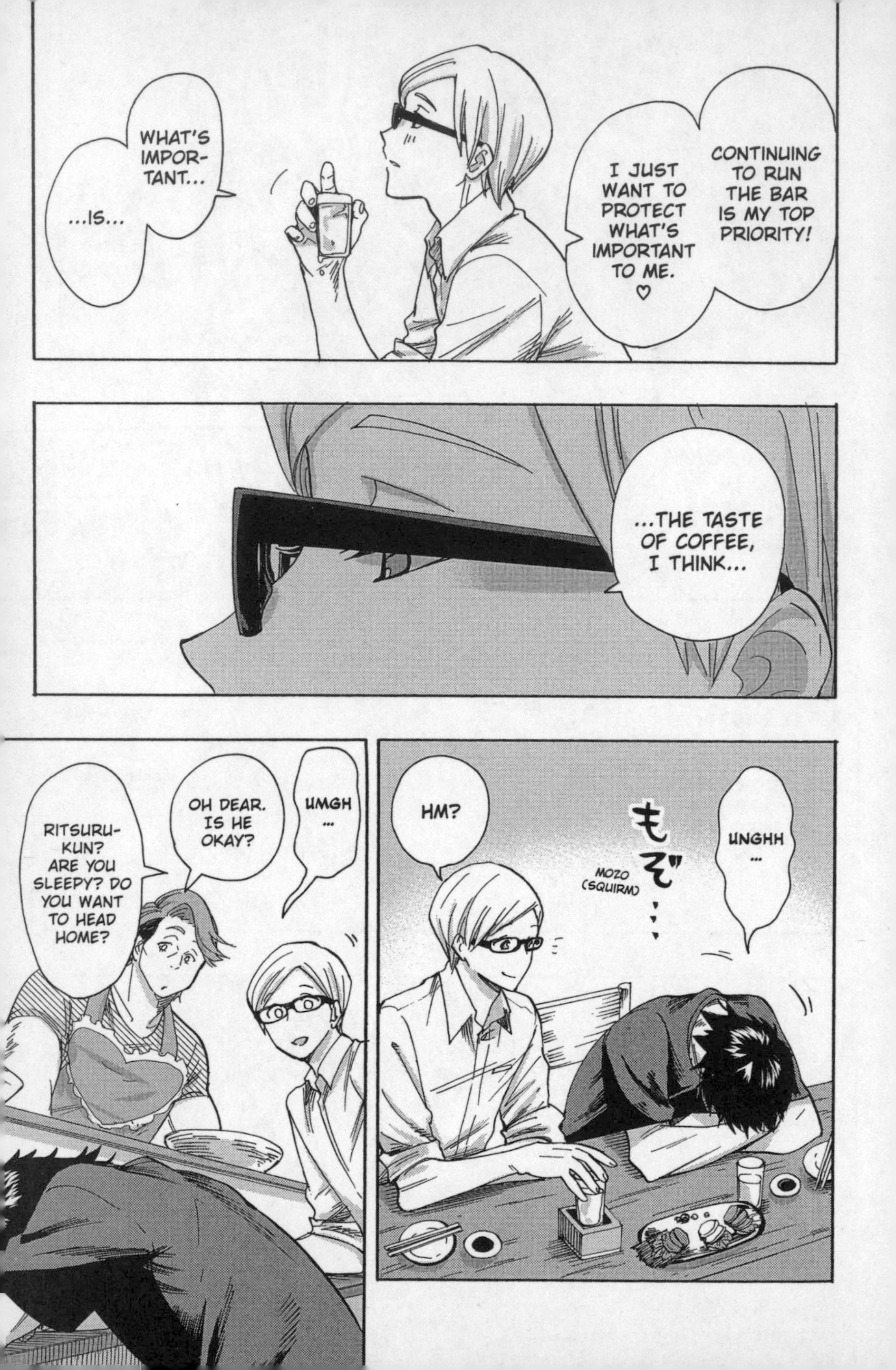

CONTINUING TO RUN THE BAR IS MY TOP PRIORITY!
I JUST WANT TO PROTECT WHAT'S IMPORTANT TO ME. ♡
WHAT'S IMPORTANT...
...IS...
...THE TASTE OF COFFEE, I THINK...
UNGHH ...
もぞ
MOZO (SQUIRM)
HM?
UMGH ...
OH DEAR. IS HE OKAY?
RITSURU-KUN? ARE YOU SLEEPY? DO YOU WANT TO HEAD HOME?

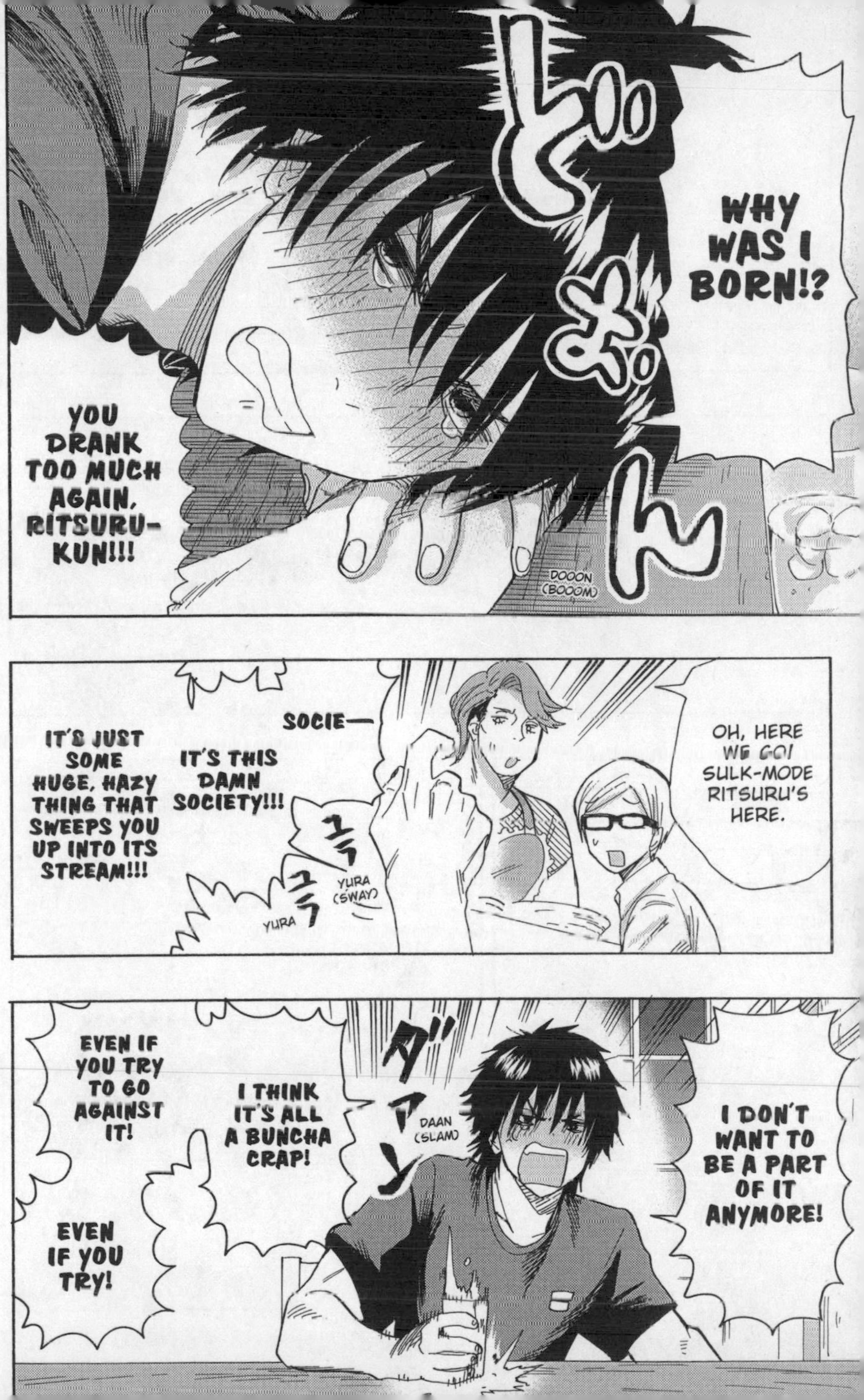
WHY WAS I BORN!?
DOOON (BOOOM)
YOU DRANK TOO MUCH AGAIN, RITSURU-KUN!!!
OH, HERE WE GO! SULK-MODE RITSURU'S HERE.
SOCIE—
IT'S THIS DAMN SOCIETY!!!
YURA (SWAY)
YURA
IT'S JUST SOME HUGE, HAZY THING THAT SWEEPS YOU UP INTO ITS STREAM!!!
I DON'T WANT TO BE A PART OF IT ANYMORE!
DAAN (SLAM)
I THINK IT'S ALL A BUNCHA CRAP!
EVEN IF YOU TRY TO GO AGAINST IT!
EVEN IF YOU TRY!

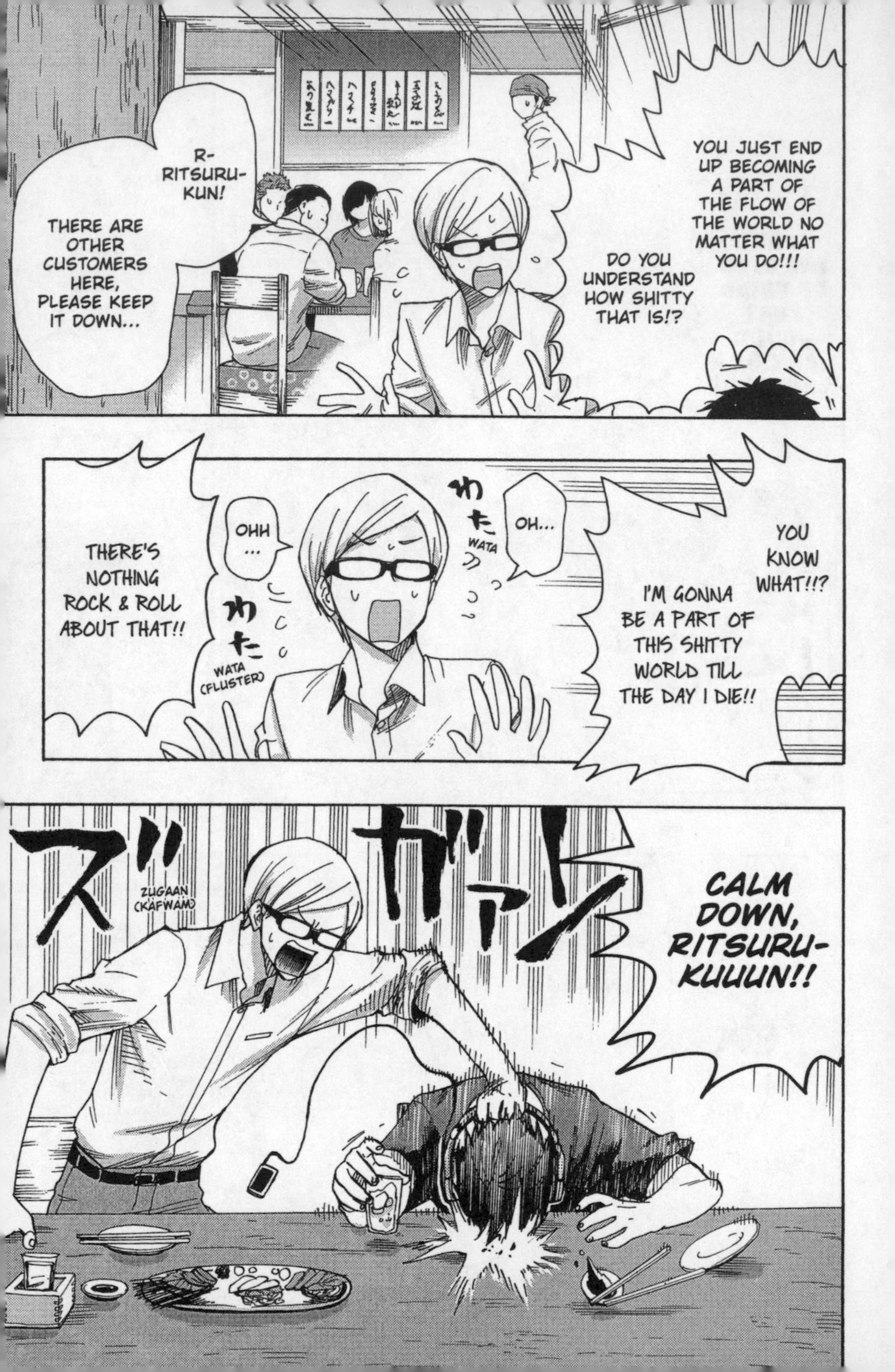
YOU JUST END UP BECOMING A PART OF THE FLOW OF THE WORLD NO MATTER WHAT YOU DO!!!
DO YOU UNDERSTAND HOW SHITTY THAT IS!?
R-RITSURU-KUN!
THERE ARE OTHER CUSTOMERS HERE, PLEASE KEEP IT DOWN...
YOU KNOW WHAT!!?
I'M GONNA BE A PART OF THIS SHITTY WORLD TILL THE DAY I DIE!!
OH...
WATA
OHH...
WATA (FLUSTER)
THERE'S NOTHING ROCK & ROLL ABOUT THAT!!
CALM DOWN, RITSURU-KUUUN!!
ZUGAAN (KAFWAM)

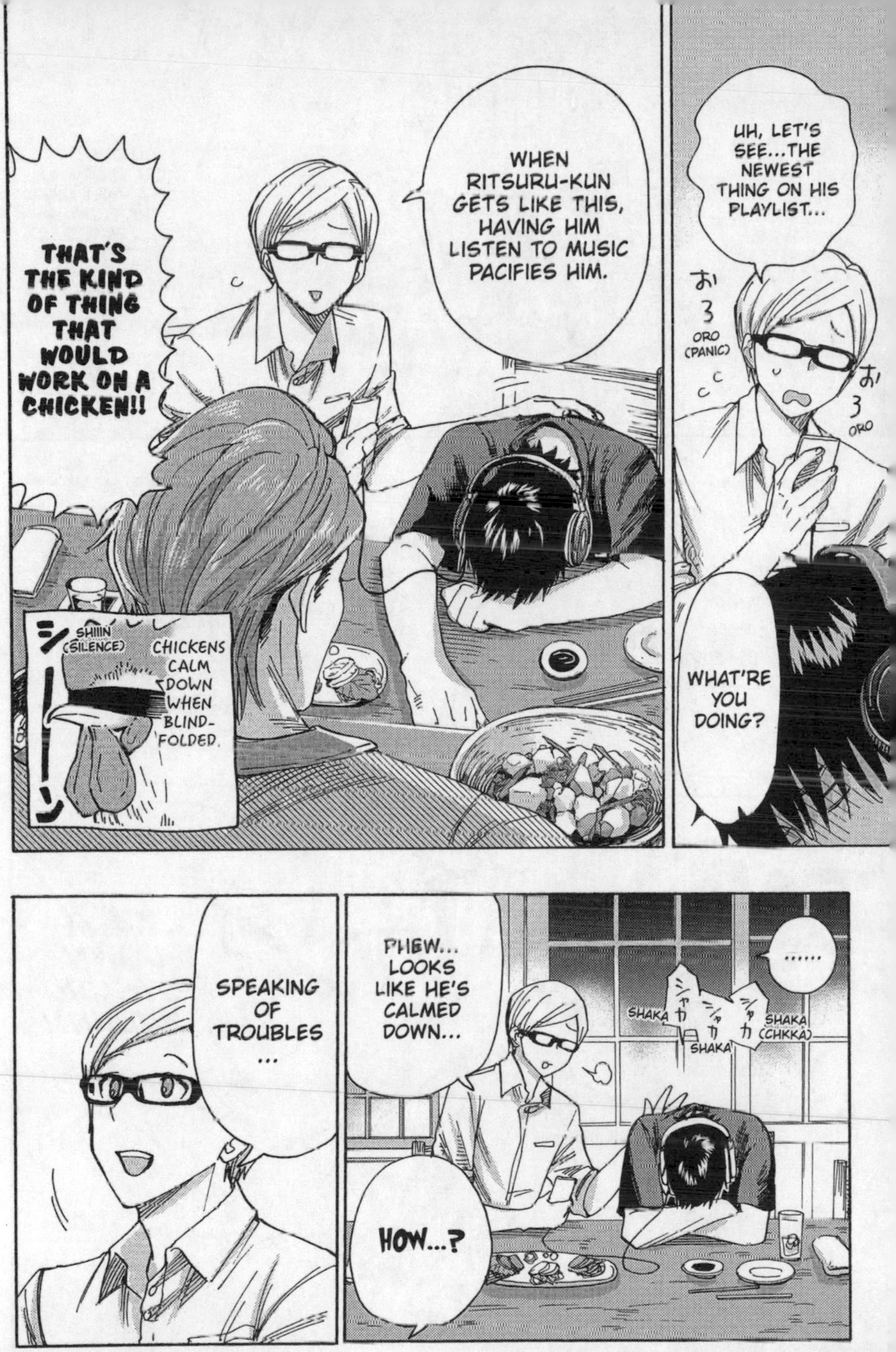
UH, LET'S SEE...THE NEWEST THING ON HIS PLAYLIST...
おろ
ORO (PANIC)
おろ
ORO
WHAT'RE YOU DOING?
WHEN RITSURU-KUN GETS LIKE THIS, HAVING HIM LISTEN TO MUSIC PACIFIES HIM.
THAT'S THE KIND OF THING THAT WOULD WORK ON A CHICKEN!!
シーン
SHIIN (SILENCE)
CHICKENS CALM DOWN WHEN BLIND-FOLDED.
......
シャカ
SHAKA
シャカ
SHAKA
シャカ
SHAKA (CHKKA)
PHEW... LOOKS LIKE HE'S CALMED DOWN...
HOW...?
SPEAKING OF TROUBLES ...

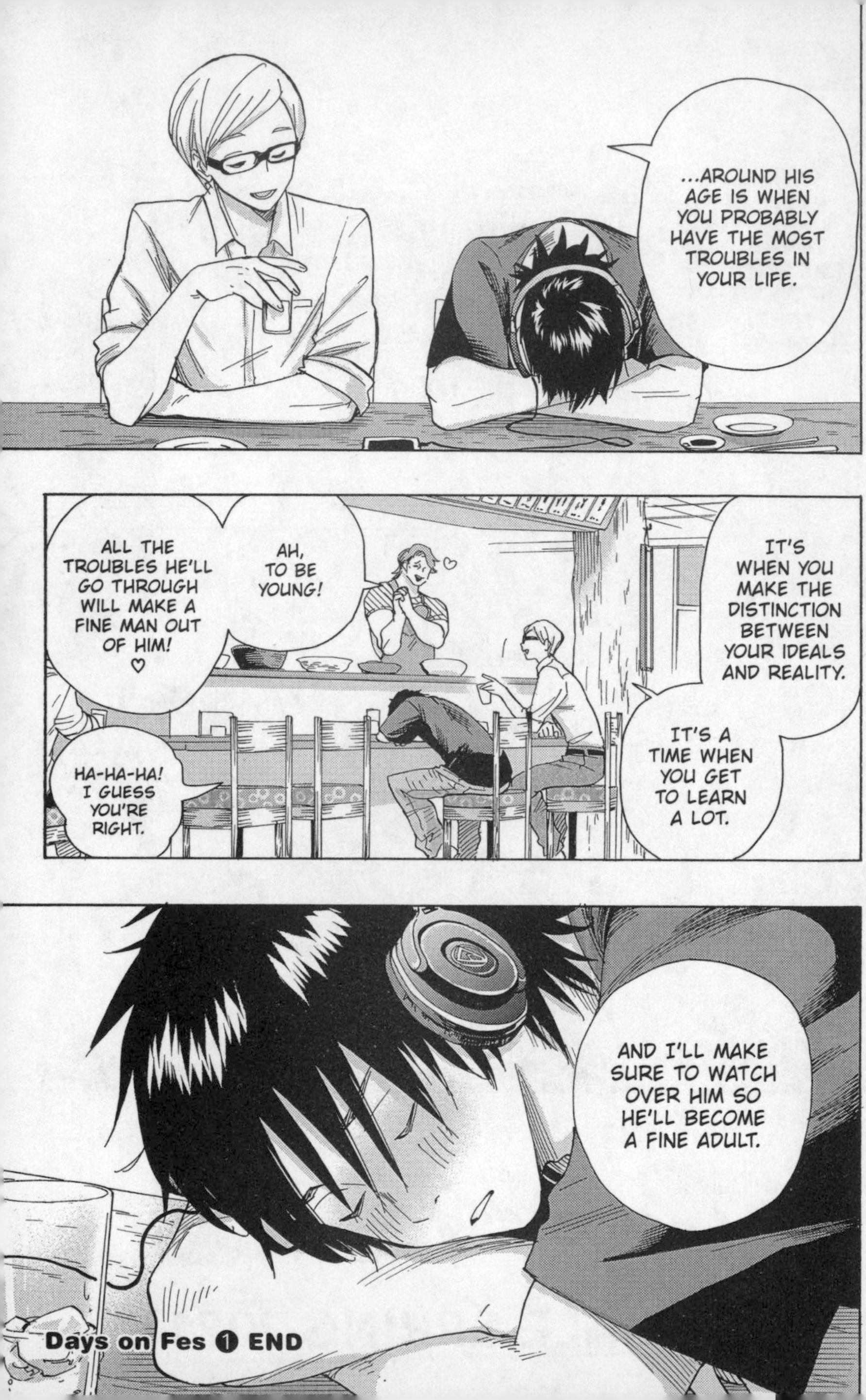
...AROUND HIS AGE IS WHEN YOU PROBABLY HAVE THE MOST TROUBLES IN YOUR LIFE.
IT'S WHEN YOU MAKE THE DISTINCTION BETWEEN YOUR IDEALS AND REALITY.
IT'S A TIME WHEN YOU GET TO LEARN A LOT.
AH, TO BE YOUNG!
ALL THE TROUBLES HE'LL GO THROUGH WILL MAKE A FINE MAN OUT OF HIM! ♡
HA-HA-HA! I GUESS YOU'RE RIGHT.
AND I'LL MAKE SURE TO WATCH OVER HIM SO HE'LL BECOME A FINE ADULT.
Days on Fes 1 END

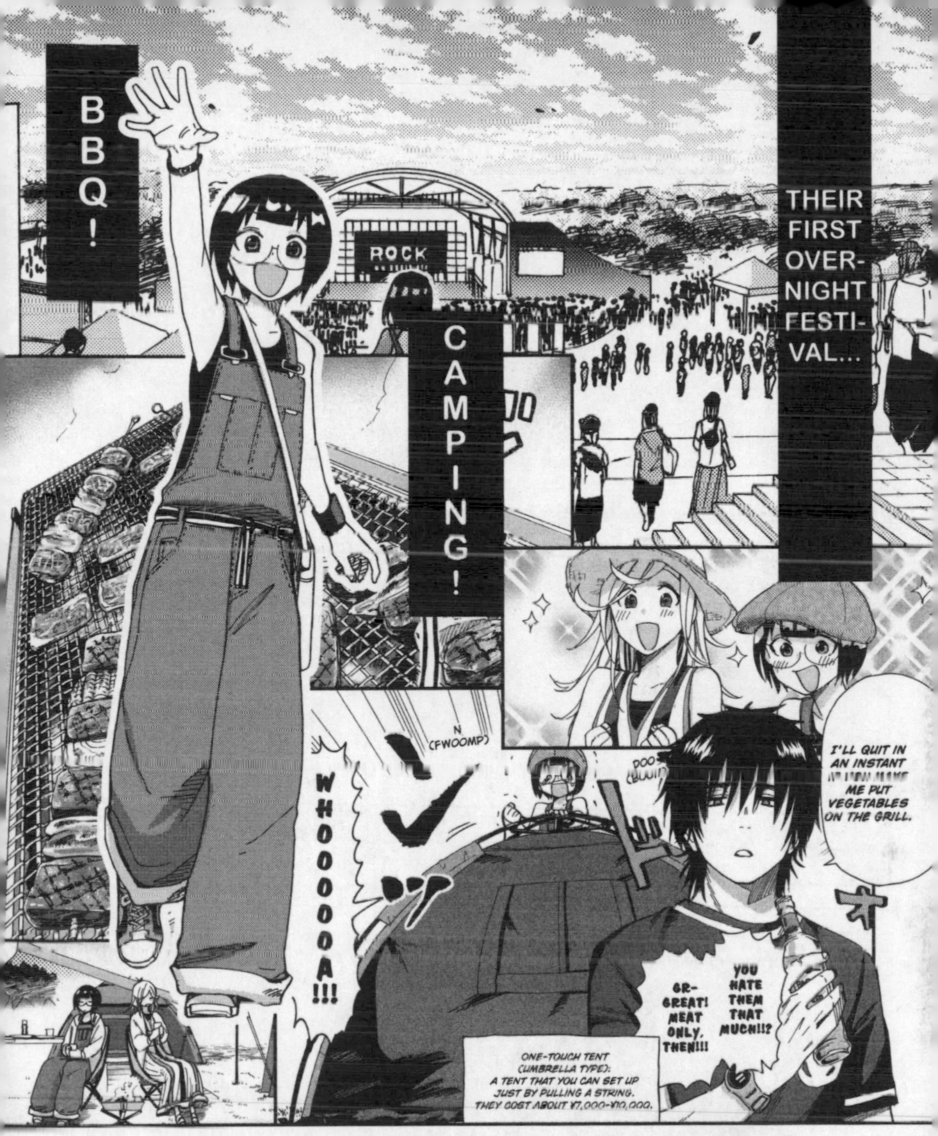
THEIR FIRST OVER-NIGHT FESTI-VAL...
CAMPING!
BBQ!
ROCK
I'LL QUIT IN AN INSTANT
ME PUT VEGETABLES ON THE GRILL.
YOU HATE THEM THAT MUCH!!?
GR-GREAT! MEAT ONLY, THEN!!!
ONE-TOUCH TENT (UMBRELLA TYPE): A TENT THAT YOU CAN SET UP JUST BY PULLING A STRING. THEY COST ABOUT ¥7,000-¥10,000.
N (FWOOMP)
WHOOOOOOA!!!

Days on Fes vol. 2

ON SALE SPRING 2021!

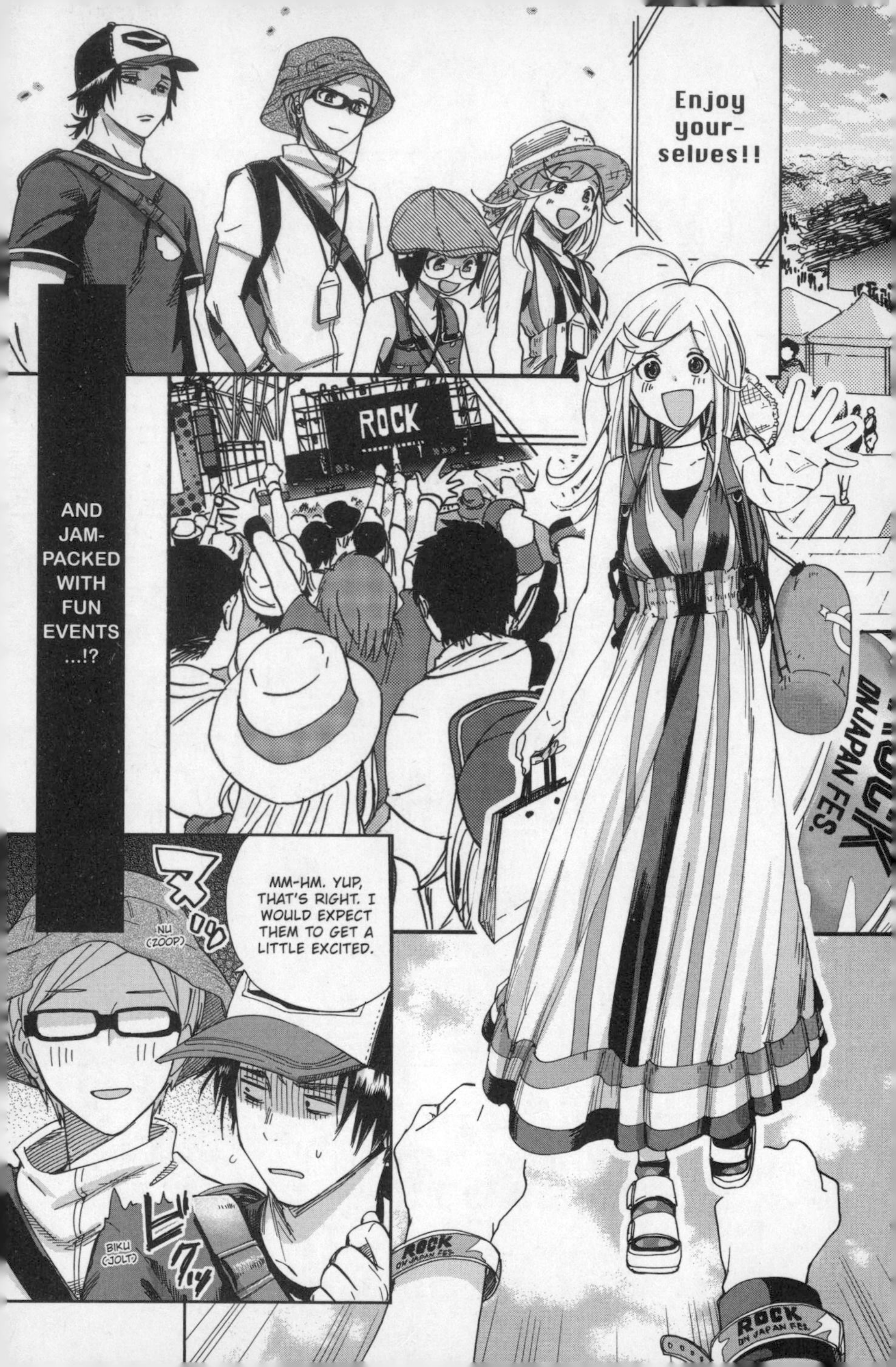

Enjoy your-selves!!
ROCK
ROCK ON JAPAN FES.
AND JAM-PACKED WITH FUN EVENTS ...!?
MM-HM. YUP, THAT'S RIGHT. I WOULD EXPECT THEM TO GET A LITTLE EXCITED.
NU (ZOOP)
BIKU (JOLT)

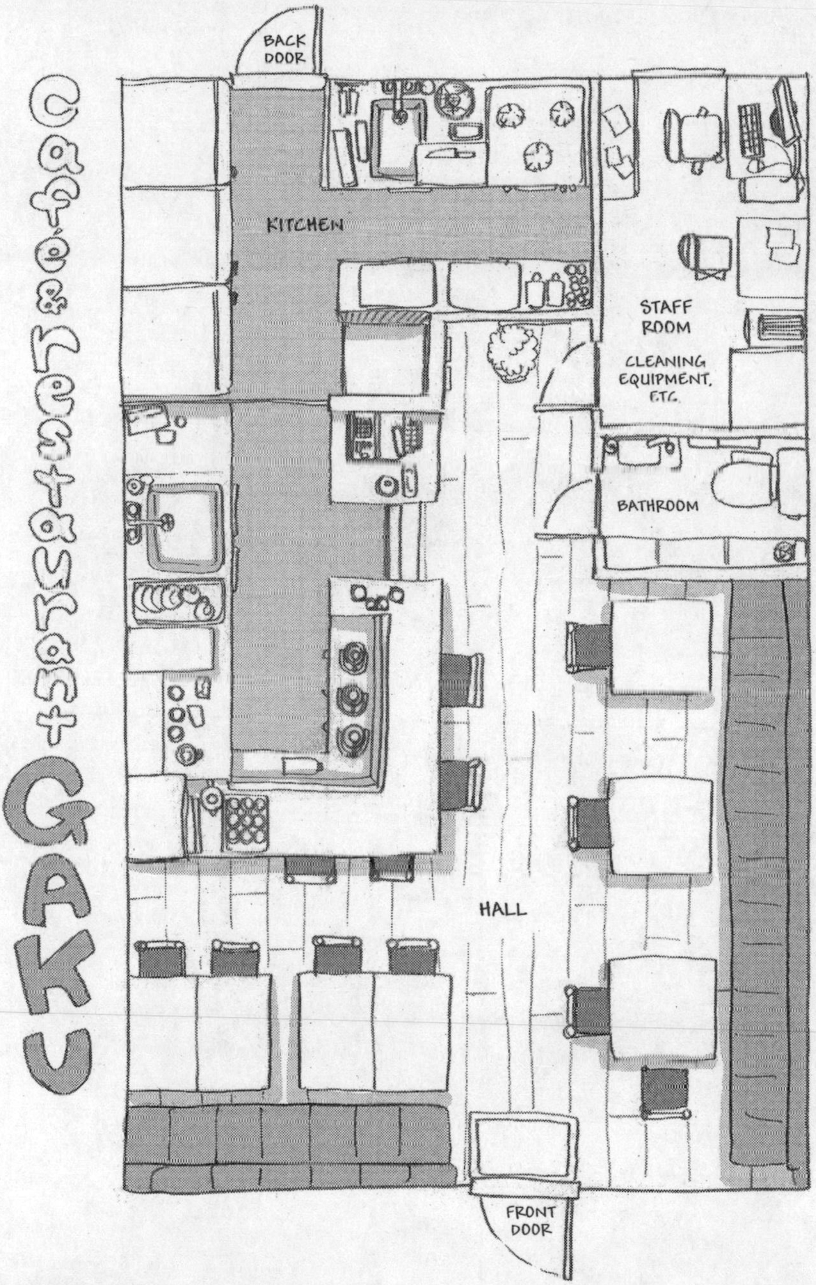

Café & restaurant GAKU
BACK DOOR
KITCHEN
STAFF ROOM
CLEANING EQUIPMENT, ETC.
BATHROOM
HALL
FRONT DOOR

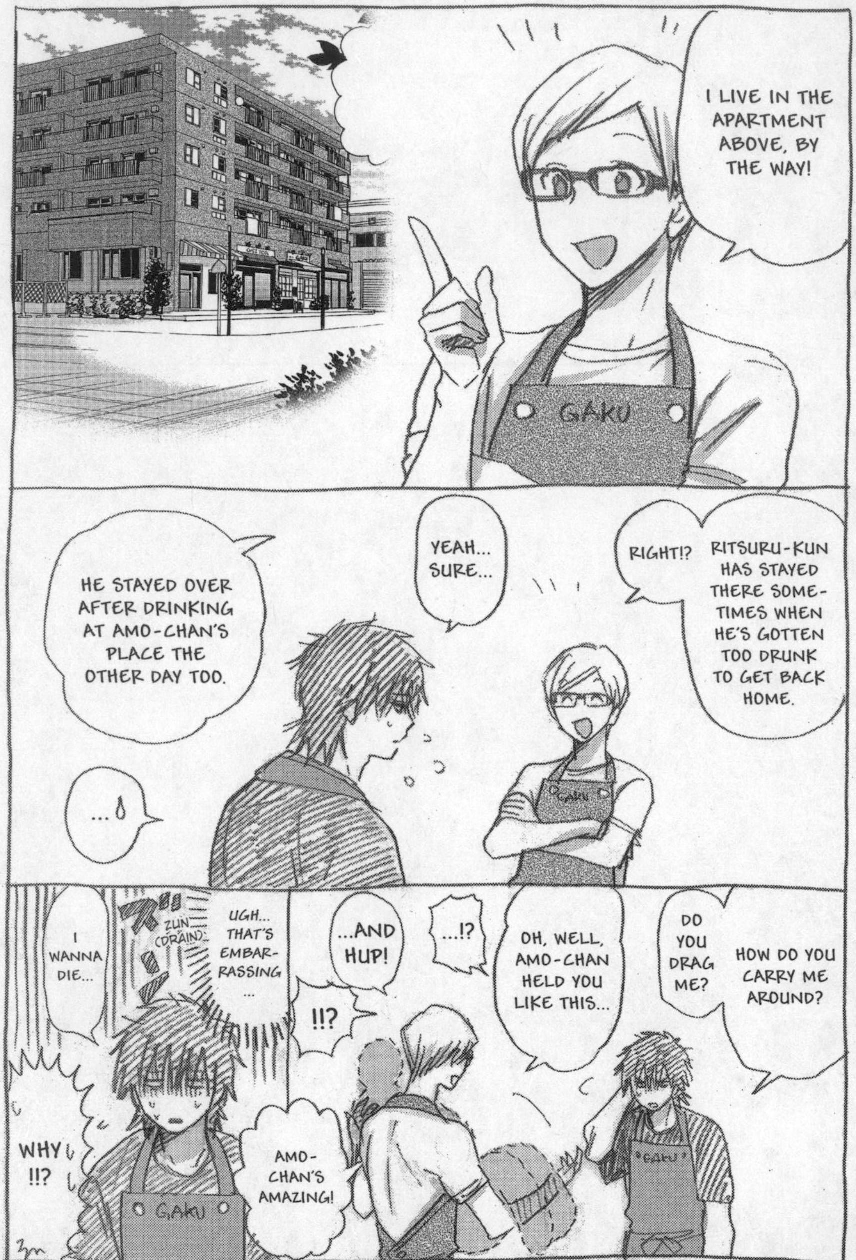
I LIVE IN THE APARTMENT ABOVE, BY THE WAY!
RITSURU-KUN HAS STAYED THERE SOME-TIMES WHEN HE'S GOTTEN TOO DRUNK TO GET BACK HOME.
RIGHT!?
YEAH... SURE...
HE STAYED OVER AFTER DRINKING AT AMO-CHAN'S PLACE THE OTHER DAY TOO.
...
HOW DO YOU CARRY ME AROUND?
DO YOU DRAG ME?
OH, WELL, AMO-CHAN HELD YOU LIKE THIS...
...!?
...AND HUP!
!!?
AMO-CHAN'S AMAZING!
UGH... THAT'S EMBAR-RASSING...
ZUN (DRAIN)
I WANNA DIE...
WHY!!?

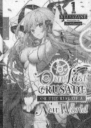
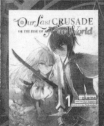

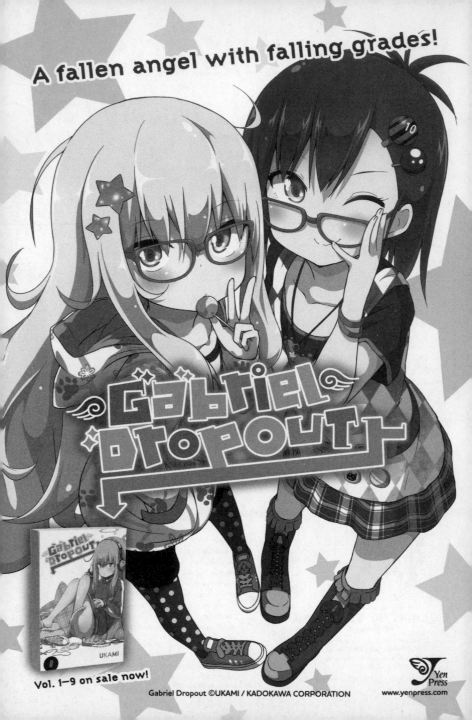

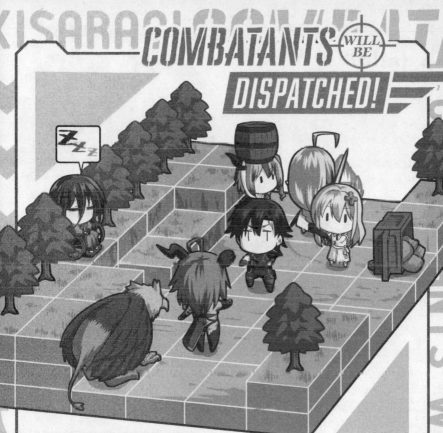

AVAILABLE WHEREVER BOOKS ARE SOLD!

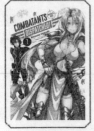 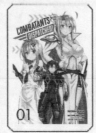

LIGHT NOVEL
VOLUMES 1-5

MANGA
VOLUMES 1-4

©Natsume Akatsuki, Kakao • Lanthanum 2017
KADOKAWA CORPORATION

©Masaaki Kiasa 2018 ©Natsume Akatsuki, Kakao • Lanthanum 2018
KADOKAWA CORPORATION

Always bring a gun to a sword fight!

With world domination nearly in their grasp, the Supreme Leaders of the Kisaragi Corporation—an underground criminal group turned evil megacorp—have decided to try their hands at interstellar conquest. A quick dice roll nominates their chief operative, Combat Agent Six, to be the one to explore an alien planet...and the first thing he does when he gets there is change the sacred incantation for a holy ritual to the most embarrassing thing he can think of. But evil deeds are business as usual for Kisaragi operatives, so if Six wants a promotion and a raise, he'll have to work much harder than that! For starters, he'll have to do something about the other group of villains on the planet, who are calling themselves the "Demon Lord's Army" or whatever. After all, this world doesn't need two evil organizations!

For more information
visit www.yenpress.com

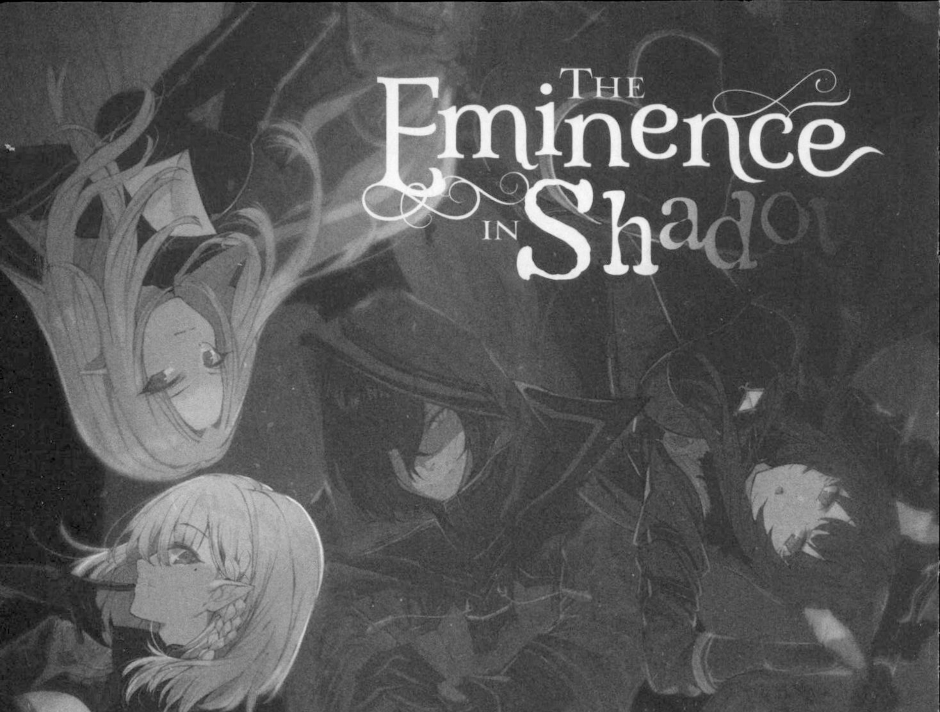
THE Eminence IN Shadow

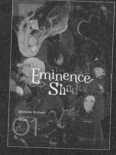

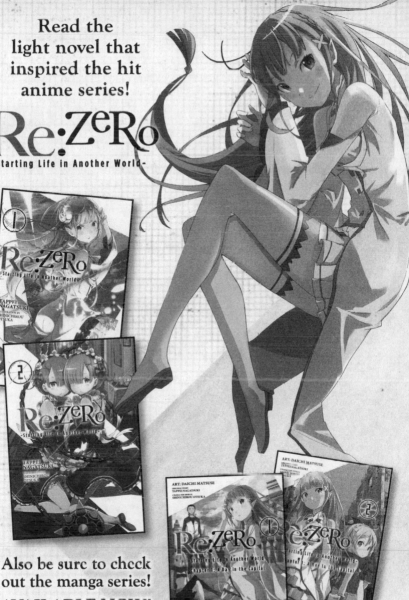

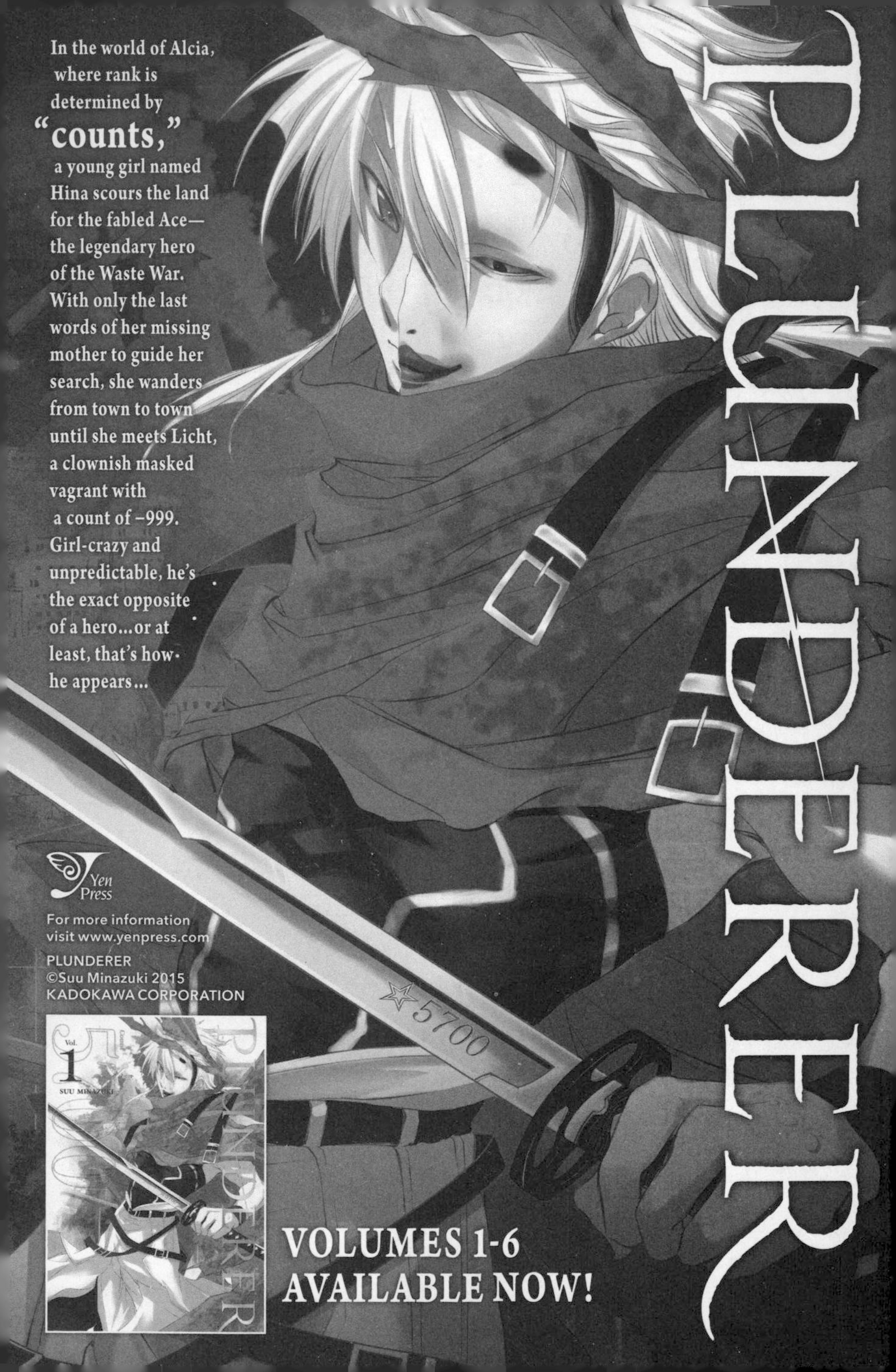
PLUNDERER
In the world of Alcia, where rank is determined by "counts," a young girl named Hina scours the land for the fabled Ace—the legendary hero of the Waste War. With only the last words of her missing mother to guide her search, she wanders from town to town until she meets Licht, a clownish masked vagrant with a count of −999. Girl-crazy and unpredictable, he's the exact opposite of a hero...or at least, that's how he appears...
5700
Yen Press
For more information visit www.yenpress.com
PLUNDERER ©Suu Minazuki 2015 KADOKAWA CORPORATION
Vol. 1
SUU MINAZUKI
PLUNDERER
VOLUMES 1-6 AVAILABLE NOW!

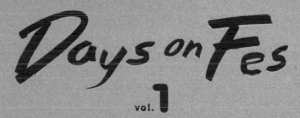

Days on Fes

vol. 1

KANATO OKA

TRANSLATION: AJANI OLOYE | LETTERING: ALEXIS ECKERMAN

DAYS ON FES Vol. 1
©Kanato Oka 2019
First published in Japan in 2019 by KADOKAWA CORPORATION, Tokyo.
English translation rights arranged with KADOKAWA CORPORATION, Tokyo
through Tuttle-Mori Agency, Inc., Tokyo.

English translation © 2021 by Yen Press, LLC

Yen Press
150 West 30th Street, 19th Floor
New York, NY 10001

Visit us at yenpress.com ♪ facebook.com/yenpress ♪ twitter.com/yenpress
yenpress.tumblr.com ♪ instagram.com/yenpress

First Yen Press Edition: February 2021

Yen Press is an imprint of Yen Press, LLC.
The Yen Press name and logo are trademarks of Yen Press, LLC.

Library of Congress Control Number: 2020950221

ISBNs: 978-1-9753-1961-8 (paperback)
978-1-9753-1962-5 (ebook)

10 9 8 7 6 5 4 3 2 1

BVG

Printed in the United States

W9-BNB-026